"This is a book no deal team should be without. It is a must for those involved in upstream oil and gas transactions, planning, budgeting, investment appraisal and portfolio management. Its step-by-step approach cuts through complexity, making it comprehensive and understandable by a wide range of users with a wide range of abilities. It can be used as a textbook, an introductory primer or as a handbook that you can dip in and out of or read cover to cover."

Michael Lynch-Bell, Senior Advisor, Oil & Gas, Ernst & Young LLP; ex-officio Chairman, UN Expert Group on Resource Classification

"This book is a terrific addition to the existing literature on the subject, and will be invaluable to a wide range of professionals, from Energy Ministry staff through NOCs to energy company economists, advisors and consultants. By far the best way to understand all the subtleties of fiscal regimes is to build one's own models of them, and then to play 'what if?' games with them. This is what the book encourages, by being set out so clearly and well, and a thorough study will take the reader from beginner to near expert status."

Graeme Simpson, Honorary Professor in Petroleum Geology / former Professor of Energy Industry Management, the University of Aberdeen, Scotland; former Business Manager, Exxon

"This book is both a reference for the various types of fiscal regimes and a how-to guide for spreadsheet modeling. Practitioners at every level will find it to be a valuable resource."

Dan Olds, Senior Vice President – International, Ryder Scott Petroleum Consultants / Past President, Society of Petroleum Evaluation Engineers

"This book gives a comprehensive and in-depth discussion of petroleum economics. It provides a step-by-step guide to understanding fiscal models similar to what many residential courses offer. The excel sheets and formulas are extremely helpful for the novice and users of economic software such as PEEP to start modeling fiscal regimes. As an experienced economist, the book has helped fill gaps in my knowledge and I would personally recommend it as a reference guide for those in commercial disciplines in the industry."

Aditya Mukherjee, Economics Analyst, Global New Business Development, Hess Services UK Limited

"Kasriel and Wood have produced a monumental set of materials for understanding how to model and analyze the impacts of upstream petroleum fiscal terms on project economics. Unique to their approach is a step-by-step guide on using Microsoft Excel that provides users with a kind of x-ray vision into the complex and sometimes unanticipated outcomes associated with various sorts of taxes, royalties, and production sharing contracts. It is a brilliant practitioner's guide to the subject."

Graham A. Davis, Professor, Division of Economics and Business, Colorado School of Mines

"I find the book a great tool for anyone who intends to initiate his/her career into the world of petroleum economics. Furthermore, I think experienced economists should always have this book on their desk for quick consultation/reference as it is very comprehensive around the modeling of oil and gas deals. This book is a must-have in every economists book shelf!"

Germán Beckmann, Business Analyst, Premier Oil PLC

"This book will be a useful, practical tool for the petroleum economics practitioner. Practitioners will find the practical spreadsheet tips, delivered in an easy-to-read, conversational style, particularly helpful."

Roy Kelly, Managing Director, Kerogen Capital

"This book fills a gap in the existing literature - a valuable work for anyone confronted with the complexities of Upstream Petroleum Fiscal and Valuation Modeling. I am impressed by the quantity of data and detailed explanations that guide the reader through the calculations. I really appreciate the authors' step-by-step approach which makes for a practical 'hands-on' tool that can be easily adapted to ones' own need"

Nadine Bret-Rouzaut, IFP School, Director of the Centre for Economics & Management, Professor, Upstream management

"This is a very enlightening textbook on Petroleum Economics. It puts a lot of financial decision making in the oil industry in perspective. The descriptions of typical economical terms such as Royalty, Abandonment and Production Sharing Contracts (PSC's) are very well explained and come to life with the abundance of examples. A must-have for every E&P professional."

Michiel Stofferis, Field Reserves Manager, CEPSA

"In this book Kasriel and Wood lay bare the complex world of petroleum fiscal systems. By leading the reader through carefully worked examples, supported by extensive Excel documentation, they share their experience to create a resource useful to the beginner and the experienced practitioner alike. Building from first principles they lay the foundation for an understanding of the differing systems in use today, whilst also acknowledging the likelihood of evolution and the need for flexibility in application."

Dr Julian A. Fennema, Lecturer in Petroleum Economics, Institute of Petroleum Engineering, Heriot-Watt University

"Kasriel and Wood have pulled together a comprehensive, well thought through and clear guide to the topic of Upstream Petroleum Fiscal and Valuation Modeling. Their use of explanation, examples and reference material makes it a very accessible guide for both beginners and experienced practioners alike. This is a very useful addition to the repertoire of writing in this area."

Tom Morris, Commercial Manager, Cairn Energy

"This clearly written, well-organized book is a valuable tool to assist governments in fiscal design and to assist investors and financiers to determine and analyze government take and its effect on the rates of cost recovery and overall profitability."

Owen L. Anderson, Eugene Kuntz Chair in Oil, Gas & Natural Resources, George Lynn Cross Research Professor, The University of Oklahoma College of Law

"*Upstream Petroleum Fiscal and Valuation Modeling in Excel* by Ken Kasriel and David Wood presents a carefully worked out set of examples that deal with a complex topic of importance for all who are engaged in the oil extraction business. The chapters lend clarity to a variety of complex topics, each of which is explained clearly and illustrated with an appropriate Excel spreadsheet. This book will prove invaluable to industry participants and analysts."

Simon Benninga, Author, *Principles of Finance with Excel* / Visiting Professor of Finance, Wharton School, University of Pennsylvania / Professor of Finance, Faculty of Management, Tel Aviv University

"This book is one of the most comprehensive I've read, that provides a generic illustrative roadmap for evaluating fiscal systems in all their intricacies that will no doubt become the reference material for those involved in understanding, applying and negotiating global fiscal systems."

Gerry F. Donnelly, Director, Institutional Research, FirstEnergy Capital LLP

Upstream Petroleum Fiscal and Valuation Modeling in Excel

For other titles in the Wiley Finance series
please see www.wiley.com/finance

Upstream Petroleum Fiscal and Valuation Modeling in Excel

A Worked Examples Approach

Ken Kasriel
David Wood

A John Wiley & Sons, Ltd., Publication

Registered office

John Wiley & Sons Ltd, The Atrium, Southern Gate, Chichester, West Sussex, PO19 8SQ, United Kingdom

For details of our global editorial offices, for customer services and for information about how to apply for permission to reuse the copyright material in this book please see our website at www.wiley.com.

Library of Congress Cataloging-in-Publication Data

Kasriel, Ken, 1965-
  Upstream petroleum fiscal and valuation modeling in Excel : a worked examples approach / Ken Kasriel, David Wood.
     pages cm
  Includes index.
  ISBN 978-0-470-68682-9 (hbk.) – ISBN 978-1-118-53768-8 (ebk.) – ISBN 978-1-118-53769-5 (ebk.) – ISBN 978-1-118-53770-1 (ebk.)
  1. Petroleum industry and trade–Valuation.   2. Microsoft Excel (Computer file)   I. Wood, David.   II. Title.
  HD9560.5.K37 2013
  665.50285′554–dc23

                                                                                    2012050120

A catalogue record for this book is available from the British Library.

ISBN 978-0-470-68682-9 (hbk) ISBN 978-1-118-53768-8 (ebk)
ISBN 978-1-118-53769-5 (ebk) ISBN 978-1-118-53770-1 (ebk)

Cover images reproduced by permission of Shutterstock.com
Trial Crystal Ball software provided with permission from the Oracle Corporation.

Set in 10/12pt Times by Aptara, Inc., New Delhi, India
Printed in Great Britain by CPI Group (UK) Ltd, Croydon, CR0 4YY

Contents

Accompanying Materials on Disk
See the file "Kasriel_Wood_disk contents.xls" on the disk

Company vs Host Company.

Introduction

The fiscal share, or "take," from an upstream petroleum project is one of the key factors determining its profitability, from the perspective of both the investors and host country governments involved. This "take" is determined not just by tax rates, but also by a number of other mechanisms (i.e., those covered in this book)[1] which collectively make up a country's fiscal regime (also called "fiscal system" or "fiscal design").

In a business which ultimately is not about producing petroleum, but rather about making money from doing so, fiscal design is all-important:

- Even assuming commodity prices are high, the fiscal regime can turn oil and/or gas fields with great underlying technical strengths (high volumes of petroleum, low costs), and thus the potential to generate significant underlying (i.e., pre-fiscal) cashflow, into an emphatically bad deal for the producer, if the fiscal rules channel too much cashflow to the state.

- For governments, understanding how their fiscal systems "behave" under different macroeconomic and project-specific conditions is essential, if they are to successfully walk the line between maximizing state revenue and deterring investors.

- The detailed calculation of investors' and governments' shares – which is imperative in understanding the true value of petroleum production projects – is the subject of this book.

Fiscal systems are often complex, due not only to the number and/or nature of the mechanisms they use, but also to the high levels of uncertainty that permeate the upstream oil and gas industries, as seen in volatile prices, and in the typically wide ranges of possible reserve sizes, production rates, and costs which characterize exploration, development and production projects.

Whereas the characteristics of each specific oil and gas field (i.e., its location, depth, reservoir and petroleum quality and reserves) are outside the control of governments and investors, these parties do have it within their power to discuss and negotiate fiscal terms, and governments can set and change them via laws and regulations.

---

[1] As seen in the Contents, these include royalties; bonuses; rentals; depreciation of costs; tax allowances and incentives; ringfencing and consolidation of tax losses; cost recovery and profit sharing mechanisms; and the funding of decommissioning (abandonment) costs.

History shows that the parties spend significant time and effort in negotiating fiscal issues and trying to optimize overall designs, and that the results have a major influence on investments being made, delayed, abandoned or avoided altogether.

Consequently, the ability to model fiscal devices and understand their impact on value to the respective parties is essential. This is the focus of our book, which takes both investor and government perspectives.

***

Our aim is *not* to provide a complete and up-to-date, country-by-country upstream petroleum fiscal "encyclopaedia." That would be huge, and quickly go out of date:[2]

- Each of the approximately 100 or so countries which explore and/or produce petroleum has its own fiscal system, and sometimes more than one – certain governments have different regimes, depending on where a project is or when permits were first awarded.
- Fiscal systems, moreover, tend to evolve over time, as:
  - economic conditions change;
  - significant discoveries are made (e.g., Brazil's "pre-salt" discoveries, as we write this, are prime examples);
  - new technologies open up new petroleum provinces with specific challenges that require new fiscal incentives (e.g., deepwater, unconventional oil and gas);
  - provinces mature and yield smaller, more marginal fields (e.g., the North Sea); and
  - governments change, or change their minds, due to political developments, upheavals, populist pressures, etc.

Despite this dynamism (which some might also call "flux"), often governments do try to design fiscal systems which are stable. To be stable, they need to be flexible, taking into account a wide range of potential economic and technical scenarios, so that the resultant fiscal "takes" vary according to a project's profitability (or lack thereof).

This flexibility, however, often leads to complexity. For example, a simple, single rate of royalty, tax or production share is usually inadequate to respond to changing conditions. Therefore, these fiscal devices are quite often expressed as formulas.

There are very many specific, often mutating fiscal formulas in use globally, but ultimately these are variations of a relatively small number of generic types of formulas. These are the focus of this book. There are less than 20 individual generic fiscal devices in common use. Different countries will "tweak" these and/or use different combinations of them. Thus the large number and variety of international fiscal systems used are like many sentences,

---

[2] Some such comprehensive information is in fact already available, for example, from the websites of governments which make this material public; from specialist consultancies, for a fee; and in free summaries, from sources such as the annual Ernst & Young *Global Oil & Gas Tax Guide*, available from www.ey.com.

using what is actually a relatively small, masterable "vocabulary list." Our choice of generic examples in this book is designed to give you this vocabulary.

Thus, to be of most immediate, practical use – without requiring at least annual revisions (and to keep it smaller than a telephone book) – this book provides what is lacking in the field, in our view: that is, detailed explanations of how these generic formulas are calculated, and how they cause fiscal systems to "behave" when input assumptions change.

- You can learn from other sources, for example, that a country has scrapped its "cumulative production-based tangible capex depreciation uplifts" and is rolling out a new "profit oil sharing scale determined by a linear R-factor scale, with contractor shares ranging from 90% and 10%." But knowing this is not the same as understanding what these changes mean in plain English, how to model them, and their impacts on fiscal take and valuation.

- This book equips the reader to understand such specific fiscal devices via transparent, well-explained spreadsheet examples, in a structured, layperson-friendly manner, which show how their generic counterparts are calculated and modeled in detail. In other words, it shows you how to make sense of and use country-specific fiscal information once you get it.

$$***$$

Fortunately, understanding, calculating and modeling petroleum fiscal designs is not rocket science, nor does it require the detailed technical knowledge involved in the geology or engineering aspects of the oil and gas industry.

The concepts behind most individual fiscal devices are usually reasonably straightforward. When, however, they are combined into multi-faceted fiscal systems and/or shrouded in fiscal and contractual jargon, they can appear to the layperson as mechanisms with many, strangely named "moving parts" which work together in ways that are far from obvious.

The key principles and methods can be learned from this book by readers with a rudimentary knowledge of spreadsheets and discounted cashflow principles. No oil and gas background is assumed. The book makes great efforts to be accessible to laypeople, while at the same time being of practical use to an array of readers, including intermediate to experienced petroleum hands. Thus it is a both a "hands-on," step-by-step course for start-to-finish readers, as well as a practitioner's reference.

The book uses Microsoft Excel as its calculation "engine." One reason is that Excel is widely used. The transparency of its calculations, moreover, makes it a very effective teaching and communications tool – clearly written models can indeed be worth (at least) a thousand words.

Many upstream petroleum companies use proprietary fiscal computer models, some of them frustratingly opaque "black boxes" which give answers that are difficult, or impossible, to check. Even if you are obliged to use a "black box" model, understanding how the detailed fiscal calculations are done in Excel, in our experience, is a great advantage when using most fiscal modeling applications. Nothing is worse than being asked to explain why a change in input assumption X leads to a Y% change in result Z, without knowing why, and without being able to know why. "This is just what the black box says" is an answer that will not inspire confidence in you as an analyst.

Excel has evolved over the past decade with the release of new and more powerful and versatile versions. In this book we provide explanations of how to perform relevant tasks in Excel 2003, Excel 2007 and Excel 2010, and cashflow models and other examples in formats which will work in all of these versions.

All calculations use "unhidden" cell formulas in our models. Much of this book is devoted to explaining these formulas. At times the discussion is dense – you probably will not be reading this book in a beach chair – but to ease understanding we tend to avoid large formulas, instead usually breaking them into smaller steps to aid understanding. Step-by-step explanations are written in plain English, with new terms clearly defined. We do not do any calculations inside Visual Basic for Applications (VBA) macros. We do, however, use Excel's VBA to make navigating and interrogating the models easier.

There is much more to *Upstream Petroleum Fiscal Cashflow and Risk Modeling in Excel* than just the physical book. In a sense, the Excel files on the disk play the lead role, with much of the text written to accompany them. The disk contains over 120 Excel files and more than 400 pages of PDF supplements and appendices covering the calculation and/or extended analysis of certain fiscal mechanisms. We have chosen to farm out some portions of the book to PDFs, both for formatting reasons (to be able to use color and larger images, e.g., clear model screenshots and charts) and to provide important material without disrupting the flow of chapters.

*** *

This book assumes you are willing to learn by getting your hands dirty – expect to spend much of your time with both the book open and the computer on. At times viewing on a larger, desktop monitor might even be helpful. Practice exercises at various points in the chapters pose problems relating to specific techniques for you to solve. Both hints and complete solutions are provided in auxiliary Excel files. There are also frequent solved exercises and interactive graphics designed to prompt and answer "what-if?" questions.

Discounted cashflow methods are standard in calculating the time value of money. Taking time value into account is crucial for oil and gas projects which involve both large, upfront capital investments and revenue streams that do not materialize until many years later, but which might last for decades. Thus when valuing oil and gas assets and evaluating the performance of petroleum fiscal systems, it is discounted post-tax cashflow calculations which usually matter most to oil companies, investors, analysts, third-party advisors and governments.

We use net present value (NPV) as our primary discounted cashflow performance indicator, but also calculate other useful economic yardsticks and other upstream petroleum-relevant benchmarks in our multi-year cashflow models.

Uncertainty and risk are crucial attributes of petroleum projects. They need to be considered when valuing projects and evaluating fiscal designs. Although they are not the main focus of this book, we do illustrate the use of Oracle's Crystal Ball add-in for Excel to add a probabilistic dimension to a few examples. We explain why probabilistic analysis can often improve our understanding of how a fiscal system or specific fiscal device performs over a wide range of input values, and how Crystal Ball lets us do this. Refer to the last page of this book for instructions on how to obtain the trial version of Crystal Ball which Oracle has kindly provided.

For those who "do not read manuals (or textbooks)," at least read the "ReadMe" file.

Some readers might prefer to dive straight into the spreadsheet models and examples, and then consult the text as needed. We strongly suggest that such readers – as well as everyone else, in fact – first take a few minutes to read the file "**Spreadsheets_ReadMeFirst.pdf**" on the disk, which covers some important Excel-related housekeeping items.

While we have made every effort to eliminate typos and other errors in the text, supplements and Excel files, some might have slipped through. For corrections to any such mistakes found since publication, visit the "Errata" tab of the webpage, http://eu.wiley.com/WileyCDA/WileyTitle/productCd-0470686820.html. (Should you find any, please let us know via the email address ken_kasriel@yahoo.com. We regret that we cannot commit to answer all correspondence.).

Those fortunate enough to be involved in the negotiation and formulation of petroleum fiscal designs, and/or in modeling their impacts on investment value, already know that it is an intellectually challenging and rewarding undertaking, involving many skilled and persuasive individuals, with diverse perspectives on what constitutes true value. This undertaking is greatly enhanced by the ability to personally build models that can quickly evaluate subtle changes to fiscal devices within an existing regime, in a comprehensive and accurate way that can be easily presented and interrogated. Good luck with your fiscal modeling endeavors!

Acknowledgements

While the views expressed here are our own, we would like to thank the following for comments and criticisms which ultimately helped shape this book: Jim Bradly, John Davies, Esther Escobar, Ed Jankowski, Juan Lopez-Raggi, Anthony Miller, Adolfo Perez and Roy Wikramaratna at RPS Energy; Otto Aristeguieta at Chevron; Manijeh Bozorgzadeh at CEPSA; Olumide Talabi at OMV; Saqib Younis at Petrofac; and Davoud Bardal at Sevenenergy. We are also grateful to the team at John Wiley & Sons, including (but not limited to) Bill Falloon, who first considered our proposal, as well as Neville Hankins, Werner Coetzee, Tessa Allen, Jennie Kitchin and Ben Hall.

Chapter 1

Introduction to Tax and Royalty Regimes

1
Introduction to Tax and Royalty Regimes

1.1 INTRODUCTION

In this book, we treat two principal types of upstream petroleum *fiscal regime* (a collection of individual *fiscal devices*, such as taxes):

- **Tax and Royalty regimes** are introduced here.

- The other major kind, known as a **Production Sharing Contract (PSC) regime**, is covered in Chapters 6, 7 and 8.

- The intervening chapters treat individual fiscal *devices* which are often used in either type of regime.

As the name implies, the main (though not necessarily only) sources of revenue for a government using a Tax and Royalty regime are income tax – payable on profits, if these occur – and **royalties**, which are usually payable as a percentage of revenue (almost always) whether the project is profitable or not.

Fiscal regimes based on royalties and taxes are a cornerstone of how governments extract their **economic rent** – here, meaning share of revenue – from petroleum producing properties. Such regimes, which are also commonly referred to as **concessionary or mineral-interest arrangements**, were the only fiscal regimes, or "fiscal designs," used, until PSCs were introduced in the mid-1960s.

In fact, in the early days of the petroleum and mineral extraction industries, a royalty was the only fiscal device applied that provided a state with any share of project revenue.

Land **rentals**, **bonuses** (both also introduced in this chapter) and income taxes were soon added, to increase the government's economic rent, or "fiscal take" (using "take" as a noun, to mean what revenue the government "takes"). As oil prices soared in the 1970s, governments saw their bargaining power grow at the expense of international oil companies, and introduced other supplementary or "special" petroleum taxes to capture "excess" profits.

Today, concessionary systems with two or more layers of taxation in addition to a royalty are not unusual. Typically there is also a complex set of tax allowances, credits and other incentives designed to encourage investors to invest in high-cost and risky projects. Most OECD countries have concessionary fiscal designs based on a combination of royalty and tax fiscal devices, as do some developing countries.

Our Approach in This Chapter

To keep things simple for the main example model in this introductory chapter – the discounted cashflow model found in the file "Ch1_Tax_and_Royalty_Model.xls" – we use simplified (though still realistic) royalty and tax rates, which are the same every year. Be aware, however, that the rates for income tax and – as we will see in Chapter 3 – royalties can vary over time, according to sophisticated formulas which make them flexible over a wide range of economic and production situations.

In this chapter we concentrate on the most common concepts and components of a basic (but reasonably typical) hypothetical tax and royalty regime, illustrated in a simplified (but reasonably granular) multi-year Excel fiscal model. This approach highlights:

- how various fiscal devices in many tax and royalty regimes are typically applied;
- the input assumptions required; and
- the allowances and deductions used in their calculation.

We include both an abstract-style summary and a flowchart-style "map" of our model for reference as we work through it, section by section.[1]

We will also pester you from time to time, asking you to make changes in the model and to decide whether the results make any sense. The ultimate goal of the model is to show how changes in the fiscal regime affect the hypothetical government's and investor's **discounted net cashflows**, the sum of which equals their **net present values (NPVs)**.

To ensure readers understand both basic and certain nuanced concepts and calculations relating to NPV, we include an introductory section on the time value of money – discounting and inflation – and why they are important in valuing upstream petroleum properties. Even if you are already familiar with discounted cashflow valuation, this section should be worthwhile for you at least to skim, to see which calculation approaches we have adopted as standard in this and other chapters.

Basic key upstream-specific model inputs are introduced in layperson's terms.

We also introduce some useful Excel techniques for making models easier to navigate and view, and ask "what-if?" questions, using interactive charts which show how specific fiscal devices and other key upstream input assumptions impact investor and government cashflow.

This chapter explains the need for, and the calculation of, an **economic limit test (ELT)**, which establishes when a project ceases to be profitable and therefore should be abandoned. The ELT thus determines when production should permanently stop (or be "shut-in") and when the site should be cleaned up and restored, by decommissioning wells and facilities. The ELT is critical in optimizing future cashflow.

---

[1] The summary is found on the "ModelSummary" sheet of the file "Ch1_Tax_and_Royalty_Model.xls." The "map" is found on the same file's "ModelMap" sheet. Note that this "map" is rather "busy," and might be a bit much to take in all at once. For this reason, we also provide different versions of it, each highlighting only a single section at a time, on pages 48–56 of the file "Ch1_Main_chapter_supplement.pdf."

Sensitivity analysis is often required to establish the impacts on NPV of ranges of uncertain input variables. Spreadsheet "spinner" controls can help make it easy to change variable settings. Excel also provides a one-way and two-way "Data Table" feature, which is more useful and powerful for showing the effects of many different variable settings in a single view. We demonstrate these tools in this chapter's main example model.

1.2   INFLATION AND DISCOUNTING: TIME VALUE OF MONEY BASICS IN THE CONTEXT OF UPSTREAM PETROLEUM MODELING

Introduction

In upstream petroleum fiscal and valuation modeling, there are three considerations which determine whether an oil or gas field is potentially a promising investment. Failure in any one area negates the strengths of the others. These areas are:

1. the parameters affecting the field's underlying performance (e.g., production volumes, commodity prices, and costs);
2. the fiscal system – which is the thrust of this book; and
3. the time value of money – how inflation but, usually more importantly, discounting can impact the investment's value to the investor today. Time value is particularly important in oil and gas field developments because they typically involve several years of upfront capital investments with no revenue, followed by many years of revenue from production.

Because we do not intend this book to be a complete course in petroleum economics – a field which actually brings in a lot of detail from other disciplines within the industry – we treat items 1 and 3 above only in overview. We shall address item 1 later in this chapter. We address item 3 here.

We introduce the time value of money in this section through examples which completely ignore the fiscal issues to which most of the rest of the book is devoted. This is deliberate, in order to isolate for examination:

- the unique "distortions" which the time value of money can have on the value of an oil or gas project to an investor and/or host government; as opposed to

- the (usually) unrelated distortions which fiscal systems (especially complex ones) can have.

Therefore, in this section, we explain the basics of the time value of money in less detail than a standard corporate finance textbook, but enough to help readers unfamiliar with the subject to proceed with this book.

We define the time value of money here, simply enough, as how the value of cashflows spent or received depends on when they occur.

Three Kinds of Money in our Models

US dollars – which generally speaking are the international currency of the upstream petroleum industry – are the "blood" of the examples and models used in this book. You will see that it consists of three "blood types":

- **"Real" dollars**, quite often the form in which a model's forecast input assumptions are denominated;

- **inflated dollars**; and

- **discounted dollars**, the calculation of which is typically our <u>valuation goal</u> when using our (and commonly, much of the upstream petroleum industry's) cashflow analysis approach, which is based on net present value (NPV), as discussed below. (Importantly, we also could have used the term "inflated, then discounted dollars" here, because in this book we only discount inflated dollars, not Real ones.)

Real Versus Inflated Dollars

"Real" dollars, also called "**constant dollars**," are dollars of a constant purchasing power at a given point in time. They ignore changes to purchasing power due to inflation/deflation and exchange rate movements. As such, values expressed in "Real" dollar terms are used to express underlying cost and price trends in terms of monetary values at a particular point in time, e.g., a specific year. This point in time is usually when the cost and price forecasts are made, which is also often the first period of a forward-looking cashflow forecast.

In contrast, **inflated dollars** – also known as "**money-of-the-day**" ("**MOD**") **dollars**, or as "**current dollars**" – are values expressed with variations in purchasing power (inflation or deflation effects) factored in. Because inflation/deflation and exchange rate movements are facts of life, this makes MOD dollars the *actual* dollar values of, for example, costs incurred, or prices realized, at a particular point in time. <u>They are the only dollars you can ever spend or receive</u>. (For this reason, you might be forgiven for calling these the "real" dollars, but do not – you will confuse everyone.)

Real Versus Inflated: Example

Suppose that, in 2015, a cost engineer is asked to forecast the cost of renting a well-drilling mechanism, or "rig," for drilling a well in 2020. She does not know much about macroeconomics, but she does know about other fundamentals of the drilling rig market.

After considering the most suitable type of rig, she reckons that, today, renting one of these would cost $125 000 per day. Because she is thinking about the price today, she is thinking about prices in today's terms, ignoring inflation.

Then, drawing on future forecasts of likely supply and demand for this kind of rig, as well as her own experience-seasoned judgment, she tries to adjust the price today for expected changes in the underlying rig rental market, to arrive at an estimated price in, say, five years' time. In the end, she forecasts that, due to expected weakening of demand for this type of rig, by 2020 the rate will actually fall, to $100 000 – *as measured in today's 2015 dollars*.

These 2015 dollars have today's constant purchasing power. In a financial modeling context, these are constant or "Real dollars." And this is why the term "Real dollars" on its own is incomplete – it always needs to be specified as **Real dollars at a given point in time**. Therefore we will correct ourselves, and call the currency used in the rig rate forecast "$100 000 Real dollars of 2015 purchasing power" or, for short, "Real 2015 $100 000."

The engineer then hands this price forecast over to the commercial analyst, who does not know much about rig rental rates, but does keep abreast of forecasts for local country and US dollar inflation and exchange rates. (In this book, because all costs and prices are assumed to be in US dollars, we will not deal with exchange rates.)

Because the analyst's job is to forecast *actual* cashflows which occur at *actual* transaction costs and prices – *not* cashflows denominated in some hypothetical unit – he applies a forecast US dollar inflation rate to the "Real" dollar amounts supplied by the engineer. We will assume that after inflating the engineer's forecast of Real 2015 $100 000 per day, the resultant inflated cost he forecasts for 2020 is MOD $115 000. Again, "MOD" is "money of the day," where "the day" is the "day"[2] when the rig rental is paid out. Assuming the forecasts are correct, the company will be writing the actual check for $115 000.

Again, to recap:
- Real dollars are not the actual values of amounts spent or received at the time these transactions occur; rather, they are these values expressed, for convenience, in the monetary value (buying power) of one specific period.

- MOD dollars *are* the values which are actually spent or received at the time these transactions occur.

Discounted Dollars

Just as inflating dollars increases their value, **discounting** decreases their value. By discounting, we mean adjusting the value of a dollar spent or received in the future to its value today, or its **present value**.

(Do not confuse the terms "real value" and "present value," at least as we use them in this book, although we can see why someone might. They are completely distinct.)

Present value in our, and the common, use of the term, is the value of a future dollar today, calculated by applying a **discount rate** to the value of a single future cashflow.
- The higher the discount rate, the lower the present (i.e., discounted) value will be.[3]

- The further from today that the cashflow occurs, the lower the present value will be.

---

[2] "Money of the day" is a loosely worded expression – it does not necessarily mean the inflated value on a specific day. The expression could be rephrased more precisely as "money of the time when it is paid or received."
[3] The discount rate actually used is likely to vary from one organization to another, as discussed in the section "What Does Discounting and NPV Tell Us?"

Terminology pause

- In this book, we only discount dollars which have already been inflated, i.e., only MOD dollars. (One can also discount Real dollars, but we do not do so here.) This is the most common way that the industry calculates and reports present value.

- Therefore, although we do sometimes go to extra lengths, especially in this introductory section, to specify, for example, that a cashflow is denominated in "inflated, discounted dollars," be aware, whenever you see a reference in this book to "discounted value," "present value" or companion terms such as **net present value** (**NPV**) or **discounted cashflow** (**DCF**), that you should understand that the values in question have been inflated to MOD values, and then discounted.

High-Level View: Using Discounted Dollars in our Valuation Models

We will show the calculations involved in discounting soon. But for the moment, let us jump ahead, and assume that we already have calculated our discounted values, so we can outline here the basic mechanics of how they are used in our valuation models.

Knowing the discounted value (or present value) of one single cashflow item – out of the many which occur in the multi-year endeavor of exploring, developing and/or producing an oil or gas field – is not very useful. Rather, here is how we, and much of the industry, use discounted values. We:

(a) discount every year's **cash inflows** (cashflow received, e.g., revenues);
(b) discount every year's **cash outflows** (cashflow spent, e.g., costs);
(c) subtract each year's (b) from each year's (a), to get annual **discounted net cashflow** values; and
(d) sum each year's (c), to get **net present value**, or **NPV**, which is one of the most commonly used valuation metrics in the upstream petroleum industry.

The basic NPV decision rule is that investments which have a positive NPV are good investments, while those with negative NPV should be avoided. Using this rule is sometimes called the **NPV method**, the **discounted cashflow method** or the **DCF method**. Importantly, **this rule only applies to future cashflows**, where "future" means starting from the date for which you wish to know the NPV (known as the **valuation date**). We ignore any past or **"sunk" costs**, unless for some fiscal reason these influence future cashflows. (We do cover such cases in this book.)

What Does Discounting and NPV Tell Us?

The subject of discounting, and ways to choose discount rates (such as basing them on an investor's weighted average cost of capital), is vast and will not be detailed here.[4] But for a quick and, we hope, intuitive understanding of why we bother discounting future cashflows, think of the process as a way of saying whether an investment is good compared to other investment opportunities available.

In other words, under this view, it is *not* enough to know that the sum of all *undiscounted* future cash inflows, minus the sum of all *undiscounted* future cash outflows – which equals **undiscounted net cashflow**[5] ("**NCF**") – is positive. Rather, you must also consider whether this NCF is more valuable to you today than NCF from one or more other investment opportunities.

One way to do this would be as follows:

- Suppose you already know of one $100 investment opportunity which you are certain is open to you – Project A – which could earn you – in *un*discounted, MOD terms – a return of 10% per year.

- This means that every year your $100 is not invested in this project, but rather in, say, Project B, which offers only 7% annual returns, you will not be losing money in an absolute sense (you will be making 7% per year), but you will be losing money in a wider, comparative sense.

- Thus you should choose investments with returns higher than Project A. The cost to you of being invested in something with lower returns than Project A is called your **opportunity cost** – the cost of a missed opportunity to do better.

Under this opportunity cost view of discounting, Project A's 10% annual returns would become the discount rate you would use to evaluate Project B, or any other investment opportunity. Again, you would use it to discount the future annual MOD net cashflows at this rate (in a way we will show soon), to get discounted MOD future annual net cashflows, which you would sum to reach NPV.

- In essence, to say that when the NPV calculated using a discount rate of 10%, for an investment other than Project A, is positive, this is just another way of saying that its returns are greater than 10%, and therefore better than Project A's.

- Hence the term, the "**time value of money**": assuming that you always have a Project A to invest in, any moment that your money is not invested there, or is invested in something with worse than 10% annual returns, means your capital is losing money compared to that benchmark.

---

[4] Good introductions can be found in most corporate finance texts. Two which we recommend are *Fundamentals of Corporate Finance* by Richard Brealey, Stewart Myers and Alan Marcus (McGraw-Hill/Irwin, 2011) and, for a more hands-on calculation approach, *Principles of Finance with Excel* by Simon Benninga (Oxford University Press, USA, 2010). An in-depth yet very readable treatment of how to choose appropriate discount rates is *The Real Cost of Capital: A Business Field Guide to Better Financial Decisions* by Tim Ogier, John Rugman and Lucinda Spicer (FT Press, 2004). (Disclosure: Tim Ogier is a former colleague of one of this book's authors.)

[5] Don't confuse **net cashflow** – which means all inflows minus all outflows, regardless of whether the values have been discounted – with **net present value**, which always means that the cashflows have been discounted. For clarity, we often specify "net cashflow" or "NCF" fully, i.e., as being "undiscounted NCF" or "discounted NCF."

There are more terminological nuances to keep in mind. Reflecting common usage, in this book we call undiscounted NCF either "undiscounted NCF" or simply "NCF." We call discounted, *annual* NCF, "discounted NCF"; we call total (all years) discounted NCF, "NPV."

Because we express the returns on a time basis, e.g., 10% annual returns, the further from today that you have to wait to receive a cash inflow, the less it is worth to you today, because in the meantime you could be investing to get at least 10% annual returns.

Timing Matters – a Lot

This is why, as we will see, the math mechanics of discounting are such that the further in the future that an undiscounted cashflow occurs, the lower its discounted (present) value will be today.

This applies whether the cashflow is an inflow or an outflow. All other things being equal:

- the further in the future that <u>inflows</u> occur, the more they will be discounted – which is bad for NPV, because, for example, revenue will be lower in present value terms; and

- the further in the future that <u>outflows</u> occur, the more they will be discounted – which is good for NPV, because, for example, these costs will be lower in present value terms.

In upstream petroleum projects – in which, commonly, there are years of upfront investment outflows before any production revenue occurs – these basic truths can become harsh facts of life from a valuation perspective.

We show a simplistic example in Figure 1.1, in which we assume, from the perspective of January 1, 2015, that:

- there are two cashflows, one a cost (an initial investment, i.e., a cash outflow) and the other, revenue (a cash inflow), each forecast to equal Real 2015 $100;

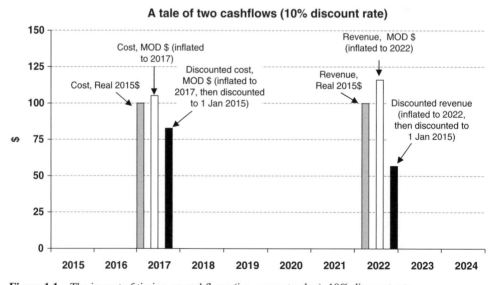

Figure 1.1   The impact of timing on cashflows (i.e., present value), 10% discount rate

- the outflow occurs in 2017 and the inflow in 2022; and

- the annual inflation rate is 2%, and the annual discount rate is 10%. (We will show how to apply these in calculations soon.)

In this example, the investment does not look very good, just knowing that the Real $ value of the outflows match the Real $ value of the inflows; after all, why would one bother, on this basis, to invest to achieve a Real net cashflow of $100 − $100 = $0?

In discounted terms, however, it looks even worse. The two black columns show that discounted revenue of around MOD $55, minus discounted costs of around MOD $80, would result in a negative discounted net cashflow of around MOD $(25). Factoring in the time value of money can really hurt sometimes when costs precede revenues, depending on the sums and timing involved. As we will illustrate in a later, more realistic upstream petroleum example, we have seen proposed investments, which look great in Real $ terms, as well as in undiscounted MOD terms, but *horrible* in discounted MOD terms.

As mentioned, the effect of discounting depends on not only the timing of the cashflows, but also on the discount rate used. Note how much smaller the discounted revenue becomes when we change the discount rate to 15%, as shown in Figure 1.2.

NPV Is the Principle Investment Decision Basis in the Upstream Petroleum Industry

Valuation is an inherently subjective endeavor, in practice sometimes drawing as much on individual judgment (based on experience, or sometimes, unfortunately, whim or bias) as on "science." Hence there are many investment metrics in addition to – and usually used in combination with – NPV. We shall focus on the NPV, i.e., the discounted cashflow method,

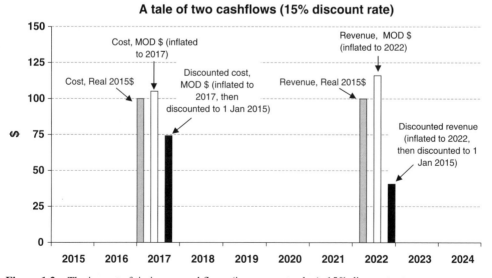

Figure 1.2   The impact of timing on cashflows (i.e., present value), 15% discount rate

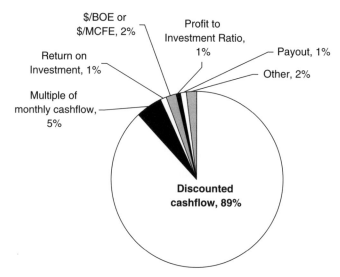

Figure 1.3   SPEE 2011 Survey, "Most Commonly Used Method for Determining Value of Oil and Gas Properties" (Reproduced by Permission of the Society of Petroleum Evaluation Engineers)
Note: (1) Values do not sum to 100% due to rounding. (2) Certain terms in this chart are explained below.

in the valuation-related portions of this book, because we believe it to be one of the most commonly used.

We base this belief on both our combined 52 years of professional experience and the literature, such as the annual *Survey of Parameters Used in Property Evaluation*, published by the Society of Petroleum Evaluation Engineers (SPEE). Results of the edition published in June 2011, presented in Figures 1.3 and 1.4, show the discounted cashflow method's clear prevalence among industry professionals.

Figure 1.3 shows that easily the largest portion of respondents favor the discounted cashflow method. This edition of the survey had 136 respondents, of which 40% were from oil and gas exploration and production companies, 38% from consultancies, 15% from banking/energy finance firms, and 7% from "Other."

Respondents said that when they use more than one investment valuation method, discounted cashflow is still the most common primary one, as shown in Figure 1.4.

Detailing the methods of choosing the discount rate, is again, beyond the scope of this book. We tend to use 10% in our examples for consistency's sake. (US and Canadian regulators require oil and gas companies to report NPVs on a 10% basis, purely to standardize comparisons across companies.) Note, however, that while the choice of discount rate can vary widely, discount rates of around 10% are fairly commonly used for upstream valuations. Again, we base this both on our own experience, and on survey results like those shown in Figure 1.5.

Figure 1.5 shows that most (64%) of the 101 respondents asked used "unrisked" discount rates between 9% and less than 10.5%.

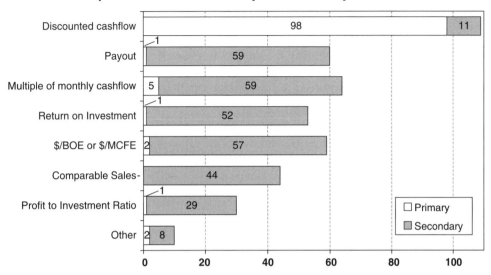

Figure 1.4 SPEE 2011 Survey, "Most Commonly Used Method for Determining Value of Oil and Gas Properties" (Reproduced by Permission of the Society of Petroleum Evaluation Engineers)

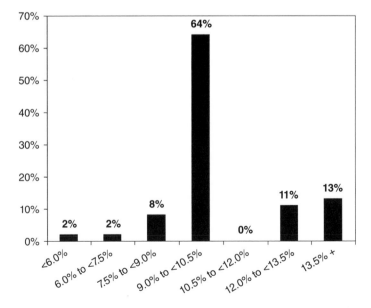

Figure 1.5 SPEE 2011 Survey, "Unrisked Discount Rate Applied to Cash Flows, Composite (101 Respondents)" (Reproduced by Permission of the Society of Petroleum Evaluation Engineers)

An Aside: Risked and Unrisked Discount Rates

"Unrisked," as used in Figure 1.5, means, in effect, that the discount rate has not been adjusted for probabilistic uncertainty. To explain with an example:

- The discount rates we use in this book – and which, unless described otherwise, is how the term is commonly understood – are "unrisked discount rates." They are used to discount (in a way we will illustrate soon) a series of future cashflows, assuming the cashflows are 100% certain to happen as forecast.

- Whereas a "risked discount rate" reflects a specialized adjustment made to the unrisked discount rate, to take into account uncertainty that the cashflows might *not* occur as forecast. For example, one could try to adjust the unrisked discount rate so that it somehow accounts for the likelihood that actual production volumes, prices, costs, timing, etc., could differ from what is forecast; or for whether certain events (such as a commercial oil or gas discovery) will even occur at all.

We do not cover risked discount rates in this book, and in fact would question whether this is the best technique for accounting for risk in valuation models. For an alternative approach to adjusting valuation models for uncertainty and risk, see the material in the "Appendix V" folder on the disk, relating to the use of the included trial version of Crystal Ball software.

Terminology pause: equivalent petroleum units

Note that "BOE" (or "boe") as used in Figures 1.3 and 1.4 means "**barrel of oil equivalent**." This unit measures combined quantities of oil, when it (as normally) is expressed in barrels, with gas, which in volumetric terms is usually measured in cubic feet or cubic meters. Looking at volumes on a BOE basis is useful because it is awkward to express, for example, total petroleum reserves as "3 million barrels + 12 billion cubic feet of gas." Instead,

- the gas is converted to BOE using a factor which depends on its energy content ("calorific value"). Although this varies according to the composition of the gas in question, common rules of thumb are that there are 6000 cubic feet per BOE, and 35.315 cubic meters per cubic feet.

- In our example, the 12 billion cubic feet of gas/6000 = 2 million BOE of gas; and this 2 million BOE of gas + 10 million barrels of oil = 12 million BOE of total petroleum reserves (or total **hydrocarbon** reserves).

"MCFE" (or "mcfe") in Figures 1.3 and 1.4 means "**1000 cubic feet equivalent**." In the upstream petroleum industry, "M" or "m" *usually* means 1000, and "MM" or "mm" *usually* means 1 million:

- We use these conventions in this book. Unfortunately, they are not universal. In fact we have even seen "M" used to be mean thousands of barrels, and "m" used to mean millions of dollars, on the same page. Ensure you know what is meant.

- We convert 3 million barrels of oil to gas equivalent units as follows. Using the same rule of thumb stated above, 3 million barrels of oil equals 3 million $\times$ 6000 = 18 billion CFE (or cfe), or 18 million MCFE.

The investment measures and methods, in addition to discounted cashflow, which appear in Figures 1.3 and 1.4 are, again, beyond our scope here. Because none, except for value per BOE or values per MCFE, are specific to the upstream petroleum industry, they can be found in many corporate finance texts.[6]

Traffic control: this section continues in PDF and Excel formats

Due to considerations of space and formatting, we continue Section 1.2 in the file "Ch1_time_value_of_money_supplement.pdf" on the disk. Its subsections are as follows:

- Basics of time value of money. Calculation of annual inflation and discounting (uses the file "Ch1_Time_value_of_money_intro.xls").

- Interactive analysis. Mechanics of inflation rates, discount rates and cashflow timing (uses the file "Ch1_Discounting_vs._inflation.xls").

- Time-shifting oil field example (uses the files "Ch1_time_shifting_example.xls" and "Ch1_IRR.xls").

  o Exercise. Guessing the impact of timing differences.

  o Sensitivity analysis. Discount rate impacts on NPV; internal rate of return.

- Monthly inflation and discounting (uses the file "Ch1_monthly_discounting.xls").

- Dealing with partial years in annual models. Annual inflation/discounting when the valuation date is not January 1 (uses the file "Ch1_Changing_the_valuation_date.xls").

- Discounting and the "Behavior" of NPV (uses the file, "Ch1_Discounting_and_NPV behavior.xls").

- Details of special formulas and Excel methods used.

Even if you are comfortable with the basic time value of money concepts and calculations, we suggest you at least "skim" this document, because in it we:

(a) explain some of the standard terms and methods we use throughout the rest of the book; and
(b) draw basic lessons from examples of some representative (albeit simplified) upstream petroleum situations. In particular, the section on the time-shifting oil field example – based loosely on a real situation – shows how the typical pattern of oil field cashflows can mean that timing can make or break a project's investment-worthiness.

---

[6] For coverage of many of them within an upstream petroleum context, good sources include: *The Economics of Worldwide Petroleum Production*, by Richard D. Seba, (OGCI Publishing, 2008), and *The Acquisition & Divestiture of Petroleum Property: A Guide to the Tactics, Strategies and Processes Used by Successful Companies*, by Jim Haag (PennWell Corp., 2005). (Disclosure: One of us is a former colleague of Jim Haag.)

1.3 INTRODUCING BASIC COMPONENTS OF UPSTREAM PETROLEUM CASHFLOW UNDER A SIMPLE TAX AND ROYALTY REGIME

The screenshot shown in Figure 1.6 is of the chart which starts in cell B603 on the "Model" sheet of **the main example model for this chapter, found in the file "Ch1_Tax_and_Royalty_ Model.xls."** If you set the model to its Base Scenario ("factory settings") by clicking the button in cell I1 (or its duplicates in cell I21), and then use the spinner control in cell G23 to raise the oil price multiplier to 150%, you should see the same results.[7]

This **"waterfall chart"** [8] assembles all the primary components of the investor's undiscounted NCF.

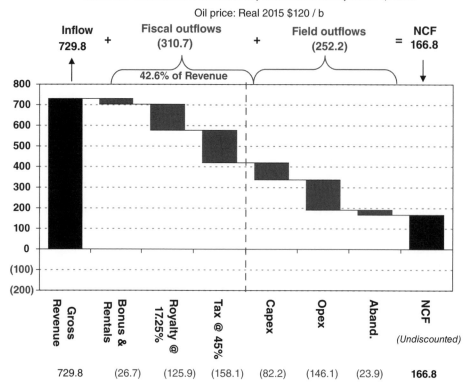

Figure 1.6   From the file "Ch1_Tax_and_Royalty_Model.xls"
Notes: Reflects Base Scenario, with oil price multiplier then set to 150%. "Aband." means abandonment costs.

[7] We will discuss some easier ways to change assumptions and view the results shortly.
[8] We made this "waterfall" chart using a method developed by Jon Peltier of Peltier Technical Services. A demo version of an Excel add-in which enables you to make such charts quickly and easily can be found at http://peltiertech.com/. The underlying data for the chart shown in this example, and for the discounted version to the right of it in the Excel file, are in rows 842–860 (the method is used by permission of Jon Peltier of Peltier Technical Services, Inc., http://peltiertech.com).

The chart is a perhaps useful reminder as we work though the model in the sections to follow that – despite its moderate complexity – ultimately, we are just looking at revenue minus seven cost items.

Let us briefly introduce the main components of NCF shown in Figure 1.6. (We shall discuss them in more detail later.)

Gross revenue is field revenue, i.e., production volumes times the price. Here we mean "gross" as in before any deductions (sometimes the term "net revenue" is used to mean "net of" (i.e., after the deduction of) royalty).

Fiscal Outflows

A **bonus** is a kind of fiscal payment made, often when some production milestone is reached.[9] Regulations usually express the amounts payable in MOD terms, as we have done in the model's assumptions section, discussed further below.

Rentals are periodic fees payable, based on the area of the license, and sometimes varying depending on what kind of activity (e.g., exploration, development or production) is occurring. Again, we (and, usually, regulations) express the sums due in MOD terms.

Royalties are fiscal payments which are usually calculated as some proportion – in this example, 17.25% – of gross revenue.

Income tax is payable as a percentage of taxable income, which is calculated as gross revenue less certain deductions, or **tax allowances**.

Note from the caption for the chart that, under these settings, the sum of the fiscal payments to the government amounts to 42.6% or gross revenue. Under a tax and royalty regime, this is known as the "**Government revenue take**" (when "take" is used as a noun, to mean "portion").

Field Outflows

Capex is capital expenditure. In this example, it is the cost of getting the field ready to produce by drilling wells and building infrastructure such as pipelines and processing facilities.

Opex is ongoing operating costs during the production years. (Opex is sometimes incurred in the pre-production years, when capex is being spent, consisting of things like administrative and managerial costs; we ignore these in our simplified example model.)

Abandonment costs are the costs of removing equipment, plugging wells and otherwise restoring the production site after production ends.

---

[9] Other kinds of bonuses, called signature bonuses, are paid when an agreement is executed. See Chapter 4 for a fuller treatment of bonuses.

A discounted view

Notice to the right of this chart (starting in cell I603) the same total (all-years) cashflow items, only discounted at the Base Scenario's default discount rate of 10% (using the mid-year discounting convention, and assuming a January 1, 2015 valuation date).

As we would expect, each discounted item is lower than its undiscounted counterpart.

But notice also – referring to <u>the value captions at the bottom of the chart</u> if needed – that not all items seem to be discounted to the same extent. For example, discounted gross revenue of MOD $546.9 mm equals 75% of undiscounted gross revenue of MOD $729.8 mm, whereas discounted capex of MOD $76.6 mm equals 93% of undiscounted capex of MOD $82.2 mm, and discounted abandonment costs of MOD $12.9 mm equal 54% of undiscounted abandonment costs of MOD $23.9 mm. Why is this so?

Get Acquainted with the Model by Playing with it

Depending on your monitor's size, if you **click the "Console View" button in cell F1** – and then perhaps the "Full screen on . . . " button row in cell F21 – you should be able to see a split view, with:

- most of the main input assumption controls and input cells visible above the split (scroll down a bit to be able to see the last few, which end in row 67); and

- a scrollable area below the split, which should be large enough for you to see analysis charts and other items of interest. In this bottom area, scroll so that the top row visible is row 602. Adjust the view as necessary (by moving the splitter bar, using Excel's full screen mode, and/or adjusting the zoom) so you can see both of the waterfall charts.

The "Console View, with waterfall charts" screenshot on page 2 of the file "Ch1_Main_ chapter_supplement.pdf" shows what you should see.

In light of the basic introduction to the time value of money, and to the components of NCF, watch the waterfall charts update as you play around with the various input assumptions, many of which should be understandable. Here are a few items, however, which might not be obvious:

- The last year of the license (cell C63) is the last year of legally permitted production by the investor.

- The distinction between tangible and intangible capex (cells I59:J60), as well as tax-related balances from prior activity in row 70, have income tax implications which we shall discuss later.

Be sure you are comfortable with how the **sensitivity multipliers** in cells F23:O23 work. These provide a quick way to ask "what-if?" questions by changing an assumption for a given parameter across all years. They multiply the variables which we have input in the

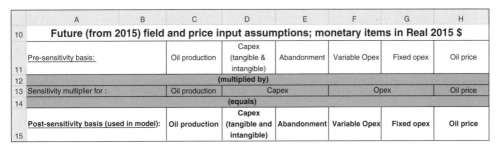

	A	B	C	D	E	F	G	H
10	**Future (from 2015) field and price input assumptions; monetary items in Real 2015 $**							
11	Pre-sensitivity basis:		Oil production	Capex (tangible & intangible)	Abandonment	Variable Opex	Fixed opex	Oil price
12	(multiplied by)							
13	Sensitivity multiplier for :		Oil production	Capex			Opex	Oil price
14	(equals)							
15	**Post-sensitivity basis (used in model):**		**Oil production**	**Capex (tangible and intangible)**	**Abandonment**	**Variable Opex**	**Fixed opex**	**Oil price**

Figure 1.7 From the "ModelSummary" sheet of the file "Ch1_Tax_and_Royalty_Model.xls"

space below them (i.e., starting in row 33) by the percentages shown. A somewhat cleaner, diagram-style view of what we mean here is shown in Figure 1.7, which is a screenshot from the "ModelSummary" sheet in the file "Ch1_Tax_and_Royalty_Model.xls."

This is the reason that many of these items – namely, the non-fiscal ones – have cells in two formats: pre-multiplier and post-multiplier. The multipliers are rather "crude" in that they each apply to their respective items equally in every year. As we shall see later, they are a quick and dirty way to analyze how changes in input assumptions affect model results:

- For example, when building our Base Scenario, we decided that Real 2015 $ capex would be 61.0 mm and 20.0 mm in 2015 and 2016, respectively, so we entered these as pre-multiplier values, using the spinners in cells I57:J57. We also entered our assumption of a Real 2015 $ 21.0 abandonment cost in cell O57. These are our pre-multiplier forecasts.

- All three of these values equal the ones immediately below them, i.e., the post-multiplier basis values in row 58, under the Base Scenario, when all multipliers are set to 100%. Raise the capex/abandonment cost multiplier (cell J23) to 105%, and you will see each of the three post-multiplier values in row 58 increase accordingly. The post-multiplier basis values are what get used in the model.

To be clear, each multiplier acts on all relevant years. Thus the oil price multiplier will affect each year's price.

Think of setting pre-multiplier inputs as fine-tuning, while setting the multipliers is a rough way of scaling a set of input assumptions up or down quickly.

With these points in mind, in the console view, vary each input from its setting under the Base Scenario (which can be restored at any time within the Console View by clicking the button in cell I21), while watching the waterfall charts, just enough for you to get a sense of whether the model behaves "sensibly":

- Do NCF and NPV increase when prices (cell G23) or production (cell O23) rise, or when the various costs fall – and vice versa?

- Get destructive: find four or five ways – using one variable, or combinations of them – to turn NCF and NPV negative.

- What is the impact on NPV of delaying the start of production to 2017 (using the spinner control in cell C43)? How about delaying the abandonment payment by a year (cell L60)?

- Do the tax deductibility switches for the rental and the bonus (cells J67 and L67) have much effect? What if you increase the bonus (cell O63) and the rentals (row 65) themselves?

- Does the difference between the discounted and undiscounted items change as you expect when you change the discount rate (cell C23)?

- Something strange, for which we have not prepared you:

  ○ Reset to the Base Scenario (cell J21).

  ○ Focus only on the undiscounted version of the waterfall chart.

  ○ Now lower the oil price multiplier (cell G23) from 100%, in steps of 5%. As you do, watch the left chart's undiscounted gross revenue column and data label.

  ○ At each multiplier setting step down through 60%, gross revenue falls – as you would expect – and by about the same amount (roughly, MOD $20–25 mm). (To see how the multiplier changes the oil price used by the model, refer to the chart which starts a bit below the waterfall charts, in cell L633.)

  ○ Change the oil price multiplier to 55%. Now undiscounted gross revenue falls sharply, by over MOD $50 mm. Keep lowering the multiplier. Between 50% and 45% is another, steeper drop. What is happening here?

Technical note: waterfall chart axis scales

It can be useful to view the two waterfall charts side by side when they use the same Y-axis scales, to clearly see the effects of discounting. For this reason, we have set them to the same scales manually (by right clicking them and making changes in the Excel dialogue boxes which appear).

One drawback of doing so, however, is that the scales might then be too small under some assumption settings (causing some columns to hit the "ceiling" or "floor"), or too large to show things in enough detail. A solution to this is to right click the Y-axis and have Excel set the scale minimum and maximum automatically; this, however, will mean that sometimes the two chart scales will not match, and/or the charts will "jump" at certain settings.

1.4 ANOTHER (IMPORTANT) MULTIPLIER – INTRODUCTION TO MODELING COMMERCIAL BEHAVIOR WITH THE ECONOMIC LIMIT TEST

Let us investigate why, as we just saw, gross revenue fell unusually sharply at certain oil price multiplier settings:

- Reset the model to the Base Scenario and, in the Console View, scroll as needed so that the oil price multiplier in cell G23 is visible above the horizontal split bar, and the small undiscounted NCF summary chart starting in cell B661 is visible below it.

- Again, lower the multiplier from 100%. Note that:

  o from 100% through to 60%, there are five years of revenue (the black columns in the chart) and thus five years of production;

  o at 55%, there are four years of revenue/production; and

  o at 45%, there are three years of revenue/production.

These three views are reproduced in screenshots on page 6 of the file "Ch1_Main_chapter_supplement.pdf," entitled "Undiscounted net cashflow, considering the economic limit test, under different oil price assumptions."

Why Is Our Production Lifespan Shrinking?

Before answering, first, let us review. In Section 1.2 we noted that:

- ultimately, the results we are most interested in are monetary values which are inflated, then discounted; and

- we implement this by multiplying all inputs which are originally expressed in Real $ by two "multiplier arrays," i.e., the annual inflation index and the annual discount factor.[10]

There is in fact a third "multiplier array" which is fundamental to our valuation models. It is based on what is called the **economic limit test (ELT)**. The ELT is a way of bringing commercial logic to our models. It is used to simulate shutting down a field when – or preferably, just before – continued production would result in losing money. "Money" as defined by the most commonly used ELT methods is a form of operating cashflow, on which we will elaborate later. For the moment, consider the example below, from the file "Ch1_Economic_Limit_Test_ELT.xls."

Consider the simplified oil field investment shown in Figure 1.8, in which all monetary values have already been inflated, i.e., put on a MOD basis. It looks like a good investment, at least initially – after an initial, "enabling" investment of $100 mm (cell E15), production starts, resulting in positive cashflow (by this simplified measure) for the next four years.

You can see that the positive cashflows of $75 mm and $55 mm in the first two production years mean that, on this basis, the investor (assumed to have a 100% equity stake, or "working interest"(WI)) makes back the initial $100 mm investment sometime by the end of 2017.

But after two more years, cashflow turns irreversibly negative in 2020, as cash costs exceed dwindling revenue. Annual cashflows are also shown in Figure 1.9.

It would be hard to imagine that a profit-minded investor would choose to continue production after 2019.

To maximize its cashflow, the investor needs to abandon the field at some point before losses can occur. The investor therefore injects some "policy" into the simplistic cashflow model, as shown in Figure 1.10.

---

[10] Note that input assumptions which are originally expressed in MOD terms – such as the bonus and rentals in this example model – are already inflated, and therefore only need to be discounted, by multiplying them by the discount factor array.

	B	C	D	E	F
11	Constant oil price, $/b				100
12			**Pre-ELT basis**		
13		Production	Revenue	Cash Costs	Cashflow
14		mm b	MOD $mm	MOD $mm	MOD $mm
15	2015	0.0	0	100	(100)
16	2016	1.0	100	25	75
17	2017	0.9	90	35	55
18	2018	0.8	80	45	35
19	2019	0.7	70	55	15
20	2020	0.6	60	65	(5)
21	2021	0.5	50	80	(30)
22	2022	0.4	40	80	(40)
23	2023	0.3	30	80	(50)
24	2024	0.2	20	80	(60)
25	**Total**	**5.4**	**540**	**645**	**(105)**

Figure 1.8   From the file "Ch1_Economic_Limit_Test_ELT.xls"
Notes: Oil price, production volumes and cash costs are assumed; revenue = price × production; cashflow = revenue − cash costs; "mm" means million; "b" (or "bbl") means barrels.

As seen in Figure 1.10, the array of 0s and 1s in column H, i.e., this **binary array**, acts like a gate – or like a bouncer at the door of a nightclub – keeping undesirable things from "passing through" by multiplying them by 0. The result is that:

- although total life-of-field production volume falls from 5.4 mmb on a pre-ELT basis (cell C67) to 3.4 mmb on a post-ELT basis (cell I67),

- the exclusion of the unprofitable barrels starting from 2020 improves total life-of-field cashflow from a loss of MOD $(105) mm (cell F67) to a profit of MOD $80 mm (cell L67).

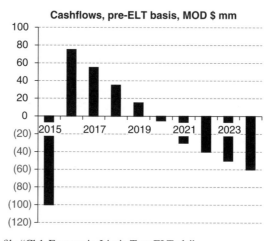

Figure 1.9   From the file "Ch1_Economic_Limit_Test_ELT.xls"

	B	C	D	E	F	G	H	I	J	K	L
50					These get multiplied...		... by this...		...resulting in these		
51											
52											
53											
54			Pre-ELT basis			ELT -- Economic Limit Test			Post-ELT basis		
55		Production	Revenue	Cash Costs	Cashflow	Continue or Quit?	Continue (1) or Quit (0)?	Production	Revenue	Cash Costs	Cashflow
56		mm b	$mm	$mm	$mm			mm b	$mm	$mm	$mm
57	2015	0.0	0	100	(100)	Continue	1	0.0	0	100	(100)
58	2016	1.0	100	25	75	Continue	1	1.0	100	25	75
59	2017	0.9	90	35	55	Continue	1	0.9	90	35	55
60	2018	0.8	80	45	35	Continue	1	0.8	80	45	35
61	2019	0.7	70	55	15	Continue	1	0.7	70	55	15
62	2020	0.6	60	65	(5)	Quit	0	0.0	0	0	0
63	2021	0.5	50	80	(30)	Quit	0	0.0	0	0	0
64	2022	0.4	40	80	(40)	Quit	0	0.0	0	0	0
65	2023	0.3	30	80	(50)	Quit	0	0.0	0	0	0
66	2024	0.2	20	80	(60)	Quit	0	0.0	0	0	0
67	Total	5.4	540	645	(105)			3.4	340	260	80

Figure 1.10   From the file "Ch1_Economic_Limit_Test_ELT.xls"
Note: All annual post-ELT basis values in columns I–K equal their pre-ELT counterparts in columns C–E, times the corresponding year's value in column H.

Multiplying the pre-ELT basis values by 0, thus shortening their lifespan, is known as "**truncating** them **to the economic limit.**"

Does the truncation of the economic field life shown in Figure 1.11 – in this case, from 2024 to 2019 – look vaguely familiar? Recall how changing the oil price multiplier in our main chapter model "Ch1_Tax_and_Royalty_Model.xls" to 55% and then to 45% shaved years off the production life. That was the model's ELT doing its job.

The criteria, or tests, which the investors in both the chapter model and the simplified example in "Ch1_Economic_Limit_Test_ELT.xls" use to decide which should be the final production

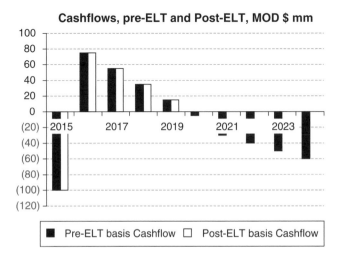

Figure 1.11   From the file "Ch1_Economic_Limit_Test_ELT.xls"

year are examples of ELTs. The ELT is there to simulate how an economically rational actor, i.e., one which wants to maximize cashflow, would behave when faced with the prospect of losses which could be avoided by abandoning the field. We consider some variant of the ELT to be essential in any serious multi-period forecast valuation model.

Note that in the underlying model in "Ch1_Economic_Limit_Test_ELT.xls" we have manually typed in the "Continue," "Quit" and 1 and 0 values columns G and H. Later we will show how to calculate these formulaically. We just note for now that while this is relatively easy, it is not necessarily done in the way that this simple example might suggest.

ELT-related terminology

The **ELT** (again, Economic Limit Test) is, as the name indicates, a test, not a point in time.

Rather, the ELT *determines* a point in time, i.e., when a field should be shut down on economic (or "commercial") grounds, sometimes called the **cutoff**. In our annual models, we call this point in time the end of the **last economic year** or **last economic production year**. In the Base Scenario of "Ch1_Economic_Limit_Test_ELT.xls" it is the end of 2020.

Therefore, the term "**pre-ELT** production" as we use it does *not* denote production occurring before the end of 2020. To be on a "pre-ELT" basis means ignoring the calculation of when the last economic year should be. Thus we use the term "pre-ELT production" to mean production in *any* year, ignoring (not applying) the ELT cutoff. In the simple example above, "pre-ELT production" could be used to describe any value in cells C57:C66. Thus we use "pre-ELT" in the same way we use "pre-tax" in the term "pre-tax cashflow" – that is, meaning cashflow in any year, ignoring (not deducting) tax.

Similarly, "post-ELT" should be understood to mean *any* value after considering (applying) the ELT cutoff, and not, in this example, as meaning after the end of 2020.

The measure of cashflow which the most commonly used variant of ELT aims to maximize, i.e., the analogue to the simplistically termed "cashflow" in Figure 1.11 – is what we term **gross operating cashflow**, or **GOCF**. We'll detail its calculation later.

The ELT is expressed in the binary array in cells H57:H66 (Figure 1.10), which we will term the similarly named **economic life flag ("ELF")**.

Calculation Flow in our Example Model – "Built Around" the ELT

Open the main example model for this chapter, found in the file "Ch1_Tax_and_Royalty_Model.xls." Look at the outline of the model found on the "ModelSummary" sheet. There is a lot of detail here; for now, what is relevant is the overall structure: calculations (which are summarized starting in row 21) are split into three main categories: pre-ELT (rows 21–33), ELT (rows 35–37), and post-ELT (starting row 39).

Pre-ELT calculations. Because the standard version of the ELT we use in this book is based on maximizing GOCF, most of the pre-ELT calculations are of items needed to determine GOCF. These include revenue, operating costs ("opex") and all fiscal costs except (for reasons we explain later) income tax.

ELT calculations. Here we determine when the last economic production year will be, and express this in the model as the binary ELF array.

Post-ELT calculations. Here, we:

- Get post-ELT versions of previously calculated pre-ELT items, by multiplying them by the ELF.
- Deal with a special item – the abandonment cost:
  - We time, based on the last economic year, and thus inflate, the abandonment payment (i.e., for removing equipment, plugging wells and restoring the site).
  - Note that the abandonment cost is on a "post-ELT basis" – not because it has been multiplied by the ELF (it has not), but rather because it has been timed to take into account when the economic production period ends.
- Calculate income tax. Income tax is on a post-ELT basis – not because it has been multiplied by the ELF (again, it has not), but rather because it is calculated using only post-ELT components.
- Calculate net cashflow (NCF) and discounted NCF, using only the post-ELT basis components determined above. Therefore our NCF and NPV results will be on a post-ELT basis as well.

1.5   CHAPTER MODEL HOUSEKEEPING NOTES

In the next few sections of this chapter, we will discuss how the model is built, section by section, and occasionally ask you to make certain changes and observe the results. Before proceeding, here are some useful points to bear in mind.

Read This in Front of the Computer, Actively

Although we try to be generous with explanatory screenshots from the model, both in the text and in the file, "Ch1_Main_chapter_supplement.pdf" on the disk, we have designed the discussion which follows assuming you will be following along while viewing the open Excel model.

You will greatly benefit from using Excel's auditing commands – as well as the shortcut keys we have designated for some of them, as explained on the "AuditingTools" worksheet of the example model file.

Essentially, these commands cause temporary blue tracer lines to appear between formulaically linked cells which are on the same sheet. (Most of our models are contained within one sheet.)

They make it much easier and quicker to follow some of our many detailed discussions about formulas, because instead of having to locate all relevant cells by their cell address, these lines point to all of them at once. When used in split-screen mode, this can be very helpful. Their use is demonstrated in the short video tutorial "Ch1_Good auditing habits.wmv" on the disk.[11]

Custom View Setting Within the Model

The model's underlying calculations, interactive charts and special analysis sections make it rather large. To ease navigation and the use of the interactive charts, we have created a number of buttons in rows 1–10 (with some duplicates elsewhere) of the "Model" sheet which trigger custom views, split the screen horizontally, and/or hide certain rows. (These custom views can be undone using the "Show all rows" buttons in cell C1 or D21.) Be sure you have set Excel to enable macros, or these will not work.

The view when you click the "Group rows" button in cell D1 is a useful format when first surveying the model's layout. The view is "semi-condensed." This means you will see:

- the most commonly used assumption input cells and controls (starting in row 22);

- starting row 83, two charts and a table for reference when making assumptions (for which you will probably have to split the screen);

- starting in row 108, many calculation subsections which show only their section headings and final results, with underlying calculations hidden; and

- the interactive charts and analysis tables which start in row 597.

We will often refer to another custom view, the Console View, which we introduced above and which you can see by clicking the button in cell F1. Although you might need to slightly adjust the horizontal split bar at times, this view should provide a convenient way to change assumptions and see the effects elsewhere in the model.

Spinner Controls

Many inputs may only be changed with spinner controls (switches) such as the one in cell C22. In cases where the variable is expressed as a percentage or contains a decimal – things which Excel's spinners do not permit directly – we have used an indirect solution, which is explained in the "Use of extra cells with spinner controls" section (page 7) of the file "Ch1_Main_chapter_supplement.pdf." This explains, among other things, what the table starting in cell Q1 is for.

If you have not built a model with spinners before, take a moment to watch the video tutorial "Ch1_Making and using spinners.wmv" on the disk in the Chapter 1 folder.

---

[11] Two other powerful auditing tools that we would urge you to investigate, both for use with this book and generally, are (a) Excel's Evaluate Formula tool (explained in the standalone file "Ch3_Evaluate_Formula_Excel_tool.xls," found in the Chapter 3 folder); and (b) a third-party Excel add-in called RefTreeAnalyser, which – provided you freeze or split the screen in half, vertically, at the right edge of the last caption column on the left – is like Excel's auditing commands on steroids. Rather than following blue lines between cells, it "flies" you past each formula component cell (this is easier to understand when it is used). A free demo and a paid version are available from the developer, JKP Application Development Services, at http://www.jkp-ads.com/RefTreeAnalyser.asp.

Only Type in Cells in Blue Font

Do not type in any cell other than those in blue font, (when permitted – note that some of these have been locked to certain values using Excel's Validation feature.)

Named Cells and Ranges

The model uses many named cells and ranges, to make formulas easier to read. These have red borders. Select a named cell or range and see its name in the box in the upper left hand corner of the Excel screen, to the left of the formula bar. You can also refer to the file's "NamedCellsAndRanges" worksheet, which lists the cell addresses of all named cells and ranges.

Be sure especially to check those named items which are visible in the assumptions part of the Console View, as many are used often in the calculation sections below.

For a quick overview of important points about how we use named *ranges* in particular – and how one should not – see "How Excel understands references to named ranges" on pages 4 and 5 of the file "Ch1_Main_chapter_supplement.pdf."

Checksums and the ROUND Function

Notice the red 0 values in column A, including the one in cell A1, as well as elsewhere in the model, and the "No errors detected" message in cell B1. The red zero cells contain formulas called "checksums," which are used to detect errors. A red zero in a gray-shaded cell means no error has been found. Often these checksum formulas use Excel's ROUND function. For details, see the Checksum pages (8 and 9) of the file "Ch1_Main_chapter_supplement.pdf."

1.6   CHAPTER MODEL ASSUMPTIONS

1.6.1   Assumptions: General Remarks

Our Assumptions Are Simplified

In real-world upstream petroleum economic models, field assumptions are the combined product of the efforts of earth scientists and petroleum reservoir and cost engineers. Each of their disciplines is a specialty in its own right and is thus beyond the scope of this book, which focuses on how to turn technical data into meaningful financial data.

Therefore, here and in other example models used in this book, we will just provide you with the raw technical data assumptions, with no attempt to make them any more detailed than needed to make our fiscal and valuation modeling points. Frequent simplifying shortcuts we have taken include:

- assuming very brief (often one- or two-year) development periods, i.e., when initial capex is spent, to enable production;

- limiting example fields' **technical production** schedules, or **profiles** – here "technical" means pre-ELT, or ignoring the economic limit – to 10 years or less (whereas many actual fields produce for decades);

- aggregating the many types of opex and capex into just a few, fiscally relevant categories;[12] and

- assuming that the Investor (which, under a type of fiscal regime called a production sharing agreement – covered in Chapters 6–8 – is also referred to as a "Contractor") has a 100% equity stake, or **working interest**, in the project in question. Note, however, that in reality often there are multiple partners, sometimes using complex shareholder/financing agreements. While these can be fiscally relevant to the individual parties, they are something of a sub-science of their own, and thus beyond our scope here.

Therefore, bear in mind the old Modeling Law: "garbage in means garbage out." The quality and validity of the input data are paramount. In real life, the analyst would get these data from in-house discipline experts if he or she is working for a petroleum company, whereas outside analysts working for banks, investment funds, potential production partners, or host governments will have to get these data from the operating company's team, from their own in-house expertise if available, or from outside consultants.

1.6.2 Assumptions: Time and the Time Value of Money

These assumptions are summarized in the screenshot from the "ModelSummary" sheet shown in Figure 1.12.

The inflation and discount rates can be input using the spinners in the "Model" sheet's cells C22 and C23. The corresponding arrays for the annual inflation index and discount factor are found in rows 28 and 29, and are named "Infl_index" and "Disc_factor" respectively. They are calculated using the mid-period method described in Section 1.2.

The valuation date, i.e., the date from which values are inflated, and to which they are discounted, is assumed to be January 1, 2015 (not changeable in this version) of the model.

	A	B	C	D	E
3	**Time related assumptions**				
4	• Inflation rate			• Inflation index	
5	• Discount rate	expressed as	--->	• Discount factor	
6	• License length			• License flag	
7	Production and Abandonment delay factors				

Figure 1.12   From the file "Ch1_Tax_and_Royalty_Model.xls"

---

[12] A wide-ranging and very readable introduction to the different kinds of equipment and processes (and thus kinds of capex and opex) involved in upstream petroleum projects is Norman J. Hyne's *Nontechnical Guide to Petroleum Geology, Exploration, Drilling and Production* (Penwell Books, 2012).

Note that the model lets you delay, compared to the Base Scenario assumptions, the start of production,[13] as well as when the abandonment payment is made, by one year, using the spinners in cells C43 and L60, respectively. The Base Case assumes production will start one year after the first capex year of 2015, and that the abandonment payment will be made in the last economic year.

Sense checks

Start each of the two checks described below by showing the Base Scenario:

(a) In the Console View, be able to see the inflation and discount rate input cells (C22:C23) above the split, and, below it, either the waterfall charts (starting in row 602) or the annual basis undiscounted and discounted NCF charts (row 661). Do you understand why these charts change as they do when you adjust the rates? Do the discounted results match their undiscounted counterparts when the discount rate is set to 0%? What (approximately) is the discount rate at which NPV equals 0 (i.e., what is the internal rate of return (IRR))?

(b) In the Console View, be able to see rows 43 and 60 in the top part of the screen, and, in the bottom part, rows 502–511 from the investor's undiscounted NCF section. Use the spinners in C43 and L60 to adjust the timings. Do the NCF components seem to shift in time appropriately?

We explain the time-shifting calculations in the sections covering production inputs and the abandonment calculation, below.

1.6.3   Assumptions: Commodity Prices[14]

Price Forecasts: General Thoughts

The oil price is one of the single most powerful parameters in an oil field valuation model in terms of its effects on NPV. In the model's Console View, note how much more a 5% increase in the oil price multiplier (cell G23) improves NPV in the waterfall chart, compared to a 5% decrease in the capex or opex multipliers (cells J23 and L23, respectively).[15]

The oil price is, however, also notoriously hard to forecast. Over the few years of writing this book, we have seen the benchmark Brent crude price range between approximately MOD $40 and $150. If we knew what the oil price would be, we would have probably dictated this book to attractive assistants from the deck chairs of yachts, if we had bothered to write at all.

---

[13] Although in this example model we express our annual production profiles (discussed below) in mmb (millions of barrels per year; also mm bbl), be aware that quite often such data are expressed in barrels per day (b/d, or bbl/d) or thousands of barrels per day (mb/d or m bbl/d). This requires an assumption about the number of days per year. One approach uses the actual number of calendar days for each year; others assume that each year has 365 days, or 365.25 days to approximate the effect of leap years.

[14] As most of our models and examples in this book assume the fields in question produce only oil, the following discussion is about oil prices, not gas prices. The main points made here, however, also apply in large measure to gas prices, except that whereas oil markets are global, gas markets tend to be more localized, and gas prices tend in many regions to vary seasonally.

[15] The degree of difference will of course depend on the field and fiscal assumptions in question, but usually the price is more influential than other input assumptions.

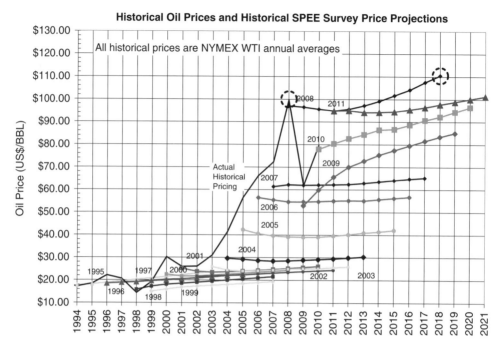

Figure 1.13   SPEE survey: respondents' oil price forecasts over time (From *Society of Petroleum Evaluation Engineers Thirtieth Annual Survey of Parameters Used in Property Evaluation, June 2011*). (For clarity, we have also reproduced this graphic on page 3 of the file "Ch1_Main_chapter_supplement.pdf")

Figure 1.13 is a screenshot from the 2011 SPEE survey we mentioned in Section 1.2. It shows respondents' average forecasts for their "NYMEX WTI" (West Texas Intermediate, the main US crude oil benchmark price, traded on the NYMEX exchange) price forecasts, made at different points in time. For example, the two blue circles, which we have added to start and end the "2008" series in the SPEE's graphic, show that:

- the average forecast made in 2008, for the 2008 oil price, was (approximating from the chart) around $98/b; and

- the average forecast made in 2008, for the 2018 oil price, was around $110.

The contrast between the forecasts and the plain black line, which represents actual historic prices, is instructive.

- The actual price is volatile – or as John Browne, former CEO of BP put it, "inherently unpredictable."

- Forecasts, on the other hand, with some variation, generally tend to "chase" the actual price as it moves up and down – that is, they tend to start at a price close to the actual price seen at, or not long (roughly 0–1.5 years) before the date the forecast was made, and then move horizontally.

This inherent volatility of the oil price is due to the fact that it is – except where governments impose local price controls – determined:

- by supply and demand; and

- due to the role of speculation, by *perceptions* of future supply and demand.

Therefore, it would seem that the most rigorous way to try to forecast global oil prices from first principles would require you to:

- assemble a base case supply/demand projection, drawing on a view of every country's future production, consumption and storage volumes;

- anticipate and quantify the impact on supply and/or demand of disruptions to the base case, e.g., on the supply side, things like wars, civil unrest, vandalism, geopolitical crises, hurricanes, accidents and their fallout, and, on the demand side, anything affecting future consumption, such as the state of the global economy;

- anticipate to what extent speculators and other buyers will themselves anticipate and respond to these disruptions; and

- then back-test the model with historic data, to see how well whatever algorithm you have devised to incorporate all these factors would have predicted actual prices. If the model passes this credibility test – and you are happy to assume that relationships which held true over the historic test period will remain in the future – you have yourself a price forecast model.

This of course is a caricature of a method we have not actually seen used, but which we cite just to show why medium- and long-term forecasts are so often wrong.

Investors, governments and other actors respond to the challenge of forecasting prices for use in valuation models in different ways. Some use quite detailed and "scientific" methods; others use probabilistic approaches;[16] while at the other extreme, others just use a price based on a consensus (often an average) of third-party forecasts, including those forecasts which are implied by exchange-traded commodity futures prices.

A common, pragmatic approach is to accept that the price is unknowable, and to use a base case, however arrived at, as well as low and high alternative cases, to try to get a feel for "expected" (however that is defined) bad and good scenarios. Sensitivity analysis, whereby one calculates NPV across a broad range of oil prices, is a prudent practice to "stress-test" a valuation.

> The oil price issue alone brings into focus the fact that, ultimately, the goal of valuation modeling is not to be able to state "NPV will equal $X," but rather to be able to answer the question "What will NPV be under any given set of explicit assumptions?" Until we learn how to see into the future, it is the best we can do.

---

[16] We provide an introduction to probabilistic modeling, including exercises for use with the trial version of Crystal Ball on the disk, in the standalone files in the Appendix V folder on the disk, and in Section 8.2 of Chapter 8.

Price Forecasts in Our Example Model

To simplify our model and keep the focus on fiscal analysis, we make no pretence of even trying to forecast the oil price. Rather, for our Base Scenario, we have pulled a number out of the air – Real 2015 $80/barrel (cell D33) – and assumed this will be the field's received oil price each year. We have also created a row for you to input your own annual price(s) in Real 2015 $ terms, and a way to choose between them. Whichever price is used will then be subject to the oil price sensitivity multiplier and inflated to MOD terms, for use in the model.

We do this in rows 33–41 of the example model:

- The spinner control in cell D33 lets you change the assumed (all-years) price in 2015 $/b which will be used, *if* you have chosen to use the Base Scenario oil price. The value in cell D33 then determines every annual cell in row 36.

- You can enter any values for the Real 2015 $/b "User custom oil price" case in cells F37:O37.

- The spinner in cell I33 lets you choose between the two forecasts to use. The selected, Real MOD $/b forecast series will appear in row 39, in which the annual cells use Excel's CHOOSE function (explained on pages 82–83 of "Ch1_Time_value_of_money_supplement.pdf).

- The selected price case in row 39 then gets multiplied in row 40 by the oil price sensitivity multiplier (or "factor," which, again, under the Base Scenario, always equals 100%).

- The resultant values in row 40 get multiplied in row 41 by the inflation index. This is what will feed the model.

Do Not Forget What "Real 2015 $" Means

Bear in mind, as we discussed in the "Real Versus Inflated Dollars" subsection of Section 1.2, above, that the term "Real 2015 $/b" on its own does *not* mean the oil price in 2015. Rather, it means an oil price – which could be for any period specified – expressed in dollars of constant 2015 purchasing power. Thus, for example, under the Base Scenario:

- the value of 80 in cell F36 means an annual average oil price of $80/b for 2015, expressed in Real 2015 dollars; and

- the value of 80 in cell I36 means an annual average oil price of $80/b for 2018, expressed in Real 2015 dollars.

These values are then inflated in row 41 for later use in the model.

Price Forecasts in Models: Differentials

Even assuming the modeler takes the "quick and dirty" approach of using a consensus forecast for a crude benchmark such as Brent crude, unless the field being modeled is one contributing physically to the Brent blend, the price in the model will likely need some adjusting. To keep our model simple, we do not make such adjustments, but you should be aware of them when building real-world models.

Adjustments are needed because Brent is only a benchmark crude, whereas there are many different grades of crude oil around the world, each with its own price. A **benchmark crude** is one:

- which is sold at a specified location; and

- for which prices are published in the public domain. Other examples include West Texas Intermediate, or "WTI" (USA), Urals (Russia) and Forcados (Nigeria).

In general, all oil prices – benchmark and non-benchmark – tend to "move together" in terms of period-on-period <u>percentage change,</u> but they have <u>different dollar values,</u> due to differences in, among other things, a crude's quality (e.g., high-sulfur or "sour" crude tends to be priced lower than low-sulfur or "sweet" crude).[17]

Therefore the modeler should base the price forecast on:

- a benchmark which has in the past shown some meaningful relationship, i.e., similar dollar pricing and percentage change trends over time, to the historic prices realized by the field being modeled; or, if the field being modeled has not produced yet,

- a benchmark of similar quality, i.e., one whose price movements could be expected to parallel those received by the field in question, once it starts producing.

In either case, an adjustment, or **price differential**, would need to be assumed. If, for example, the crude in question has historically sold at a price 10% lower than, say, Brent crude, then one might assume that, in the future, the differential will continue to be equal to 10% of Brent, i.e., the crude in question would sell at a 10% discount to Brent. If on the other hand the crude has historically traded at 10% higher than Brent, the assumed differential could be an assumed "10% premium to Brent."[18]

Price Forecasts in Models: Where Is This Price Realized?

Crude is priced at a specific location. The location matters from a fiscal and valuation standpoint:

- Most fiscal devices such as royalties, which are calculated as some percentage of revenue, specify that the location where the sales price is realized is to be used in their calculation. This could be at the **wellhead** (right were the crude comes out of the ground), or it could be somewhere outside the license area, such as a third-party pumping station, or a pipeline juncture. To correctly calculate royalties and other fiscal devices based on the received price, you need to know this price.

- Location also matters because the cost of transportation to a selling point costs money. In such a case, for cashflow purposes, the cash inflow should be the price received at the selling

---

[17] Note that in some cases, though, regional differences in inventory values can and do lead to benchmark oil prices moving in opposite directions. In such a case, you need to "take a view" as to which trend should be assumed for forecasting purposes.

[18] Note, however, that differentials between oil price benchmarks may vary significantly over short periods of time (e.g., Brent and WTI over the 2010–2012 period).

point, and the cash outflow would be the handling (i.e., transportation and storage) opex incurred in getting it there.

In our example models in this book, we assume that the assumed oil prices, i.e., those chosen for use in row 39, are the same prices used by fiscal devices, and that these are the <u>wellhead prices</u>, so the investor incurs no transport costs.

1.6.4   Assumptions: Production Profile

Up to seven years of annual oil production volumes, in mmb, can be entered on a pre-multiplier, pre-ELT basis in the gray-shaded cells F46:L46. To enable time-shifting,

- These annual volumes are entered on a <u>generic year</u> basis, i.e., for production year 1, production year 2, etc.

- They are then converted to a <u>calendar year</u> basis in row 49, based on the starting calendar year of production which you specify in row 43.

The method used to shift the production profile to the specified timeframe is explained on pages 11–13 of the file "Ch1_Main_chapter_supplement.pdf."

1.6.5   Assumptions: Capex

Capex Scheduling Issues

For a given production "stream," **capex** or **capital expenditure** consists of the costs of services and/or long-life assets incurred:

- before production starts, as an initial enabling investment, i.e. to find and appraise oil and gas and to get commercial production up and running; typical items include wells and ancillary items, pipelines and treatment/storage facilities; and

- after production starts, to maintain production; this includes certain categories of maintenance/reinvigoration of wells though "recompletions" and "workovers"; these costs are usually incurred only occasionally (i.e., they are not a recurrent annual expense).

In such a simplified single "stream" view, often most of the capex will be spent before production starts (meaning the investor starts off "in the red" – see for example the cumulative undiscounted and discounted NCF charts which start in cells B669 and L669).

Often, however, large and/or complex fields will require a phased approach, i.e., consisting of different "streams" starting at different times, meaning pre-production capex for one stream might be incurred at the same time that another is in its post-production phase. Some "streams" will also share common facilities. Multi-"stream" capex scheduling can get complex, and require solving timing and capacity optimization problems.[19] In nearly all the examples used in this book, we have kept things simple by using the single "stream" assumption.

Capex Classification for Fiscal Purposes: Intangible vs. Tangible

For fiscal purposes, a key distinction is whether capex is classed as intangible or tangible:

- Intangible capex consists of items, the essence of which cannot be touched – for example, seismic data and its processing and interpretation; a facilities plan; the drilling of a well bore, etc. Intangible capex is usually "expensed for tax purposes." This means that, for example, the full value of a $10 mm intangible capex item is eligible to be an income tax deduction, or **tax allowance**, in the year that it is incurred.

- Tangible capex, on the other hand, can be touched – for example, the steel casing which is placed in the well bore; well platforms and facilities, pipelines, compressor stations, etc.

- Often – though not always – tangible capex is "capitalized for tax purposes," which means that the tax allowances which arise from tangible capex will be phased over time via depreciation. For example, under a common variant known as "straight line" depreciation:

  ○ if the depreciation rules in the country's tax code state that a $10 mm tangible capex item has a 10-year "useful life" for depreciation purposes,

  ○ then for each of the 10 years, starting with the year the item is first used, there will be 10 equal annual tax allowances of $1 mm each.

This is a simplification. We treat depreciation in more detail below.

In our example model, capex is assumed to be incurred only in 2015 and 2016. Assumptions are input in pre-multiplier, Real 2015 $ terms, along with an assumed tangible/intangible percentage split each year, as shown in Figure 1.14.

	F	G	H	I	J
55	**costs (Real 2015 $)**				
56	**Capex , $mm**			2015	2016
57	Pre-multiplier			61.0	20.0
58	**Post-multiplier**			61.0	20.0
59	of which tangible, %			60.0%	90.0%
60	of which intangible, %			40.0%	10.0%

Figure 1.14 Capex inputs under Base Scenario (Real 2015 $ mm), from the file "Ch1_Tax_and_Royalty_Model.xls"
Note: Reflects Base Scenario.

[19] A good source on generic project timing modeling in Excel is *Spreadsheet Modeling and Applications: Essentials of Practical Management Science*, by S. Christian Albright and Wayne L. Winston (South-Western, 2005). In addition, the trial version of Crystal Ball on the book's disk contains tutorials for solving schedule optimization problems using the included OptQuest software.

1.6.6   Assumptions: Opex

Field operating expenses, or **opex**, are the ongoing costs incurred once production has begun. Opex is usually often divided for modeling purposes into two categories:

- fixed opex; and
- variable opex.

Fixed field opex (cell C57) is usually forecast in terms of total cost per accounting period. In our example model, it lives up to its name, i.e., the cost is a "fixed," or constant, amount incurred for each period of operation, regardless of how much oil is produced.

Be aware, however, that in the real world, the amount is only "fixed" *within certain ranges* of production volumes involved:

- For example, a processing facility might cost Real 2015 $10 mm per year to operate, when the annual volumes processed are between, say, 0 and 1 mmb, but $15 mm per year when they are between 1 and 2 mmb etc.
- Thus what is commonly called "fixed opex" is actually "fixed" only over certain ranges of production, and can vary in a step-like manner between thresholds.

Other examples of such fixed field opex include administrative overheads, operating staff, safety, security, environmental monitoring and facility insurance.

In contrast, **variable field opex** (cell D57) always varies continuously according to production volumes. For oil production, variable field opex is normally expressed on a unit basis, which in the case of an oil-only development would mean cost per barrel of oil production.[20]

Simplifications Used in Our Example Model

We have ignored any operating costs incurred in the pre- and post-production years. In real life there would be, at minimum, managerial and administrative overheads incurred to consider.

In our Base Scenario, fixed opex of Real 2015 $15 mm per year (cell C57) is assumed incurred in all production years, i.e., it is truly "fixed," and does not vary depending on a year's production volume.

> While this assumption might be plausible in light of the Base Scenario's assumed volumes, be aware that it might not make sense in the real world, for example, to increase the oil production sensitivity multiplier in cell O23 from 100% to 500%, while leaving fixed opex unchanged.

---

[20] With fields producing a significant amount of water, variable operating costs are sometimes expressed as cost per barrel of total fluid production (i.e., oil plus water). So be sure you are clear what "per barrel" means!

To remedy this in a real-world Excel model, one would need to ensure that fixed opex charges vary formulaically with the appropriate production thresholds – using, for example, IF statements, or LOOKUP tables.[21] Note that while writing the formulas might be easy, the underlying inputs would likely require somewhat detailed cost engineering expertise.

1.6.7   Assumptions: Abandonment

The assumptions for the **abandonment costs** – also called **decommissioning costs** and/or **site restoration costs** – are input on a Real 2015 $, pre-multiplier basis in cell O57. Under our Base Scenario, they are Real 2015 $21.0 mm.

Abandonment costs are the costs incurred to meet the requirement for oil and gas producers to clean up after themselves when production has finished, usually by plugging disused wells and dismantling facilities. By definition, much of this constitutes the last activity in the life of the field, most of which occurs after revenue from production has ceased.

In our example model, the abandonment cost is paid in a single "lumpsum," either in the last year of economic (i.e., post-ELT) production, or one year later, as the user specifies using the spinner in cell L60.

Note that:

- The relevant sensitivity multiplier is the combined capex/abandonment multiplier in cell J23. We use a combined multiplier as a simplification, though one which makes some sense, as the size of abandonment costs is often linked to the scale of capex involved in developing a field.

- We do not inflate the abandonment cost at this stage in the model. We cannot, because we do not yet know when it will be paid – we will know this only after we determine when the last economic production year will be, which is calculated later, in the model's ELT section. We will inflate the abandonment cost there.

Looking ahead: abandonment costs' impact on NPV

Discharging abandonment obligations via such a single, end-of-life lumpsum is fairly common practice, but there are several variations used as well. One is to require payments from the producer in advance, i.e., while the field is still producing. This and other abandonment funding arrangements are important as they can impact cashflows in a number of ways:

- As cash outflows in their own right, which in some cases can be quite material. For example, a long-producing field, nearing the end of its life, can have large accumulated "lumpsum" abandonment liabilities due in the near future, "looming on the horizon."

- The timing of abandonment payments influences their discounted cost to the investor, and thus the investor's NPV; this aspect of the time value of money can, in fact, sometimes

---

[21] See the standalone file "VLOOKUP_HLOOKUP_examples.xls" in the Chapter 1 folder for more details on LOOKUP tables.

give investors incentives to seek legitimate ways to delay abandonment payments, when permitted.

- Abandonment costs are usually tax deductible, as we assume in our example model.
  - o Abandonment costs paid as an end-of-life lumpsum, however, will be incurred at a time when the field will have little or no revenue, and thus little or no taxable income. When there is no taxable income, a tax deduction does not benefit the taxpayer (unless there are special fiscal mechanisms in place to help remedy this, which our example model does *not* assume).
  - o Whereas if, in contrast, abandonment costs are paid over the producing life, when there *is* (hopefully) taxable income, then the abandonment costs paid will benefit the taxpayer as tax deductions.

Thus the impact of how abandonment costs are funded will depend on the interplay between the size of the costs, their timing, the ability to make use of the associated tax benefits, and the effects of inflation/and discounting on both the outflow itself and on any tax benefits.

Chapter 5 is devoted entirely to abandonment funding.

Coming Up: Overview of Fiscal Assumptions

The screenshot reproduced in Figure 1.15 shows the main items which we shall introduce in the next few sections.

1.6.8   Assumptions: Royalty

	A	B	C	D	E	F	G	H
16								
17					**Fiscal assumptions**			
18		Royalty rate %	Rental amount, MOD $	Bonus amount, MOD $	Tax loss end of 2014	Income tax rate, %; Depreciation rules	Prior balances: Tax loss and Undepreciated balance end of 2014, MOD $	Capex as tax allowances: Intangible is expensed; Tangible is depreciated
19	Usable as tax allowances?	Yes	Maybe	Maybe	Yes			

Figure 1.15   From the "ModelSummary" sheet of the file "Ch1_Tax_and_Royalty_Model.xls"

The royalty payment is one of a few "off-the-top" fiscal devices in our example model.

Royalties are payments to the government – and sometimes to third parties ("overriding royalties") – based on a rate which is a percentage of the value of commercial production. Their cash value per barrel (in the case of oil) is usually based on the producer's received sales price. Hence the term "off the top" – such royalty payments are usually made from revenue before any other deductions are made.

Government royalties provide a guaranteed revenue stream for the state, regardless of a field's profitability. (In formal petroleum economics terminology, this means they are **regressive** devices.)

Royalties can take many different forms – Chapter 3 is devoted to some of the most common ones. For this chapter's introductory model, we have used the simplest version – a constant percentage of the wellhead price in all years. Under the Base Scenario, it is 17.25%, input in cell H63 of the "Model" sheet.

Sense check

Set the model to the Base Scenario and, in the Console View, move the oil price multiplier above and below 100% while watching the waterfall charts below the split. Do the royalty columns (and value captions at the bottom) update as you would expect?

Reset the oil price multiplier to 100%, and then scroll down in the top part of the screen, so that you can see the royalty rate (cell H63). At which royalty rates do the investor's NCF and NPV – shown in the waterfall charts' captions – turn negative?

Note that in cell N67 we have assumed that the royalty is tax deductible. This is not changeable in the model. We have never seen a case where royalty was not tax deductible. It would be cruel indeed for a government to tax an investor based on income which was taken "off the top," i.e., never actually received by the investor.

1.6.9   Assumptions: Rentals

Area rentals – not to be confused with opex, which can include the costs of renting equipment or facilities – are a second fiscal device in our example tax and royalty regime which takes money "off the top" of the investor's cash inflows, without any direct link to field profitability or the lack thereof.

As the name implies, area rentals are periodic, area-based fees payable to the government, usually based on the area of the acreage[22] in question, and the phase of the fields' lives, which in our example is divided for these purposes into the pre-production phase and the production phase.

Rental assumptions for the area and the annual rental rates payable during each type of period are entered in row 65 of the model. Note that:

- as is common in many fiscal regimes with rentals, the annual per-unit payments required are small relative to project cashflows – in this case MOD $50 000–100 000, depending on the period – and are expressed in the regulations (and thus in the model) in MOD terms; and

---

[22] Note that in upstream petroleum, the term "acreage" is sometimes used to mean "area," even when the regulations use other units, such as square kilometers in our example model.

- we simplify in our example model by assuming that the license area is the same every year. Be aware, though, that often in real exploration licenses which result in a discovery, the investor is required to **relinquish**, or give back to the government, any acreage it no longer needs for further exploration and/or development and production. In some cases, relinquishments are required after certain deadlines. At all events, the license area can shrink over time.

Sense check

Note that, in cell J67, you can assume whether rentals are tax deductible. Reset the model to the Base Scenario. Then in the Console View, arrange the split so that rows 65–67 are visible above it and, below it, the waterfall charts (including the value labels at the bottom of the charts, which should be possible in full screen mode). Make the rentals non-deductible by changing the value in cell J67 from 1 to 0, while noting the changes in the waterfall charts. Note that doing so will not change the amounts shown in either chart for "Bonuses & Rentals," but it will have a modest impact on the income tax charge, and thus on NCF and NPV.

1.6.10 Assumptions: Bonuses

Bonuses are the third "off-the-top" fiscal device in our example model's assumed tax and royalty regime. Bonuses are payments – again, usually denominated in MOD terms – made to the government which correspond to some project milestone.

Bonuses take many forms. A few common ones include:

- Signature bonuses (paid when the investor formally joins a license, or signs a production sharing contract).
- Bonuses payable upon first commercial[23] production (like the one in our example model). While not always large, they can have symbolic/"public relations" value to governments which wish to show the public, early in a project, that the host country is receiving cashflow.
- Bonuses based on reaching a level or levels of cumulative production.

Chapter 4 is devoted entirely to bonuses.

In this chapter's example model, the assumed bonus amount is entered using the spinner in cell O63. Bonuses are not always tax deductible; therefore the user may decide whether this one is or not, using the spinner in cell L67.

---

[23] "Commercial production" in this sense usually means production which is sold during a field's main production period, as opposed to early volumes produced on a test basis during the preceding appraisal period.

Sense check

In the Console View, make row 43 – where you decide when first production will be – visible above the split, and the timed bonus payment in row 160 visible below the split. Change the production date and be sure the bonus timing changes appropriately. Note that because we have entered the assumed bonus assumption in MOD terms, its MOD value in the model does not change according to when it is paid.

Assumptions: per-barrels basis "reality check" table

If you click the "Show all rows" button in cell C1, and then click the "Console View" button in cell F1, you should see below the horizontal split (perhaps most clearly in full screen mode) a table starting in cell G83. This expresses all the results of all the assumptions, excluding income tax and related items, on a (take a deep breath) post-sensitivity multiplier, pre-ELT, life-of-field, Real 2015 $/barrel basis. The table is shown in Figure 1.16. It reflects the Base Scenario.

In other words, we get a "raw" or "underlying" view of the weighted average field economics, based on assumptions feeding the model, but before the model "acts" on them by introducing "distortions" due to the economic limit, taxation and the time value of money.

	Real 2015 $/b	% of gross revenue
82 Reflects post-multiplier basis assumptions		
83 Memo: Total (all years) results of assumptions, IGNORING the economic limit, in Real 2015 $		
84 Item	Real 2015 $/b	% of gross revenue
85 Gross field revenue	80.00	100.0%
86 Capex	13.79	17.2%
87 Fixed opex	17.88	22.3%
88 Variable opex	8.00	10.0%
89 Abandonment	3.58	4.5%
90 Field costs	43.24	54.1%
91 Field operating cashflow	36.76	45.9%
92 Royalty @ 17.25%	13.80	17.3%
93 Rentals	2.12	2.6%
94 Bonus	2.48	3.1%
95 Fiscal costs	18.39	23.0%
96 Field pre-tax cashflow	18.36	23.0%

Figure 1.16   From the "Model" sheet of the file "Ch1_Tax_and_Royalty_Model.xls"
Note: Reflects Base Scenario.

This per-barrel view puts into perspective the relative size of different cost items in relation to revenue, which otherwise would be hard to do, since we are inputting our assumptions in so many different formats, namely:

- variable opex in Real 2015 $ per barrel;

- fixed opex in real 2015 $ mm per producing year;

- capex per year in Real 2015 $ mm in specific years;

- abandonment costs in Real 2015 $ mm (to be spent in a year we do not know yet);

- royalty as a percentage of the oil price; and

- rentals and the bonus in MOD $ mm.[24]

The "raw" view in this table is only a starting point for analysis – after all, we are building a fiscally detailed valuation model, so we will only discount and thus derive a value from inflated, post-ELT, post-tax cashflows. But the "raw" view still can give useful insights, and help check the credibility of some of the inputs.

- For example, if you reset the model to the Base Scenario and, in Console View, lower the oil price (cell D33), you will see that the field's "raw" pre-tax cashflow (cell J96) first goes negative at Real 2015 $(0.67) mm, when the price is Real 2015 $57.00/b.

- You will also see why. Field operating cashflow (i.e., ignoring fiscal costs) in cell J91 is positive at this oil price; therefore the loss shown in cell J96 must be due to the fiscal costs.

- If you continue lowering the oil price you will see that at Real 2015 $43.00/b, cashflow goes cash negative on a field basis as well, i.e., the result in cell J91 also turns negative, to Real 2015 $(0.24) mm.

- Getting such a feel for the field's "underlying" (i.e., non-fiscal) "breaking point" can help inform investors who have an opportunity to negotiate aspects of the fiscal regime.

1.6.11   Assumptions: Income Tax and Related Items

Before detailing our Base Scenario's specific income tax assumptions, first let us get a sense of how they will ultimately be used in the model, by jumping ahead to look at the outline of the income tax calculation. Refer to the screenshot from the "ModelSummary" sheet shown in Figure 1.17. Note that income taxes are calculated on a post-ELT basis, meaning that all the components of the calculation are on a post-ELT basis.

Conceptually, the income tax calculation is quite straightforward. The investor's **tax position** in any given year equals gross revenue minus the sum of **tax allowances** (i.e., deductions). When the annual result is positive, the tax position is one of **taxable income** (or **taxable**

---

[24] In order to get the rentals and bonus from their input format of MOD $ into the "reality check" table's Real 2015 $ format, we had to go a bit further down, into the calculations section of the model, to where we time and sum these items in MOD terms (as discussed below), and then deflate them to get them in Real 2015 $ terms. We deflate them by *dividing* each annual MOD result by the appropriate year's inflation index. We do this in the workspace in rows 142–146. Note also how we have calculated the fixed opex cost per barrel in cell J87, using the COUNTIF function. See the comment in this cell, or Excel's online help, regarding how this function works here.

	A	B	C	D	E	F	G	H
47				**(Post-ELT) Income tax calculation**				
48				**Income tax allowances (i.e., deductions) MOD $ =**				
49	(Post-ELT, MOD $:	Royalty + Rental (maybe) + Bonus (maybe)	+	Total Opex + Intangible capex + Aband. costs	+	Depreciation of Tangible capex	+	Tax loss carryforward)
50	Tax position, MOD $	=	(Post-ELT, MOD $:		Gross Revenue	-	Income tax allowances)	
51				**Income tax liability, MOD $**				
52	• if Tax position > 0,	=	Post-ELT, MOD $:		Tax position, MOD $	x	Income tax rate, %	
53	• if Tax position < = 0,	=		0				

Figure 1.17   From the "ModelSummary" sheet of the file "Ch1_Tax_and_Royalty_Model.xls"
Note: Reflects Base Scenario.

profit), which gets multiplied by the tax rate (45% in our Base Scenario (cell C67 of the "Model" sheet)) to result in the income tax charge. When the annual result is negative, the tax position is an **untaxable loss** (or **tax loss**), so the investor pays no tax. All inputs are on a post-ELT basis, because we only want to forecast tax liabilities for the years of actual activity, based on the shutdown date which the ELT will tell us (once we've calculated the ELT.)

We have already detailed some of the tax allowances: opex; intangible capex (assuming, as we do, that all intangible capex is expensed for tax purposes); abandonment costs; royalty; and – depending on the user's choice – the rental and bonus payments.

Tax allowances: two "funny ones"

There are, however, two other types of tax allowance which require a bit more explanation. These are depreciation and tax loss carryforwards:

- Depreciation, as already mentioned, is a way of spreading over multiple periods the tax allowances arising from tangible capex, once this capex has been incurred in a particular period. Under our Base Case, the number of periods over which costs are depreciated is assumed to be eight years (cell C75).

- Tax loss carryforwards are historic tax losses which can, under certain circumstances (i.e., depending upon prevailing tax regulations), be used to reduce future taxable income.

Thus these two items – uniquely among the tax allowances shown in Figure 1.17 – sometimes require us to directly take certain *historic* costs into account:

- This might at first sound unusual, because, as discussed in Section 1.2, the NPV result we are working toward is the sum of discounted *future* net cashflows.

- There is in fact no inconsistency; this is because the historic costs in question (under our Base Scenario, as we will detail in a moment) have a direct impact on future tax payments, which of course do influence future net cashflow. Their impacts, under our Base Scenario, are as follows:

○ It is assumed that before the valuation period, some tangible capex was incurred, and partly depreciated; that as of December 31, 2014, the undepreciated amount remaining is MOD $6.0 mm (cell O70) and that this sum has two more years (during which there is production) to fully depreciate (cell G77). This, as we shall see more clearly later, means that there is the potential for the investor to benefit from up to $6.0 mm in deductions to offset future tax bills.

○ It is assumed that before the valuation period, losses for tax purposes were made from prior activity, which as of December 31, 2014 totaled MOD $10.8 mm (cell I70). Again, as we will detail later, this means that there is the potential for the investor to benefit from up to an additional $10.8 mm in deductions to offset future tax bills.

While the basic ideas at work here are clear, there are some nuances to consider and a few, perhaps not obvious, calculation steps involved. We will deal with these in later sections.

For now, just be aware that these assumed two prior balances in row 70:

• are exceptional among our other assumptions, because they are historic; and

• can end up having a material effect on NCF and NPV.

In a real-world model, you will need to know details of any such "prior" (i.e., pre-valuation date) items.

Where We Are Heading: Pre-ELT Calculation of GOCF (Gross Operating Cashflow)

Over the next few pages we will cover the steps in calculating the components of GOCF, which, as defined in row 33 of Figure 1.18, is gross field revenue minus the cash royalty, rentals, bonus and opex. As mentioned in Section 1.4, GOCF is the basis for the version of the ELT we will calculate later.

	A	B	C	D	E	F	G	H
21		**Pre-ELT (Economic limit test) calculations**						
23	(For later use): Total Capex , MOD $	=	(Post-sensitivity, Real 2015 $:	*Capex)*		x	Inflation index	
25		**Cash items for GOCF (Gross operating cashflow) calculation MOD $**						
27	Opex MOD $	=	(Post-sensitivity, Real 2015 $:	*Total Opex)*		x	Inflation index	
28	Fiscal cost: Royalty MOD $	=	Gross Revenue MOD $	x	Royalty rate (%)			
29	Other non-tax fiscal costs MOD $	=	*Rental MOD $*	+	*Bonus MOD $*			
31	Gross Revenue MOD $	=	(Post-sensitivity, Real 2015 $:	Oil price x Inflation index)		x	Post-sensitivity Oil production	
33	**GOCF MOD $**	=	(MOD $:	Gross Revenue	-	(Royalty + Rentals + Bonus + Opex))		

Figure 1.18   From the "ModelSummary" sheet of the file "Ch1_Tax_and_Royalty_Model.xls"
Note: Italics indicate a timing adjustment is made at that calculation stage.

1.7 PRE-ELT CALCULATIONS

1.7.1 Pre-ELT Calculations: Opex and Capex Timing/Inflation

The calculations for timing, in a dynamic model, of opex – relative to production– and of capex – as determined by our assumed spending schedule – are straightforward, although two formulas initially look imposing. Refer to Figure 1.19.

	B	C	D	E	F	K	L	M	N	O
113		**Timing/inflating of opex and capex**								
115			**Total/other**		**2015**	**2020**	**2021**	**2022**	**2023**	**2024**
116	Field production	mm b	5.9		-	0.6	0.2	0.2	-	-
118	Fixed opex	MOD $ mm	114.9		-	16.7	17.1	17.4	-	-
119	Variable opex	MOD $ mm	50.1		-	5.1	2.1	1.4	-	-
120	**Total opex**	**MOD $ mm**	165.0		-	21.8	19.1	18.8	-	-
121										
122	Tangible capex	Real 2015 $ mm	54.6		36.6	-	-	-	-	-
123	Intangible capex	Real 2015 $ mm	26.4		24.4	-	-	-	-	-
124	Tangible capex	MOD $ mm	55.5		37.0	-	-	-	-	-
125	Intangible capex	MOD $ mm	26.7		24.6	-	-	-	-	-
126	**Total capex**	**MOD $ mm**	82.2		61.6	-	-	-	-	-

Figure 1.19 From the "Model" sheet of the file "Ch1_Tax_and_Royalty_Model.xls
Notes: Reflects Base Scenario. Some columns (for 2016–2019) are hidden.

Key/typical formulas used ("•" indicates the end of the formula):
K116. =K53 K118. =(IF(K116>0, Fixed_opex_per_year_real, 0)) * Infl_index •
K119. =(K116 * Variable_opex_real_per_bbl) * Infl_index • K120. =SUM(K118:K119) •

F122. =IF(year = First_Capex_Year, Capex_year1_real_total *
Capex_year1_real_percent_tang,
IF(year = Second_Capex_Year, Capex_year2_real_total *
Capex_year2_real_percent_tang, 0)) •

F123. =IF(year = First_Capex_Year, Capex_year1_real_total *
Capex_year1_real_percent_Intang,
IF(year = Second_Capex_Year, Capex_year2_real_total *
Capex_year2_real_percent_intang, 0)) •

F124. =F122*Infl_index • F125. =F123*Infl_index • F126. =SUM(F124:F125) •

We defined fixed opex in the model's assumptions section as an annual charge, equal in Real 2015 $ terms, incurred only during production years.[25] We named the post-multiplier version of this assumed value, found in cell C58, $\boxed{\text{Fixed\_opex\_per\_year\_real}}$. This named cell is referenced by the annual formulas in row 118, to mean that, if it is a production year, the answer equals $\boxed{\text{Fixed\_opex\_per\_year\_real}}$, times the corresponding annual inflation index, to give us the answer in MOD $; otherwise, the answer is $0.

Annual variable opex (row 119) in MOD $ mm is calculated as annual production in mmb, times our assumed post-multiplier Real $ per-barrel cost in cell D58 (named $\boxed{\text{Variable\_opex\_real\_per\_bbl}}$), times the corresponding annual inflation index.

Capex

We will shortly use the opex results just calculated in the GOCF calculation. We do not use capex in the GOCF calculation, so we shall time and inflate capex in this section just to get the task "out of the way"; we will use these timed/inflated capex results soon enough.

Whereas for opex we combined the timing and inflation of each item into a single formula, for capex, we split things up to keep the formulas from getting too long.

First, in row 122, we calculate tangible capex in Real 2015 $ mm. The typical formula, e.g., the year 2015 in cell F122, is the long and – at first – slightly hostile-looking IF statement:

```
=IF(year = First_Capex_Year, Capex_year1_real_total * Capex_year1_real_percent_tang,
IF(year = Second_Capex_Year, Capex_year2_real_total *
Capex_year2_real_percent_tang, 0))
```

Because our example formula in cell F122 is for 2015, and the input assumption in the cell named "First_Capex_Year" is also 2015, let us just focus on the first line of the formula.

In a somewhat friendlier format, the formula means that if it is the first year in which capex is spent – which we assumed to be in 2015 – then, in 2015, Real 2015 $ tangible capex equals total real 2015 $ capex, times the percentage of that which is tangible:

- Under our Base Scenario, total 2015 capex – $\boxed{\text{Capex\_year1\_real\_total}}$ (cell I58) – is assumed to be real 2015 $**61.0** mm,

- of which **60%** – $\boxed{\text{Capex\_year1\_real\_percent\_tang}}$ (cell I59) – is assumed to be tangible,

- so that the 2015 tangible capex outflow is Real 2015 $61.0 mm × 60% = Real 2015 $**36.6** mm (cell F122).

The second IF statement in the formula works the same way, except that it only gives an answer when the year is the assumed second year of capex spending, i.e., 2016, and it references the capex inputs relevant to this second year. The results are shown in cell G122 of the model (which is hidden in the screenshot).

---

[25] In our simplified version used in this example, we ignore fixed general and administration (G&A) costs in the Base Scenario's single pre-production period year of 2015.

If the year is neither of the two years of capex spending, the answer in the annual cells of row 122 is **$0**.

Annual <u>MOD $ tangible capex</u> is calculated in row 124, by multiplying the annual Real 2015 $ tangible capex just calculated in row 122, by the inflation index. We inflate these values in a separate step here, because the formulas in the first step are already long enough.

<u>Intangible capex</u> in Real 2015 $ and MOD $ is calculated in rows 123 and 125, respectively, in exactly the same way as tangible capex, except that the formulas reference the intangible percentage of total capex.

Each year's MOD $ tangible and intangible capex is summed in row 126 to give total MOD $ capex, which in our example year of 2015 is MOD $61.6 mm (cell F126).

1.7.2 Pre-ELT Calculations: Bonus and Rentals

To calculate the bonus and both kinds of rental payments in rows 132–139:

- we create timing rows, which return a 1 in the year when a payment is due; and

- in the next rows, we multiply the corresponding year's 1 or 0 by the amount of the payment.

Recall that we assume, as is common, that the fiscal regulations express the amounts due in MOD $, so there is no need to inflate them.

In light of this, Figure 1.20, and the formulas beneath it, should require little explanation. Note, however, that:

- the checksum in cell A132 uses the formula $\boxed{= 1\text{-}D132}$ to ensure that the one-time bonus is indeed paid only once;

- the named cell $\boxed{\text{Bonus\_MOD}}$ referenced in row 133 is the cell O63 in the assumptions section, where we input the Base Scenario bonus of MOD $15.0 mm;

- cells D134 and D135 are named $\boxed{\text{Rental\_pre\_production\_MOD}}$ and $\boxed{\text{Rental\_production\_}}$ $\boxed{\text{MOD}}$ respectively; they calculate each rental as the assumed area of the license, in km^2 (square kilometers) times the appropriate per-km^2 MOD payment due each year;

- in each annual cell of row 140, we use a checksum formula to ensure that in any given year, only one type of rental is paid.[26] The formula for the typical year of 2016, for example, is $\boxed{= \text{IF(G116=0, 0, 1-G138-G136)}}$.

---

[26] Note that this approach, simplified for use in our annual model, assumes that a calendar year will be either 100% pre-production period or 100% post-production period. Therefore only one kind of rental will be paid in any given year. When – as is common, and therefore assumed in our example model – rentals are usually rather small relative to other cashflows, this approximation should not result in material error. If desired, however, when first production is expected to start at specific point *within* a calendar year, you can adjust the rental calculation for the first production year (assuming that the license terms provide for charging rentals on a fractions-of-period basis). For example, if production were to start at the end of the first calendar quarter, you could calculate the total rentals payable for that year as (the pre-production period's annual rental charge × 25%) + (the post-production period's annual rental charge × 75%).

	A	B	C	D	E	F	G	H	I
				Total/other		2015	2016	2017	2018
116		Field production	mm b	5.9		-	1.8	1.4	1.0
129						**Calculation of Rental and Bonus payments**			
131				Total/other		2015	2016	2017	2018
132	0	Is it the first year of production?	1 = yes	1		-	1	-	-
133		**Bonus, payable first production year**	**MOD $ mm**	15.0		-	15.0	-	-
134		Annual Rental, pre-production period	MOD $ mm	0.9					
135		Annual Rental, production period	MOD $ mm	1.8					
136		Is it the pre-production period?	1 = yes			1	-	-	-
137		**Rental payment, pre-production period**	**MOD $ mm**	0.9		0.9	-	-	-
138		Is it the production period?	1 = yes			-	1	1	1
139		**Rental payment, production period**	**MOD $ mm**	12.6		-	1.8	1.8	1.8
140	0	Check	(0=ok)			0	0	0	0

Figure 1.20   From the file "Ch1_Tax_and_Royalty_Model.xls"
Notes: Reflects Base Scenario. Some rows and columns are hidden.

Key/typical formulas used ("•" indicates the end of the formula):
G132. =IF(year=Production_first_year, 1, 0) • G133. =Bonus_MOD*G132 •
A132. =1-D132 •

D134. =M$65*G65 • D135. =M$65*J65 • F136. =IF(year<Production_first_year, 1, 0) •
F137. =F136*Rental_pre_production_MOD •
G138. =IF(G136=1, 0, IF(year<=Production_last_year_pre_ELT, 1, 0)) •

G139. =G138*Rental_production_MOD • G140. =IF(G116=0, 0, 1-G138-G136) •

1.7.3   Pre-ELT Calculations: GOCF

The calculation of GOCF (again, gross operating cashflow) is shown schematically in Figure 1.21 and in detail in the model screenshot in Figure 1.22.

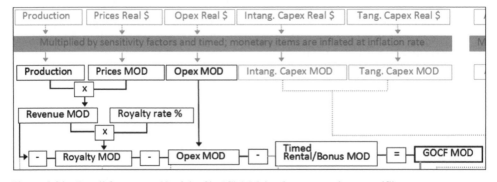

Figure 1.21   Detail from page 49 of the file "Ch1_Main_chapter_supplement.pdf"

B	C	D	E	F	G	H	I
116 Field production	mm b	5.9		-	1.8	1.4	1.0
149			Calculation of GOCF (Gross Operating Field Cashflow)				
151		Total/other		2015	2016	2017	2018
152 Oil price	MOD $/b			80.80	82.41	84.06	85.74
154 Gross field revenue	MOD $ mm	500.9		-	148.3	113.5	86.6
156 Royalty @ 17.25%	MOD $ mm	86.4		-	25.6	19.6	14.9
157 Fixed opex	MOD $ mm	114.9		-	15.5	15.8	16.1
158 Variable opex	MOD $ mm	50.1		-	14.8	11.3	8.7
159 Rentals	MOD $ mm	13.5		0.9	1.8	1.8	1.8
160 Bonus	MOD $ mm	15.0		-	15.0	-	-
161 Total costs (for GOCF purposes)	MOD $ mm	279.9		0.9	72.7	48.5	41.5
163 Field gross operating cashflow (GOCF)	MOD $ mm	221.1		(0.9)	75.7	65.0	45.1
164		Maximum					
165 Cumulative GOCF	MOD $ mm	233.5		(0.9)	74.8	139.8	184.9

Figure 1.22   From the file "Ch1_Tax_and_Royalty_Model.xls"
Notes: Reflects Base Scenario. Some rows and columns are hidden.

Key/typical formulas used ("•" indicates the end of the formula):
H152. =H41 • H154. =H116*H152 • H156. =Roy_rate*H154 • H157. =H118 •
H158. =H119 • H159. =SUM(H137,H139) • H160. =H133 •
H161. =SUM(H156:H160) • H163. =H154-H161 • D165. =MAX(F165:O165) •
H165. =G165+H163 •

Let us look at the annual GOCF calculation shown in Figure 1.22 as consisting of three basic steps:

- *Collection of previously calculated MOD $ (i.e., inflated) components.* These include the oil price (row 152), fixed and variable opex (rows 157–158) and rentals and the bonus (rows 159–160).

- *Calculation of remaining components: gross field revenue and royalties:*

  ○ Annual gross field revenue, in MOD $ mm (row 154), equals annual field production, in mmb (row 116), times the year's oil price, in MOD $/b (row 152).

  ○ Annual royalty payments, in MOD $ mm (row 156), equal gross field revenue in MOD $ mm, times the assumed royalty rate, which is in the cell named Roy_rate (cell H63, in the assumptions section).

- *Calculation of GOCF.* Annual GOCF, in MOD $ mm, is calculated in row 163 as gross revenue (row 154) minus all relevant cash costs (row 161). Note that we calculate cumulative GOCF in row 165. This will be the basis of our commercial shutdown mechanism, the ELT, in the next section.

1.8   ELT CALCULATION AND ROLE IN ECONOMIC MODELING

The ELT calculation is summarized schematically in Figure 1.23.

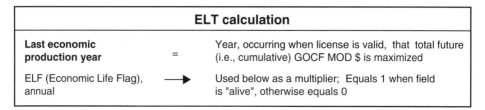

Figure 1.23   From the "ModelSummary" sheet of the file "Ch1_Tax_and_Royalty_Model.xls"

The ELT in Action – Knowing When to Quit

> **Refer to the "ELT calculation" screenshot on page 14 of the file "Ch1_Main_chapter_supplement.pdf" for the following discussion.**

As discussed earlier, the ELT is used to determine when to shut down the field. The goal in doing so is to maximize cashflow – in particular, GOCF.

Before we detail the formulas used in the ELF (i.e., economic life flag) section, first let us "jump ahead", and watch an already-completed ELF do its job.

In essence, the ELF is just a multiplier applied to annual pre-ELT cashflow items, i.e., revenue, royalty, opex, rentals, the bonus and total capex. These are all are multiplied by a 1 when the field is economically "alive," or by 0 afterwards, to result in their post-ELT equivalents.

If this sounds a bit abstract, refer to the "ELT calculation" screenshot on page 14 of the file "Ch1_Main_chapter_supplement.pdf" for the following discussion. (Note that certain columns are hidden to make the screenshot fit the page, but all relevant years are shown.)

- First, focus on row 203 – the binary "ELF" or economic life flag – which simply implements the (similarly named) ELT. This is the main result we are working toward in this section of the model. We will explain its calculation soon, but, for now, recall our analogy likening the ELF to a bouncer, implementing the "orders" of the ELT, to only let annual items occurring during the economic lifespan "pass through."

- According to the ELT, the last year of economic life is 2020 (cell D204). Therefore the ELF equals 1 up to and including that year, and 0 thereafter.

- Thus, for example, in 2015, pre-ELT basis GOCF of MOD $(0.9) mm (cell F163) occurs while the field is considered economically alive; therefore it is multiplied by the 1 in cell F203 to give a post-ELT basis of MOD $(0.9) mm (cell F206).

- But the pre-ELT basis GOCF of MOD $(3.7) mm in 2021 (cell L163) occurs after the last economic year of 2020, and so is multiplied by the 0 in cell L203 to give a post-ELT basis of GOCF of $0.

Thus we can say that the ELF truncates the field's lifespan to the economic limit. In doing so, it maximizes the field's total (all years) GOCF, i.e., its cumulative GOCF at the end of the field life.

This truncation by the ELF maximizes project GOCF as follows:

- Before considering the ELT, the field produces through the end of **2022** (cell M163), achieving a total GOCF of **MOD $221.1 mm** (cell D163), which is the same as the cumulative GOCF value at the end of that year (cell M165).

- This is less than the maximum pre-ELT basis, cumulative GOCF of **MOD $233.5 mm**, which occurs earlier, in **2020** (cell K165, and captured in cell D165). It is less than this maximum because, after the maximum is reached in 2020, the field goes on to produce two years of losses (cells L163:M163). If only the field had stopped at that maximum!

- The ELF does just that – subject to the license term being valid, which it is (as detailed below): it stops the field life at the end of the period (2020) in which post-ELT GOCF has reached its cumulative maximum, hence the MOD $0 values in cells L206:0206. The result is that post-ELT GOCF totals **MOD $233.5 mm** (cell D206), which is the same as the cumulative GOCF value at the end of 2020 (cell K208).

- In other words, the ELF stops production before the loss-making years of 2021 and 2022 can occur, and thus maximizes project GOCF.

ELF Calculation Details

Because the investment's lifespan depends not only on its commercial viability, but also on how long it is permitted to occur, our calculation strategy is to combine:

- the information that 2020 is the year of peak cumulative GOCF, with

- the information about the length of the license period, to determine the ultimate answer to the question, **when will the field be shut down?**

We do this by calculating two "sub-multipliers," one considering the year of peak cumulative GOCF (row 201) and the other considering the license length (row 202). Both of these determine our "final" multiplier, i.e., the ELF, in row 203:

- First, we capture in row 200 the fact that 2020 is the year of peak cumulative GOCF:

  ○ In each annual cell of this row, we use a formula which answers with the year, if the year in question is the year when this peak GOCF value occurs; otherwise, the answer will be the text, "n.a."

  ○ For example, the typical annual formula used in 2020 (cell K200) is $= \text{IF}(\text{K199} =$ $\$ \text{D199}, \text{year}, \text{"n.a."})$, where $\boxed{\text{K199}}$ is cumulative GOCF in 2020, and $\boxed{\text{D199}}$ is the maximum cumulative GOCF of all years. Since in this example 2020 is in fact the year when maximum cumulative GOCF occurs, the answer in cell K200 is 2020, while the answer in all the other years is "n.a."

  ○ We then capture the information, that 2020 is the peak year, in cell D200, which uses the formula $\boxed{=\text{MIN}(\text{F200:O200})}$. This formula ignores the "n.a." text in the annual cells, and so only records the answer of 2020.

- We express that 2020 is the last economic year – *ignoring the license length* – in row 201, in which each annual cell uses the formula $\boxed{= \text{IF}(\text{year} < = \$ \text{D200}, 1, 0)}$, where $\boxed{\text{D200}}$ is the year of peak cumulative GOCF. In our Base Scenario, this results in values of 1 in each year up to and including 2020 (cell K201), and values of 0 thereafter. This **binary range** or "binary array" is the first of the two "sub-multipliers."

- Similarly, we use a binary range in row 202 to create a license flag, i.e., a row where the annual cells show a 1 when the license term is ongoing, and a 0 otherwise. Each annual cell in row 202 uses the formula =IF(year <=Last_license_year, 1, 0), where Last_license_year is the named assumption cell C63. Because our Base Scenario assumes the license is valid through to the last year in our timeline, i.e., 2024, every annual cell in row 202 shows a value of 1. The license flag thus becomes our second "sub-multiplier."

- Next, we express **the economic lifespan,** *considering* **the license length** – that is, the most sensible commercial lifespan which is permitted by the license length – with a "final" third binary range, in row 203. Each annual cell in row 203 just multiplies the relevant year's value in row 201 by the one in row 202. Thus the annual cells in row 203 make up the **economic life flag (ELF),**[27] which we have already seen "in action."

- We have named the red-bordered range F203:O203, "ELF." We will use the ELF in the next section of the model as a multiplier to truncate the field inputs (production, costs, etc.) to the economic lifespan, considering the license length. In other words, under the Base Scenario, the ELF will remove various post-2020 items from the model by multiplying them by 0, which will have **the effect of modeling a field which shuts down in 2020**.

Finally, we capture, as a "memo" (information) item, the last year of economic life, considering the license length, i.e., our "ultimate" stopping year, which from now on is what we will call the **last economic year** for short – in cell D204. We can see that the answer is 2020 just by noticing that the last year in the ELF range which contains a 1 is 2020 (cell K203), but it will be useful to have this recorded it in a cell. Therefore we calculate as follows:

- In each of the annual cells in row 204, we use a formula which, in essence, says, "If this year is the last year when the ELF equals 1, then the answer is this year; otherwise, the answer is 'n.a.'" To frame this as a formula:

  o we could expand this into, "If this year, the ELF equals 1, and in each of the following years, the ELF equals 0, then the answer is this year; otherwise, the answer is 'n.a.'";

  o which in turn expands into, "If this year, the ELF equals 1, and the sum of the ELF values in all following years equals 0, then the answer is this year; otherwise, the answer is 'n.a.'";

  o which we write as the following Excel formula (using the typical example of cell K204, for 2020): =IF(AND(K203=1, SUM(L203:$P203)=0), year, "n.a.") .

- Under the Base Scenario, this results in a value of 2020 in cell K204, and the text "n.m." ("not meaningful") in the other annual cells in row 204.

---

[27] To reclarify terminology: "ELT" is the economic limit test, which tells us the economic limit (i.e., the last year when it makes economic sense to produce); "ELF" is the economic life flag, i.e., the mechanism which communicates the ELT's findings to the rest of the model.

- We capture this result of 2020 in cell D204 with the formula $\boxed{= \text{MIN(F204:O204)},}$ and name cell D204 "Production_last_economic_year." Again, the MIN function ignores the text and captures only the numerical value of 2020.

Why Base the ELT on Peak Cumulative *GOCF?*

Some analysts use a version of the ELT which is not based on peak cumulative GOCF, but rather a version which shuts down the field the *first time* GOCF goes negative. This is incorrect, because it ignores the possibility that the field could recover in subsequent periods, generating enough GOCF to offset the loss.

Let us consider an example. Reset the model to the Base Scenario. Then set up the view as follows:

- Use the button in cell C1 to show all rows on the "Model sheet," split the screen using the button in row 4, and adjust the view so that rows 33–37 are visible in the top part of the screen, and the chart starting in row 170 is visible in the bottom.

- Right click the chart's Y-axis, and manually set the scale to a minimum of -125 and a maximum of 375, if this is not already the case.

In the top part of the screen, change the chosen oil price scenario to the "User Custom price" using the spinner in cell I33. This will use the Real 2015 $120/b price assumption for each year, which we have supplied as a default value. You will notice that the chart's cumulative GOCF line (white, with black diamonds) goes off the scale; that will change in a moment.

Now let us assume the oil price collapses in 2018. In cell I37, enter 20 (i.e., Real 2015 $20/b).[28] The chart will appear as shown in Figure 1.24.

The impact is that annual GOCF in 2018 is negative – the underlying value is MOD $(8.6) mm, which you can see either by hovering the cursor over 2018's white triangle, or by looking at the underlying value a bit below the chart, in cell I187.

Would you really want to shut down the field at the end of 2018 (or the end of 2017, to avoid the 2018 loss), when GOCF, as noted in the chart's caption, recovers enough to reach a cumulative peak of MOD $341.5 mm in 2021 (cell L188)?

You might reply that we are ignoring the time value of money, since GOCF here is undiscounted. You would be right.[29] We prepared for that. In this example, discounted cumulative GOCF also peaks in 2020 (at MOD $263.5 mm (cell L190)). So, again, why would you shut down before then? It would be a mistake to shut down the field just because there has been one year of GOCF losses.

---

[28] This is not far-fetched; note that the benchmark Brent crude price reached close to MOD $10/b in 1998.
[29] Basing ELTs on undiscounted values appears to be rather common in practice, although NPV maximization "purists" might argue that this is wrong.

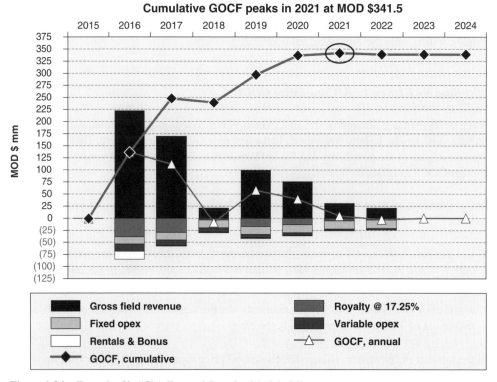

Figure 1.24   From the file "Ch1_Tax_and_Royalty_Model.xls"
Note: The chart's Y-axis scale has been manually set to a minimum of (125) and a maximum of 375 for this screenshot. Not all the colors reproduced here match those in the Excel file.

Another, similar approach – also incorrect, in our opinion – tries to set a number of periods of GOCF losses which can be tolerated before shutting down. This approach is intended to prevent being "fooled" by a single, perhaps exceptionally bad period, like 2018 in the case just described.

For example, suppose an analyst modeled such that one period of GOCF losses is tolerable, but any more are not.

Suppose further that the oil price crash is forecast to continue into 2019. Change the price in cell J37 to $20. The chart will now look like the screenshot in Figure 1.25.

Even after two years of annual GOCF losses, cashflow starting in 2020 is still strong enough to recover: cumulative GOCF goes on to peak in 2021 at MOD $272.7 mm (cell L188, as does discounted cumulative GOCF, at MOD $218.7 mm (cell L190)).

An analyst could, effectively, say, "Ok, then, let's tolerate *three* years of annual GOCF losses, to avoid getting fooled by two exceptional years." At which point it becomes clear that setting a number of periods of tolerance for losses before finally shutting down the field is an arbitrary

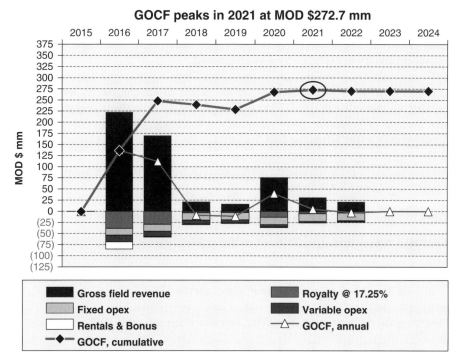

Figure 1.25 From the file "Ch1_Tax_and_Royalty_Model.xls"
Note: The chart's Y-axis scale has been manually set to a minimum of (125) and a maximum of 375 for this screenshot. Not all the colors reproduced here match those in the Excel file.

approach, because what matters is not the number of periods of production, but rather the value of the cashflow you are trying to maximize.

Therefore, the best version, in our opinion, of the GOCF method for determining the economic limit is based on the maximum *cumulative* GOCF, which takes into account all years, including those which follow perhaps exceptional losses. If there is any positive cumulative GOCF to be generated, this method will maximize it.

(Do not forget to change the custom prices in row 37 back to $120, unless you want to keep the $20 years in place for your own custom price scenario.)

ELT Exercise: Playing with the Field Life

For this exercise, first set up as follows.

Reset the model to the Base Scenario. Show all rows, then use the Console View (cell F1) and full screen mode (cell F21).

In the bottom part of the screen, scroll so that, again, you can see the chart which starts in row 170. Right click the Y-axis, and set the Y-axis scale's minimum and maximum values to automatic.

Now, make changes to various assumptions in the top, console part of the screen which will cause GOCF to peak earlier than under the Base Scenario's result of 2020. (You can see the peak year at each setting in the chart's caption.) Stop and inspect at each setting what causes this to happen, and try to explain why it has happened.

For example, let us re-enact the exercise we did earlier in the chapter, by lowering the oil price sensitivity multiplier in cell G23 to 60%, and then to 55%. (Note that you can see the resultant average (all-years) received oil price, for reference, change in the "thermometer" chart in column D, to the left of the GOCF chart.)

As we cross these oil price thresholds, we cause GOCF in 2020 to turn negative enough to lower peak cumulative GOCF from:

- MOD $79.3 mm, occurring in 2020, when the multiplier is 60%, to

- MOD $60.5 mm, occurring in 2019, when the multiplier is set to 55%.[30]

Inspect the chart at each of the two settings. What seems to be the "culprit" causing cumulative GOCF to peak a year earlier, when the multiplier is set to 55%?

Keep lowering the oil price multiplier. What happens when it reaches 45%, and, again, why?

Continue lowering the oil price multiplier. Notice what happens when it reaches 35%, or lower:

- Cumulative GOCF never becomes positive. (Why not?)

- As the caption shows, cumulative GOCF "peaks" at MOD $(0.9) mm in 2015. Notice that this value equals the amount of the rental paid that year (cell F186).

- If this is the best the field can do, the advice to stop at a negative "peak" GOCF year is another way of saying, this investment, under this price outlook, should not be made at all.

> Play with other variables in the console section and see what else you can do to change the year of peak cumulative GOCF, i.e., to change the field's economic lifespan.

Sensitivity Analysis with Excels' Data Tables Feature: The Impact of Fixed Opex on Economic Field Life

As you did the last exercise, or went on to practice finding ways to shorten the economic field life, you might have noticed that the level of fixed opex has a big impact. This is to be expected in situations like our Base Scenario, where a constant, material cost is incurred in each production year, regardless of the volume – meaning that at low enough volumes, or prices, fixed opex can push GOCF into negativity.

---

[30] Note that in cases when the multiplier is set to 55%, it can be hard to see from the chart's cumulative GOCF line exactly where the peak cumulative GOCF year is – in this case, 2020 or 2019. Although the chart's caption records the peak value, you can check this and in fact see any year's value by hovering your mouse over the line's black diamonds.

Let us focus a bit more on how fixed opex can impact the economic lifespan. Open the file "Ch1_Tax_and_Royalty_Model_Small_Data_Table.xls." This is a duplicate of our main chapter example file, except that in rows 235–256 it has an array of values produced by Excel's **Data Tables** feature, and a chart based on it.

Behind the rather unremarkable name, "Data Table", is a fast and powerful way to conduct sensitivity analysis. If you wished to see in a single view, e.g., NPV at every oil price assumption between MOD $0 and $200/b, in increments of MOD $5/b:

- you could do it the long way, i.e., change the oil price 40 times, and copy and paste the result 40 times as values into a table somewhere; or

- you could do the same thing with the Data Table wizard in a few mouse-clicks.

The tradeoff is that Data Tables use a lot of computer resources, and so can slow down the calculation of models, so much so that we are putting this one in its own file, to allow our main example file to work faster.[31]

In this case, our Data Table shows the length in years of the field's economic life – on a post-ELT basis – under fixed opex assumptions ranging from Real 2015 $0 to $100 mm per production year, in increments of Real 2015 $5 mm. (We show how to create Data Tables like this one in the short video file "Ch1_Using_Data_Tables.wmv" in the Chapter 1 folder.)

The results are shown graphically in Figure 1.26.

Notice that when the annual fixed opex per production year is between Real 2015 $0 and $5 mm, the last economic production year is 2022. This is the same last production year of

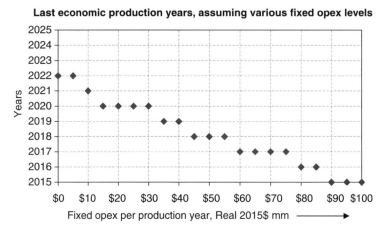

Figure 1.26   From the file "Ch1_Tax_and_Royalty_Model_Small_Data_Table.xls"
Note: Reflects Base Scenario except for different opex assumptions.

---

[31] When you open "Ch01_TaxRoyModel_v05_with 1 data table.xls" be sure that Excel's calculation mode is set to Automatic, otherwise the results in the Data Table might not display/update as expected.

our Base Scenario *pre*-ELT field production life shown in cell D54. In other words, under these two particular fixed opex assumptions, the field shuts down on technical grounds (i.e., it is out of oil), not on economic grounds.

But rising levels of fixed opex steadily shorten the economic field life so that, by the time we reach the extreme assumptions of Real 2015 $90–100 mm, the ELT's advice is that the economic field life ends in 2015, which is before production even starts. In other words, again, the ELT's "advice" is not to produce (i.e., not to invest) at all.

Can we trust a Data Table?

Note that, due to how Data Tables work, the chart will *not* update when you change the fixed opex assumption in cell C57. (It will change when you change other assumptions, depending on the changes you make.) You can, however, check the Data Table's results against the "live model."

Starting from the Console View, arrange the split so you can see row 57 above the split, and, below it, rows 204–229. Use full screen mode if necessary.

Pick a fixed opex value from the chart, e.g., Real 2015 $50 mm, and note from the chart that the Data Table tells us that this would result in an economic lifespan ending in 2018.

Use the spinner to enter Real 2015 $50 mm in cell C57. Now inspect cell D204. It shows that the last economic year has indeed changed to 2020. You can check any other Data Table result this way.

What Is Missing from Our GOCF Calculation?

Note that in arriving at GOCF, we ignore some cashflow items which we do consider when calculating NCF (net cashflow).

One of these is capex. Why exclude such an often very material cash outflow? The reason for doing so, under the commonly used ELT approach, is that the ELT is supposed to measure the commercial viability of an upstream petroleum investment based on its *operating* cashflows, i.e., once the field is *already* "up and running." Capex – specifically upfront development capex – is what *gets it* up and running, and thus, the reasoning goes, should not be considered.

Two other very real cash outflows which are not deducted from revenue when calculating GOCF under common methods are the abandonment cost and income taxes.

We have some ideas why this is so. Regarding abandonment payments:

- One cannot know the inflated value of an abandonment payment, or series of payments, until one knows when it, or they, will be made. But one does not know when it, or they, will be made until one knows when the field has reached the economic limit, which in turn is knowable only by calculating GOCF.

- Thus trying to deduct timed and inflated abandonment payments from GOCF, which tells us when to quit and thus when to time the abandonment payments, is a circular calculation.

- It is circular because, to know when to quit, one must know the inflated value of the abandonment payments. But to know the inflated value of the abandonment payments, one must know when to quit.

Regarding income taxes, we suppose that these are excluded from the standard approach to GOCF calculation due to the problem with abandonment payments just mentioned. Abandonment payments are, as mentioned, often tax deductible. If one cannot include abandonment as an outflow in the GOCF calculation, then one cannot correctly calculate the tax position and thus the tax charge, in order to count the tax charge as an outflow in the GOCF calculation. The tax calculation would be wrong, as it would ignore the tax deductions from abandonment payments.

Whatever the reasoning, this approach – that is, to ignore abandonment costs and income taxes when calculating GOCF in order to determine the economic limit – has been codified as recommended practice by an unofficial but influential group of upstream petroleum industry associations,[32] most recently in reporting guidelines published in November 2011, from which we quote below.

From *Guidelines for Application of the Petroleum Resources Management System, November 2011*

Sec. 7.4.1. Economic limit is defined as the production rate beyond which the net operating cashflows (net revenue minus direct **operating costs**) from a project are negative, a point in time that defines the project's economic life.

The project may represent an individual well, lease, or entire field.

Alternatively, it is the production rate at which net revenue from a project equals "out of pocket" **cost to operate** that project (the direct costs to maintain the operation) as described in the next paragraph ...

Operating costs should include property-specific fixed overhead charges if these are actual incremental costs attributable to the project and any production and property taxes **but (for purposes of calculating economic limit) should exclude depreciation, abandonment and reclamation costs, and income tax**, as well as any overhead above that required to operate the subject property (or project) itself. [Emphasis in bold added] (Yasin Senturk, "Evaluation of Petroleum Reserves and Resources," *Guidelines for Application of the Petroleum Resources Management System*, Society of Petroleum Engineers, Richardson, Texas, USA (November 2011), p. 112. This can be found online on at www.spe.org/industry/docs/PRMS_Guidelines_Nov2011.pdf.)

[32] The Society of Petroleum Engineers, the Society of Petroleum Evaluation Engineers, the American Association of Petroleum Geologists, the World Petroleum Council, and the Society of Exploration Geophysicists.

We shall revisit this topic later, in Section 1.11. For the time being, be sure that you are able to calculate the ELT and the ELF according to the common industry approach as we have shown above.

1.9 POST-ELT CALCULATIONS

1.9.1 Post-ELT Calculations: Abandonment

Having calculated the ELT, we will now apply it, directly or indirectly, to every component of NCF. The method for calculating all items except for income tax and tax-related depreciation is summarized in the screenshot from the "ModelSummary" sheet of our example file, shown in Figure 1.27.

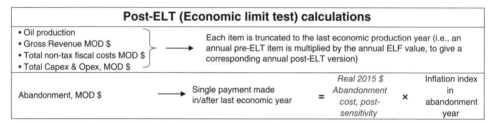

Figure 1.27   From the "ModelSummary" sheet of the file "Ch1_Tax_and_Royalty_Model.xls"

The actual calculations of the items shown schematically in Figure 1.27 – *except* for the abandonment payment – can be found in the section of the "Model" sheet which starts in row 276. These calculations are straightforward – as you can see from the typical formula captions in column P, we simply multiply each item's pre-ELT counterpart by the ELF.

Calculating the abandonment cost is only slightly more involved, due to the simplicity of the single "lumpsum" abandonment funding arrangement which the Base Scenario assumes. The method used is shown in Figure 1.28.

	B	C	D	E	F	G	H	I	J	K
264		Abandonment calculation								
265 266				Total/other	2015	2016	2017	2018	2019	2020
267	Abandonment payment made in ..	year		2020						
268	Abandonment payment	Real 2015 $ mm		21.0	-	-	-	-	-	21.0
269	Inflation index				1.010	1.030	1.051	1.072	1.093	1.115
270	**Abandonment payment**	MOD $ mm		23.4	-	-	-	-	-	23.4

Figure 1.28   From the file "Ch1_Tax_and_Royalty_Model.xls"
Notes: Reflects Base Scenario. Some columns are not shown.

Key/typical formulas used ("●" indicates the end of the formula):
D267. =Production_last_economic_year + Abandonment_delay ●
D268. =Abandonment_cost_real ●
K268. =IF(year=Abandonment_payment_year, $D268, 0) ● K269. =Infl_index ●
K270. =K268*K269 ●

The purpose of the abandonment calculation section, shown in Figure 1.28, is to time the abandonment payment and then inflate it appropriately to give a MOD value.

We time the payment based on the year in cell **D267**, which we have named Abandonment_payment_year . This is calculated as:

* the last economic production year, which we calculated in cell D204 (named Production_last_economic_year) as 2020 under the Base Scenario; plus

* any delay we assumed in cell L60, which we named Abandonment_delay . Under the Base Scenario, this is a "delay of 0 years," hence no delay. Therefore Abandonment_payment_year equals **2020** (cell D267).

The "formula flow" of row 268, in which we time the Real 2015 $ abandonment payment, is atypical. Usually, the value in the Total column is determined by (is the sum of) the annual values. In this case, however, the Real 2015 $21.0 mm in cell D268 is the starting point, i.e., it is our assumed value, which determines values in the annual columns:

* The value in cell **D268** brings down the assumed **Real 2015 $21.0 mm** from the named cell, Abandonment_cost_real (cell O58).

* The annual cells in row 268 capture the timing with the typical formula (using 2020 as an example) of IF(year = Abandonment_payment_year, $D268, 0) . Thus the Real 2015 $21.0 mm abandonment payment appears in 2020 (cell K268), while the rest of the annual cells in row 268 return zero values.

* We inflate the timed abandonment payment by multiplying each annual cell in row 268 by the inflation index, which we brought down to row 269 for clarity of presentation. The inflated value of the abandonment payment is thus MOD $21.0 mm (cell K268) × 1.115 (cell K269) = MOD $23.4 mm (cell K270). The total in cell D270 is a "normal" total.

Note that we do not multiply the abandonment payment by the ELF. This is because the way we have calculated it, it is already on a "post-ELT basis," in that it is already timed in relation to the field's shutdown year.

Sense check

Reset the model to the Base Scenario, use the Console View, and arrange the screen so that you can see row 60 above the split and the waterfall charts, starting in row 603, below it. As you change the assumed abandonment timing from 0 to 1 year post-production (cell L60), you will see that NCF and NPV – recorded in the charts' captions – change as follows:

MOD $ mm	NCF	NPV
0-year delay	61.3	37.4
1-year delay	60.8	38.4

The later the abandonment occurs, the lower NCF will be, but the higher NPV will be. Why?

1.9.2 Post-ELT Calculations: Depreciation

We have now calculated every cashflow item needed to calculate NCF, with the exception of income tax. To calculate income tax, we need to calculate two more items, both tax allowances: namely, depreciation and tax loss carryforwards. We treat depreciation here.

Notice that the model actually calculates depreciation two ways, and lets the user choose, using the spinner in cell B433, which method's results will be used by the model:

- The first is calculated in the section entitled "Method 1) Straight line depreciation charge, SIMPLIFIED method, for demonstration ONLY (i.e., "quick and dirty")" which starts in row 294.

  o Be forewarned – as the heavily qualified title suggests, this is not fully correct. Among other things, it fails to get the timing quite right for a model like ours, which uses the mid-year inflation and discounting conventions. It is useful, at best, as a starting point approximation of the depreciation charges.

  o The simplified method is used here because it provides a way for us to show you most of the important calculations in a reasonably small space.

- The second method is calculated in the section entitled "Method 2) Straight line depreciation charge, "proper" version (ok for real models)" starting in row 339. This method involves some details omitted from the quick and dirty method. This "proper" method has one clear advantage – it is right. Otherwise, it is rather involved and frankly tedious.

We detail the "quick and dirty" method on pages 15–18 of the file "Ch1_Main_chapter_supplement.pdf."

We detail the proper method in "Appendix I: Depreciation.pdf." It is not strictly necessary for you to turn to this now – you will still benefit from this chapter without doing so. It is, however, something you will need to tackle at some point, especially as we will see it again – a lot – in our production sharing contract example models in Chapters 7 and 8. Although we do not discuss this method here, we include it as an option in the example model, so that when you do turn to it, you will have a working example for a basic tax and royalty regime.

Take a moment to review the depreciation assumptions in cell O70 and in rows 74–77, and then turn to the "Quick and dirty depreciation calculation" (pages 15–18) from the file, "Ch1_Main_chapter_supplement.pdf." (Return here when you are done.)

Now that you have seen how to do the quick and dirty method, we do not want you to get too comfortable with it. To encourage you to eventually learn the proper one, we will show you – a bit later, after covering the income tax calculations, below – that under the Base Scenario assumptions, the choice of method can in fact make a material difference to the investor's tax liability.

1.9.3   Income Tax: Basic Concepts and Calculations

Income tax is one of the key sources of revenue for a state applying a tax and royalty regime.[33]

In this section we will step away temporarily from the main example model in the file "Ch1_Tax_and_Royalty_Model.xls" in order to explain some important basics of income taxation, and then return to the example model in Section 1.9.4.

Here we will show how to calculate two basic versions of income tax. These are income taxes both <u>without</u> and – as is more common – <u>with</u> **income tax loss carryforwards**.

Loss Carryforward: Simple Example

The idea behind tax loss carryforwards is straightforward. Suppose that a company is started in 2015, during which its costs – all assumed to be tax deductible – are $12 mm and its revenues are $10 mm. It has made a **$2 mm tax loss**, so it will pay no income tax.

This loss not only prevents it from paying taxes in 2015, but also will provide, under a tax regime which permits it, a form of future tax relief – that is, the **$2 mm** loss will be *carried forward* as a tax deduction for the 2016 tax year. Thus:

- if in 2016 the company generates $10 mm in taxable profit, then its taxable 2016 income will be $10 mm − **$2 mm** = $8 mm (and if the tax rate is 50%, it will pay $4 mm in taxes);

- if in 2016 the company generates $2 mm in taxable profit, then its taxable 2016 income will be $2 mm − **$2 mm** = $0 (and will pay no taxes);

- if in 2016 the company generates $1 mm in taxable profit, then its taxable 2016 income will be $1 mm − **$2 mm** = $(1) mm, i.e., a tax loss (on which no income tax will be payable). In this case, $1 mm of the $2 mm tax loss from 2015 gets used up, leaving <u>$1 mm</u> in unused tax losses from the 2015 tax year.

  o If the tax rules permit carrying forward tax losses for one year only, then that is the end of the story for this remaining <u>$1 mm</u> tax from the 2015 tax year – it will not be used for any future tax relief, and so "dies on paper";

  o If, however, the tax rules *do* permit carrying forward tax losses for more than one year – and, say, the company's 2017 operations generate $5 mm in taxable income – then taxable income for 2017 will be $5 mm – the remaining <u>$ 1mm</u> loss from 2015 = $4 mm (and so taxes payable, at a 50% tax rate, will be $2 mm).

Indefinite and Time-Limited Carryforwards

Most regimes permit tax loss carryforwards, and usually permit them to be carried forward indefinitely, until the tax loss is fully used up ("amortized"). We show how to model such loss carryforwards these in this section.

---

[33] As we shall see in later chapters, income taxes also feature in some production sharing regimes.

We discuss a less common variant – in which there is a time limit on how far into the future tax losses may be carried – later in this section.

Generic Income Tax Equations and Terminology

Income Tax Liability

$$\boxed{\text{Income tax liability} = \text{Income tax rate} \times \text{Taxable profit}}$$

where the **income tax liability** – which we use interchangeably with the term "income tax charge"[34] – is the income tax payment due.

Taxable Position

We use "tax position" to mean either a **taxable profit** – sometimes called "pre-tax profit" – or an **untaxable loss**, which is also called a "tax loss":

$$\boxed{\text{Taxable profit} = (\text{Taxable revenue}) - (\text{Tax deductions}) \text{ when the result if positive}}$$

$$\boxed{\text{Untaxable loss} = (\text{Taxable revenue}) - (\text{Tax deductions}) \text{ when the result if negative}}$$

Following common practice, our examples assume that royalty payments are tax deductible.

Therefore "taxable revenue" – in our examples which feature royalties – is field <u>revenue minus royalty</u>. (This is also called "revenue, net of royalty" or sometimes "net revenue," though we do not like the latter term, because sometimes "net revenue" is used to mean net of royalty, but at other times, to reflect a net working interest (equity) share. It is therefore often best to clarify what is meant by the prefix "net.")

Tax Deductions

$$\boxed{\begin{array}{c}\text{Tax deductions} = (\text{Costs and charges occurring in the present year}) \\ + (\text{Any prior period tax losses, carried forward})\end{array}}$$

Income **tax deductions** are also called "income **tax allowances**." Different income tax regimes define income tax deductions in different ways, but they usually include components of the cost of supply (e.g., operating expenses, or "opex"), other production costs, and, as mentioned in Section 1.6.5, above, intangible capex. (We treat intangible capex in more detail when discussing depreciation.)

Let us now look at some simple calculation examples.

---

[34] Our examples in this book assume that all tax liabilities are paid, so we consider the liabilities to be cash charges. In addition, as some tax regimes require a given year's tax liability to be paid in instalments throughout that year, we effectively assume in our annual models that total tax charges for the full year – like any other cashflow, using our standard mid-period inflation/discounting method – are actually made in the middle of that year. Therefore, be aware that if you wish to assume later payment – for example, that taxes owed for the full year 2015 are paid sometime in 2016 – you will need to adjust the example templates we provide.

	B	C	D	E	F	G
1	**Assumptions**					
2	Item	Unit	Value			
3	Revenue	$	100			
4	Opex	$	160			
5	Annual tax rate	%	50%			
6	Only profit is taxed; losses are not taxed					
8	**Calculations -- single year's tax liabilty**		Income tax liability		Formulae used	
9	Item	Unit	Wrong	Right	Wrong	Right
10	Revenue	$	100	100	D10. =D3	E10. =D3
11	Tax deduction: opex	$	160	160	D11. =D4	E11. =D4
12	Taxable profit / (untaxable loss)	$	(60)	(60)	D12. =D10-D11	E12. =E10-E11
13	Annual tax rate	%	50%	50%	D13. =D5	E13. =D5
14	**Tax liability**	$	(30)	0	D14. =D12*D13	E14. =IF(E12<0, 0, E12*E13)

Logic to prevent taxing losses

Figure 1.29   From the file "Ch1_tax basics.xls"

Excel Logic to Prevent the Taxation of Losses

In Figure 1.29, which comes from the example file "Ch1_tax basics.xls," we show a simple one-year model, in which we ignore loss carryforwards for the moment.

Note that, in this and the following examples in this section 1.9.3, all revenue is assumed to be taxable revenue.

In the Assumptions section, we can see that there is only one deductible item, opex, which has been set in cell D4 to $160. Revenue is $100, and the tax rate is 50%.

Column D shows what happens without any adjustment to the tax liability formula in cell D14. Even though the $(60) loss in cell D12 is untaxable, it gets taxed at 50% anyway, resulting in the "negative tax liability" of $30 (cell D14).

What does a "negative income tax liability" mean? That the government will write the loss-making company a check for $30 in that year? That would be very unusual – imagine the strain on public finances and perverse business incentives if this were the case. Most of the time, the term "negative income tax liability" is meaningless.[35] Usually, the maximum benefit a company can expect when it makes an income tax loss – again, *ignoring* loss carryforwards for the moment – is that it will not be charged for income tax that year, but it will not be *rewarded* for losing money.

[35] Some governments in certain circumstances do issue companies with tax credits associated with certain qualifying losses (e.g., for exploration expenditures in Norway and Alaska), but these are exceptions to the general rule.

The formula in cell E14 fixes the mistake seen in cell D14. The IF statement in cell E14 $= \text{IF(E12} < 0, 0, \text{E12} * \text{E13)}$ means that:

- if the pre-tax position value in cell $\boxed{\text{E12}}$ is less than $\boxed{0}$ (i.e., is a loss), then the tax liability is $\boxed{0}$;

- otherwise (i.e., if the pre-tax position is positive (a profit), or equals 0) the income tax liability equals the tax position in $\boxed{\text{E12}}$ times the income tax rate in cell $\boxed{\text{E13}}$, in this case correctly resulting in a tax liability of $0 (cell E14).

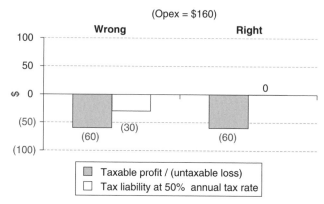

Figure 1.30   From "Ch1_tax basics.xls"

Figures 1.30 and 1.31 reproduce a chart from the Excel file under two different opex settings. Take a moment to use the spinner in cell D4 to scroll from the minimum opex permitted ($40) to the maximum ($160) and back again, to check that the "Right" method logic works.

We know the "Right" formula logic is working when:

- losses are not taxed (Figure 1.30), but

- taxable profits are taxed (Figure 1.31, in which case the "Wrong" method also happens to give the right answer).

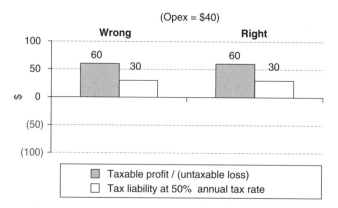

Figure 1.31   From "Ch1_tax basics.xls"

Calculating Indefinite Income Tax Loss Carryforwards

Our model in the file "Ch1_tax basics.xls" was only for a single year. In the following, still much simplified, two- and three-year examples, we have assumed that:

- there were no tax losses before Year 1; and

- when tax losses may be carried forward, they may be carried forward indefinitely.

But first, let's look at another example which ignores loss carryforwards.

Income tax without carryforwards	Year 1	Year 2
Revenue	100	100
Tax deduction 1: current year opex	160	20
Taxable profit/(untaxable loss), ignoring loss carryforward	(60)	80
Tax rate	50%	50%
Tax liability	0	40

Figure 1.32   Tax calculation without loss carryforwards

Because the example in Figure 1.32 assumes tax losses may *not* be carried forward, there is no connection between the two years' calculations. The Year 1 tax loss of $60 "goes nowhere," and so provides no tax relief. Having calculated each year's tax liability, our work is done.

Now let us try an example with loss carryforwards.

First, let us just focus on the vertical flow of calculations *within* years in Figure 1.33, below, ignoring for the moment the flow *between* years. In either year, note the two-stage calculation which results in the final annual tax position in row 6. There is one stage for each of the two types of tax deduction:

- Tax deduction 1 relates to underlying operations (opex in row 3). The tax position, considering only this deduction, is calculated in row 4.

- Tax deduction 2 relates only to carried forward losses (row 5). These are subtracted from the corresponding year's result in row 4, to give the year's "final" tax position in row 6.

Now let us turn to the flow between years, i.e., tax loss carryforwards. There is assumed to have been no loss in "Year 0" (not shown) to carry forward, so this means only Year 1's $60 tax loss (cell B6) gets carried forward to cell C5. This happens via the formula in cell C5, =IF(B6 < 0, (-B6), 0), which means:

- if the prior year's final tax position in B6 is negative i.e., is a loss, then the answer is the value of that loss, expressed as a positive;

- otherwise, the answer is 0 (i.e., there is no loss to carry forward).

> Year 1 "final" pre-tax position – a \$60 loss – is carried forward to Year 2, expressed as a positive, and subtracted from this (i.e., from C4)…

	A	B	C
1	**Income tax with carryforwards, Example 1**	**Year 1**	**Year 2**
2	*Revenue*	*100*	*100*
3	*Tax deduction 1: current year opex*	*160*	*20*
4	Taxable profit/(untaxable loss), ignoring loss carryforward	(60)	80
5	Tax deduction 2: tax loss from prior year (shown as a positive)	*0*	60
6	**Taxable profit/(untaxable loss), considering loss carryforward**	**(60)**	**20**
7	*Tax rate*	*50%*	*50%*
8	Tax liability	0	10

> … resulting in this final taxable profit for Year 2.

Figure 1.33   Indefinite income tax with loss carryforward, Example 1

Note: All values in italics are *assumptions* (including cell B5). The "•" symbol marks the end of a formula.
Typical formulas used (e.g., in Year 2): **C4.** = C2-C3 • **C5.** = IF(B6 <0, (-B6), 0) •
C6. = C4 – C5 • **C8.** = IF(C6 < 0, 0, C6 * C7)

Thus in this example, \$(60) in cell B6 becomes \$60 in cell C5.

Regarding this change in sign (from negative to positive):

- The tax loss is negative in cell B6 because…well, that is how losses are calculated! This has the bonus here of telling us whether cell C5 should consider it to be a loss to be carried forward to Year 2, which should only happen when B6 is negative.

- The reason we change any loss in B6 into a positive value in cell C5 is that we – almost uniformly in this book – format both revenues and costs/other deductions as positives, and then obtain results by subtracting the latter from the former (as opposed to formatting revenues as positives; costs etc. as negatives; and obtaining results by adding the two). Therefore we express both types of deductions (carried forward losses) as positives.[36]

Let us look at another example.

---

[36] This applies to how we *calculate* items. Some charts we use, however, draw on data which are reformatted so that costs and other outflows are shown as negative. In our models and examples, such reformatting is normally done under the heading "For chart".

	A	B	C
1	**Income tax with carryforwards, Example 2**	Year 1	Year 2
2	*Revenue*	*100*	*100*
3	*Tax deduction 1: current year opex*	*160*	*160*
4	Taxable profit/(untaxable loss), ignoring loss carryforward	(60)	(60)
5	Tax deduction 2: tax loss from prior year (shown as a positive)	0	◀ 60
6	**Taxable profit/(untaxable loss), considering loss carryforward**	(60)	(120)
7	*Tax rate*	*50%*	*50%*
8	Tax liability	0	0

Figure 1.34   Indefinite income tax with loss carryforward, Example 2

Note: All values in italics are assumptions (including cell B5). The "•" symbol marks the end of a formula.
Typical formulas used (e.g., in Year 2): **C4.** = C2-C3 • **C5.** = IF(B6 <0, (-B6), 0) •
C6. = C4 – C5 • **C8.** = IF(C6 < 0, 0, C6 ∗ C7)

In Example 2 (Figure 1.34), we use the same formulas, but revise our scenario:

• As before, we have a Year 1 untaxable loss of $60 (cell C6). But now suppose that Year 2's *operations* result in another tax loss of $60 (cell C4).

• When we carry forward the Year 1 tax loss of $60, it combines with the Year 2 tax loss from current year operations of $60, to result in a total Year 2 tax loss of $60 + $60 = $120 (cell C6).

• Because we end Year 2 with an untaxable loss of $120, the Year 2 tax liability is **$0** (cell C8).

Let us add another year.

In Example 3 (Figure 1.35):

• Year 3's operating pre-tax profit of $100 (cell D4), minus the $120 *cumulative* tax loss carried forward from the end of Year 2 (cell C6), equals a Year 3 end-period tax loss of $20 (cell D6).

• Because it is an untaxable loss, the Year 3 tax liability is $0.

• This $20 tax loss at the end of Year 3 would then be carried forward to any fourth business year. If there were no fourth year, the $20 tax loss would "die in the books."[37]

---

[37] When we say that the Year 3 tax loss never gets used as a benefit, in a scenario in which there are only three tax years, we are assuming that a special variant of tax loss benefit transfer, called a **tax loss carryback**, is *not* applicable. Tax loss carrybacks are discussed at the end of this section.

	A	B	C	D
		Year 1	Year 2	Year 3
1	**Income tax with carryforwards, Example 3**			
2	*Revenue*	*100*	*100*	*200*
3	*Tax deduction 1: current year opex*	*160*	*160*	*100*
4	Taxable profit/(untaxable loss), ignoring loss carryforward	(60)	(60)	(100)
5	Tax deduction 2: tax loss from prior year (shown as a positive)	0	60	120
6	**Taxable profit/(untaxable loss), considering loss carryforward**	(60)	(120)	(20)
7	*Tax rate*	*50%*	*50%*	*50%*
8	Tax liability	0	0	0

Figure 1.35   Indefinite income tax with loss carryforward, Example 3

Note: All values in italics are assumed (including cell B5). The "•" symbol marks the end of a formula.
Typical formulas used (e.g., in Year 2): **C4.** = C2-C3 • **C5.** = IF(B6 <0, (-B6), 0) • **C6.** = C4 – C5 • **C8.** = IF(C6 < 0, 0, C6 * C7).

In Example 4 (Figure 1.36):

- The Year 3 operating pre-tax position is positive $120 (cell D4). This $120, minus the $120 cumulative tax loss carried forward from the end of Year 2 (cell D5), is $120 − $120 = $0, i.e., a Year 3 taxable position of $0 (cell D6). The Year 3 tax liability is therefore $0.

	A	B	C	D
		Year 1	Year 2	Year 3
1	**Income tax with carryforwards, Example 4**			
2	*Revenue*	*100*	*100*	*300*
3	*Tax deduction 1: current year opex*	*160*	*160*	*180*
4	Taxable profit/(untaxable loss), ignoring loss carryforward	(60)	(60)	(120)
5	Tax deduction 2: tax loss from prior year (shown as a positive)	0	60	120
6	**Taxable profit/(untaxable loss), considering loss carryforward**	(60)	(120)	0
7	*Tax rate*	*50%*	*50%*	*50%*
8	Tax liability	0	0	0

Figure 1.36   Indefinite income tax with loss carry forward, Example 4

Note: All values in italics are assumed (including cell B5). The "•" symbol marks the end of a formula.
Typical formulas used (e.g., in Year 2): **C4.** = C2-C3 • **C5.** = IF(B6 <0, (-B6), 0) • **C6.** = C4 – C5 • **C8.** = IF(C6 < 0, 0, C6 * C7).

A	B	C	D
Income tax with carryforwards, Example 5	Year 1	Year 2	Year 3
2	*Revenue*	*100*	*100*	*300*
3	*Tax deduction 1: current year opex*	*160*	*160*	*100*
4	Taxable profit/(untaxable loss), ignoring loss carryforward	(60)	(60)	200
5	Tax deduction 2: tax loss from prior year (shown as a positive)	*0*	60	120
6	**Taxable profit/(untaxable loss), considering loss carryforward**	(60)	(120)	80
7	*Tax rate*	50%	50%	50%
8	Tax liability	0	0	40

Figure 1.37   Indefinite income tax with loss carryforward, Example 5

Note: All values in italics are assumed (including cell B5). The "•" symbol marks the end of a formula.
Typical formulas used (e.g., in Year 2): **C4.** = C2-C3 • **C5.** = IF(B6 <0, (-B6), 0) • **C6.** = C4 – C5 • **C8.** = IF(C6 < 0, 0, C6 * C7).

- In Example 4, the cumulative $120 **tax loss** carried forward from the end of Year 2 gets "used up," or **amortized**, in Year 3, so there is no tax loss to carry forward to any fourth business year.

In <u>Example 5</u> (Figure 1.37):

- The Year 3 operating pre-tax position of positive $200 (cell D4), minus the $120 cumulative tax loss carried forward from the end of Year 2 (cell D5), is $80, i.e., a Year 3 taxable profit of $80 (cell D6). At 50%, the Year 3 tax liability is $40 (cell D8).

- Again, the $120 tax loss gets amortized at the end of Year 3, so there is no tax loss to carry forward to any fourth business year.

In <u>Example 6</u> (Figure 1.38, below):

- The Year 2 operating pre-tax position is positive $80 (cell C4), and the Year 3 operating pre-tax position is positive $200 (cell D4).

- In Year 2, the $80 pre-tax position, minus the $60 cumulative tax loss carried forward from the end of Year 1 (cell C5), is $80 − $60 = $20, i.e., <u>a Year 2 taxable *profit* of $20</u> (cell C6), on which tax of 50% × $20 = $10 is payable (cell C8).

- Because Year 2 ends with a taxable profit, there is <u>no loss to carry forward</u> to Year 3, so the carried forward tax loss for Year 3 is $0 (cell D5). Year 3's taxable profit = $200 − $0 = $200 (cell D6), 50% of which makes for a Year 3 tax liability of $100 (cell D8).

This is how <u>indefinite tax loss carryforwards</u> work. They are a quite common investment incentive for petroleum producers in many countries. We will use them as <u>standard assumptions in many of the models in this book.</u>

	A	B	C	D
1	**Income tax with carryforwards, example 6**	Year 1	Year 2	Year 3
2	*Revenue*	*100*	*100*	*300*
3	*Tax deduction 1: current year opex*	*160*	*20*	*100*
4	Taxable profit/(untaxable loss), ignoring loss carryforward	(60)	80	200
5	Tax deduction 2: tax loss from prior year (shown as a positive)	*0*	60	0
6	**Taxable profit/(untaxable loss), considering loss carryforward**	**(60)**	20	**200**
7	*Tax rate*	*50%*	*50%*	*50%*
8	Tax liability	0	10	100

Figure 1.38   Indefinite income tax with loss carryforward, Example 6

Note: All values in italics are assumed (including cell B5). The "•" symbol marks the end of a formula.
Typical formulas used (e.g., in Year 2): **C4.** = C2-C3 • **C5.** = IF(B6 <0, (-B6), 0) • **C6.** = C4 – C5 • **C8.** = IF(C6 < 0, 0, 6 * C7)

Changing Formats – Same Calculations, Different Presentation

We chose the modeling format used in the preceding examples to help ease explanation. This format, however, is not one we have commonly seen or used ourselves in real-world models. Therefore, **from now on in this book, we shall use (a more common) standard format**. We introduce it by showing an Excel screenshot of Example 6 in both formats, in Figure 1.39. Note how they result in the same tax liabilities (rows 8 and 21).

Exercise: Calculate These Yourself

Enough passive learning! On the "Exercise_setup" worksheet of the file "Ch1_Indefinite_tax_loss_carryforward_format.xls" find a version of the "Model" sheet which has new input assumptions, but no formulas. Supply the formulas at least in the standard format version. Check your answers against those in the "Exercise_solution" sheet.

Tax Loss Carryforwards: Calculation and Analysis – The Value of Prior Tax Losses

In the preceding examples, we had assumed that activity starts in Year 1, and that therefore there was no prior tax loss arising before Year 1, to carry forward to Year 1. We represented this by using values of $0, e.g., in cells B5 and B14 in Figure 1.39.

But if, for example, a model's timeframe starts in 2015, and there *has* been activity before then, we need to know the value of any tax loss as at the end of 2014, to carry forward to 2015.

Our next example shows how to model this. It also gives a graphic view of how tax losses can grow, shrink and have "ripple effects" across multiple tax years.

	A	B	C	D	E / F / G
1	Income tax with carryforwards, Example 6 – introductory format	Year 1	Year 2	Year 3	Typical formulae
2	*Revenue*	*100*	*100*	*300*	(using Year 2
3	*Tax deduction 1: current year opex*	*160*	*20*	*100*	as example)
4	Taxable profit/(untaxable loss), ignoring loss carryforward	(60)	80	200	C4. =C2-C3
5	Tax deduction 2: tax loss from prior year (shown as a positive)	0	60	0	C5. =IF(B6<0, (-B6), 0)
6	Taxable profit/(untaxable loss), considering loss carryforward	(60)	20	200	C6. =C4-C5
7	*Tax rate*	*50%*	*50%*	*50%*	
8	Tax liability	0	10	100	C8. =IF(C6<0, 0, C6*C7)
9					
10	Income tax with carryforwards, Example 6 – standard format used elsewhere in this book	Year 1	Year 2	Year 3	
11	*Revenue*	*100*	*100*	*300*	
13	*Opex*	*160*	*20*	*100*	
14	Tax loss from prior year (shown as a positive)	0	60	0	C14. =(-B19)
15	Total tax deductions for current year	160	80	100	C15. =SUM(C13:C14)
17	Taxable profit/untaxable loss	(60)	20	200	C17. =C11-C15
19	Tax loss, to be carried to next year (shown as a negative)	(60)	0	0	C19. =IF(C17<0, C17, 0)
20	*Tax rate*	*50%*	*50%*	*50%*	
21	Income tax liability	0	10	100	C21. =IF(C19<0, 0, C20*C17)

Figure 1.39 Indefinite tax loss carryforwards: introductory and standard formats, from the "Model" sheet of the file "Ch1_Indefinite_tax_loss_carryforward_format.xls"
Notes: (1) The arrows are Excel audit ("trace precedent") lines. (2) It should be understood that "Taxable profit/untaxable loss" in row 17 is the final tax position, which considers the tax loss carryforward, even though this is not stated explicitly. (3) Italics, which here indicate hard-coded values, will not normally be used this way in the Excel files; rather, this is the job of the blue font in the Excel files. We used italics here and in the preceding examples because blue is not distinguishable in this black and white book.

The **main points** to take away from this are that:

- one always needs to **know the value of any such prior carried forward tax loss**; and

- this **focus on past** (pre-valuation date) activity is an **exception to the general rule** that we normally **ignore the past** in a NPV model, which by definition discounts only future cashflows occurring starting from the valuation date. We make this exception precisely **because the past in this case can impact future cashflows** – that is, the end-2014, carried forward tax loss can impact future tax payments.

This section is continued on the disk

For formatting reasons (relating to size and the use of color), we have put the material for this example into a PDF file on the disk. Go to the file "Ch1_Indefinite_tax_loss_carryforward_examples.pdf" which uses the model in the file "Ch1_Carryfoward_prior_losses.xls."

Related Topics and Techniques: Fiscal Consolidation; Time-Limited Tax Loss Carryforwards; Loss Carrybacks

It is important that you feel comfortable modeling indefinite tax loss carryforwards. As mentioned earlier, they are a very common incentive for investors which we use in many of the example models in this book.

In fact, we will soon see in Chapter 2 that the ability to apply tax loss carryforwards from one license to the pre-tax positions of another is a key feature of **fiscal consolidation** regimes.

In addition, there are two "cousins" of the indefinite tax loss carryforward. Neither are used in this chapter, but we introduce them here and then detail them later in standalone files:

- One is the **time-limited loss carryforward**. So far we have covered indefinite loss carry-forwards, whereby tax losses may be carried forward until they are amortized. This is a very common approach. Some regimes, however, use time-limited loss carryforwards. For example, a loss may be carried forward for a maximum of three years, but no more. This would be a case of "use it (in time) or lose it." Although the idea is simple, time-limited loss carryforwards can be quite tricky to model (so much that you might consider this device to be more like an "evil twin" than a "cousin"). We show how in the supplemental file "Appendix III_time_limited_tax_loss_ carryforwards.pdf."

- Another is the **tax loss carryback**:

  ○ Assume a field produces for 10 years, and that in the last year it has a tax loss of $100. Because it is the last year of business, the loss cannot be carried forward to a next year, and so there are no future taxable profits which this tax loss can reduce.

  ○ If loss carrybacks are not allowed, this tax loss cannot benefit the producer – the producer has not used it, and therefore has lost it.

  ○ But if loss carrybacks *are* allowed, the loss can be carried back to offset any *prior* taxable profits. How is this done, if one cannot travel back in time? Essentially, the tax man compares:

    – the producer's total (from all-years) tax position, ignoring the tax loss carryback, to

    – the producer's tax position if the producer *had* been able to deduct $100 from any prior taxable profits.

  ○ If the second option would have resulted in a lower tax liability than the first, then at the end of Year 10, the tax man would write the producer a check for an amount equal to the amount of the reduction.

- Again, this is harder to model than it sounds. We give an example in the file "Appendix II_tax_loss_carrybacks.pdf."

1.9.4   Returning to Main Model – Post-ELT Calculations: Income Tax

The income tax calculations format will be the same as that shown near the end of Section 1.9.3, from which we repeat, for reference, part of the screenshot shown in Figure 1.40.

The only difference is that in this simplified example, there are only two kinds of tax allowance – opex, and tax loss carryforwards – whereas, as seen in Figure 1.41, below, under our main chapter model's Base Scenario, we have not only opex and tax loss carryforwards, but also royalty, the bonus, rentals, expensed intangible capex, abandonment and the depreciation of tangible capex. (Recall that the Base Scenario uses the option to make the bonus and rentals tax deductible.)

	A	B	C	D	E	F	G
10	**Income tax with carryforwards, Example 6 – standard format used elsewhere in this book**	**Year 1**	**Year 2**	**Year 3**			
11	*Revenue*	*100*	*100*	*300*			
13	*Opex*	*160*	*20*	*100*			
14	Tax loss from prior year (shown as a positive)	*0*	*60*	*0*	C14. =(-B19)		
15	Total tax deductions for current year	160	80	100	C15. =SUM(C13:C14)		
17	**Taxable profit/untaxable loss**	(60)	20	200	C17. =C11-C15		
19	Tax loss, to be carried to next year (shown as a negative)	(60)	0	0	C19. =IF(C17<0, C17, 0)		
20	*Tax rate*	*50%*	*50%*	*50%*			
21	Income tax liability	0	10	100	C21. =IF(C19<0, 0, C20*C17)		

Figure 1.40 From the "Model" sheet of the file "Ch1_Indefinite_tax_loss_carryforward_format.xls"

The calculation principles are the same, however. Again, revenue minus the sum of all tax allowances equals the tax position, which:

- if it is a taxable profit, is taxed at the income tax rate; and

- if it is a loss, is not taxed, but carried forward as a tax allowance to the next year.

	A	B	C	D	E	F	G	H
47			**(Post-ELT) Income tax calculation**					
48			**Income tax allowances (i.e., deductions) MOD $ =**					
49	(Post-ELT, MOD $:	Royalty + Rental (maybe) + Bonus (maybe)	+	Total Opex + Intangible capex + Aband. costs	+	Depreciation of Tangible capex	+	Tax loss carryforward)
50	Tax position, MOD $	=	(Post-ELT, MOD $:	Gross Revenue	-	Income tax allowances)		
51			**Income tax liability, MOD $**					
52	• if Tax position > 0,	=	Post-ELT, MOD $:	Tax position, MOD$	x	Income tax rate, %		
53	• if Tax position < = 0,	=	0					

Figure 1.41 From the "ModelSummary" sheet of the file "Ch1_Tax_and_Royalty_Model.xls"
Note: Reflects Base Scenario.

Take a quick look at pages 52–53 of the file "Ch1_Main_chapter_supplement.pdf," in which this section's income tax calculations are highlighted on a version of the "model map" introduced earlier.

Then, for the following discussion, refer to the "Income tax calculation" page (page 19) of "Ch1_Main_chapter_supplement.pdf," which reproduces a view of rows 476–495 of the model. (Note that some columns are hidden in this screenshot.)

Some of the items in the income tax calculation section are essentially just carried down from above, including:

- gross field revenue;

- intangible capex;

- the abandonment payment;

- depreciation; and

- the tax position at the end of 2014 (cell F489, i.e., the MOD $10.8 mm tax loss which we input as an assumption in cell I70).

All of these items are on a post-ELT basis.

Total opex in row 483 is the sum of post-ELT fixed opex and post-ELT variable opex in rows 284 and 285, respectively.

The three fiscal items – royalty, rentals and the bonus – take into account whether or not they are in fact tax deductible:

- Each one equals its post-ELT version, multiplied by the relevant, named, binary (0 or 1) tax deductibility assumption cell in row 67.

- For example, each annual rental charge in row 485 equals the corresponding annual post-ELT rental charge in row 286, times the cell "Tax_deduction_rental" in cell J67, which equals 1 when rentals are assumed to be tax deductible, and 0 when they are not.

- The royalty and bonus calculations in rows 482 and 486 work the same way as the rentals.

The actual tax calculation, including the carryforward of tax losses, is done in rows 489–495, in the same way as described in Section 1.9.3, resulting, under the Base Scenario, in a total, post-ELT investor tax charge of **MOD $66.6 mm** (cell D495).

Unused Tax Losses at Project End

Notice that under the Base Scenario, at the end of the project in 2024, the field life has an accumulated carried forward tax loss of **MOD $36.9 mm** (cell L489). We capture this as a memo item in cell D493. Under our Base Scenario's assumed fiscal regime, that is the end of the story, i.e., this represents MOD $36.9 mm of potential tax benefits, in the form of tax allowances, which will never get used, because the "dead" field will never produce any more taxable income for these allowances to reduce.

Be aware, however, that – as mentioned at the end of Section 1.9.3 – some regimes have ways to let the investor benefit from such unused, end-of-project tax losses:

- One is known as a **tax loss carryback**, which we treat in "Appendix II_Tax_loss_carrybacks.pdf" on the disk.

- The other is a very important mechanism for "sharing" tax losses among fields or reservoirs, when the investor has more than one field or reservoir generating revenue. This is known as **income tax consolidation**, and is the focus of Chapter 2.

Sense check

With the model set to the Base Scenario, split the screen so that above the split you see rows 67–70, and below it, the waterfall charts. Increase the MOD $ values for the historic tax losses and the undepreciated balance, using the spinners in cells I70 and O70, while watching the charts' columns and/or value labels. Does the income tax charge, and thus NCF/NPV, behave as expected? The point to take away is that <u>these historic items can have real value to an investor</u>.

Reset to the Base Scenario (there is a duplicate switch for this just above the left waterfall chart, in cell B600), and then set the tax rate to 75%, using the spinner in cell C67. Then make the same increases to the prior balance items in row 70 as before. For each click of the spinner, is the dollar impact on the tax charge greater or smaller than when the tax rate was 45%?

Once again, reset to the Base Scenario, and set the tax rate to 0%. Again, change the values in I75 and O75 while watching the charts. Nothing happens. Why not?

Assumptions about the "Cashiness" and Timing of Tax Liabilities

In this example model, we assume that the investor pays 100% of tax liabilities in cash, which is why we use the terms "tax liability," "tax charge" and "tax payment" interchangeably.

We also assume that the tax year is the same as the calendar year, and that tax is paid in installments throughout the year (which in fact is common practice in some oil-producing countries, such as Nigeria). This approach is consistent with the mid-year discounting convention which we use in the model, because this convention, you will recall from Section 1.2, approximates cashflows occurring throughout the year. If in your own models the time-related assumptions and/or discounting methods differ from those used here, you will need to adjust the timing of tax payments accordingly.

Variations among Income Tax Regimes

Be aware that we are focusing on the tax liabilities arising only from field activity. In real life, some tax regimes have comprehensive provisions which can greatly complicate the picture, such as:

- tax treaties between the host country and an investor's home country for tax purposes;
- tax incentives focused on specific activities or geographic areas;
- time-limited tax incentives;
- general tax allowances applied to all industries within a specific jurisdiction;
- loopholes; etc.

These are beyond the scope of our book (and in fact, for some countries, could make a book of their own). Bear in mind, however, that these exist and can result in differences between the field-based tax liabilities we calculate here and the investor's final corporate tax bill paid.

To keep our model simple, we have assumed that a single tax rate is applicable each year. In practice, however, in some countries, annual income tax rates can vary: for example, according to how many years a license has been producing; the period's production rate; cumulative production levels; commodity prices; and a device known as an "R-factor," which is some measure of cumulative revenue divided by some measure of cumulative costs.

Because some of these same tax rate-setting mechanisms also apply to royalties – and to prevent overloading this chapter – we detail their calculation in Chapter 3 on royalties. You will find the methods shown there transferrable to income tax calculations.[38]

Analysis: Comparing the Impacts of the "Quick And Dirty" and "Proper" Depreciation Methods on the Tax Liability

As seen in the boxed caption of the chart reproduced in Figure 1.42, the two methods' (all-years) *total* depreciation charges are the same at MOD \$61.51 mm, but the timing of *individual, annual* depreciation charges differs under the two methods. As the data labels show, the quick

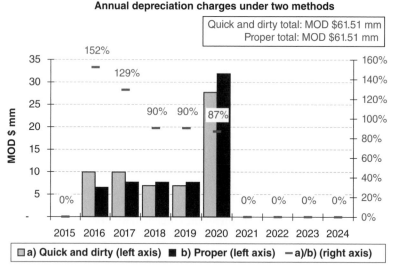

Figure 1.42   From row 436 of the file "Ch1_Tax_and_Royalty_Model.xls"
Note: Reflects Base Scenario.

---

[38] (1) Some regimes offer tax benefits based on these factors, not by lowering the tax rate, but by using them as the basis for creating additional tax allowances; by excluding certain portions of revenue from taxation (in which case the exempted portions would need to be subtracted from the values found in row 479 of our example model); and / or by creating tax credits (amounts subtracted from the tax liability). (2) Some regimes base a period's tax rate on the period's IRR. This can be problematic in cases where IRR is incalculable, as discussed earlier on pages 55–56 of the file, "Ch1_time_value_of_money_supplement.pdf".

and dirty method overstates the properly calculated depreciation charges for 2016 and 2017 by 52% and 29%, respectively, and understates it by 10–13% in the remaining years.

To overstate a tax allowance is to understate tax liabilities, and vice versa.

Importantly, the fact that the total (all-years) allowances from depreciation, calculated both ways, are equal, does _not_ mean these annual distortions "even out in the end," as far as the investor's tax charges, and thus NCF, are concerned. There are too many other "moving parts" in the model to support such a generalization.

For example, from Section 1.9.3 on tax loss carryforwards, we know that how much – if any – of a tax allowance can be used to reduce taxable income in a given year depends on that year's level of taxable income, which in turn depends on many factors unrelated to depreciation, such as annual prices, volumes and costs, as well as any prior tax losses.

Total (all-years) results		
MOD $ mm	Tax charge	NCF
a) Quick and dirty	64.7	63.2
b) Proper	66.6	61.3
a) – b)	(1.87)	1.87
a)/b)	97.2%	103.1%

Figure 1.43   From row 465 of the file "Ch1_Tax_and_Royalty_Model.xls"
Note: Some columns not shown. Values in the table are hard-coded, reflecting the results of each depreciation method under the Base Scenario.

The Tax charge column of Figure 1.43 shows that, in this case, the quick and dirty method's distortions of tax allowances from depreciation would lead the investor to believe that its tax charge would be MOD $1.87 mm lower than if depreciation were calculated properly.

(Notice, by the way, that the "a) – b)" row highlights that the only effect which the depreciation method has on cashflows is via the tax charge.)

Another reason _not_ to assume that the annual distortions even out in the end is that the depreciation charges shown in Figure 1.43 are undiscounted, and therefore ignore the time value of money:

- Of course, it only makes sense to calculate them on an undiscounted basis – the taxpayer has to, because they are used to calculate tax liabilities, which are payable on an undiscounted basis. (Imagine trying to get away with declaring "discounted income" on your annual personal tax return.)

- Irrespective of how tax liabilities are actually calculated, the fact remains that the timing of when tax benefits are available, and thus the timing of any taxes paid, can – like anything with a cash impact – affect discounted results.

- All other things being equal, the earlier a tax benefit occurs, and can be used to reduce taxable income, the greater its discounted value to the taxpayer will be, and vice versa.

- From row 29, using a 10% discount rate and the mid-year discounting convention, note that the present values of a (MOD) $1.00 tax benefit arising in 2015 or 2016 are $0.95 or $0.87, respectively, but for one arising in 2020, it is $0.59.

Just knowing this, and looking at the undiscounted values in Figure 1.42, you might guess that the net effect of the quick and dirty method's distortions is to <u>overstate</u> the <u>discounted</u> sum of all-years discounted depreciation charges, reasoning that the two big overstatements are in the early years, and so get discounted less than the one big understatement, which is in 2020.

If this guess is correct, the quick and dirty method's overstated (compared to the proper method) discounted tax benefit would show up as an understated discounted tax charge. In fact, this is what we see in the discounted results added to Figure 1.44.

MOD $ mm	Tax charge	Disc. tax charge	NCF	NPV
a) Quick and dirty	64.7	**49.3**	63.2	**39.1**
b) Proper	66.6	**51.0**	61.3	**37.4**
a) – b)	(1.87)	**(1.67)**	1.87	**1.67**
a) / b)	97.2%	**96.7%**	103.1%	**104.5%**

Figure 1.44   From row 465 of the file "Ch1_Tax_and_Royalty_Model.xls"
Note: Values in the table are hard-coded, reflecting the results of each depreciation method under the Base Scenario.

The main point of this analysis is that:

- although we have used and explained the quick and dirty depreciation method in this chapter, because it covers most of the steps needed to calculate depreciation correctly, and

- we have placed the full explanation of the proper method outside this chapter, in "Appendix I_Depreciation.pdf" for reasons of space,

the differences between the methods are not merely academic, as they can give materially different results. For this reason, you should be sure to familiarize yourself with the material in Appendix I. We shall use the proper method in a number of the production sharing models in Chapters 7 and 8.

1.9.5   Post-ELT Calculations: NCF and Discounting

The calculation of both the investor's and government's NCF and discounted NCF is outlined in Figure 1.45 and implemented in the model as shown in Figure 1.46.

Because we have finished calculating all post-ELT components of the cashflow, the undiscounted NCF calculations are entirely straightforward, consisting mainly of collecting these components, and then subtracting all the costs from gross revenue.

(Post ELT) Investor net cashflow, discounted net cashflow and NPV calculation				
Net cashflow, MOD $	=	(Post-ELT, MOD $;	Gross Revenue	− (Rentals + Bonus + Tax + Opex + Capex + Abandonment))
Discounted Net cashflow, MOD $	=	Annual net cashflow, MOD $	× Annual discount factor	
NPV	=	Sum of annual discounted Net cashflows		

Figure 1.45   From ModelSummary sheet of the file "Ch1_Tax_and_Royalty_Model.xls"

The undiscounted NCF calculations, shown in Figure 1.46, below, using the typical annual formulas for 2020 (column K) as examples, are as follows (all items are on a post-ELT basis):

- Gross revenue, royalty, the abandonment payment and income tax are all just carried down from above.

- Total opex (row 506) is the sum of fixed and variable opex.

- Total capex (row 507) is the sum of tangible and intangible capex.

- Bonuses and rentals are summed into one line item in row 508.

- The investor's undiscounted NCF in row 514 equals gross revenue less all costs.

- Because in this example model we assume that the investor bears all costs, the government's undiscounted NCF (row 515) is the sum of its undiscounted revenues, i.e., royalty, rental, bonus and tax income.

If we only wanted to know the investor's and government's NPVs, we could multiply the annual values in rows 514 and 515, respectively, by the annual discount factors, and sum the resultant discounted annual values.

But as we mentioned in Section 1.2, the time value of money is a sometimes subtle, sometimes powerful "distorter" of the "story" of the field's underlying undiscounted cashflow generation. Different components of cashflow get discounted to different degrees, making it at times hard to understand the "discounted story" – that is, why NPV behaves as it does under different assumptions – by just comparing two lines, undiscounted and discounted NCF.

Therefore, to aid our analysis, we calculate NPV "the long way" by:

- multiplying each undiscounted cashflow component by the discount factor, as seen in rows 540–547;

- subtracting total annual discounted cash outflows from discounted annual revenue to get discounted annual investor NCF (row 551), and summing the discounted annual royalty, rentals, bonus and income tax to get discounted annual government NCF (row 552);

Undiscounted net cashflow (NCF)

			2015	2016	2017	2018	2019	2020	2021	
501 Undiscounted net cashflow (NCF)		Total								
503 Gross field revenue	MOD $ mm	465.7	-	148.3	113.5	86.6	66.5	50.8	-	K503. =K279
505 Royalty @ 17.25%	MOD $ mm	80.3	-	25.6	19.6	14.9	11.5	8.8	-	K505. =K281
506 Total Opex	MOD $ mm	127.0	-	30.3	27.1	24.7	23.0	21.8	-	K506. =SUM(K284:K285)
507 Total Capex	MOD $ mm	82.2	61.6	20.6	-	-	-	-	-	K507. =SUM(K282:K283)
508 Bonus & Rentals	MOD $ mm	24.9	0.9	16.8	1.8	1.8	1.8	1.8	-	K508. =SUM(K286:K287)
509 Abandonment payment	MOD $ mm	23.4	-	-	-	-	-	23.4	-	K509. =K270
510 Income Tax @ 45%	MOD $ mm	66.6	-	13.8	25.8	16.8	10.1	-	-	K510. =K495
511 Investor's total cash outflows	MOD $ mm	404.4	62.5	107.1	74.3	58.3	46.4	55.8	-	K511. =SUM(K505:K510)
514 Investor NCF	MOD $ mm	61.3	(62.5)	41.2	39.2	28.3	20.0	(5.0)	-	K514. =K503-K511
515 Government NCF	MOD $ mm	171.8	0.9	56.2	47.2	33.6	23.4	10.6	-	K515. =SUM(K505,K508,K510)

Discounted NCF and NPV

			2015	2016	2017	2018	2019	2020	2021	
539 Discounted NCF		Total								
540 Gross field revenue	MOD $ mm	353.4	-	128.6	89.4	62.0	43.3	30.1	-	K540. =K503*Disc_factor
542 Royalty @ 17.25%	MOD $ mm	61.0	-	22.2	15.4	10.7	7.5	5.2	-	K542. =K505*Disc_factor
543 Total Opex	MOD $ mm	93.3	-	26.3	21.4	17.7	15.0	12.9	-	K543. =K506*Disc_factor
544 Total Capex	MOD $ mm	76.6	58.7	17.9	-	-	-	-	-	K544. =K507*Disc_factor
545 Bonus & Rentals	MOD $ mm	20.4	0.9	14.6	1.4	1.3	1.2	1.1	-	K545. =K508*Disc_factor
546 Abandonment payment	MOD $ mm	13.9	-	-	-	-	-	13.9	-	K546. =K509*Disc_factor
547 Income Tax @ 45%	MOD $ mm	51.0	-	12.0	20.3	12.1	6.6	-	-	K547. =K510*Disc_factor
548 Investor's total cash outflows	MOD $ mm	316.0	59.6	92.8	58.5	41.8	30.2	33.0	-	K548. =SUM(K542:K547)
		NPV								
551 Investor Discounted NCF	MOD $ mm	37.4	(59.6)	35.7	30.9	20.3	13.1	(2.9)	-	K551. =K540-K548
552 Government Discounted NCF	MOD $ mm	132.3	0.9	48.7	37.2	24.1	15.2	6.3	-	K552. =SUM(K542,K545,K547)

Figure 1.46 From the file "Ch1_Tax_and_Royalty_Model.xls"
Notes: Reflects Base Scenario. Some rows and columns are hidden.

- and summing the annual NCF values to get investor and government NPV of MOD $ 37.4 mm and MOD $132.3 mm, respectively (cells D551 and D552).

1.9.6   Post-ELT Calculations: Financial Metrics

Starting in row 518 of the model, we calculate the following metrics.

Internal Rate of Return (IRR)

Under the Base Scenario, the investor's IRR of 42% in cell D518 is, as described in Section 1.2, the discount rate at which the investor's NPV equals 0. (When the IRR is incalculable, the formula used returns "n.m." ("not meaningful").)

Recall that IRRs need to be treated with some caution, as it is possible, when a series of undiscounted net cashflows changes signs (i.e., goes from positive to negative, or vice versa), more than once, for there to be more than one correct answer. Note that the investor's Base Scenario NCF in row 514 changes signs twice: in 2015–2016 and 2020–2021.

Breakeven

The investor's **breakeven** – also known as **payback** – is the point in a field's life when the investor's cumulative net cashflow first turns positive. In our Base Scenario, this happens sometime in 2017, giving that year the first black column in the cumulative undiscounted investor NCF chart, reproduced in Figure 1.47.

All other things being equal, the sooner breakeven occurs, the better for the investor.

While knowing the time it takes to break even is useful both in and of itself, and when comparing competing investment opportunities, it is only *so* useful, because it ignores what

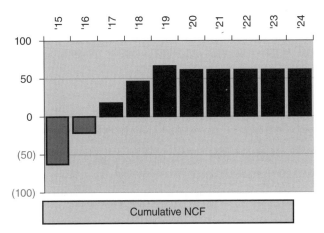

Figure 1.47   Investor's cumulative undiscounted NCF, MOD $ mm, from row 668 of the file "Ch1_Tax_and_Royalty_Model.xls"
Note: Reflects Base Scenario.

happens *after* the field breaks even. Does it go on to generate years and years of positive NCF? Is it abandoned as loss making immediately after breaking even? Or something in between? It is therefore used by some in capital budgeting, but usually as a secondary metric.

We calculate the investor's undiscounted breakeven year in rows 521–525. We explain the method on page 20 ("Approximate breakeven calculation") of the file "Ch1_Main_chapter_supplement.pdf," to which you should now turn. We call the approach shown the "approximate" method because it tells you in which period breakeven occurs, but not when within that period.[39]

Maximum Exposure

An investor's undiscounted **maximum exposure** is the most negative level of investor undiscounted cumulative NCF over the investment lifespan. It is meaningful when – as in our example model, and in many other upstream petroleum situations – an initial investment is required before production can start.

Maximum exposure thus measures the deepest that the investor is "in the hole," and tells us how much of a loss it would sustain if, in a worst case scenario, it made its full enabling investment, but then for some reason had no chance to recoup it by generating positive cashflow.

In our example model, undiscounted maximum exposure is calculated in cell D530 as being **MOD \$62.5** mm in the Base Scenario. It is seen as the lowest column in the chart shown in Figure 1.47.

The formula used to calculate it in cell D530 is $\boxed{\text{=IF(MIN(F529:O529)>=0, "n.m.",}}$ $\boxed{\text{-MIN(F529:O529))}}$ where $\boxed{\text{F529:O529}}$ is each year's cumulative undiscounted NCF:

- The second expression is the "main" part of the formula; note how the minus sign means the maximum exposure will be expressed as a positive.

- The first expression is an error trap, which returns $\boxed{\text{"n.m."}}$ in cases where cumulative undiscounted NCF is never negative, in which case the investor is never "exposed" in the sense of this metric.

---

[39] Sometimes it is not enough to know only that breakeven, as measured by some item – whether it is NCF, or another measure of profitability – occurs "sometime" within a period; it is necessary to know more about *when* within the period. This is because some countries base royalty, income tax and other fiscally relevant rates on the *quantified* extent to which an investor has broken even, e.g., whether it has only 50% broken even (i.e., cumulative revenues are only half of cumulative costs); it has fully broken even; or it has 150% broken even (i.e., cumulative revenue equals 1.5 times cumulative costs). In such a case, knowing the specific breakeven date is necessary to calculate correctly when a specified breakeven milestone is reached.

For example, if a tax rate is stated to be 30% before breakeven, and 50% after, and if the company breaks even at the end of the first quarter of the tax year, then it would only enjoy the 30% tax rate for the first 25% of the tax year, and be taxed at 50% thereafter.

This linkage of some measure of breakeven to another fiscal device is a "sub-device" often known as an "R-factor." We cover R-factors in detail as they apply to royalties and production sharing contracts in Chapters 3 and 8, respectively.

We show how to calculate an estimate of a specific breakeven time-point in the standalone file "Ch1_breakeven_methods.pdf" and its companion Excel files in the "Ch1_breakeven" sub-folder on the disk.

Note that in row 531 we determine the year in which undiscounted maximum exposure occurs, using simple logic in the annual cells. This logic:

- returns the calendar year if cumulative undiscounted cashflow equals the maximum exposure, and otherwise returns "n.a."; and

- captures, in cell D531, this year of maximum exposure, by taking the minimum value of the annual cells. The MIN function used ignores the text in the annual "n.a." cells.

(This will make more sense when you inspect the actual model!)

Thus under the Base Scenario, maximum exposure occurs in 2015 (cell D531), which in this case is the first capex year.

Sense check

Reset the model to the Base Scenario. In the Console View, adjust the split so you can see row 43 above the split and rows 661–684 below it.

Production starts in 2016. Change this to 2017, using the spinner in cell C43 (i.e., changing it to the value of 2).

What happens to (a) the amount and timing of maximum exposure, and (b) the timing of the breakeven year (shown in cells B681:B682)?

Experiment with how at least five other input assumptions in the Console View affect each of these two metrics.

Two other undiscounted metrics calculated are:

- **The PIR, or profit–to-investment ratio.** It is calculated in cell D534, with the formula =IF(D507<0, 0,   D514/D507), which divides total (all-years) investor NCF by total (all-years) capex, subject to a 0 denominator "error trap." Under the Base Scenario, PIR is 0.75, which means that over the field's economic life, each dollar of undiscounted capex invested generates an undiscounted 75 cents of economic profit, measured as undiscounted NCF – in other words, a NCF undiscounted 75% cash return on cash invested.

- **NCF per barrel.** This is calculated as MOD $11.17/barrel[40] in cell D535. The formula is straightforward – on a post-ELT, total, life-of-field basis, it divides undiscounted investor NCF (cell D514) by post-ELT field production in mmb (cell D276), again, subject to a zero-denominator error trap.

---

[40] Note that the volumetric unit used reflects the fact that our example model produces only oil, whereas a gas field would use NCF per MCF, and a mixed oil and gas field would use NCF per BOE or NCF per MCFE.

In parallel calculations using discounted components, we calculate in rows 555–569 the discounted breakeven year, discounted maximum exposure, discounted PIR ("DPIR") and NPV per barrel.

These ratios are most commonly used for capital budgeting purposes, i.e., for making decisions which affect a portfolio of investments. While capital budgeting is not the focus of this book – except indirectly, in that capital budgeting models rely on inputs from properly executed fiscal models of individual investments – we calculate them in our example model here to make readers who are new to the subject aware of them.

Many analysts prefer to calculate discounted breakeven metrics. Discounted breakeven often occurs later than undiscounted breakeven. Whereas fiscal instruments tend to be linked to undiscounted breakeven metrics, it is the discounted breakeven measures that are more useful for capital budgeting, project performance evaluation and investment decision making.

1.9.7   Post-ELT Calculations: Volumetric Outcomes

In Figure 1.48 (from the section of the model starting in row 629), we show four different ways of measuring the field's total (all-years) production (a term which some might loosely refer to as "reserves," although we hesitate to do so here, as "reserves" is often a legal/reporting term which means different things in different jurisdictions). They are calculated in the section of the model starting in row 572:

- Gross pre-ELT volumes consist of the "technical production" volumes which we entered, and timed and applied a sensitivity factor to, in the assumptions section of the model.

- Gross post-ELT volumes are the gross pre-ELT annual volumes multiplied by the ELF, i.e., truncated to the economic limit.

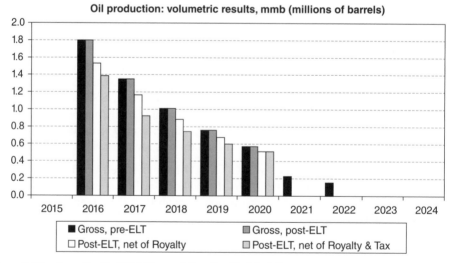

Figure 1.48   From the file "Ch1_Tax_and_Royalty_Model.xls"
Note: Reflects Base Scenario.

- The post-ELT volumes, net of royalty deduct the volumetric equivalent of the royalty payment:

  ○ Here is a "shortcut" calculation example: if gross post-ELT production is 10 mmb, and the royalty rate is 20%, then the royalty equivalent in barrels is 2 mmb; therefore, post-ELT, net of royalty volumes equal 8 mmb.

  ○ Some jurisdictions require that investors' reports to stock exchanges provide data on a net of royalty (also called "after-royalty" or "post-royalty") basis. The reasoning is that because the government takes a royalty – either in cash or "**in kind**" (i.e., as volumes) – from "off the top" of the gross revenue stream, the investor is never entitled to the royalty component of the volumes to begin with. Therefore, the investor should deduct the royalty component from reported reserves; otherwise, the investor would overstate the volumes to which it is actually entitled. Under such definitions, the investor's **working interest** volumes would equal the investor's equity stake in the license (assumed 100% in this model), multiplied by the post-ELT volumes, net of royalty volumes.[41]

- The post-ELT volumes, net of royalty and tax, deduct the volumetric equivalent of both the royalty and the income tax charge. The latter is calculated in row 581 of the model as the period's tax charge in MOD $ mm, divided by the period's oil price in MOD $/b. This is also a reporting requirement in some jurisdictions.

The total (all-years) Base Scenarios volumes under each of these four measures are shown in the "Ignored" row (we will explain in a moment) in Figure 1.49, which starts in row 631 of the model.

Note that many jurisdictions require reporting future production volumes on a post-ELT basis as one requirement for them to be called "Reserves" in a strict, regulatory sense. This means that changing economic conditions – or changing forecasts of *expected* economic conditions – can be one factor causing companies to revise their reported reserve estimates from year to year.

For example, suppose that in 2015, a company forecast that the ELT would cause the last expected economic production year to be 2020, but in 2016 the company raises its oil price forecast, which would make two more years of production appear in its model to be commercially viable. In this case the reported reserves would increase by an amount equal to the company's working interest (however defined) in the volume from those two extra years worth of production.[42]

---

[41] It is always good to ask whether what a company claims to be its "working interest" reserves have had the royalty component deducted – that is, to ask whether the reserves quoted are "net of royalty" – as reporting standards vary, and some companies will publish figures which do not deduct the royalty component, i.e., they publish reserves, gross of royalty, as this can make the reserves look larger.

[42] Conversely, the company's reported reserves could fall, if in 2016 it lowered its oil price forecast enough to cause the forecast last economic year to occur before 2020.

Note that some reporting jurisdictions such as the US – in order to limit the scope for manipulating reported reserve volumes by "playing" with the commodity price forecast – require that all companies calculate economic reserves using price forecasts which reflect the *historic* average prices realized in the reporting year. This does have the effect of putting each company's reported reserves on an "equal footing" in this respect. However, the resultant reserves volumes reported will not necessarily be that meaningful – unless you happen to believe that, for example, a 20-year oil price forecast, made at the end of 2016, somehow gains "realism" by being based on the average 2016 historic received price.

Points to Consider Regarding Reported Volumes

Although royalty and income tax are both fiscal cash outflows from the investor's point of view, so are other fiscal costs, such as rentals and bonuses; yet stock exchange and other rules seldom (if at all) require that investors deduct the volumetric equivalents of these other fiscal costs to arrive at reported working interest volumes.

- On the one hand, it strikes us as inconsistent to require the deduction of volumes corresponding to some fiscal costs but not others.

- On the other hand, it might be just as well not to require things like volumes net of all fiscal charges.

- One reason is that too many volumetric measures would be likely to confuse outside investors.

- Another is that, from a valuation point of view, calculating ever more finely sliced measures of volumes is only so useful. It is important not to lose sight of the fact that in fiscally detailed upstream petroleum cashflow valuations, volumes are usually not "the point"; rather, they are stepping stones to reach "the point," which is the monetary value of those volumes, as measured by NCF and ultimately NPV and related discounted metrics. From a cold investment perspective, an oil field investment is not about oil, it is about cashflows.[43]

The Positive-NPV Test for Reporting Reserves

Another adjustment to reported production volumes is the positive-NPV test, which, simply put, means that if the project is NPV-negative, the investor may not report *any* future production volumes. The thinking behind this is that if the investment is NPV-negative, the investor will not proceed with the project, and so will not ever produce.

Total (all years) oil production, mmb				
	Pre-ELT	Post-ELT		
Positive-NPV test:	Gross of royalty	Gross of royalty	Net of royalty	Net of royalty & tax
Ignored	5.9	5.5	4.8	4.2
Applied	Not relevant		4.8	4.2

Figure 1.49 From rows 631–635 of the "Model" sheet of the file "Ch1_Tax_and_Royalty_Model.xls"
Note: Reflects Base Scenario.

The model provides the option whether to apply this test, using the spinner in cell C590. If the test is selected, simple formula logic is applied to the post-ELT volumes, net of royalty, and the post-ELT volumes, net of royalty and tax, in cells D594 and D595, respectively. These are the values in the "Applied" row of Figure 1.49. Note that under the Base Scenario, NPV is positive, and so the results are the same, whether the positive-NPV test is applied or ignored.

---

[43] For further discussion on volumetric outcomes, see Sections 6.5 and 6.7 of Chapter 6 on PSCs.

Note that in Figure 1.49 we have written "Not relevant" because the positive-NPV test is not usually applied to pre-ELT, gross of royalty volumes, or to post-ELT, gross of royalty volumes.

Sense check

Reset the model to the Base Scenario. In the Console View, be able to see row 23 above the split, and rows 590–595 below the split. Apply the positive-NPV test by selecting "Yes" with the spinner in cell C590. Now lower the oil price multiplier (cell G23) from 100% until the values in cells D594 and D595 equal 0. Scroll down below the split to check, in the discounted waterfall chart just below, that NPV is indeed negative at this multiplier setting.

Concluding sections

Turn to pages 21–46 of the file "Ch1_Main_chapter_supplement.pdf" on the disk for the following three, concluding sections of this chapter:

- 1.10 Multivariable Sensitivity Analysis Using a Two-Way Data Table
- 1.11 The ELT – Questions to Consider
- 1.12 Review Exercise: Key Calculations

Chapter 2
Tax Consolidation and Incremental Value

2

Tax Consolidation and Incremental Value

2.1 TOM AND CARMEN MIX LOVE AND MONEY: A ROMANTIC INTRODUCTION TO FISCAL CONSOLIDATION

Tom and Carmen are each self-employed, running separate businesses. Although they never married – "it's just a piece of paper," they say – they have lived happily together for years, and pool their incomes in a joint bank account.

Until recently, each made annual taxable income of $60 000, or, to express all money in this example in thousands of dollars, $60. Because the tax rate is 50%, they each paid annual taxes of $30 and kept the other $30. Thus their combined annual post-tax "cashflow" was $30 apiece, for a combined total of $60.

That is, until Tom had a bad year last year. Not only did a series of disastrous business mistakes leave him with a $50 loss, but, under a court-imposed curfew (long story), he is prevented from working for the next three years.

The only potential comfort for Tom (beyond his love of Carmen) is theoretical – the tax laws in their country allow tax losses to be carried forward for three years. As discussed in Chapter 1,[1] this means that his $50 loss could be used as a tax allowance, to reduce the taxable income Tom earns over the next three years. But as Tom will not be working, he will not have any taxable income to reduce, so this gives no practical benefit over the coming three years.

The couple worry how they will manage over the next three years with only Carmen's annual post-tax cashflow of $30. Carmen and Tom talk each other out of suicide and prostitution, respectively. Then suddenly they have an idea – maybe marriage isn't just a "piece of paper" after all.

Carmen recalls that, while once browsing a copy of the tax code in a plastic surgeon's waiting room, she saw that if they file jointly as a married couple, they can combine the best of both worlds -- they can apply Tom's tax loss against Carmen's taxable income. Their three-year analysis of post-tax cashflow is shown in Figure 2.1.

Take a moment to review the formulas before proceeding. (Note that they assume Carmen will not have any tax losses.)

---

[1] You will need to understand the basic mechanics of tax loss carryforwards to follow this chapter. We cover them in Chapter 1, Section 1.9.3, "Income Tax: Basic Concepts and Calculations."

	B	C	D	E	F	G	H	I	J
2	**To wed, or not to wed: filing income taxes separately, or as a married couple**								
3	*Note:"LCF" means "loss carried forward"*		Tax rate:		50%	← cell name: Tax_rate			
4	All figures in $	Total/other	Year 1	Year 2	Year 3	**Typical formulae**			
5	**Not married**					(example: Year 1)			
6	Tom's taxable income, ignoring LCF	Loss from pre-year 1	0	0	0	(assumed)			
7	Tom's LCF (shown as a positive)		50	50	50	D7. =(–C9)			
8	Tom's taxable income, considering LCF		(50)	(50)	(50)	D8. =D6–D7			
9	Tom's loss, carriable forward to next year	(50)	(50)	(50)	(50)	D9. =IF(D8<0, D8, 0)			
10	Tom's tax charge at 50% tax rate	0	0	0	0	D10. =IF(D8<0, 0, Tax_rate*D8)			
11	Tom's post-tax cashflow	0	0	0	0	D11. =D6–D10			
13	Carmen's taxable income	180	60	60	60	(assumed)			
14	Carmen's tax charge at 50% tax rate	90	30	30	30	D14. =IF(D13<0,0, Tax_rate * D13)			
15	Carmen's post-tax cashflow	90	30	30	30	D15. =D13–D14			
17	**Tom & Carmen's post-tax cashflow**	90	30	30	30	D17. =D11+D15			
18	**Married**								
19	Tom's taxable income, ignoring LCF		0	0	0	D19. =D6			
20	Carmen's taxable income, ignoring LCF		60	60	60	D20. =D13			
21	Couple's taxable income, ignoring LCF		60	60	60	D21. =D19+D20			
23	Tom's LCF (shown as a positive)	Loss from pre-year 1	50	0	0	D23. =(–C25)			
24	Couple's taxable income, considering LCF		10	60	60	D24. =D21–D23			
25	*Tom's loss, carriable forward to next year*	(50)	0	0	0	D25. =IF(D24<0, D24, 0)			
26	**Combined tax charge at 50% tax rate**	65	5	30	30	D26. =IF(D24<0, 0, Tax_rate * D24)			
28	**Tom & Carmen's post-tax cashflow**	115	55	30	30	D28. =D21–D26			

Figure 2.1 Tax bill: filing separately vs. as a married couple, from the file "Ch2_Tax_consolidation_introduction.xls"

From the analysis above, we can see that:

- *If they do not marry*, together, over the three years, they will pay combined taxes of Tom's $0 (cell C11) + Carmen's $90 (cell C14) = $90, leaving them with a post-tax cashflow of **$90** (cell C17).

- *If they do marry*:

  ○ in <u>Year 1</u>, Carmen's taxable income of $60 (cell D20), minus Tom's $50 loss from the prior year ("Year 0" – his bad year), carried forward to Year 1 (cell D23), means Year 1 taxable income will be $10 (cell D24), which, when taxed at 50%, means taxes due of $5 (cell D25), resulting in a Year 1 combined post-tax cashflow of $60 – $5 = <u>$55</u> (cell D28);

  ○ by the end of Year 1, the tax loss has already been used up, so it cannot be carried forward to Year 2, thus Tom plays no role in <u>Year 2</u>, when the couple's combined post-tax cashflow equals Carmen's <u>$30</u> (cell E28);

  ○ <u>Year 3</u> is the same as Year 2, so, again, combined post-tax cashflow is <u>$30</u> (cell F28);

  ○ at the end of three years, the total combined post-tax income is <u>$55 + $30 + $30</u> = **$115** (cell C28).

Comparing the two outcomes, the **$115 – $90 = $25 benefit of marrying**, because it "unlocks" the benefits of Tom's prior $50 loss, is clear. If marriage is just a piece of paper, it is a pretty valuable one.

2.2 PETROLEUM TAX AND ROYALTY REGIMES: "RINGFENCING" VS. CONSOLIDATION

The tax rules and cashflow implications for Tom and Carmen <u>as individuals</u> are analogous to the upstream petroleum income tax treatment known as **income tax "ringfencing,"** in which each project is assessed fiscally on a "standalone" basis.

The <u>married couple's</u> regime, on the other hand, is analogous to upstream petroleum **income tax consolidation** treatment, whereby tax losses from one project may be used to offset the taxable profit of another project.[2]

For example, suppose an investor develops two oil fields, Field 1 and Field 2, in the same country. (To keep things simple, we will say the two fields are in different regions, with no infrastructure or anything else in common except that they are subject to the same tax rules).

Under a tax and royalty regime using <u>ringfencing rules</u>, tax deductions – including (but not limited to) tax losses carried forward – from one field <u>may not</u> be used to reduce the taxable income from the other. It is as though there is a fiscal wall ("ringfence") around each field.

- Thus the investor's total income tax charge from its activities in the country in any single tax period – like Tom and Carmen's combined tax bill if they did not marry – is the <u>sum of two separately calculated individual tax charges</u> for each field during that period.

- In fact, the investor's <u>total post-tax cashflow</u>, for a given period's activities in the country under <u>ringfencing rules</u>, is simply the sum of each field's separately calculated post-tax cashflow for that period.

Whereas under fiscal <u>consolidation</u> rules, tax deductions from one field <u>may</u> be used to reduce the taxable income from the other. In which case, the investor's total income tax charge from its activities in the country in any given tax period – like Tom and Carmen's combined tax bill after they got married – is calculated by summing the *components* of each field's income tax calculation, and then using these sums in a *combined-basis* taxable income/(untaxable loss) calculation, which, if taxable, is then taxed. Put as formulas:

(a) Consolidated taxable income/untaxable loss =
    (Field 1 revenue + Field 2 revenue) – (Field 1 tax deductions + Field 2 tax deductions)
(b) Consolidated tax charge when (a) is positive (i.e. taxable) = a) × tax rate
(c) Consolidated tax charge when (a) is negative (i.e. untaxable) = 0

Tax deductions include:

- "normal" tax deductible costs (e.g., from operations); as well as

- tax loss carryforwards (when regimes permit them).

---

[2] Be aware that income tax is not the only fiscal device which can work on a ringfenced or consolidated basis. Another example is the recovery of contractor costs under some production sharing agreements (which are covered in Chapter 6).

The total post-tax cashflow for activities in the country in any single tax period under consolidation rules is calculated as:

> (Field 1 revenue + Field 2 revenue)−
> (Field 1 cash costs excluding tax + Field 2 cash costs excluding tax)−
> Consolidated tax charge

For Tom and Carmen, filing separately or as a married couple made a big difference to their three-year post-tax cashflow.

Similarly, **whether ringfenced or consolidated fiscal rules are used can materially affect the post-tax cashflows and thus NPV of upstream petroleum projects.**

We will soon see this by examining an oil production valuation model, which is more nuanced than the simplistic Tom and Carmen example, although the same principles apply.

2.3 RINGFENCING, CONSOLIDATION AND INCREMENTAL VALUE

Suppose on that on January 1, 2014, an investor already owns Field 1 and is considering buying Field 2.

Again, we have assumed that − apart from being in the same country, and thus subject to the same fiscal regime − the fields have nothing in common; they have no synergies; they lie hundreds of miles apart and share no infrastructure or any other common costs. The *pre-tax* commercial viability of one field does not affect that of the other, therefore each will have distinct, independently calculated economic limits (as discussed in Chapter 1, Sections 1.4 and 1.8).[3]

Suppose further that the government is considering changing from a ringfenced to a consolidated fiscal regime − or, put another way, effectively making the ringfence the country's national border, so that the whole country can be considered as one consolidation area for oil taxation purposes.

If the change comes, it is expected to happen very soon, and to take effect retroactively, starting January 1, 2014.

The company therefore needs to model twice − once, assuming ringfencing rules remain in place, and then again, assuming the change to consolidation rules happens.

---

[3] If, on the other hand, Field 1 and Field 2 *did* share infrastructure or some other common element which impacted each of their costs, such as a processing facility, their commercial viability would be interdependent to an extent. In such a case, it would be necessary to calculate a common economic limit for the two fields as one combined producing entity. Using the GOCF-based method discussed in Chapter 1, GOCF would equal (Field 1 + Field 2 revenues) − ((Field 1 + Field 2) ELT-relevant cash costs).

The investor has produced oil price, production volume, cost and other forecasts for Fields 1 and 2, and now wants to know, what is the maximum acquisition price it should pay – basing its value on post-tax NPV – for Field 2, under each fiscal regime?

Phrased another way, what is the **incremental** NPV of Field 2 to the investor which owns Field 1?

Before turning directly to the new example model which answers this question, let us preview its generic modeling approach to fiscally ringfenced vs. consolidated investment combinations.

Fiscal Consolidation and the Incremental Value Approach

Incremental value in this example is the change in value to the investor's total portfolio caused by adding Field 2 to its existing portfolio, which now consists only of Field 1.

Expressed as a formula:

> Incremental value to investor's portfolio of Field 2 =
> NPV of portfolio consisting of Field 1 and Field 2 – NPV of portfolio consisting of Field 1

This might seem like an unnecessarily complicated way of stating the obvious; after all, to say that

A: (Value of Field 2) = (Value of (Field 1 + Field 2)) − (Value of Field 1)

is just a restatement of

B: (Value of (Field 1 + Field 2)) = (Value of Field 1) + (Value of Field 2)

Right?

From the Tom and Carmen saga, we know that the answer is that B is right **only sometimes**.

Refer back to Figure 2.1. Suppose Tom – cunningly – wanted to assess the monetary value of the proposed marriage, i.e., he wanted to know the value, measured by total three-year post-tax cashflow, of (Married Tom & Carmen), as opposed to just the value of (Single Tom).

If they filed their taxes separately – which, again, is comparable to a ringfenced tax regime – then the value of (Married Tom & Carmen) would be $90, calculated as:

> (Single Tom's income − Single Tom's taxes) + (Single Carmen's income − Single Carmen's taxes) =
> (Single Tom's post-tax cashflow)+
> (Single Carmen's post-tax cashflow) =
> ($0) + ($90)

In this case, we *can* use the "Tom & Carmen version" of statement B, above; that is, we can always say that the value of (Married Tom & Carmen) always equals the value of (Single Tom) + (Single Carmen).

If, however, they filed their taxes as a couple – which is analogous to a consolidated tax regime – we *cannot* use the format of statement B to calculate the value of (Married Tom & Carmen).

Why not? Consider that under the consolidation rules, the value of the post-tax cashflows of (Married Tom & Carmen), which is **$115**, is calculated as:

> (Single Tom's income + Single Carmen's income) − ((Married Tom & Carmen's)taxes) =
> ($0 + $180) − ($65) =
> $115

Under consolidation rules, we cannot reach this answer using the format of statement B, because statement B requires us to know both the post-tax value of Single Tom's cashflow and the post-tax value of Single Carmen's cashflow.

But we do not know either of these – we only know the value of each on a *pre-tax basis*.

- Because the taxation occurs on a combined, consolidated basis, it is not possible to say how much of the tax charge is due to just Tom or to just Carmen, because the tax charge is the result of the interaction between their finances as a married couple.

- Trying to assign portions of the tax charge to each of them, in order to work out their individual post-tax values and thus solve in the format of statement B, would be like trying to identify individual eggs in an omelet.

Therefore we have to "back out the answer" to our question, which is, what is the incremental value to Tom of marrying Carmen? (which is analogous to the incremental value to the owner of Field 2 of owning Field 2 under consolidation rules). We use the format of statement A:

> Value of marrying Carmen = (Value of (Married Tom & Carmen) − (Value of Single Tom))

which is just another way of Tom asking himself, "What difference does it make to me if I marry Carmen?"

Therefore, he solves as follows:

> Value of marrying Carmen = (Value of(Married Tom & Carmen)−(Value of Single Tom))
> Value of marrying Carmen = ($115) − ($0) = **$115**

* * *

To apply all this to answer our original question, "what is the incremental value to the owner of Field 1 of acquiring Field 2?", based on NPV, <u>what should the owner of Field 1 pay for Field 2</u>:

- on a <u>ringfenced basis</u>? The answer is simple – it is NPV of Field 2. Whereas

- on a <u>fiscally consolidated basis</u>, we:
  (a) calculate Field 1 NPV;
  (b) calculate combined, consolidated (Field 1 & Field 2) NPV; and
  (c) calculate Field 2 NPV incrementally as (b) minus (a).

This method honors the definition of incremental value stated above, i.e., the change in value to the investor's total portfolio caused by acquiring Field 2.

2.4 RINGFENCED VS. CONSOLIDATED INCREMENTAL VALUE MODEL: ASSUMPTIONS

The oil field model we now turn to – found on the "Model" sheet of the file "Ch2_Tax_consolidation_model.xls" – shows each method in action.

It will also be a <u>useful review</u> of how to model items already covered in Chapter 1, including:

- simple royalties;

- fixed and variable opex;

- economic limit tests ("**ELT**s") using the GOCF method;

- abandonment cost timing;

- tax loss carryforwards; and

- mid-year inflation/discounting.

Assumptions are detailed in the section starting in row 32 of the file "Ch2_Tax_consolidation_model.xls." We have constructed a scenario – the "Base Scenario"[4] – for our example, using some very <u>simplistic assumptions</u> in order to limit the number of "moving parts" which might distract us from our main focus here, which is on the effects of income tax consolidation. Therefore we assume a constant oil price, 0% inflation,[5] and perfectly flat oil production profiles, as shown in Figure 2.2.

In the Base Scenario, it is, as mentioned, January 1, 2014. The investor already has a <u>100%</u> equity share (or <u>working interest</u>) in <u>Field 1</u>.

---

[4] Note that if you change any of the input assumptions, you can restore the model to the "factory settings" discussed here by pressing the "Reset to Base Scenario" button in cell C29.

[5] In this example, because the Base Scenario inflation rate is 0%, real 2014 dollars and MOD dollars are the same. The example model *does* "inflate" items at 0% (or any other rate chosen), but in our text discussion we do not describe the values as being in real or MOD terms.

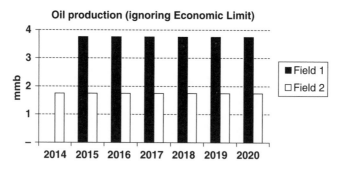

Figure 2.2 Assumed production profiles, mmb/year, from the file "Ch2_Tax_consolidation_model.xls"

The investor expects that Field 1, after a $350 mm investment this year, will start producing a technical volume (i.e., ignoring the ELT; a "pre-ELT" volume) of 3.75 mmb (or mm bbl, meaning million barrels) per year for each year, from 2015 through to the end of 2021 (row 49).

The investor now has the option to buy a 100% working interest in Field 2, an old field with a long prior production history.

Field 2 had at one point been "shut in" (i.e., production was suspended) as it had been thought to be uneconomic.

Another investor, however, then invested in a new enhanced recovery (i.e., production) technology, which is believed to enable 1.75 mmb of technical production for the seven years starting 2014 (row 50), but due to a shift in geographic focus, this investor now wishes to sell its 100% WI and pursue opportunities elsewhere.

Detailed assumptions are shown in Figures 2.3 and 2.4.

Warning: depreciation "shortcut" used. To limit the model's size, and to keep the learning focus on consolidation, we have used a simplified, approximate (i.e., "quick and dirty") method

	B	C	D	E	F	G	H	I	J	K	L
31				Total/other	2014	2015	2016	2017	2018	2019	2020
32	**Assumptions common to both fields**										
33	Last year of license	2020									
34	Valuation date is 1 January 2014										
35	Inflation/discounting year	year #			0.5	1.5	2.5	3.5	4.5	5.5	6.5
36	Inflation rate	%	0.0%								
37	Mid-year inflation index	x.x			1.00	1.00	1.00	1.00	1.00	1.00	1.00
38	Discount rate	%	10.0%								
39	Mid-year discount factor	x.x			0.95	0.87	0.79	0.72	0.65	0.59	0.54
40	Oil price	Real 2014 $/b			70.0	70.0	70.0	70.0	70.0	70.0	70.0
41	Oil price	MOD $/b			70.0	70.0	70.0	70.0	70.0	70.0	70.0
42	Royalty rate	% of revenue	12.5%								
43	Depreciation: Straight line period (useful life)	years	5	<--- Note: simplified depreciation method is used;							
44	Undepreciated balance in terminal year assumed not to be written off in that year			see comment in cell B8							
45	Income tax rate	%									
46	Tax losses are carriable forward indefinitely		50.0%								

Figure 2.3 Base Scenario assumptions from the file "Ch2_Tax_consolidation_model.xls"

	B	C	D	E	F	G	H	I	J	K	L
47	**Field-specific assumptions (before Economic Limit)**										
48	**Production and capex**		**Total/other**		**2014**	**2015**	**2016**	**2017**	**2018**	**2019**	**2020**
49	Field 1 oil production	mmb	22.5		-	3.75	3.75	3.75	3.75	3.75	3.75
50	Field 2 oil production	mmb	12.3		1.75	1.75	1.75	1.75	1.75	1.75	1.75
51	Field 1 future capex (all depreciable)	Real 2014 $mm	350.0		350.0	-	-	-	-	-	-
52	Field 2 future capex (all depreciable)	Real 2014 $mm	0				(None)				
53											
54	**Opex and abandonment**		**Field 1**	**Field 2**							
55	Annual fixed opex	Real 2014 $mm	45.0	15.0							
56	Variable opex	Real 2014 $/b	15.0	24.0							
57	Abandonment cost (lumpsum)	Real 2014 $mm	35.0	40.0	<--- (Paid in each field's last economic production year)						
59	Other tax deductions: balance of prior year items on 1 January 2014		**Field 1**	**Field 2**							
60	Balance of prior capex left to depreciate	MOD $mm	0	300	Field 2 prior capex assumed to have X years left to depreciate:						3
61	Balance of prior, carriable forward tax losses (enter as positive values)	MOD $mm	30	220							

Figure 2.4   Base Scenario assumptions, continued, from the file "Ch2_Tax_consolidation_model.xls"

to calculate straight line depreciation. This is the "quick and dirty" shortcut method discussed in Section 1.9.2 of Chapter 1. Do not mistake it for an example of fully correct practice.

Although the distortions caused by using this shortcut, under this model's Base Scenario assumptions, are not very material, be aware that the method used here is *not* consistent with the mid-year inflation and discounting methods also used here. In addition, it is inflexible in that it assumes that there will only be one year's capex (2014).

A full example of the correct straight line depreciation calculation method can be found in the file "Appendix_I_Depreciation.pdf" on the disk.

Rows 60 and 61 are **where this starts to get interesting**.

Whoever acquires Field 2 gets not only production, but also $520 mm in tax allowances for *potential* use starting in 2014. These consist of $300 mm in historic (i.e., pre-2014) capex (cell E60) which has three more years (starting 2014) to depreciate (cell L60), as well as $220 mm in tax losses which can be carried forward to offset any taxable income occurring starting 2014 (cell E61).

Note that we say "potential use".

- One reason is that we do not yet know whether the government will, in fact, change the income tax rules from their present standalone basis to a consolidated basis – which is why we model both ways.

- If the basis does change, we still do not know whether:

   o Field 2 will be shut down by the economic limit test before all three years of depreciation can occur. Note that in this model – unlike the one in Chapter 1 in file "Ch1_Tax_and_Royalty_Model.xls" – we do *not* assume that terminal year write-offs apply. (Recall the explanation of this write-off rule from page 18 of the "Quick and dirty depreciation calculation" discussion in the file "Ch1_Main_chapter_supplement.pdf.")

The fact that this rule is assumed *not* to apply in our present example means that if the field shuts down before all three years of depreciation occur, then the tax benefits from the years when depreciation does not occur will be "lost."

○ There will be any opportunities to use the tax loss carryforwards, i.e., whether there will be any taxable profits for the loss carryforwards to reduce. If there are not, under the assumptions used in this example, these loss carryforwards will "die unused" at the end of the economic production period.

2.5 RINGFENCED VS. CONSOLIDATED INCREMENTAL VALUE MODEL: CALCULATIONS

Note: The auditing macros might be especially helpful here

This is one of the longer models we have encountered in the book so far, because we are modeling the fields both individually (i.e., on a standalone basis) and under two different fiscal combination methods (i.e., ring-fenced vs. consolidated).

The formulas are generally straightforward, and many have been covered in previous material, but there are a lot of them.

Therefore we suggest that using the Excel auditing macros (see the "AuditingTools" sheet of the example file), perhaps with the screen split horizontally at times, will greatly help as you review this model.

Step 1: Standalone NPVs for Each Field

First, NPVs are calculated for each field on a standalone basis, in the section starting in row 86 for Field 1 and in the one starting in row 136 for Field 2. For each field, the following are calculated – as explained in Chapter 1 – in this order:

• Gross operating cashflow (GOCF) on a pre-economic limit test (ELT) basis.

• The ELT, and an economic life flag (**ELF**) based on this ELT.

• The calculation and timing of the lumpsum abandonment cost based on the economic life.

• On a post-ELT basis, all cash items, as well as depreciation.

○ As mentioned, these depreciation calculations have been simplified. In rows 112–114 (Field 1) and 162–164 (Field 2) we have "manually" chosen in which cells to place formulas. This means that the depreciation sections are not fully flexible – you should *not* type in the gray cells in these rows, or change the Base Scenario timing assumptions for capex (all of which is assumed depreciable). Again, our shortcuts here are not standard recommended modeling practice. They are specific to this example, to help limit the model's size and complexity.

○ Generically, each annual depreciation charge is calculated as:

  – the relevant new capex (in the case of Field 1) or undepreciated historic capex (Field 2), divided by

  – the relevant number of years to depreciate, times

  – the corresponding year's ELF value. This last operation ensures that depreciation stops when the economic field life ends. (Again, the depreciation terminal year write-off rules used in the Chapter 1 model are assumed not to apply here.)

• Income taxes based on post-ELT revenue and deductions.

• Undiscounted net cashflow (NCF) based on all post-ELT values.

• Discounted NCF, summed to NPV.

If you press the "Reset to Base Scenario" button in row 30, you will see that for **Field 1**, **standalone NPV is $63.0 mm** (cell D134) and for **Field 2**, it is **$234.7 mm** (cell D182).

A quick point of preliminary analysis

We will analyze these results further later. For now, we will mention that, if it seems strange that Field 2, with much less production, has a much larger NPV than Field 1, bear in mind that, uniquely, Field 2 enters the valuation period starting January 1, 2014:

• with all of its capex spending behind it; and

• in a "privileged," inherited tax position, due to the combined $520 mm in tax deductions from prior years.

Step 2: Combined, Ringfenced NPV

Next, NPVs are calculated for Fields 1 and 2 on a combined, ringfenced basis, in the short section starting in row 185.

Here we could have shortened this section to a single row, in which we just add the annual discounted NCF values already calculated for Field 1 (row 134) and Field 2 (row 182), and then summed the resulting annual figures to reach NPV. With ringfenced combinations like this one, it really is that simple.

But for the analysis we will do later, we need to see some of the individual components of the calculation. Therefore we have made this section slightly longer:

• First, in row 187, we sum each field's post-ELT revenue.

• Next, we sum each field's post-ELT cash outflows: royalties, opex, capex, abandonment costs and income tax charges (rows 188–192).

- Note that there is no need for us to calculate combined depreciation here, because, for ringfenced combinations, the only role which depreciation plays in our calculations is that of a tax deduction, which by definition is not shared between the ringfenced fields. Instead we ignore depreciation at the combined ringfenced level, and instead determine the combined ringfenced tax charge just by summing the standalone Field 1 and Field 2 tax charges.

- We then subtract these combined outflows from the combined revenue to reach undiscounted NCF (row 193).

- Finally, in row 194, we discount the resultant annual NCF values, and sum them to reach a combined, ringfenced NPV.

Under the Base Scenario settings, the resultant **combined, ringfenced NPV is $297.8 mm** (cell D194). The checksum in cell A194 confirms that this is the same result we would have reached if we had taken the shortcut of simply adding Fields 1's standalone NPV of $63.0 mm (cell D134) to Field 2's standalone NPV of $234.7 mm (cell D182).

Step 4: Combined, Consolidated NPV

We calculate a combined, consolidated NPV for Fields (1 & 2) in the section starting row 196.

Our calculation strategy is to first calculate consolidated, undiscounted NCF. To do this:

- we calculate, in rows 198–206, all cashflows *except income tax* the same way we calculated them for the ringfenced combination, i.e., we just added each Field 1 (standalone basis) item to its Field 2 (standalone basis) counterpart; however,

- we calculate the *consolidated income tax* charge, in rows 208–214, by summing the necessary Field 1 and Field 2 items, and then calculating the combined tax charge from these summed items.

We then use all these consolidated items to calculate consolidated, undiscounted NCF (row 223), which we then discount in the next row to obtain NPV.

In detail:

- In rows 199–202 and 206, we obtain the sum of Field 1 and Field 2 standalone, post-ELT revenue, royalties, opex, capex and abandonment charges.[6] We already calculated these sums in the previous section, so rather than do so again, we merely use equal signs to link these rows to the previous section's corresponding rows.

---

[6] Recall our mentioning that a combined, consolidated ELT is inappropriate in this example. This is because the fields share no infrastructure, and otherwise are commercially independent of each other on a *pre-income tax basis* – which is the basis for the ELT calculation recommended by a number of upstream industry professional bodies, and so is the standard ELT method used in this book, as explained in Section 1.8 of Chapter 1.

Having said that, here is a question to think about: in cases like this fiscal consolidation example of Fields 1 and 2, where the income tax impacts of the combination can be quite material, is it a good idea to use a version of the ELT which ignores income taxes? We address this question in detail in "Appendix_IV_Knowing_when_to_quit_Alternative economic limit test.pdf" in the "Appendix_IV_Alternative_economic_limit_test" folder on the disk.

- In rows 203–205, we sum Field 1 and Field 2's post-ELT depreciation charges.

- In rows 208–214, we calculate the combined, consolidated income tax charge, using:

  ○ the combined revenues and tax deductions just described; and

  ○ in 2014, the sum of each field's initial, "inherited" tax losses (i.e., carriable forward tax losses incurred before our model starts in 2014); these losses sum to $250 mm (cell F211).

- Note that the resultant $73.5 mm total (all-years) combined, consolidated basis tax charge (cell D214) is *not* the same as the combined, ringfenced tax charge of $177.8 mm (cell D192); this **is the whole point of fiscal consolidation**.

- In rows 216–224, we calculate the combined, consolidated NCF and NPV based on these preceding items. NPV is $374.8 mm (cell D224) versus the combined, ringfenced NPV of $297.8 mm (cell D194) we saw above.

We now turn to **Step 5** – the calculation of incremental value – in the next section.

2.6 MODEL RESULTS AND ANALYSIS

As seen in the summary of total (all-years) cashflows in Figure 2.5:

- The only difference in each case's undiscounted NCF is due to the income tax charge. Again, we've designed the example this way to keep the focus on fiscal consolidation, which in this case would give an acquirer $104.3 mm of income tax savings over the ringfenced combination (cell AE237), and thus a $104.3 mm NCF advantage (cell AE238).

- Accounting for the time value of money, discounted NCF (i.e., **NPV**) **is $77.0 mm higher than in the ringfenced combination** (cell AE239).

	AA	AB	AC	AD	AE
229	**Cashflow: Comparison of fiscal combination method results (life-of-field totals)**				
230	Memo: oil price = $70		A) Fields 1+2 **Ringfenced**	B) Fields 1+2 **Consolidated**	**B)-A)**
231	Oil production	mmb	34.8	34.8	0.0
232	Revenue	MOD $mm	2,432.5	2,432.5	0.0
233	Royalty	MOD $mm	304.1	304.1	0.0
234	Total Opex	MOD $mm	1,006.5	1,006.5	0.0
235	Capex	MOD $mm	350.0	350.0	0.0
236	Abandonment cost	MOD $mm	75.0	75.0	0.0
237	Income tax charge	MOD $mm	177.8	73.5	(104.3)
238	Net cashflow	MOD $mm	519.1	623.5	104.3
239	**Discounted Net Cashflow (NPV)**	**MOD $mm**	**297.8**	**374.8**	**77.0**

Figure 2.5   Base Scenario combination results: ringfenced vs. consolidated NCF and NPV, from the "Model" sheet of "Ch2_Tax_consolidation_model.xls"

	AF	AG	AH	AI	AJ	AK
15			Summary: Life-of-field totals, MOD $ mm			
16		Item		Undiscounted tax charge	Undiscounted net cashflow	Discounted net cashflow
17	A) Field 1 alone			177.8	207.8	63.0
18	B) Field 2 alone			0.0	311.3	234.7
19	C) Fields 1 & 2 combined, ringfenced			177.8	519.1	297.8
20	D) Fields 1 & 2 combined, consolidated			73.5	623.5	374.8
21	E) = D)-C)			(104.3)	104.3	77.0
22	F) = D)/C)			41.3%	120.1%	125.9%
23	**G) = C)-A) = Incremental NPV of Field 2, ringfenced regime**			n.m.	n.m.	**234.7**
24	**H) = D)-A) = Incremental NPV of Field 2, consolidation regime**			n.m.	n.m.	**311.8**

Figure 2.6 Base Scenario combination results: ringfenced vs. consolidated incremental value of Field 2, from the file "Ch2_Tax_consolidation_model.xls"

Step 5: Incremental Value

Figure 2.6 answers the original question – what is the incremental value, to the investor in Field 1, in acquiring Field 2?

As seen in Figure 2.6 (which repeats a few of the results just seen in Figure 2.5):

- Presented for information only, and not used in the incremental value calculation:
  - ○ the consolidated case has a 20.1% undiscounted NCF advantage over the ringfenced case (cell AJ22);
  - ○ the consolidated case has a 25.9% discounted NCF (i.e., NPV) advantage over the ringfenced case (cell AK22).
- The **incremental value of Field 2** to the investor under a **ringfenced** fiscal regime, as measured by total discounted net cashflow (NPV), is **$234.7 mm** (cell AK23). As mentioned, this is simply the same as the standalone NPV of Field 2 (cell AK18).
- The **incremental value of Field 2** to the investor under a **consolidated** fiscal regime is **$311.8 mm** (cell AK24).

Notice that this $311.8 mm − $234.7 mm = **$77.0 mm** extra value in the consolidated case (note the slight rounding effects, due to values being displayed to only one decimal place) is identical to the **$77.0 mm** NPV advantage of the combined consolidated case seen in cell AE239 of the previous Figure 2.5.

Thus if the government does change the fiscal laws to permit consolidating income tax allowances, Field 2 will become worth $77.0 mm more to the investor than it would be under ringfence rules.

2.7   EXERCISE – TRY MODELING SCENARIO 2 YOURSELF

We have covered a lot of ground regarding fiscal consolidation in the last few sections. Now it is your turn to calculate ringfenced and consolidated investment combinations, and incremental value, as measured by incremental NPV, for each.

Again, assume there are two fields – the investor owns Field 1 and is considering buying Field 2 – which again must be valued on a combined, ringfenced basis and on a combined, consolidated basis, so that the incremental value of Field 2 can be determined for each basis.

We have created short and long versions of this exercise (in terms of how much work is required).

The short version emphasizes mainly the new points covered in this chapter. It is in the file "Ch2_Exercise_setup_short_version.xls." Here, the standalone Field 1 and Field 2 NPVs are already calculated; you only need to supply the formulas for calculating:

- the ringfenced combination's NPV;

- the consolidated combination's NPV; and

- the incremental value of Field 2, to an investor which already owns 100% of Field 1 for each combination.

The cells to fill in are the orange-shaded ones in rows 186–224, as well as cells AK23:AK24, which give us our final incremental values.

The long version is in the file "Ch2_Exercise_setup_long_version.xls." It is identical to the short version, except here you also calculate the underlying, standalone Field 1 and Field 2 NPVs. This is not necessary to get the main points of this chapter, but is a good review/consolidation of some basic modeling methods we introduced in Chapter 1. This time, fill in the orange-shaded cells in rows 88–224, and again, cells AK23:AK24.

In either case:

- Assumptions, cell and range names, spinner controls and charts are already in place. Assumptions are somewhat less simplified this time, however – there is now annual inflation, and more realistic (though still atypically short) declining production profiles for each field.

- We have calculated depreciation for you, using the same shortcut as in our example model. (It is not that we think you cannot do it this way; rather, we just do not want you to.) Therefore, do not change the timing of any capex.

- Note that until you have filled in certain cells, cells A1 and B1 will indicate that errors have been found. When you finish, these error messages should disappear.

- Check your answers against those in the solution file "Ch2_Exercise_solutions.xls." To be safe, use the button in row 29 to reset the files to Scenario 2.

2.8   INCOME TAX CONSOLIDATION AND INCREMENTAL VALUE (INTERACTIVE ANALYSIS)

Continue to the file "Ch2_Tax_consolidation_analysis.pdf" on the disk, which concludes this chapter. The section continues to use the file "Ch2_Tax_consolidation_model.xls."

Chapter 3

Royalties

3

Royalties

3.1 INTRODUCTION

Royalties are one of several fiscal instruments widely used by governments to raise revenue from oil and gas projects.

Royalties Are Paid as a Slice of Revenue or Production

A **royalty** is a payment made by a permit holder, which is usually a corporation, either "in cash" (as a monetary payment) or as a payment "in kind" (meaning actual volumes of oil or gas which the permit holder has "won" (i.e., produced, processed and exported from the permit area) and sold.

Thus in essence, a royalty is a specified (by law or contract) portion of gross sales revenue, or of the actual volume of oil and gas produced, which the permit holder hands over to the party to whom the royalty is paid.

In the case of **state royalties**, the permit holder pays the royalty to some government entity (e.g., national or local governments)[1] in return for the right to explore and/or produce or otherwise exploit oil and gas present in the permit area. Thus a state royalty is the share of production from the permit area reserved for the state which grants the permit (i.e., the "grantor," in legalese) to the permit holder.

Royalties which the permit holder pays, not to a government entity, but rather to another private party, are called **overriding royalties** or **overrides**. These usually follow the same principles (explained below) as state royalties, differing only in whom gets paid.

As mentioned, royalties are generally levied as a portion of either the total *value* or, if the royalty is paid "in kind," the total *volume*, of oil and/or gas production, usually as measured close to the wellhead (i.e., the point where it comes out of the ground, as mentioned in Chapter 1), at the production site, or at an export point (e.g., entry or exit point to a pipeline).

A Simple Example

If a royalty rate on oil production is 5%, and the point where the production is measured is at the wellhead:

---

[1] Originally royalties were paid to the monarch, hence the origin of the term "royalty."

- an in-cash royalty paid by the permit holder for each barrel of production would be equal to 5% of the gross revenue which the permit holder receives at the wellhead;

- an in-kind royalty paid by the permit holder would be 5% of each barrel produced, as measured at the wellhead.

Whether the royalty is paid in cash or in kind makes no difference to the permit holder's cashflow. This is because the permit holder's revenue after royalty – also known as **revenue, net of royalty** – is simply gross revenue minus the royalty payment. Suppose that in our example, using a 5% royalty rate, production is 1000 "bbl" (or b, barrels), and the oil price at the wellhead is $100/bbl.

When the permit holder pays the royalty in cash:

- its gross revenue = 1000 bbl × $100 = $100 000;

- the royalty it pays is 5% × $100 000 = $5000;

- so the permit holder's revenue, net of royalty = $100 000 − $5000 = **$95 000**.

When the permit holder pays the royalty in kind:

- its gross production = 1000 bbl;

- the portion of which it pays as a royalty = 1000 bbl × 5% = 50 bbl;

- this leaves the permit holder with production, net of royalty, of 1000 bbl − 50 bbl = 950 bbl;

- so the permit holder's revenue, net of royalty = 950 bbl × $100 = **$95 000**.

> The examples in this chapter assume that royalty is paid in cash.

Royalties Are Usually Taken "Off the Top"

Whether in cash or in kind, royalties are often one of the first deductions to be made in a cashflow calculation.

This means that royalties are commonly taken "off the top," i.e., before most, if any, of the costs of production are deducted in calculating the net revenue or cashflow of the project. It is this "off the top" characteristic of a royalty which makes royalties particularly appealing to governments as stable fiscal instruments to extract a reasonably steady levy from production that is unaffected by costs and other fiscal instruments. Royalties paid in monetary terms sometimes fluctuate with oil and gas prices, but not nearly so much as other fiscal elements linked to profitability or revenue, net of royalty.

Not all fiscal regimes include royalties, but many do. This makes understanding the different royalty mechanisms used and how they work important for the petroleum economist.

As in our simple example above, royalties may be calculated by simple fixed percentage rates. If that were the only method, this chapter would be very short. Alas, there are many different royalty mechanisms, some of them rather complicated. These include royalties determined by a wide range of more complex variable percentage rates, which depend on changes in production volumes, commodity prices, measures of profitability, or some combination of these factors.

The fixed rate royalties are easy to calculate, but lack flexibility and can be **regressive** (see the boxed section "Fiscal progressivity and regressivity" in Section 3.2, below). On the other hand, variable rate royalty mechanisms introduce flexibility to respond to various measures (oil price, profitability, production rate, cumulative production, water depth, etc.), but are harder to calculate.

This chapter provides a detailed insight into how the different types of royalty mechanisms work and how they can be effectively calculated and modeled using Excel.

Be aware that royalties are also often used in agreements between private companies, such as in some asset acquisition or **farm-in**[2] agreements, when an acquirer or "farminee" agrees to pay the seller or "farmor" an overriding royalty equal to an agreed percentage from a field's future production. Although such corporate royalties are not specifically addressed here, calculating them in Excel is similar to calculating the examples shown in this chapter.

Chapter Materials Included on the Disk

Excel files: These are the core of our example-based approach.

Supplementary figures: Because much of this chapter consists of detailed explanations of the Excel models, you must refer either to the models themselves or to the screenshots taken from them. Some of the screenshots are too large to fit on these pages, so we have collected them into the file "Ch3_Supplement_to_roy_examples.pdf," which you might want to print out or open before starting to work through the examples.

Other PDF sections: For reasons of space and formatting, we present certain sections of this chapter in other PDF files rather than in the printed text.

3.2 ROYALTY BASED ON COMMODITY PRICES

Figure 3.1, from the file "Ch3_roy_price_example.xls," shows a schedule of rates for a royalty based on the price – in this case, the price received for oil sold at the wellhead. (Press the Scenario 2 or 3 buttons in row 17.)

---

[2] To "farm in" to an oil and gas investment simply means to join an existing investor on specified terms. In such cases, the joining party is called the "farminee" and the original party which is joined is called the "farmor."

Oil price at wellhead, $(MOD)/bbl		Royalty rate
>=	<	%
0	10	0.0%
10	15	5.0%
15	20	7.5%
20	30	10.0%
30	50	12.5%
50	75	15.0%
75	100	17.5%
100	120	20.0%
120	10 000	25.0%

Figure 3.1   Royalty schedule based on the received oil price, Scenarios 2 or 3

Under this regime, the oil price and royalty rate rise and fall together. When the oil price is greater than or equal to $0, but less than $10, the royalty rate is 0%; when the oil price is greater than or equal to $10, but less than $15, the royalty rate is 5%; and so on. The value of 10 000 in the second column of the last row means there is effectively no upper limit, i.e., the maximum royalty rate is 25%, no matter how much over $120 the oil price goes.

Calculating the Royalty Rate: Using Excel's VLOOKUP Function

Given an average oil price for each year, we need to apply the appropriate royalty rate. What formula will calculate the rate? Suppose you have named the oil price row in your model "Price." You could *not* use a long IF statement, such as

=IF(AND(Price > = 0, Price < 10), 0%, IF(AND(Price > = 10, Price < 15), 5% ... etc.))

(which would mean, "If the price is greater than or equal to 0 and less than 10, the answer is 0%; if the price is greater than or equal to 10 and less than 15, the answer is 5%; etc."), even if you wanted to, because Excel only permits a maximum of seven "nested" IF statements within a single formula, whereas we have nine price bands in the royalty schedule.

In any case, we prefer short formulas to long formulas whenever possible. A good Excel modeling principle is that needlessly long formulas increase the chance of error, and reduce auditability.[3]

A nested IF statement would indeed be needlessly long here, because Excel has two concise but powerful functions for looking up values in tables and returning the appropriate answers. These are VLOOKUP, where "V" means it is used for vertically formatted tables, and HLOOKUP, for horizontal ones.

---

[3] There are, however, some occasions when, in order to produce a compact model involving many different calculations, and make a model look tidier and easier to take in at a glance, compressing certain calculations into single rows or columns is desirable.

> **Be sure you understand Excel's LOOKUP functions**
>
> We quickly walk through the use of the VLOOKUP function in the discussion below. If, however, you find it is still unclear, turn to the self-explanatory file "VLOOKUP_ HLOOKUP_examples.xls" in the Chapter 1 folder. It is *important* that you do so, because *we use these functions* not only in this example, but *in many models in this book.*

Let us put the VLOOKUP function to work.

> Refer to the screenshot from "Ch3_roy_price_example.xls," reproduced in **Figure 3.1**, on page 2 of the file "Ch3_Supplement_to_roy_examples.pdf."

The royalty schedule from Figure 3.1 is in cells C6:E14. It has been given the range name "Royalty_table". It reflects Scenario 3.

- Price and production assumptions, and some buttons used to invoke certain scenarios (discussed below), are in rows 17–24. (These buttons will not work unless you choose to enable macros when you open the file.)

- Gross field revenue is calculated in a straightforward way in row 28.

- The royalty rate for each year is calculated in row 29. For example, the formula for the rate in 2014 (cell G29) is $\boxed{\text{VLOOKUP(G23, Royalty\_table, 3)}}$, where $\boxed{\text{G23}}$ is the wellhead oil price, and $\boxed{\text{Royalty\_table, 3}}$ indicates column $\boxed{3}$ of the royalty schedule named $\boxed{\text{Royalty\_table}}$. In other words, the formula:

  o looks at the oil price of $70.66 in cell $\boxed{\text{G23}}$;

  o then looks in the first column (this is the default action for the VLOOKUP function) of the range $\boxed{\text{Royalty\_table}}$ for the highest number which is less than or equal to $70.66, and finds it in cell C11 of $\boxed{\text{Royalty\_table}}$;

  o and finally looks across row 11 to column $\boxed{3}$ of $\boxed{\text{Royalty\_table}}$ for the answer, which is the royalty rate of 15% in cell E11.

- The resultant royalty rate in row 29 is multiplied by gross field revenue (row 28) to give the royalty payment in dollars (row 30).

- This payment is then subtracted from gross revenue to give revenue, net of royalty (row 31).

- The weighted average royalty rate (cell E29) is calculated as the sum of all-years royalty payments, divided by the sum of all-years gross field revenue. (Notice the **error trap** in the first part of the formula for E29, $\boxed{\text{=IF(E28 = 0, 0, E30/E28)}}$, where $\boxed{\text{E28}}$ is total gross field revenue and $\boxed{\text{E30}}$ is the total royalty payment. As already discussed in Chapter 1, the error-trap expression $\boxed{\text{=IF(E28 = 0, 0 \ldots}}$ means that if $\boxed{\text{E28}}$ is 0, the answer will be 0. This prevents the division-by-zero error message $\boxed{\text{\# DIV/0!}}$ which Excel would give us if E28 were 0, and we tried to divide something by it.)

Analysis

To illustrate the dynamics of this kind of royalty, we will look at three scenarios, within which you can adjust the oil price. We suggest you arrange the screen as follows:

- Scroll so that row 17, with the three buttons, is the first row visible at the top.

- Place the cursor in cell A25 and split the screen horizontally.

- Make at least two of the four charts (starting in row 36) visible below the split. (Note that this might work better on a desktop monitor which is larger than a laptop screen, as zooming out to make everything visible on the latter could cause the chart headings to truncate at small zoom settings.)

The first two scenarios we will examine are simplistic. They have a constant production volume in all years, and an oil price which increases steadily each year. Keeping production flat in these two scenarios makes it easier to see the effects of changing only the price and thus the royalty rate.

Press the button to show Scenario 1, which is actually pretty boring, as it has no royalty at all. It is there to show, by comparison, the effect of adding the royalty regime in Scenario 2. So with your eye on Chart C, press the button to show Scenario 2. You will see that the black columns for annual revenue, net of royalty will get shorter, as the white royalty payment columns on top of them absorb a portion of gross revenue. (The total height of the (black + white) columns equals gross revenue.)

Before any adjustments to the weighted average oil price of $60 (calculated in cell E32, and displayed in the title of each chart), Scenario 2 produces a weighted average royalty rate of 16.7% (also shown in the chart titles). Now, use the spinner control (cell D22) to increase the oil price multiplier to 150%, while watching Chart C. Chart C will now look like Figure 3.2.

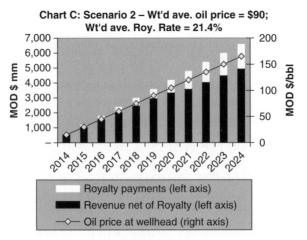

Figure 3.2   Chart C from "Ch3_roy_price_example.xls"

Note how, when you increase the oil price, the total absolute height of each stacked column increases, as does the relative height of the white portion of each column. This makes sense, because, when the oil price rises, both gross revenue (again, the combined height of the black and white columns) and the royalty rate (which determines the size of the royalty payment) should also both rise. With the weighted average oil price now up from $60 to $90, the weighted average royalty rate grows from 16.7% to 21.4%. You can also see the effect of a price change on the weighted average royalty rate by watching the pie graph in Chart D as you change the oil price multiplier.

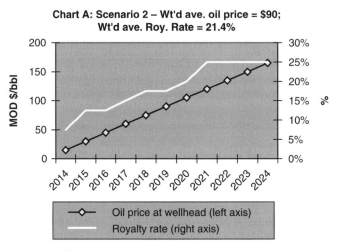

Figure 3.3   Chart A from "Ch3_roy_price_example.xls"

Still using Scenario 2, with the oil price multiplier set to 150%, Chart A (reproduced in Figure 3.3) shows that the annual royalty rate trend line looks like an irregular staircase, with slopes interrupted by plateaus. The slopes occur whenever the annual oil price passes into a new band from the royalty schedule. The plateaus occur when the oil price, although always rising, remains within the same band as the year before. The reason for the long, final plateau starting in 2021 is that, in this year, the oil price reaches $120, the price at which the highest possible royalty rate starts.

Finally, click the button to show Scenario 3. This is a more realistic scenario, with declining production and an erratic oil price trend. Note in Chart A how the royalty rate roughly tracks the oil price. (It would track the price more closely if the royalty rate schedule consisted of more, and narrower, oil price bands.)

The preceding discussion should enable you to understand the changes in Charts A, C and D as you adjust the oil price using the multiplier switch in cell D22.

Notice that, under Scenario 3, with the oil price multiplier set to 150%, Chart B (see Figure 3.4) reveals that the state's take of revenue rises sharply as oil production (and thus revenue) falls. This makes the royalty regime in our example a potentially **regressive** fiscal instrument.

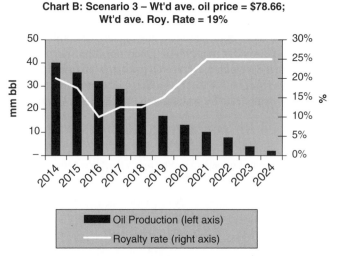

Figure 3.4   Chart B from "Ch3_roy_price_example.xls"
Note: Results reflect Scenario 3, with the oil price multiplier set to 150%.

Fiscal progressivity and regressivity

What does it mean for a fiscal system to be "regressive?" The question is best answered in the fuller context of two key concepts – **progressivity** versus **regressivity**.

A *progressive fiscal system* is one in which as profits go up – due to either lower costs or higher revenues derived from higher product prices – a government's fiscal take in percentage and absolute terms increases. As project profitability decreases, however – due to either higher costs or lower revenues derived from lower product prices – a government's fiscal take in percentage and absolute terms should also decrease. Such designs are attractive to investors because they help to maintain the commercial viability of projects in adverse economic conditions.

In contrast, a *regressive fiscal system* is one in which as profits go up – due to either lower costs or higher revenues derived from higher product prices – a government's fiscal take in percentage terms goes down (although in absolute terms it may increase). More significantly, as project profitability decreases under a regressive fiscal system – due to either higher costs or lower revenues derived from lower product prices – a government's fiscal take in percentage terms of project profits increases (even if in absolute terms it might decrease). Such designs are generally less attractive to investors, because they can help to push projects further into non-commercial positions in adverse economic conditions.

Governments often prefer to structure their fiscal systems to consist of a **combination of progressive and regressive fiscal elements**, to enable them to secure some fiscal revenues in adverse economic conditions (e.g., a regressive royalty component) and to take a larger share of revenues in favorable economic conditions (e.g., a progressive tax component). How progressive or regressive a fiscal element, or an entire fiscal system, actually is requires an analysis of its performance at different levels of profitability, which is influenced by costs, production volumes and prices.

Some people incorrectly think fiscal instruments like the royalty schedule in our example, which is linked to commodity prices, are **progressive**, reasoning that as prices rise, the government takes more on a unit (per barrel or barrel of oil equivalent ("boe")) basis, and that as prices fall, the government takes less on a unit basis. **Progressive versus regressive characteristics, however, are determined based on** *profitability*, **not** *price or production per se*. It is likely, in a case like Scenario 3, that as production declines, a fixed component of operating costs will lead to per-boe profitability also declining. If this is indeed the case, then this royalty instrument linked to oil price is in fact regressive, not progressive.

Exercises

1. The file "Ch3_roy_price_setup.xls" has a royalty regime similar to the one covered here, and four oil price cases. Try to fill in the blanks in order to calculate the weighted average (over the field life) royalty rate and oil price for each price case. Compare your answers to those in the file "Ch3_roy_price_solution.xls." Use the ready-made charts and spinner control to check that you understand what the model is doing.
2. A somewhat longer and more elaborate exercise in the file "Ch3_roy_price_SPT_exercise.xls" deals with a fiscal device which works in a very similar way to a royalty based on the oil price, but with a slight difference. Again, solutions are provided.

3.3 ROYALTY BASED ON LENGTH OF PRODUCTION

Some countries levy royalties based on how long a field has been producing. Under rules which have been used in Australia, for example, the first five production years were royalty-free. In Year 6 the rate was 6%. It then rose by one percentage point annually through Year 10, when it reached 10%, and stayed there for all subsequent production years. This structure can be interpreted as a **royalty holiday** – a period during which royalty does not apply – for the first five years, followed by a partial royalty paid in Years 6 through 9, with the full royalty rate applied from Year 10. This mechanism can therefore be used to model periodic royalty holidays.

This is not hard to model. Here is the basic solution strategy:

• Determine each year how many years a field has been producing (accounting for any past production, i.e., production before the first year in the model).

• Calculate the applicable royalty rate for each year. The "cleanest" way might be to translate the rules expressed above into a table, like the one which is shown in Figure 3.5, for use with the VLOOKUP function.

• Multiply the resultant rate by gross revenue to determine the royalty payment.

Year of production		Royalty rate
>=	<	%
0	6	0.0%
6	7	6.0%
7	8	7.0%
8	9	8.0%
9	10	9.0%
10	1000	10.0%

Figure 3.5   Royalty schedule based on time producing, from the file, "Ch3_roy_time based_Oz_solution.xls"

An example is in the file "Ch3_roy_time based_Oz_solution.xls" In the Assumptions section of the sheet, you will find the following:

- The royalty schedule shown in Figure 3.5, in cells B7:D12; it has been given the range name "Royalty_table."

- The number of years of historic production (i.e., pre-2014) for four fields (cells D17– D20), and corresponding forecast production profiles (before any adjustments for delays, discussed below) covering 2014–2023 (rows 23–26). (You will see that there are gap years in the production. For Fields 1 and 3, we assume production at some point in the pre-2014 past, with production resuming in 2017 and 2019 respectively, while Field 4 has a year's gap in 2018. Such long gaps are uncommon in real life, but have been assumed to help test the model's logic.)

- Inputs, controlled by spinners, for setting a delay (in years) to the start of each field's forecast production, are located in cells D30:D33. This will have the effect – later, in rows 42–45 – of shifting the entire profiles in rows 23–26 by the specified number of years' delay.[4] Again, this is introduced to test and verify the model's logic. To keep things simple, we have assumed each field begins producing on January 1. (In real life – this being unlikely – you would need to know the actual production start date, and use this to determine what portion of a production year falls within a tax year.)

- An oil price forecast in row 35, kept flat for simplicity's sake.

The royalty calculations for all four fields are performed in the same way, so we will only walk you through those for Field 1.

---

[4] The delay is achieved using Excel's OFFSET function. (See the self-contained examples in the Chapter 1 folder, "Ch1_Delays using OFFSET".) This technique requires empty columns to the left of the start of the timeline – this is the reason for the blank, gray columns F–K in "Ch3_roy_time based_Oz_solution.xls."

Refer to Figure 3.6 in the file "Ch3_Supplement_to_roy_examples.pdf," which matches the view in the Excel file when you close all the grouped rows by pressing the boxed ⬚1 button to the left of column A.

Field 1 had produced for six years (cell D17) before the start of the unadjusted forecast in 2014 (row 23). Here, a one-year delay to this forecast is set in cell D30, and is applied using the OFFSET function in row 42.

Row 49 uses a simple IF statement to return a 1 if there is (adjusted) production in a given year, and a 0 if there is not. These results are used in row 55 to determine the cumulative number of production years. Note that the formula for 2014 (cell L55) is unique in that it references the pre-2014 number of production years (cell D17). Also note that cell D55 calculates the maximum, not total, of row 55. (This maximum value will be used in a chart later.)

The royalty rate for the typical year of 2019, for example, is calculated in cell Q61 with the formula =VLOOKUP(Q55, Royalty_table, 3). This matches the cumulative number of production years (8, in cell Q55) to the corresponding royalty rate in column 3 of the royalty schedule ("Royalty_table," which is not shown in Figure 3.6 to save space, but which we saw on the previous page). Thus this rate is 8% in 2019. Note that cell D55 calculates the maximum, not total, of its row, again for use in a chart.

In cell Q74, this 8% royalty rate is then multiplied by gross revenue (row 67) – which, as usual, equals price times production volume – to calculate the 2019 royalty payment of MOD $144mm. Revenue, net of royalty is calculated in a straightforward way in row 81.

Visual check

The results feed into charts starting in row 88. Split the screen so that above the split you can see the production delay spinner for Field 1 in row 30 (or, if you wish, those for its companion fields as well in rows 31–33), and the charts below the split. Satisfy yourself that you understand what the charts tell you when you apply the delay factor(s).

Exercise

The file "Ch3_roy_time based_Oz_setup.xls" has the same assumptions – except that the delay values in cells D30:D33 are each set to 0 – and charts as our example file, but we have left it for you to do the calculations (except for the delaying of the production profile, which we have done for you). Fill in the blanks for a few – if not all four – of the fields, and compare your answers to those provided in the file "Ch3_roy_time based_Oz_solution.xls" (when its delay values are also set to 0).

3.4   ROYALTY BASED ON PERIOD-END CUMULATIVE PRODUCTION

Another form of variable royalty is based on cumulative production.

An example is provided in the file "Ch3_roy_cuml_prod_example.xls."

The royalty rates from this file (cells C11:E22) are as shown in Figure 3.7 below.

Cumulative oil production, mm bbl		Royalty rate
>=	<	%
2.0	4.0	5.0%
4.0	10.0	7.0%
10.0	15.0	8.0%
15.0	25.0	10.0%
25.0	35.0	12.0%
35.0	45.0	14.0%
45.0	55.0	16.0%
55.0	65.0	18.0%
65.0	75.0	20.0%
75.0	9999.00	22.0%

Figure 3.7   Royalty schedule based on cumulative production

At first glance, you might think that this royalty is "fair," in that the royalty rate rises as the investor produces more. The latter statement is potentially misleading – because the rate is based on *cumulative* production, the rate is largely determined on how much the investor has *already* produced. And because usually oil production rates start high early in a field's life, and then tail off dramatically in later years, such royalty regimes often have the effect of imposing the highest royalty rates when current annual production volume is low, near the end of the field's life.

A government's rationale in applying such a mechanism is that field development capex is likely to be paid back as a field matures, so that barrels produced later in a field's life are "burdened" only by ongoing opex. This rationale, however, makes no allowance for the higher unit opex (i.e., opex per barrel) costs which are likely to occur due to the impact of fixed costs (discussed in Chapter 1) as maturing fields' production declines. In fact, the mechanism is highly regressive. We will see this more clearly soon.

Assumptions and Calculations

Refer to the Excel file, and/or Figure 3.8 in the file "Ch3_Supplement_to_roy_ examples.pdf," which for reasons of space does not show all columns and rows. Figure 3.8 shows the Low Production case (cell D33).

In the Assumptions section of our example Excel file, you will find the following:

- The royalty schedule shown in Figure 3.7, in cells C13:E22, with the range name "Royalty_table."

- A switch in cell C25 which lets you change between the cumulative production-based royalty regime and, for comparison, a flat royalty rate of 10% (cell D7).

- Three production cases, and a switch for selecting one of them, in rows 29–33. Note that – although it is assumed the model is dated January 1, 2014 – in column F we show *historic* production (i.e., cumulative as at the end of 2013), as distinct from the *forecast* volumes starting in 2014 (columns G–Q). We include the cumulative historic value in this example to highlight the need for the analyst to know prior production volumes when calculating cumulative production and things based on it. (We will face this issue again when we discuss production bonuses in Chapter 4.)

- The wellhead oil price – assumed to be flat, to make it easier to see how the royalty regime works – in row 34.

In the Calculations section of the Excel file:

- Gross revenue and cumulative oil production are calculated in straightforward ways in rows 38 and 40.

- The annual royalty rate calculation is in row 41. Depending on the royalty regime chosen in cell C25, it either applies the 10% flat rate, or uses the VLOOKUP function to apply the cumulative production-based royalty schedule to a given year's cumulative production volume. The formula for 2015 (cell H41), for example, is $=IF(\$C25 = Flat$ "rate," $\$D7,$ VLOOKUP(H40, Royalty_table, 3)). This means that if the flat royalty rate regime is chosen in cell C25, then the answer is 10% (cell D7); otherwise, the answer is the royalty rate, found in column 3 of the range "Royalty_table," which corresponds to cumulative production in 2015 (cell G40). When the cumulative production-based royalty regime and the low-case production forecast are chosen, cumulative production of 12.7 mm bbl at the end of 2015 (cell H40), for example, will translate into a 2015 royalty rate of 8%.

- The royalty rate is used to calculate the royalty payment, which in turn is used to calculate revenue, net of royalty, in straightforward ways in rows 42–43.

- Lastly, gross revenue, royalty, and revenue, net of royalty are calculated on a per-barrel basis of annual (not cumulative) production in the annual columns of rows 46–48, and on a field life basis (starting with 2014) in column E of those rows.

Visual Check and Analysis

To see the effect of changes in the chosen royalty regime and the chosen production case, scroll until row 24 is the first visible row at the top of the screen; hide rows 26–32 using the grouping button at the far left side of the screen; place the cursor in cell A35; split the screen; and scroll in the bottom part of the screen until the charts starting in row 50 are visible.

The charts show that the model is working as you might expect. If you select "Flat rate" in cell C25, and then scroll through the three production cases using the spinner in cell C33, you will see that the royalty rate stays the same regardless of the cumulative production volume:

- the white horizontal lines in Charts A and B do not move;
- the white royalty portions of the stacked columns in Chart C stay the same;
- in Chart D, the absolute value of total royalty payments always looks to be the same proportion of gross revenue (which equals the total height of the stacked column); and
- the weighted average royalty rate, displayed in the title of each chart, is always 10%.

If you select "Rate based on cumulative production" in cell C25, and then again scroll through the three production cases, you will see that the higher the cumulative production is:

- the higher the annual (Chart A) and weighted average royalty rates (all charts' titles) are – for example, the weighted average royalty rates for the low, mid- and high production cases are respectively 9.3%, 14.6% and 18.8%;
- the larger the proportion of gross revenue paid out as royalty payments is (see the white columns in Charts C and D).

Moreover, as noted earlier, when the mid- or high production case is chosen, you can see in Chart B (shown in Figure 3.9) that the highest royalty rates are levied on the years of lowest production – not very equitable from the investor's point of view.

A government which does not wish to deter investors would likely consider imposing such a regime only in mature producing areas, where production costs are low and production is highly profitable. The risk for the government, however, is that such a mechanism could lead to early abandonment of fields in low-price/high-cost environments, because the regressive royalties could make low levels of production uneconomic. The early abandonment, of course,

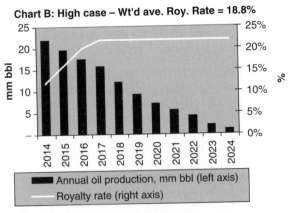

Figure 3.9   Cumulative production-based royalty regime, high production case

could mean less revenue for the government, as less production could result in less cumulative royalty paid.

Exercise

In the file "Ch3_roy_cuml_prod_setup.xls" find royalty rate, price and production assumptions. Calculate gross revenue, royalty payments, and revenue, net of royalty on both an absolute and per-barrel basis. Explain how the charts change when you change the price cases using the spinner control. Compare your answers to those in "Ch3_roy_cuml_prod_solution.xls."

3.5   ROYALTY BASED ON CUMULATIVE PRODUCTION THROUGHOUT THE PERIOD

Introduction: Top-Rate and Tranche Methods

In Section 3.4 of this chapter, we looked at a regime in which *a single royalty rate for a given period* is determined by the *highest level* of cumulative production in that period. We call this the **top-rate method**.

In this section, we will look at one in which *multiple royalty rates can apply within a given period*. We call this the **tranche method**, where **tranches** are different bands of production, each associated with a different royalty rate. It can require us to calculate a "blended" or weighted average royalty rate for each period. The ideas behind tranche method calculations are simple, although the calculations themselves can become complex.

Before illustrating with a multi-year dynamic model and a full royalty schedule, let us first walk through the following simple examples. The tranche method is best explained by comparison to the top-rate method, which we revisit in a short model for one year.

Refer to the Excel file "Ch3_roy_cuml_prod_CROSSOVER_simple_example.xls," from which we have created Figure 3.10, which is shown in the file "Ch3_Supplement_to_ roy_examples.pdf."

There is not much to the top-rate method. The applicable royalty rate is the one corresponding to the highest rate of cumulative production in the year. By definition, this is cumulative production at the end of the year, or 3.50 mm bbl (cell F8). We can easily see that, because 3.50 mm bbl falls between the Tranche 2 lower limit of 2.00 mm bbl (cell D6) and the Tranche 2 upper limit of 4.00 mm bbl (cell E6), a 5% royalty rate (cell F6) applies to all production for the year. In the Calculations section, we formally determine the rate in two ways:

- The first is by simple visual inspection (cell F15). Here we just decided that it equals the 5% rate shown in cell F6, so the formula is =F6 . Obviously, however, you cannot use this approach in a dynamic model.

- The second way (cell F16) uses the formula $\boxed{\text{=VLOOKUP(F11, D5:F6, 3)}}$, which looks in column $\boxed{3}$ of the row in the range $\boxed{\text{D5:F6}}$ for the rate corresponding to cumulative production of 3.50 mm bbl in cell $\boxed{\text{F11}}$. Again, the answer is 5%.

Both methods give the same answer – the royalty rate applicable to all production for the year is 5%. This rate is multiplied by gross revenue of $350 mm (cell F12) to return the royalty payment for the year of **MOD $17.50 mm** (cell F17).

Now let us try the tranche method.

> Refer again to the Excel file "Ch3_roy_cuml_prod_CROSSOVER_simple_example.xls," from which we have created Figure 3.11, which is shown in the file "Ch3_Supplement_to_roy_examples.pdf."

Tranche Method Steps

1. *Determine how much cumulative production is relevant to each tranche.* That is, allocate production to tranches:

   - We know that total cumulative production of 3.50 mm bbl at the end of the year is greater than the 2.00 mm bbl upper limit for Tranche 2 (cell E5); therefore, we know that production entirely "fills" Tranche 1. The amount relevant to **Tranche 1** is thus calculated in cell F20 as 2.00 mm bbl minus 0.00 bbl (i.e., as $\boxed{\text{=E5-D5}}$), or **2.00 mm bbl**.[5]

   - The allocation to **Tranche 2** is calculated in cell F21 as $\boxed{\text{=F8-D6}}$, i.e., as end-year cumulative production of 3.50 mm bbl (cell F8) minus the Tranche 2 lower limit of 2.00 mm bbl (cell D6), or **1.50 mm bbl**.

   Note that this method assumes the production occurs at a constant rate throughout the year.

2. *Calculate the percentages of each tranche's volumes as a percentage of the total volume.* This is done in a straightforward way in cells F22:F23. (We don't use error-trapping expressions in these two formulas, as we know that in this simple, static example model, the denominators of these cells will not be 0.) The result is that a little over half of the total (57.1%) of the total is in Tranche 1 (cell F22), while the remaining 42.9% (cell F23) is in Tranche 2.

3. *Determine the royalty rate applicable to each tranche.* Although we can plainly see that the rates for Tranches 1 and 2 are 0% and 5% respectively (cells F5:F6), we determine the rates formulaically in this example, to help prepare you for the method used in the fuller, dynamic example model we will use later in this section. Note that we have

---

[5] You might notice that it is technically incorrect to calculate the "capacity" of Tranche 1 as 2.00 mm bbl minus 0.00 bbl, because the upper limit, as specified in cells E4:E5, is *not* 2.00 mm bbl, but rather any number *up to, but less than* ($<$) 2.00 mm bbl. But consider that cumulative production of 1.9 mm bbl *would* fall within Tranche 1, as would cumulative production of 1.99 mm bbl, or 1.999 mm bbl, or 1.999 999 999 mm bbl, etc. So while technically this is wrong, any error resulting in calculating the capacity of Tranche 2 as 2.00 mm bbl minus 0.00 bbl would be infinitesimal, and thus immaterial.

typed 1 and 2 in cells E24 and E25. These are referenced by VLOOKUP formulas in cells F24:F25:

- For example, the formula in cell F24 is $\boxed{\text{=VLOOKUP(E24, C5:F6, 4)}}$, meaning column $\boxed{4}$ of the row in the range $\boxed{\text{C5:F6}}$ which corresponds to the 1 in cell $\boxed{\text{E24}}$. This gives the answer of **0%**.

- The VLOOKUP formula in cell F25 works the same way, giving the answer of **5%**.

- Note that the range being looked up (cells C5:F6) is one column larger than the range which was looked up under the top-rate method. This is because the former range includes the tranche index numbers (cells C5:C6).

4. *Calculate the blended royalty rate.* There are two ways to do this:

- In cell F26, we use a "manually coded" weighted average formula. This takes the form:

> (% of production in Tranche 1) × (Tranche 1 royalty rate)
> +
> (% of production in Tranche 2) × (Tranche 2 royalty rate)

or, as written in cell F26, $\boxed{\text{=(F22*F24) + (F23*F25)}}$. The result is **2.14%**.

- In cell F27, we use Excel's SUMPRODUCT function, which does the same calculation as the "manual" formula, but – when there are many cells from which to calculate the weighted average – is more compact and less error-prone. The formula, $\boxed{\text{=SUMPRODUCT(F22:F23, F24:F25)}}$, also gives the answer of **2.14%**.

5. *Calculate the total royalty payment for the year.* The formula used in cell F28 is $\boxed{\text{=F27*F12}}$, where $\boxed{\text{F27}}$ is the blended royalty rate and $\boxed{\text{F12}}$ is gross revenue. The result is **MOD $7.50 mm.**

Note that the results of the tranche rate – a blended royalty rate of 2.14% and a royalty payment of MOD $7.50 mm – result in a lower royalty burden for the producer than the top-rate method results of a 5% blended royalty rate and a royalty payment of MOD $17.50 mm. This will always be the case if more than one tranche is applicable when using the tranche method. Why do you think this is so?

Can We Trust the "Blended Rate" Calculation?

Yes. The check of the tranche method in our example file shows that the same results are obtained by calculating the royalty rate and payment explicitly, i.e., by calculating the rate and royalty payment for each tranche, and then summing the royalty payments.

> Refer again to the Excel file "Ch3_roy_cuml_prod_CROSSOVER_simple_example.xls," from which we have created Figure 3.12, which is shown in the file "Ch3_Supplement_to_roy_examples.pdf." Study the simple calculations in rows 30–40.

Note that our previous answers in cells F27 and F28 match their counterparts in cells F40 and F39, respectively.

Clarifying terms: "weighted average rate" and "blended rate"

In this book we use the term **weighted average royalty rate** to mean the *weighted average over the producing life of the field*. The **blended royalty rate** we have just calculated is also, mathematically, a weighted average, but to avoid confusion we use the term "blended rate" to mean the *weighted average for a single period*.

There are different ways to calculate weighted averages in Excel. All of these ways give the same answer. We show an example of this in the self-explanatory file "Ch3_weighted_averages.xls."

Tranche Method – More Complex Example

Model Assumptions

Refer to the Excel file "Ch3_roy_cuml_prod_CROSSOVER_full_example.xls"which contains the assumptions also shown in Figure 3.13 in the file "Ch3_Supplement_to_roy_examples.pdf."

These assumptions are as follows:

- A royalty schedule is shown in cells C8:E18. Note that, for reasons we will explain later, we have created two named ranges: (1) cells C8:E18, named "Royalty_table"; and (2) cells B18:E18, named "Enlarged_table."

- A choice of low, mid- and high oil production cases (rows 22–24, not shown in Figure 3.13), one of which is chosen for use in the model in row 26. (Note that in each case, in column F, there is production of 1 mm bbl from before our timeframe begins in 2014, which needs to be considered when calculating *cumulative* production.)

- An oil price forecast (row 27).

Note that, in this example, the mid-production case is used, and that only three of the seven years of forecast field life are shown (for reasons of space) in Figure 3.13 and all other screenshots referred to in this section.

For Comparison: Calculation Using the Top Rate

Although this section is about royalties based on tranches of cumulative production, in our example file we also take a moment to study the simple calculations in rows 30–40. Calculate for comparison, the royalty based on the schedule shown in Figure 3.13 using the top-rate method, in exactly the same way as described earlier in this section.

These calculations appear in "Section 1) Calculations – Top rate method" in rows 29–35 (not shown in Figure 3.13) of our current example model "Ch3_roy_cuml_prod_CROSSOVER_full_example.xls." Note that the VLOOKUP formula in row 33 references the range "Royalty_table" (cells C8:E18). It results in a weighted average royalty rate of 14.8% (cell E33) and a total royalty payment of MOD $236 mm (cell E34).

Calculation Objective – With Caveats

Our ultimate goal is to calculate annual royalty payments, based on annual blended royalty rates, using the tranche method. Before we begin, be aware of the following:

(a) In cases when cumulative production remains within only one royalty tranche during the year, this is easy. Just use a simple VLOOKUP formula, exactly as when using the top-rate method.

(b) In other cases, however, when cumulative production in one year passes through one or more royalty tranche thresholds – causing different tranches to apply during the year – a blended rate must be calculated. This takes more steps.

(c) What makes parts of this example model even more complex is that it is dynamic, and must be flexible enough to accommodate different production profiles, some of which require the approach described in point (a), while others require the approach in point (b). So for each year, the model must be able to apply *either* approach as appropriate. This requires using some formulas which are longer than what we usually prefer.

Calculation Strategy

Our approach is probably best described by discussing, in *reverse order*, the steps we will take for any given year:

- (The last step): calculate in each year the royalty payment from a blended royalty rate.

- Before that, calculate the blended rate, using the percentage(s) of cumulative production falling within the relevant royalty tranche(s) from the royalty schedule.

- Before that, calculate the percentage(s) from the volumes, in barrels, in each relevant tranche.

- Before that, calculate this allocation of barrels to tranches. Figure 3.14, from our example file, shows what we mean. For example, we can see in this chart that over the pre-2014 period, cumulative production rises such that the applicable royalty rate starts at 0%, then changes to 5%, then to 7% and finally to 8%. Thus during this period the "barrels" belong, at one point or another, to the 0–5% tranche, then to the 5–7% tranche, then to the 7–8% tranche and finally to the 8–10% tranche.

This allocation of barrels to royalty rate tranches is actually the trickiest part, because the calculation method varies, depending on whether:

- only one tranche is relevant; or

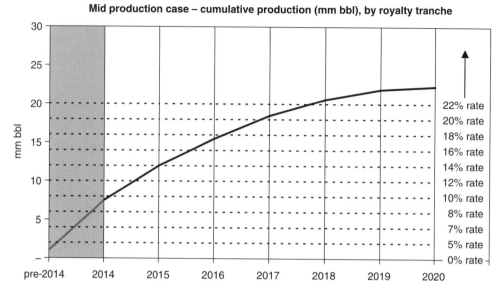

Figure 3.14   Allocation of mid-case cumulative production to tranches, from row 142 of "Ch3_roy _cuml_prod_CROSSOVER_full_example.xls"

  o if more than one tranche is relevant, whether:

  – the tranche is the lowest tranche in the ascending royalty schedule;

  – the tranche is the highest in this schedule; or

  – the tranche is between the lowest and the highest.

• Continuing to list the steps in reverse order, before we allocate barrels to royalty tranches, we must first establish the order of the relevant tranches by numbering them in ascending order.

• To number a relevant tranche, we must first identify if the tranche is relevant in the year, making this the first step.

Calculations: Model Section 2a): Determination of Relevant Tranches

Refer to Figure 3.15 on page 9 of the file "Ch3_Supplement_to_roy_examples.pdf" which helps explain Section 2a) of the example Excel file "Ch3_roy_cuml_prod_CROSSOVER _full_example.xls."

The goal of this section of the model, which starts in row 38, is simple: for each year, we need to identify which royalty tranches are relevant to the level of cumulative production as it changes through the year. Put another way, we want to know which tranches' *lower* limits (cells C8:C18, of which cells C13:C17 are not shown in Figure 3.15) does cumulative production meet or exceed over the course of each year?

Before worrying about the calculation mechanics, let us look at the end result we want. For 2014, for example, we want to identify the relevant tranches by placing a 1 in the appropriate cells in column G, starting with cell G45, and to put a 0 in any irrelevant cells.

Just "by eye" this is easy to do. Look at how cumulative production changes over the course of 2014. It starts at 1.00 mm bbl (cell G41) and ends at 7.50 mm bbl (cell G42). We can see which tranches in the royalty schedule (columns C and D, starting row 8) apply: Tranches 1–4 (rows 8–11). Tranche 5 is the first irrelevant tranche, as its lower limit of 8.00 mm bbl (cell C12) is *not* exceeded by 7.50 mm bbl.

To do this formulaically, first we have set up cells for cumulative production at the start and end of 2014, in cells G41:G42, as well as tranche numbers in column B, both in Section 2a) (starting in row 45) and in the royalty schedule (starting in row 8). Note that with the addition of the tranche rows to the royalty schedule, the range B8:E18 has been named "Enlarged_table." The fact that the column index numbers of 1–11 are the first column (column B) in this named range will let us use VLOOKUP formulas when we want information about a tranche, referring to it by its index number.

Things are now set up to let us identify, in rows 45–55, for each year, the relevant tranches with 1s and irrelevant tranches with 0s. This is done with a single formula which can be copied into each annual cell starting in row 45. Here are two examples.

Example 1: Determining the Relevance of Tranche 1 in 2014 (Cell G45)   In cell G45 we use the double-condition lookup formula

> =IF(AND(G$41 < VLOOKUP($B45, Enlarged_table, 3), G$42 > VLOOKUP($B45, Enlarged_table, 2)), 1, 0)

Let us calculate the values; translate the terms of this formula into English; and then make an English sentence:

- G41 is cumulative production at the start of 2014, or **1.00 mm bbl**.

- VLOOKUP($B45, Enlarged_table, 3) looks in column 3 (i.e., column D) of the range "Enlarged_table" for the value corresponding to B45, where B45 is the tranche number of 1; in other words, it looks for the *upper* limit of Tranche 1, and finds that it is **2.00 mm bbl** (cell D8).

- G42 is cumulative production at the end of 2014, or **7.50 mm bbl**.

- VLOOKUP($B45, Enlarged_table, 2) looks in column 2 (i.e., column C) of the range "Enlarged_table" for the value corresponding to B45, where, again, B45 is the tranche number of 1; in other words, it looks for the *lower* limit of Tranche 1, and finds that it is **0.00 mm bbl** (cell C8).

Thus the formula means:

- if (cumulative production at the start of the year < Tranche 1's upper limit) AND
- if (cumulative production at the end of the year > Tranche 1's lower limit), then the answer is 1; otherwise, the answer is 0.

Plugging in the values, we get:

- if (1.00 mm bbl < 2.00 mm bbl) AND
- if (7.50 mm bbl > 0.00 mm bbl), the answer is 1, otherwise the answer is 0.

Both of the conditions are true, so the answer for 2014 is Tranche 1 (cell G45) = **1**, meaning yes, **Tranche 1 is relevant in 2014.**

What's happening inside this formula? Excel's Evaluate Formula tool

Sometimes it can be hard to know what formulas like these are doing. The Audit Trace Dependents command, as useful as it is, has its limits when used with formulas which use the VLOOKUP function, because the tracer lines point to the entire lookup array (i.e., the table being looked up), not to just the relevant part of it. Moreover, if a formula contains multiple IF statements, the tracer lines point all over the place, including to cells relating to conditions which are not met.

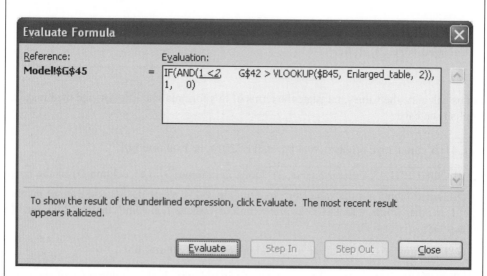

Figure 3.16   Screenshot of the Evaluate Formula tool, halfway through evaluating the formula in cell G45

Excel's Evaluate tool (Figure 3.16) is very useful in these cases. In a special window, it solves a formula step by step, so you can see how it works. Try it with, for example, the cell we just evaluated – cell G45 from our example file. Select the cell, and then, in Excel 2003, go to Tools/Formula Auditing/Evaluate Formula. (In Excel 2007 and Excel 2010, go to Formulas/Formula Auditing/Evaluate Formula.) You will see the formula from cell G45 in a dialogue box. As you click the Evaluate button repeatedly, you will see each element of the formula identified (i.e., a cell address reference will be replaced by the value in the cell), and each arithmetic, logical or function expression solved individually. In short, it will translate the formula in a way similar to what we have just done above.

This is **one of Excel's best tools for helping read and write complex formulas**. It will, in fact, come in handy in this chapter again very soon. We urge you to get comfortable using it if you are not already. For a more detailed illustration of the Evaluate Formula tool's usefulness, see the self-explanatory file "Ch3_Evaluate_Formula_Excel_tool.xls."

Example 2: Determining the Relevance of Tranche 5 in 2014 (Cell G49)   Just to reinforce our explanation, let us look at an example where a tranche is *not* relevant. From the example file, you will see that the formula in cell G49 for 2014, Tranche 5, is

=IF(AND(G$41 < VLOOKUP($B49, Enlarged_table, 3), G$42 > VLOOKUP($B49, Enlarged_table, 2)), 1, 0)

This means:

- if (cumulative production at the start of the year < Tranche 5's upper limit) AND
- if (cumulative production at the end of the year > Tranche 5's lower limit), then the answer is 1; otherwise, the answer is 0.

This reduces as follows:

- if (1.0 mm bbl < 10.0 mm bbl) AND
- if (7.50 mm bbl > 8.0 mm bbl), the answer is 1, otherwise the answer is 0.

The first condition is true, but the second is not – so the answer is, for 2014, that Tranche 5 in cell G49 = **0**, meaning, no, **Tranche 5 is not relevant in 2014**.

After determining in each year the relevance of each tranche in this manner, we sum the number of relevant tranches in row 56, for reasons we shall see in Section 2c), below.

Calculations: Model Section 2b): Numbering of Relevant Tranches

As mentioned, when we reach the stage (in Section 2c) of our example file) to allocate production to relevant tranches, our calculation method will depend on whether:

- there is only one relevant tranche per year;

- or, if there is more than one relevant tranche, on whether a tranche is the first, second, etc., tranche which is relevant in the year.

So we need to number the relevant tranches in ascending order. Let us do this now, in Section 2b) of the model. The calculations are straightforward.

> Refer to Figure 3.17 in the file "Ch3_Supplement_to_roy_examples.pdf" which helps explain Section 2b) of the example Excel file "Ch3_roy_cuml_prod_CROSSOVER_full_example.xls."

For 2014, for example, we can see that each value of 1 in column G in Section 2a) of the model is assigned an ordinal number in Section 2b). Thus, in 2014, for example, Tranche 1 is the first relevant tranche for the year, Tranche 2 is the second, etc. In 2015, Tranche 4 is the first relevant tranche and Tranche 5 is the second relevant tranche.

> ## Keep the terms clear: "Tranche N" versus "the Nth tranche"
>
> Do not confuse the terms: for example, "Tranche 4" with "the fourth tranche" or "the fourth relevant tranche."
>
> The "4" in "Tranche 4," for example, is an *index number*, used for reference purposes. Thus "Tranche 4" means the tranche within the range of cumulative production shown in row 11 of the royalty schedule in the model. It is denoted by the index numbers in the shaded cells in cells B8:B18, which then recur in column B throughout the model.
>
> Conversely, the "four" in "the fourth tranche" or "the fourth relevant tranche" is an *ordinal number* which describes, within any single year, the order in which a tranche becomes relevant within that year. For example, when the model is set to the mid-production case (using the spinner in cell C26):
>
> - In 2014, Tranche #4 is the fourth relevant tranche that year, as shown by the value of 4 in cell G67.
>
> - In 2015, Tranche #4 is the first relevant tranche that year, as shown by the value of 1 in cell H67.
>
> - In 2020, Tranche #11 is the first relevant tranche that year, as shown by the value of 1 in cell M74.
>
> And so on.

The row 64 formula for numbering Tranche 1 in all years is unique in Section 2b) of the model. In 2014, for example, the ordinal number of Tranche 1 (cell G64) simply equals the corresponding value in Section 2a) of the model, i.e., cell G45. This is **1**, so Tranche 1 is the **first** relevant tranche for 2014.

For the remaining tranches, starting with Tranche 2, in all years, numbering is done with **truncated accumulation formulas**. These are simply formulas which stop counting (or some other form of accumulation) when there is nothing more to count (or accumulate).

- This works like a standard accumulation formula, which adds a new annual value to the last year's cumulative result.

- But it also multiplies the answer by a 1 or a 0. The 1 or 0 acts like a signal – 1 means count, 0 means do not count. If 1 is the multiplier, the sum is recorded. If 0 is the multiplier, the sum is "ignored."

We will take Tranche 2 in 2014 (cell G65) as an example:

- The formula in G65 is $=(G46+G64)*G46$, or $(1 + 1) \times 1 = \mathbf{2}$, meaning Tranche 2 is the **second relevant tranche in 2014**.

- Note that the 1 in cell G46 thus plays two roles: it is both the thing being counted as relevant, and the signal that it *should be* counted as relevant.

Now look at another example, Tranche 5 in 2014 (cell G68):

- The formula in G68 is $=(G49+G67)*G49$. The 0 in cell G49 says that the sum should not be counted. The formula thus resolves as $(0 + 4) \times 0 = \mathbf{0}$, meaning Tranche 5 is **not a relevant tranche in 2014**, and therefore does not get an ordinal number; instead it gets designated as the "0th" relevant tranche, i.e., as an irrelevant tranche.

- If we had used a standard accumulation formula in cell G68, i.e., simply $=(G49+G67)$, the answer would have been $(0 + 4) = 4$, meaning Tranche 5 would be the fourth relevant tranche in 2014. Because Tranche 5 is not relevant, and we already have Tranche 4 as the fourth relevant tranche in 2014 (cell G67), this is not what we want.

The checksums in row 75 ensure that, for each year, the highest ordinal number in Section 2b) of the model equals the total number of relevant tranches, calculated in row 56 of Section 2a).

Calculations: Model Section 2c): Allocation of Volumes (Barrels) to Tranches

Our goal here is to get the results we have already seen in Figure 3.14: "Allocation of Mid case cumulative production to tranches," above. This is the most complex step in our example model, but what mainly makes it challenging is that the single, copied formula requires some concentration to translate into English – it combines multiple IF statements which use the VLOOKUP function. The underlying logic is actually fairly simple. It is a good example of how implementing a basic idea in Excel can become complicated in the context of a dynamic model. **Using the Evaluate Formula tool might help you as you go through the formulas discussed below**.

Refer to Figure 3.18 in the file "Ch3_Supplement_to_roy_examples.pdf," which helps explain Section 2c) of the example Excel file "Ch3_roy_cuml_prod_CROSSOVER_full_example.xls."

As shown in Figure 3.18, in Section 2c) of the model, we have used a long, multiple-condition IF statement (a nested "IF statement") to allocate barrels of production to the relevant tranches. Although this formula has been copied to every annual cell in columns G–M of Section 2c) of the model (except for the totals in row 89), we will discuss different cells in different examples to show how the formula works under different conditions.

Example 1: The Tranche is not Relevant in the Given Year   First, let us examine the formula for Tranche 5 for year 2014 (cell G82, with the formula shown in row 94). This one is easy. The formula for cell G82 starts with $\boxed{\text{=G49* ...}}$ and is followed by a long list of IF statements. Cell $\boxed{\text{G49}}$ equals 0. We have already seen that, being in Section 2a) of the model, this 0 means that the Tranche 5 is not relevant in 2014. So multiplying the rest of the formula by 0 gives us the result of **0 bbl** for Tranche 5 in 2014. There is nothing more to consider.

Example 2: There is Only One Relevant Tranche in the Given Year   Our example is 2020, Tranche 11 (in cell M88, with the formula shown in row 93). (Normally we would keep all our examples in the same year, but 2014 lacks a relevant example.)

This is another easy one. The formula in cell M88 begins $\boxed{\text{=M55*(IF(M\$56=1, M\$40, ...}}$ and is followed by the other IF statements, all of which are all inapplicable in this case.

- Multiplying the expression by $\boxed{\text{M55}}$ means we are multiplying it by 1, signifying again that Tranche 11 *is* relevant in 2020.

- Cell $\boxed{\text{M56}}$ is the total number of relevant tranches in 2020. It equals $\boxed{1}$. Because there is only one relevant tranche in 2020, allocating production volumes is simple – all production goes into it.

Since $\boxed{\text{M56} = 1}$, the answer is the value found in cell $\boxed{\text{M40}}$, i.e., 0.40 mm bbl, which is the total production for 2020. Thus the total production allocated to Tranche 11 in 2020 is **0.40 mm bbl**.

Importantly, **the order in which IF statements appear in a formula affects the result**. Because we precede the IF statements with a 0 multiplier when there are *no* relevant tranches in a given year, and because our first IF statement translates as "IF there is only one relevant tranche in the relevant year . . . ; *IF NOT* . . . ," the "IF NOT" means that all of the IF statements which follow assume, logically, that there is *more than one* relevant tranche for the year. The importance of this becomes clear in the next example.

Calculating Volume Allocations to Tranches When There Is More than One Relevant Tranche

Before walking through the formula workings for the remaining examples (3–5), we will highlight again the basic idea: that is, the calculation of how many barrels get allocated to a relevant tranche in a given year depends on whether the tranche is the first relevant tranche that year, the last relevant tranche, or an "in-between" tranche.

If this is not intuitive, consider the following. Four students arrive at, and leave, a classroom in a particular order. None stay for the entire class. Two also spend some time in the classroom when the class is not in session. We calculate how much time each student spends in the room *while the class is ongoing*, in Figure 3.19, which comes from the "Analogy" sheet of "Ch3_roy_cuml_prod_CROSSOVER_full_example.xls."

Examine the formulas used in column F, as shown in column G. The time spent can be calculated three ways. The first is used for Ling Noi, in cell F10. The second is used for Roberto and Olumide, in cells F11:F12. The third is for Ed, in cell F13.

Satisfy yourself that you understand why these methods differ. You will find, as you go through the remaining examples of tranche allocation which follow, that if we had combined all the formulas in column G in Figure 3.19 as a single nested IF statement, e.g., IF (order of arrival = 1, E10-D5,   IF(order of arrival = 2, E11-D11 . . . etc), this formula would look much like the one we will discuss in the next three examples. We will revisit Figure 3.19 later to help complete the analogy.

	A	B	C	D	E	F	G	H
1								
2				Class starts	Class ends			
5				9:00	10:00			
6								
7		Student	Order of arrival	Arrives	Leaves	Total time spent in CLASS (<u>not</u> total time in the room)	Formulae	Remark
10		Ling Noi	1	8:45	9:15	0:15	F10. = E10-D5	Time of leaving minus Class start time
11		Roberto	2	9:16	9:30	0:14	F11. = E11-D11	Time of leaving minus Time of arrival
12		Olumide	3	9:31	9:45	0:14	F12. = E12-D12	Time of leaving minus Time of arrival
13		Ed	4	9:46	10:15	0:14	F13. = E5-D13	Class end time minus Time of arrival

Figure 3.19   Different ways to calculate the same parameter, depending on circumstances
Note: Some rows and columns are hidden.

Example 3: The Tranche is the First Relevant Tranche (When There is More Than One Relevant Tranche)   Our example here is 2014, Tranche 1 (cell G78). The relevant portion of the formula is shown in black:

=G45*(IF(G\$56 = 1, G\$40, IF(G64 = 1, VLOOKUP(\$B78, Enlarged_table,3) - G\$41, . . .

Again, multiplying the IF statement by the 1 in cell G45 means that Tranche 1 is relevant in 2014.

And again, the first IF statement (which is grayed out in the box above) IF(G56=1 . . . tests for whether there is only 1 relevant tranche for the year by checking the sum of relevant tranches for the year in cell G56. Because this is *not* the case (i.e., because G56 = 4), Excel sees that this is inapplicable; it "knows" that there is in fact more than one relevant tranche for the year, and moves on to evaluate our next IF statement. (Using the Evaluate Formula tool on cell G78, as described above, might help you see this more clearly.)

Our next IF statement, which is the one applicable to this example, is =IF(G64=1, VLOOKUP(\$B78, Enlarged_table,3)-G\$41, ... The value of 1 in cell G64 means that Tranche 1 is the first relevant tranche for 2014. The condition is met. Therefore the answer is:

- the value found in column 3 of the row in the range "Enlarged_table" (cells B8:E18) which corresponds to the index number of our tranche (the 1 found in cell B78), *minus* cumulative production at the start of 2014 (cell G41); in plainer English, this means
- the upper limit of Tranche 1 (cell D8, i.e., the result of the VLOOKUP expression) *minus* cumulative production at the start of 2014 (cell G41), which means:
  - 2.0 mm bbl (cell D8) *minus* 1.0 mm bbl (cell G41);
  - which equals 1.0 mm bbl. Thus the production volume allocated to Tranche 1 for 2014 in cell G78 is **1.0 mm bbl**.

Example 4: The Tranche is the Last Relevant Tranche (When There is More Than One Relevant Tranche)   Our example here is 2014, Tranche 4 (cell G81). The relevant portion of the formula is shown in black as

=G48*(IF(G\$56=1, G\$40, [inapplicable expression], IF(G67=G\$56, G\$42-VLOOKUP(\$B81, Enlarged_table, 2) . . .

The multiplication by the value of 1 in cell G48, and the fact that the condition G56 = 1 is *not* met, have the same significance here as they did in the last example; i.e., that the tranche in question is relevant, and the first IF statement is inapplicable.

We therefore test the next expression, i.e.,

=IF(G67=G$56, G$42-VLOOKUP($B81, Enlarged_table, 2) . . .

The condition to be met is whether the tranche is the last relevant tranche, i.e., whether G67=G56 , where:

- G67 is the ordinal number of the relevant tranche, which is 4 (cell G67), making it the fourth relevant tranche; and

- G56 is the total number of relevant tranches for the year, which is also 4.

In other words, if the tranche in our example is the fourth relevant tranche, and there are only four relevant tranches, then it must be the last relevant tranche in the year. This condition is met.

Because the condition is met, the second part of our IF statement becomes applicable. So our answer will be the solution to G$42-VLOOKUP($B81, Enlarged_table, 2) .

G42 is the cumulative production of 7.50 mm bbl at the end of 2014.

The expression VLOOKUP($B81, Enlarged_table, 2) finds the lower cumulative production limit for the relevant tranche in the royalty schedule. It does this by looking in column 2 of the row in the range " Enlarged_table " (cells B8–E18) which corresponds to the index number of our tranche (the 4 found in cell B81). It finds that the answer is 6.00 mm bbl (cell C11).

Thus the production allocated to Tranche 4 in 2014 is 7.50 mm bbl minus 6.00 mm bbl = **1.50 mm bbl** (cell G81).

Example 5: The Tranche is an "in-between" Relevant Tranche – Neither the First Nor the Last
Our last example is for 2014, Tranche 2 (cell G79). The relevant portion of the formula, shown in black, is

=G46*(IF(G$56=1, G$40, [inapplicable expression], [inapplicable expression],
VLOOKUP($B79, Enlarged_table, 3)-VLOOKUP($B79, Enlarged_table, 2))) . . .

Multiplication by cell G46 , and the fact that the condition G56=1 is *not* met, have the same significance here as they did in the last two examples.

Excel "knows" that our final expression is intended to deal with "in-between" tranches because it is the last expression in the formula following the IF statements; it is only true when none of the preceding IF statement conditions apply (i.e., if it is not the first tranche, and not the last tranche, it must be an in-between tranche.)

Because the condition of "in-betweeness" applies, the answer in cell G79 is the answer to VLOOKUP($B79, Enlarged_table, 3)-VLOOKUP($B79, Enlarged_table, 2).

This says to find the applicable tranche in the royalty table, and subtract its lower cumulative production limit from its upper cumulative production limit. Put more plainly, it says to use the total volume in the applicable tranche.[6] The expression is resolved as follows:

- VLOOKUP($B79, Enlarged_table, 3) means column 3 of the row in the range "Enlarged_table" (cells B8–E18) which corresponds to the index number in B79, which means the upper limit of Tranche 2, or 4.0 mm bbl (cell D9).

- From this 4.0 mm bbl, we subtract the result of VLOOKUP($B79, Enlarged_table, 2), or column 2 of the row of the range "Enlarged_table" which corresponds to the index number in B79, which means the lower limit of Tranche 2, or 2.0 mm bbl (cell C9).

Thus the production volume allocated to Tranche 2 for 2014 in cell G79 is 4.0 mm bbl minus 2.0 mm bbl = **2.0 mm bbl**.

Summary of calculations used in Examples 3–5

In Figure 3.20, we summarize the production volume calculations in the shaded additions to Figure 3.19 which we saw above.

The Ling Noi calculation is analogous to that in Example 3, when the tranche is the first relevant tranche (and there is more than one relevant tranche). The Roberto and Olumide calculations are analogous to that in Example 5, when the tranche is an "in-between" relevant tranche – neither the first nor the last. And the Ed calculation is analogous to that in Example 4, when the tranche is the last relevant tranche (and there is more than one relevant tranche).

Final Production Tally and Check   To be sure that we have accounted for all production in a given year, in row 89 we sum each tranche's allocations, and, in row 95, check that the results in row 89 equal the production volumes in row 40.

Calculations: Model Section 2d): Allocation of Volumes (Percentages) to Tranches

In this (considerably easier) step, we use our *barrel* volume allocations by tranche, from Section 2c), to calculate *percentage* allocations by tranche.

This step is straightforward – each tranche's production volume from Section 2c) of the model is divided by the relevant year's total production volume (row 89). An error trap

---

[6] Why the total? Because, in an "in-between" tranche, we do not have to worry about where the actual cumulative volume starts or ends, relative to the applicable tranche upper or lower limits, as we did with the last two examples. The in-between tranche volumes are thus fully included within the upper and lower limits set by the royalty schedule. They are analogous to the two students, Roberto and Olumide, whose time spent in the classroom began and ended while the class was ongoing.

	B	C	D	E	F	G	H	I
1								
2			Class starts	Class ends				
3			(Analogous to ...)					
4			Cuml. production at start of year	Cuml. production at end of year				
5			9:00	10:00				
6								
7	Student	Order of arrival	Arrives	Leaves	Total time spent in CLASS (not total time in the room)	Formulae	Remark	(Analogous to ...)
8			(Analogous to ...)					
9	Tranche	Nth relevant tranche	Lower limit	Upper limit	Production in relevant tranche			
10	Ling Noi	1	8:45	9:15	0:15	F10. =E10-D5	Time of leaving minus Class start time	Upper limit minus Cuml. production at start of year
11	Roberto	2	9:16	9:30	0:14	F11. =E11-D11	Time of leaving minus Time of arrival	Upper limit minus Lower limit
12	Olumide	3	9:31	9:45	0:14	F12. =E12-D12	Time of leaving minus Time of arrival	Upper limit minus Lower limit
13	Ed	4	9:46	10:15	0:14	F13. =E5-D13	Class end time minus Time of arrival	Cuml. production at end of year minus Lower Limit

Figure 3.20 Different ways to calculate the same parameter, depending on circumstances (expanded version)

is included in case total production is 0. For example, in 2014, Tranche 1 (cell G98), $=IF(G\$89 = 0, 0, G78/G\$89)$ gives the answer of **15%**.

The percentage allocations for each year are then summed in row 109. Checksums in row 110 ensure that the sum of each year's percentage allocations is either 100%, or, if production in that year is 0, then 0%.

Calculations: Model Section 2e): Calculation of Blended Royalty Rates, and Royalty Payments

We can now calculate the blended royalty rate for each year, and then, finally, the royalty payments.

> Refer to Figure 3.21 in the file "Ch3_Supplement_to_roy_examples.pdf," which helps explain the relevant part of Section 2e) of the example Excel file "Ch3_roy_cuml_prod_CROSSOVER_full_example.xls."

We can calculate the blended royalty rate two ways:

- The first way uses a long weighted average formula. For 2014 (cell G113, with the formula shown in row 114), for example, it:

  ○ calculates the product of the Tranche 1 royalty rate (cell E8) and the 2014 Tranche 1 percentage allocation (cell G98);

  ○ adds this to the product of the Tranche 2 royalty rate (cell E9) and the 2014 Tranche 2 percentage allocation (cell G99);

  and so on, for all 11 tranches. It is not our preferred method – it is tedious and error-prone. For 2014, it gives the answer of **5.5%**.

- The second way uses Excel's SUMPRODUCT function. For 2014 (cell G115, with the formula shown in row 116), for example, the formula is =SUMPRODUCT(G98:G108, $E8:$E18) , where the range G98:G108 contains each tranche's percentage allocation for 2014, and the range E8:E18 contains each tranche's royalty rate. It gives the same answer of **5.5%** as the long formula (as shown by the checksum formulas in row 117), but is faster to use, and less error-prone.

The royalty payments are calculated for each year in the usual way – as the royalty rate multiplied by gross revenue – in row 121. For the entire field life, royalty payments total **MOD $203 mm** (cell E121) for the mid-production case.

By summing each year's royalty payments in cell E121, we can then calculate the weighted average royalty rate for the entire field life, back up in cell E115, with the formula =IF(E120 = 0, 0, E121/E120) , where E120 is total gross revenue for the field life, and E121 is the sum of each year's royalty payments. Under the mid-case production profile, the weighted average royalty rate using the tranche method is **12.7%**. This compares to **14.8%** using the top-rate method (cell E118). Why is the top-rate method's result higher?

Visual check

Reveal all rows and columns. Then split the screen so that the production case chooser (row 26) is visible in the top part, and the charts starting row 124 are in the bottom part.

You can see that in each production case, for the life of the field:

- the weighted average tranche-based royalty rate is lower than the top-rate-based royalty rate (both are recorded in the title of the chart on the left);

- and that, therefore, the total royalty payments (recorded in the title of the chart on the right) are lower as well.

The difference in the total results of the two methods increases as you move from the low- to the high production cases. The differences in annual results occur in the earlier years of production. In the later years, they are the same, because in those years cumulative production falls within only one relevant tranche.

In the high case, as shown in Figure 3.22 on the next page, the tranche method results in a weighted average royalty rate of 14.8% and total payments of MOD $308 mm, versus 16.7% and MOD $348 mm for the top-rate method.

These differences are already material enough in this case to justify the extra effort needed to calculate royalties under the tranche method. Moreover, bear in mind that the payments are on an undiscounted basis. Because the rates diverge most in the early years, then on a discounted basis, the difference between the total value of the royalty payments made under the tranche method and under the top-rate method is even larger.

Exercise

Try to fill in the blanks in the file "Ch3_roy_cuml_prod_CROSSOVER_exercise_setup.xls" to calculate the royalty payments due using the tranche method. Compare your answers to those in the file "Ch3_roy_cuml_prod_CROSSOVER_exercise_solution.xls."

3.6 ROYALTY RATES BASED ON THE PRODUCTION RATE

Another, very common type of royalty regime bases the royalty rate in a given period on that period's petroleum production rate. In contrast to regimes based on cumulative production – where the rate is determined largely by how much you *have produced already* – this regime is based on how much you are producing *now*.

An example of such a regime is shown in Figure 3.23, which comes from our example file "Ch3_roy_prod_rate_example.xls."

Recall that "m bbl/d" means thousands of barrels per day. Also note that, as usual, the implausibly large number in the second column of the last row signifies that there is no upper limit, i.e., the top royalty rate is 25%, no matter how much over 50 m bbl/d production goes. Note further that while this royalty schedule is based on daily production averaged over the course of each year, some fiscal systems use shorter periods (e.g., a quarter or a month).[7]

Again, "Top Rate" or "Tranches"? (But with Different Kinds of Tranches)

As we saw in our previous two sections on royalties based on cumulative production, a question about royalty schedules, such as the one shown above, which *always* must be answered is: which of the two following conventions are used?

- Is this a **top-rate** royalty regime? Again, this would mean that only one rate – the rate corresponding to the production rate – is ever used in any period. For example, if production

---

[7] In some cases, the timeframe used to calculate a fiscal device, or its **periodicity**, can affect financial results materially. For an illustration of this, see Chapter 4 on bonuses, Section 4.6: "Bonuses Based on the Production Rate for a Specified Period." The same principles explained there also apply to the royalties discussed here.

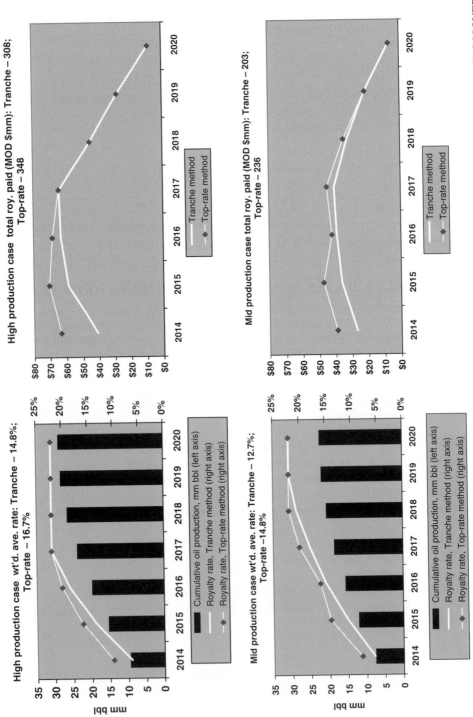

Figure 3.22 Comparison of tranche and top-rate royalty method results, high production case, from the file "Ch3_roy_cuml_prod_CROSSOVER_full_example.xls"

Annual average oil production rate, m bbl/d		Royalty rate
>=	<	%
0	10	5%
10	25	10%
25	50	20%
50	1 000 000 000	25%

Figure 3.23 Royalty schedule based on average annual daily production rate

in Period X is 26 m bbl/d, then the royalty rate to use would be 20%, and you can ignore all other rates in the schedule for that period.

- Or rather, is this regime based on **tranches**? Again, by "tranches" we mean the bands of production rates shown in the first two columns of Figure 3.23 (i.e., 0–10 m bbl/d, 10–25 m bbl/d, etc.). If so, then, potentially, multiple royalty rates are used in the calculation. If for example annual production averages 26 m bbl/d, then, according to our rate schedule:

  ○ a 5% royalty rate is levied on *the first 10 m bbl/d* of production;

  ○ a 10% royalty rate is levied on *the next 15 m bbl/d* of production (i.e., from the second row of the schedule, 25 m bbl/d – 10 m bbl/d); and

  ○ a 20% royalty rate is levied on *the remaining 1 m bbl/d* of production.

  This results in the rate applied each year being a *blended* royalty rate.

The idea of a tranche-based regime resulting in a blended royalty rate is similar to the tranche method cumulative production-based regime we saw in our last section, but is not exactly the same. In the last section, the use of tranches applied to changes over time; in this section they will apply to components of a single average production rate. To elaborate:

- In the last section, we used the tranche method to account for changes in cumulative production levels within a modeling time period (e.g., a year), causing multiple royalty rates to apply within that period. If, for example, cumulative production changes within the year so that it crosses a royalty threshold (i.e., enters a new tranche) during the year, one royalty rate will apply to the portion of the year before the threshold is crossed, and another rate will apply to the portion after it is crossed. The rates are "blended" according to the percentages of the year when they apply, to give an effective annual royalty rate.

- Whereas with one of the regimes we will discuss in this section – that is, the tranche-based variant of a royalty schedule basing the royalty rate on the period average production rate – the tranches denote different components of a single average production rate over the whole period. Again, assume the royalty is calculated based on the average production rate for one year. How this production rate might change within this year is made irrelevant by the fact that the royalty is based on the annual average. The tranches, however, come into play because one royalty rate applies – as in the example shown in Figure 3.23 (assuming it is tranche based) – to the first 10 m bbl/d of this single average production rate; another royalty rate applies to the next 15 m bbl/d; and so on. The royalty rates are "blended" according to their percentages of the total average production rate for the year to give an effective annual royalty rate.

If you had a hard time mastering the tranche-based calculations in the previous section, we have some good news – those we will use in this section are easier.

Reclarifying terms

As noted in the last section, mathematically the "blended rate" is a weighted average rate. But do not confuse this with the "weighted average royalty rate" as we use the term, which refers to the full field life. To clarify:

- We use the term "blended rate" to describe – when using *the tranche method* – the effective royalty rate for a *single period*, which we will show you how to calculate soon, and which, you will see, equals *that period's* royalty payment divided by *that period's* gross revenue.

- We use "weighted average rate" to describe – when using *any royalty method* – the effective royalty rate over the *entire field life*, which equals the sum of all royalty payments made over the field life, divided by the sum of all gross revenue received over the field life.

Unfortunately, some fiscal legislation and contracts provide a rate schedule like the one shown above, *without* stating clearly whether the top-rate or the tranche method should be used. Although the latter is much more common, we have seen top-rate regimes used as well, e.g., in West Africa. Knowing which regime is used can make a big difference to the actual royalty paid. We will show this by calculating the royalty both ways. Meanwhile, we invite you to guess why the results could differ.

Production Rate-Based Royalty Example Model: Assumptions and Initial Calculations

The file "Ch3_roy_prod_rate_example.xls" is longer than some of our example files, as it calculates royalty payments using different regimes (and in some cases, different ways to calculate the same thing):

- a flat rate of 10% (cell D9; again, this is for comparative purposes);

- the rate schedule from Figure 3.23 (rows 17–22), using the top rate method; and

- the same rate schedule, but using the tranche method. We show three different ways to calculate the tranche method. The first is very transparent but takes a lot of space. The second and third are increasingly condensed. We shall see that they all give the same answers.

A switch for choosing the royalty regime is in cell C25. Note that each type of royalty will be calculated in its own section of the file, regardless of how this switch is set; what the switch does is pick the result of the chosen regime for use in the analysis section starting in row 191, and in the charts which follow.

Other assumptions include:

- a days-per-year cell (cell D5, named "Days_per_year");

- a choice of low, mid- and high oil production cases (rows 30–32) and a switch for choosing one of them (cell C35);

- a multiplier for adjusting the chosen case's volumes (cell D36); and

- an oil price time series (row 39), given the range name "Oil_price." As in prior examples, the price is kept flat to make it easier to see how the royalty dynamics work. For now, select the mid-case production profile and set the multiplier to 100%.

The first three rows (43–45) of the Calculations section convert the chosen annual production profile (after it has been adjusted by the multiplier) from m bbl/d (1000 barrels/day) to mm bbl (millions of barrels per year), and calculate gross revenue. These steps are straightforward.

Calculating the Royalty, Based on a Flat Royalty Rate

This is done in the usual way, as seen in Chapter 1, i.e., as each year's gross revenue times the flat royalty rate, in rows 48–49. Using the mid-production case, the weighted average royalty rate is 10% (cell E48) – which is appropriate, since the flat rate is assumed to be 10%.

Calculating the Production Rate-Based Royalty, Assuming a Top Rate Regime

In row 52, we use the VLOOKUP function to calculate the royalty rate, assuming this is a top-rate regime. The formulas used take the same form as those in the last section's top-rate calculation of royalties based on cumulative production.

> Refer to Figure 3.24 on page 13 of the file "Ch3_Supplement_to_roy_examples.pdf," which shows the relevant part of the model in file "Ch3_roy_prod_rate_example.xls." (Note that the setting shown in cell C25 is irrelevant to this example.)

The formula for the royalty rate in 2014 (cell G52), for example, is =VLOOKUP(G43, $C$19:$E$22, 3). This says that the royalty rate corresponding to the 2014 production rate of 56.8 m bbl/d (cell G43) is found in column 3 of the rate schedule (cells C19:E22). The rate for 2014 is thus 25%.

Next, the royalty payment is calculated in the usual way, i.e., the royalty rate times gross revenue, in row 53. Under the mid-case production profile, with the multiplier set to 100%, the weighted average royalty rate (cell E52) – which accounts for all years in the field life (including those not shown, to save space in Figure 3.24) – is 18.3%.

Calculating the Production Rate-Based Royalty, Assuming a Tranche Regime – Version 1 (Longest)

Tranche-based calculations of the kind addressed here are somewhat (though not horribly) more complex than top-rate-based calculations. **Mastering them is important**, though, as we will use a similar technique to calculate certain kinds of production sharing splits in Chapter 8.

Here are the steps – listed here using the numbering of the sections in the model – for the first of three ways to calculate a royalty based on production tranches. We devote most space to the first, Step 1a), using 2014 as an example.

Refer to Figure 3.25 in the file "Ch3_Supplement_to_roy_examples.pdf," which shows calculation Step 1a) in the Excel model, "Ch3_roy_prod_rate_example.xls."

Step 1a). Allocate each year's production, *in m bbl/d*, to the individual tranches. Refer to Figure 3.25 as we walk through how to do this, using 2014 as an example.

Notice that in rows 58–63 we have:

- reproduced the royalty rate table from the Assumptions section;
- added tranche reference numbers in cells B60:B63 (these are for convenience only; they are not referenced by any formula);
- named the cells in E60:E63 "Roy_rate_tranche1," "Roy_rate_tranche2," "Roy_rate_tranche3" and "Roy_rate_tranche4," to help make the formulas we will write easier to read; and
- added a column to the rate schedule in column F, in which we calculate the maximum possible volume or capacity of each tranche, in m bbl/d (cells F60:F63). Each of these cells simply subtracts the values in the relevant row of column C from those in column D.

We can now allocate portions of the 2014 (for example) total production volume of 56.8 m bbl/d (cell G43) to Tranches 1–4 (cells G66, G68, G70 and G72).

The allocation to Tranche 1 (cell G66), for example, is done with the formula =MIN($F60, G43), where F60 is the maximum possible production in Tranche 1, and G43 is the total volume of 2014 production to be allocated among all tranches. The MIN (minimum) function simply gives the smaller of the two values.

Why use the MIN function?

If the use of the MIN function in this formula, or the sense behind it, is not immediately intuitive, consider this analogy. Suppose 70 people on an organized tour are waiting for buses. Three empty buses arrive. Each has a maximum capacity of 30 passengers.

- The first bus opens its doors. The total number of passengers waiting to be "allocated" to it is 70; the capacity of the first bus is 30; the number of passengers who actually get allocated seats is the lower of the two values, i.e., 30.

- The second bus opens its doors. The total number of remaining passengers waiting to be allocated to it is now $70 - 30 = 40$; the capacity of the second bus is 30; the number of passengers who actually get allocated seats is the lower of the two values, i.e., 30.

- The third bus opens its doors. The total number of remaining passengers waiting to be allocated to it is now $70 - 30 - 30 = 10$; the capacity of the second bus is 30; the number of passengers who actually get allocated seats is the lower of the two values, i.e., 10.

In each case, the number of remaining passengers awaiting the allocation of a seat when a bus opens its doors equals the total number initially waiting, less any who have already been seated.

Our model works the same way, except that – instead of an initial 70 people to be allocated among three buses, each with a maximum capacity of 30 – we have an initial 56.8 m bbl/d of production in 2014, to be allocated among four tranches, the first with a maximum capacity of 10 m bbl/d; the second with a maximum capacity of 15 m bbl/d; the third, 25 m bbl/d; and the fourth, effectively limitless (cells F60:F63). The amount of 2014 production "awaiting" allocation at the start of each tranche (cells G43, G67, G69 and G71) equals the initial volume of 56.8 m bbl/d, less any production already allocated to a tranche.

Before the buses depart, the conscientious tour organizer checks that there are no passengers remaining after the allocation to buses; similarly, in cell A73 (which sums all the annual values in row 73), we check to be sure that the post-allocation production volume is 0. And just as the organizer, to be extra safe, also does a headcount to ensure that the total number of passengers on the three buses equals the total number initially waiting, in our model we use formulas – for example, in cell G75 – to check that the total volume allocated to the four tranches in 2014 equals total production in 2014. The other formulas in row 75, and the checksum in cell A75, which sums their results, show us this is the case for all years.

Finally, we have done a visual check of the production allocation (see the section starting row 77) for good measure as shown in Figure 3.26, below.

That takes care of the first and perhaps most complicated step of allocating production to tranches. For the remaining Steps 1b)–1e), refer to Figure 3.27 (which also again shows the results from Step 1a), because they are referenced in the following discussion.)

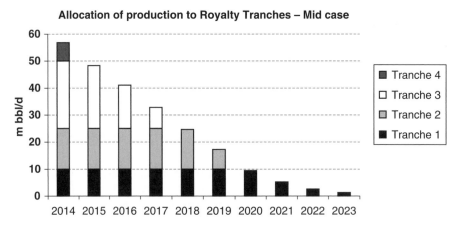

Figure 3.26 Visual check of production allocation, from the file "Ch3_roy_prod_rate_example.xls"
Note: Results shown here reflect the mid-case production profile with the production multiplier set to 100%.

> Refer to Figure 3.27 in the file "Ch3_Supplement_to_roy_examples.pdf," which shows the remaining Steps 1b)–1e) in the Excel model "Ch3_roy_prod_rate_example.xls."

Step 1b). Convert the production which has been allocated to each tranche in Step 1a) to mm bbl (rows 105–109). In 2014, for example, the 10.0 m bbl/d allocation to Tranche 1 (cell G66) becomes 3.7 mm bbl per year (cell G105).

Step 1c). In rows 113–116, multiply the volumes, in mm bbl, in each tranche by the corresponding years' oil price in the named range "Oil_price" (row 39; not shown in Figure 3.27) to calculate the gross revenue for each tranche. The results for each tranche are totaled in row 117. In 2014, for example, gross revenue is MOD \$1557 mm (cell G117). The checksum in cell A117 ensures that the sum of all tranches' gross revenue (row 117) matches the total gross revenue already calculated in row 45 (also not shown in Figure 3.27).

Step 1d). In rows 121–125, for each tranche, multiply the gross revenue just calculated in Step 1c) by the appropriate royalty rate (the cells named "Roy_rate_tranche1," "Roy_rate_tranche2," etc., in cells E60–E63) to calculate the royalty payments. Sum these payments to reach the total royalty payment (row 125). In 2014, the total royalty payment is MOD \$239 mm.

Step 1e). Derive the blended royalty rate for each year in row 128, and the weighted average royalty rate for the total field life (cell E128). This step is not essential, but is useful for analytical purposes. Under the mid-case production profile, with the multiplier set to 100%, the weighted average royalty rate is **11.8%** (cell E128). **Compare this to 18.3% for the top-rate method (cell E52). Why is there such a large difference?**

Calculating the Production Rate-Based Royalty, Assuming a Tranche
Regime – Version 2 (Shorter)

The main difference between this shorter approach and Version 1 is that:

- in Version 1, we calculated the royalty payments arising from each tranche, and used the sum of these payments to derive a blended royalty rate for each year (which acts basically as a memorandum item, as no calculations depend on this blended rate);

- whereas here, we will calculate a blended royalty rate, and use this to calculate the total royalty payment – saving ourselves some steps in the process.

Here are the steps – again, listed using the numbering from the model sections – for a shorter way to calculate the royalty payments using the tranche method.

> Refer to Figure 3.28 in the file "Ch3_Supplement_to_roy_examples.pdf," which shows the shorter method (Steps 2a)–2d)) in the Excel model "Ch3_roy_prod_rate_example.xls."

- **Step 2a).** As in the longer version's Step 1a), allocate each year's production, in m bbl/d, to the individual tranches. Rather than repeat the calculation, we have just brought the previously calculated results down to this part of the model using equals signs (rows 135–138).

- **Step 2b).** Convert the allocated production for each tranche to its percentage of total production in each tranche. Thus in rows 142–145, we divide each of the values in Step 2a) by the corresponding total annual production values (in row 43, not shown in Figure 3.28). Note that we have added an error-trapping expression – for example, in 2014 (in any of the cells G142–G145), $\boxed{\text{=If(G43} = 0, 0, \ldots)}$ – to these formulas in case production in a given year is ever 0. The percentage of total annual production allocated to Tranche 1 in 2014, for example, is 18% (cell G142). Also note the check formulas in row 147, which ensure that in years with production, the percentages for a given year sum to 100%.

- **Step 2c).** Calculate the blended royalty rate for each year. As in this method we are ultimately only concerned with the actual royalty paid for all production in a given year – and not with the payments for each tranche – by calculating the blended rate we get the information we need without having to calculate the payment for each tranche, as we did in Version 1. As we saw earlier in the chapter, there are two ways to calculate the blended rate:

  - using a long formula, which in 2014 (cell G150), for example, is

  > $$= (G142*Roy\_rate\_tranche1) + (G143*Roy\_rate\_tranche2)$$
  > $$+(G144*Roy\_rate\_tranche3) + (G145*Roy\_rate\_tranche4)$$

  where G142–G145 are the percentages of production in Tranches 1–4, respectively; or

  - using the SUMPRODUCT function, which does the same as the long formula, but in less space. For 2014, the formula (cell G152) is

$$= \text{SUMPRODUCT}(\text{Roy\_rate\_tranche1} : \text{Roy\_rate\_tranche4}, \text{G142} : \text{G145})$$

The check formulas in rows 154 and 155 ensure that the two methods give the same answer – in 2014 it is 15.3% (cells G150 and G152) – and that these equal the blended rates calculated in Step 1e), above. (Note that we have calculated the weighted average rate (again, this is for the full field life) in cell E152, but we had to wait until we finished the remaining steps below, in rows 159–160, in order to do so.)

- **Step 2d).** In row 160, for each year, calculate the total royalty payment as the blended royalty rate calculated in Step 2c) times gross revenue (row 159). For 2014, for example, the answer is MOD \$239 mm. The check formulas in row 161 show us that this answer is the same as for Version 1.

Calculating the Royalty, Assuming a Tranche Regime – Version 3 (Very Short Alternatives)

The section starting in row 163 presents more compact, though perhaps less initially intuitive, ways to calculate royalties based on the production rate, assuming a tranche regime.

The strategy here is to expand the calculation in the lookup table itself in such a way that we can calculate each year's blended royalty rate with three rows, each of which has a formula which references the table using the VLOOKUP function. We also show a way to make the calculation even more compact, by compressing the three formulas into one long one.

> Refer to Figure 3.29 in the file "Ch3_Supplement_to_roy_examples.pdf," which shows the even shorter method (Steps 3a)–3c)) in the Excel model "Ch3_roy_prod_rate_example.xls."

Modifying the lookup table (cells C168:G172) is the key initial step in this approach. Note that it has two more columns (F and G) than the one used in previous methods. We have numbered each column in the table in row 165. (This is for ease of reading only; these numbers are not referenced by any formula.)

Column F (or column #4) in the table calculates the royalty due, in volume terms, for each full tranche. For example, cell F169 references the first three columns of the table to calculate the royalty due for the production tranche 0 m bbl/d to 10 m bbl/d, with the simple formula =(D168-C168)*E168. This takes the difference between the upper and lower production limits of the tranche, and multiplies that value by the appropriate royalty rate.

Column G (or column #5) is simply the cumulative sum of column F, adding the royalty production volumes for each full tranche of production.

Values from columns 1, 3 and 5 of this lookup table, and total annual oil (row 176), give us enough information to calculate the weighted average royalty in only three steps. Taking 2014 as an example:

1. The first reference to the lookup table (cell G177) selects the column 5 value relevant to the full oil production of the period (cell G176) with the formula =VLOOKUP(G176, $C$168:$G$172, 5).

2. The second reference to the lookup table (cell G178) selects the column 1 value (i.e., the low limit of the production tranche appropriate for the full oil production of the period (cell G176)), and subtracts that value from the full oil production for the period (cell G176) with formula

=G176-VLOOKUP(G176, $C$168:$G$172, 1)

3. The third reference to the lookup table (cell G179) selects the column 3 top tranche royalty rate value relevant to the full oil production of the period (cell G176) with formula

=IF(G176=0, 0, VLOOKUP(G176, $C$168:$G$172, 3))

(note the error-trap expression at the start of the formula).

These three results are then combined in cell G180 to give the blended royalty rate with the formula =IF(G176 = 0, 0, (G177 + (G178 * G179)) / G176) (again, note the initial error-trap expression). This formula takes the product of the second and third references to the lookup table, adds that product to the first reference to the lookup table, and divides that sum by the full oil production for the period.

This whole calculation can be compressed further into one line if the analyst only wants to display the blended royalty rate but not the intermediate steps in the calculation. This is shown in the formula in cell G182

=IF(G176=0, 0, (VLOOKUP(G176, $C$168 : $G$172, 5)
+(G176-VLOOKUP(G176, $C$168:$G$172, 1))*IF(G176=0, 0,
VLOOKUP(G176, $C$168:$G$172, 3)))/G176)

(Note the initial error-trap expression, in case G176 equals 0.) The check formulas in rows 181 and 183 show that the blended rates resulting from both the three-step and single-formula methods equal the results of Step 2c). The checksum in cell A182 shows that the weighted average rate also equals that from Step 2c).

Tradeoff: compactness vs. complexity

In using these shorter methods, you can save time and calculation space. But in doing so, you are compressing a lot of calculations into a small space; be sure you understand this method and can explain it to others if questioned. Rigorous testing is also important, especially for the single-formula version just shown, as errors (e.g., misplaced commas or parentheses) can easily creep into long formulas, and it can be time consuming to re-establish the logic required to correct them. In long and complex models, though, some users prefer the compactness of a single-line complex formula once they are confident through testing that the formula works correctly.

Visual Analysis: Interactive Examples of Royalties Based on the Production Rate

Some examples using the interactive graphics starting in row 206 should help to consolidate your understanding of production-based royalties and calculations using both top-rate and tranches methods.

For these exercises, refer to the file "Ch3_roy_prod_based_exercises.pdf" and the Excel file "Ch3_roy_prod_rate_example.xls."

Calculation Practice

We have covered a lot of ground in this section. To consolidate, we suggest you try the calculation methods yourself, by filling in the blanks in the file "Ch3_roy_prod_rate_exercise_setup.xls," where we provide new assumptions and interactive charts to display your results. Check your answers against those in "Ch3_roy_prod_rate_exercise_solution.xls."

3.7   ROYALTY BASED ON PRICE AND PRODUCTION RATES (VERSION 1)

Some royalty regimes are based on more than one factor. We have already covered those based on price and on production rates. This one is based on both. The objective of introducing an oil price as well as a production factor is to make the royalty rates more responsive to market conditions, so that high royalty rates are not applied in low oil price environments and vice versa.

An example of a royalty regime based on both the oil price and the production rates is shown in Figure 3.37, which comes from the file "Ch3_roy_price_prod_rate_example.xls." It uses the tranche method described in the last section of Section 3.6, with one major difference:

- in that section, we had a single schedule, or set, of royalty rates which was applied in all years to tranches of production;

- whereas in this example, there is a choice of one of four rate schedules to apply to tranches of production in a given year, depending on the oil price in that year.

Here are some examples of how to interpret the rate schedule shown in Figure 3.37:

- when the oil price is $25/bbl and production is 20 m bbl/d, the royalty rate is 2.5% on all production;

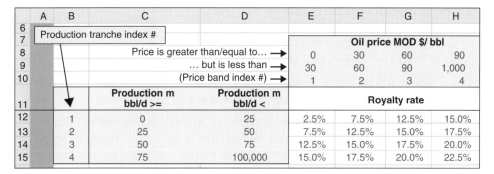

Figure 3.37 Royalty rates based on price and production, from the file "Ch3_roy_price_prod_rate_example.xls"

- when the oil price is $50/bbl and production is 20 m bbl/d, the royalty rate is 7.5% on all production;

- when the oil price is $25/bbl and production is 40 m bbl/d, the royalty rate is 2.5% on the first 25 m bbl/d of production and 7.5% on the remaining 15 m bbl/d;

- when the oil price is $80/bbl and production is 20 m bbl/d, the royalty rate is 12.5% on all production;

- when the oil price is $80/bbl and production is 90 m bbl/d, the royalty rate is 12.5% on the first 25 m bbl/d of production, 15% on the next 25 m bbl/d, 17.5% on the next 25 m bbl/d, and 20% on the remaining 15 m bbl/d.

Calculation – The Longer Way

Just as in the last section on production tranche-based royalties, we will show you two ways to calculate royalties under this regime. The first, described here, breaks the formulas down into small steps. The second way is more compact. As both are very similar to their counterparts in the last section, we will not describe all steps here in great detail.

In our example file, after the royalty schedule shown above, the Assumptions section has choices of low-, mid- and high-production cases (rows 19–21) and rising, flat and falling oil price cases (rows 26–28).

In the Calculations section, the chosen production profile is converted to mm bbl and multiplied by the chosen price to calculate gross revenue (rows 35–38).

The new "twist" to our method is in the section of the file "Royalty calculation: 1) Determination of applicable rate schedule," starting in row 40.

Refer to Figure 3.38 on page 18 of the file "Ch3_Supplement_to_roy_examples.pdf," which draws on the Excel file "Ch3_roy_price_prod_rate_example.xls."

To determine which royalty rates to use for each year:

- First, we determine which price band, i.e., which of the four possible sets of royalty rates (those in E12:E15, F12:F15, G12:G15, or H12:H15), will apply in each year.

- This is done in row 42 with a formula which gives the index number (1, 2, 3, or 4, in cells E10:H10) of the price band which corresponds to that year's oil price.

- We do this by treating the range E8:H10 as a small lookup table – which we have named "Price_bands" – so that we can use a LOOKUP function, specifically a horizontal or HLOOKUP function.[8] For 2015, for example, we use the formula =HLOOKUP(H37, Price_bands, 3) in cell H42.

- This formula looks in the first row (i.e., row 8) of the range Price_bands for the lower end of the band corresponding to the 2015 oil price of $95 (cell H37). It finds that this corresponding price band is the one described by cells H8:H9 of Price_bands . It then returns the value found in row 3 of H8:H10, i.e., the value in cell H10, which is the index number 4.

Well, what good is the index number of 4?

> Refer to Figure 3.39 in the file "Ch3_Supplement_to_roy_examples.pdf," which draws on the Excel file "Ch3_roy_price_prod_rate_example.xls."

The index number of 4 tells us, for a given year and production tranche, which column of royalty rates applies from the schedule in cells E12:H15. Thus we use the CHOOSE function in rows 43–46 to translate the index number into the relevant rates.

The syntax of the CHOOSE function (of which examples are shown in the file "Ch3_CHOOSE_function_examples.xls") is

> =CHOOSE([an "index" i.e., the order in which the chosen value appears in the following list of values], [1st value], [2nd value], [3rd value], etc.)

We use the CHOOSE function to determine the royalty rate for the first production tranche in 2015, e.g., in cell H43, with the formula =CHOOSE(H$42, $E12, $F12, $G12, $H12) . This means that, because H42 is 4, we choose the fourth item in the list E12, F12, G12, H12 of possible royalty rates applicable to the first production tranche. The fourth rate is H12, or 15%.

We have copied this formula down, using dollar signs, to rows 44–46, to determine the applicable rate for each production tranche for each year. Notice that the end result is to reproduce one of the four columns of the rate schedule (cells E12:H15) in each year (i.e., cells G43:G46 for 2014, cells H43:H46 for 2015, etc.). For example:

---

[8] Recall that HLOOKUP works just like a VLOOKUP function turned on its side; see the file "VLOOKUP_HLOOKUP_examples.xls" in the Chapter 1 folder on the disk for an illustration.

- In 2015, because the oil price is $95 (cell H37), the calculated price band index of 4 (cell H42) effectively says to use the rates corresponding to the rate table's stated price band index of 4 (cell H10); that is, it says to fill cells H43:H46 with the rates in cells H12:H15.

- In 2016, because the oil price is $76 (cell I37), the calculated price band index of 3 (cell I42) effectively says to use the rates corresponding to the rate table's stated price band index of 3 (cell G10); that is, it says to fill cells I43:I46 with the rates in cells G12:G15.

Calculating the Royalty Rates and Payments

After filling in the rates for each year in rows 43–46, these are our remaining steps:

1. Allocate each year's total production (in m bbl/d) to its component tranches, i.e., the tranches in cells C12:D15 of our current file. (Note that the tranche index numbers in cells B12:B15 are not used in any formulas; they just serve as labels enabling us to refer to "Tranche 1, Tranche 2," etc.) This step – along with using checksums to be sure all production has been allocated – is done in rows 48–67. (This step uses the same tranche allocation method discussed earlier in the subsection "Calculating the Production Rate-Based Royalty, Assuming a Tranche Regime – Version 1 (Longest)" of Section 3.6, and as shown as the section starting in row 57 of the file "Ch3_roy_prod_rate_example.xls.")

2. Determine each tranche's percentage of total production (rows 98–101), and then calculate the effective royalty rate for each year using either a "manual" formula or the SUMPRODUCT function (rows 104–105). (This is done the same way as in rows 142–152 of "Ch3_roy_prod_rate_example.xls.")

3. Calculate the royalty payments and revenue, net of royalty, in rows 111–112.

Calculation – The Shorter Way

We show a more compact alternative calculation method starting in row 115. (This is essentially the same very short approach as the one described in the last section, and shown starting in row 163 of the file "Ch3_roy_prod_rate_example.xls".) The checksums in rows 140 and 142 of our current example file show that this method gives the same effective royalty rates and payments as the shorter method.

Visual Check and Analysis

In the current example file "Ch3_roy_price_prod_rate_example.xls," split and otherwise adjust your screen so that the spinners controlling the production and price cases in rows 23 and 30, respectively, are visible above the split (you might want to use the grouping buttons to hide rows 24–28), and that the chart, starting in row 144, is visible below the split.

Choose the high production and falling price cases (cells C23 and C30, respectively). The chart should look like Figure 3.40. Note that the left axis scale is denominated in m bbl/d with reference to production, and in MOD $/ bbl with reference to the oil price, while the right axis refers to the effective percentage annual royalty rate.

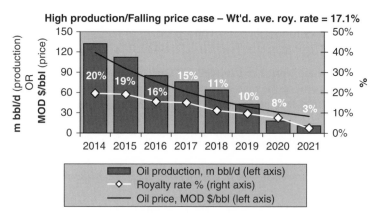

Figure 3.40   From "Ch3_roy_price_prod_rate_example.xls"

With your eye on this chart, use the spinner to scroll among the three price cases. (Keep production set at the high case.) The charts under the flat and rising price cases are shown in Figures 3.41 and 3.42.

First, notice the changes in the annual royalty rates. The rate schedule is designed so that:

(a) all other things being equal, the lower the production rate, the lower the annual royalty rate will be; and
(b) all other things being equal, the lower the oil price, the lower the annual royalty rate will be.

The charts show how both the price and the production rates work in combination. In Figure 3.40, both production and prices fall, resulting in steeply falling annual royalty rates. In Figure

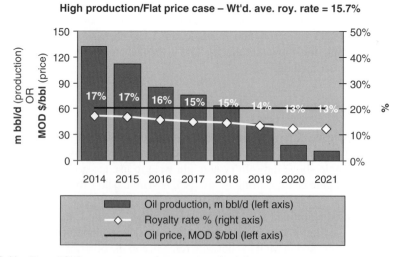

Figure 3.41   From "Ch3_roy_price_prod_rate_example.xls"

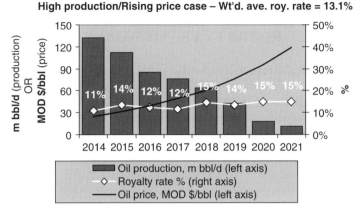

Figure 3.42   From "Ch3_roy_price_prod_rate_example.xls"

3.41, the oil price flattens, so that it is lower than in Figure 3.40 in the early years (when it pushes royalty rates down, compared to Figure 3.40) and higher in the later years (when it pulls royalty rates up). In Figure 3.42, where prices start low and rise, both effects are even more pronounced.

Notice further that the weighted average royalty rates (noted in the chart titles) for the entire field life in Figures 3.40, 3.41 and 3.42 are 17.1%, 15.7% and 13.1%, respectively. This might seem counterintuitive at first glance, as the annual royalty rates rise over time in Figures 3.41 and 3.42, compared to Figure 3.40 (and in Figure 3.42, compared to Figure 3.41). There are two overlapping reasons for the *decline* in the weighted average royalty rates over Figures 3.40–3.42:

1. As you move though these figures in sequence, you will see that although the later years have relatively higher royalty rates, the early years in the falling price case have relatively higher rates.
2. These higher, early rates in the falling price case are applied to the years when production is highest, which pushes up the weighted average rate.

Exercise

On the disk you will find two exercise files:

- **"Ch3_roy_price_prod_rate_exercise_long.xls."** This leaves blank cells for you to fill in which relate to most steps in the example file, including the allocation of production to tranches, calculating the royalty payments in both the long and short ways, etc.
- **"Ch3_roy_price_prod_rate_exercise_short.xls."** This only leaves blank cells for you to fill in which relate to determining which royalty rate to use for each production tranche in each year (i.e., rows 42–46).

The answers to both exercises are in "**Ch3_roy_price_prod_rate_exercise_solution.xls**."

3.8   ROYALTY BASED ON PRICE AND PRODUCTION RATES (VERSION 2 – BASED ON CANADA'S NEW ROYALTY FRAMEWORK)

Another example of a royalty regime based on both production volumes and oil prices is based on Canada's New Royalty Framework (NRF) for conventional oil as at the time of writing. It calculates two components of the royalty rate – one based on the oil price, the other on production volumes – and adds them together to give the final royalty rate. Although it sounds conceptually simple, it is a bit tricky to model.

> This section appears in the file "Ch3_roy_Canadian_NRF.pdf."

3.9   ROYALTY BASED ON A MEASURE OF CUMULATIVE PROFITABILITY: THE "R-FACTOR"

The variable rate royalty regimes we have looked at so far have two things in common. One is that they allow the producer to calculate royalties by dealing with items found near "the top" of the model, i.e., production volumes, prices and revenues. The other is the shared idea (even if it does not always work out in reality) that the higher the producer's turnover is (due to high oil prices, high production, or both), the more royalty the producer should pay.

An alternative to this idea is to link the royalty not only to some proxy for *revenue* (e.g., prices or production rates), but also to something which reflects the producer's *costs*. Hence the idea to base the royalty rate on some **measure of "profitability."** Calculating such a royalty, as we shall soon see, requires delving deeper into the model than we have done so far.

Imagine that in the early years of an oil field development and production project, the fiscal regime is more lenient to the producer, until the producer has made its money back (i.e., recovered its investment or "broken even"), but thereafter is less lenient as the producer's profit grows. Imagine further that the extent to which the producer has "broken even" or is "profitable" is measured according to a simple ratio *of cumulative revenue to cumulative costs*:

- If, for example, the producer invests $10 mm the first year, and produces nothing that year, the producer has no revenue, so the producer is $10 mm down. Expressed as a ratio, the producer's cumulative profitability that year is (revenue/costs) = (0/10) = 0.

- To keep the example simple, assume the producer never incurs any additional costs. The next year the producer receives $5 mm in revenue. At the end of the second year, the producer's cumulative profitability ratio, accounting for all previous cashflows, is ((0 + 5)/10) = 0.5.

- The next year the producer makes another $5 mm in revenue. The producer's cumulative profitability ratio is now ((0 + 5 + 5)/10) = 1.0. In these terms, 1.0 = "breakeven" (on an undiscounted basis).

- The next year the producer again makes \$5 mm in revenue. The producer's cumulative profitability ratio is now $((0 + 5 + 5 + 5)/10) = 1.5$. Because the ratio is greater than 1.0, the producer is now "profitable" according to this measure.[9]

Such a cumulative "profitability ratio" is used in many oil and gas fiscal regimes, and is most commonly referred to as an **R-factor**. Some countries (e.g., Tunisia) have used R-factors to determine royalty rates.[10]

Calculating the R-factor

Our example calculation is found in two files, "Ch3_roy_R_factor_1st_step.xls" and "Ch3_roy_R_factor_2nd_step.xls."

In the former, we start with a table showing the royalty rates which correspond to different R-factors. This range in cells C14:E20, named "Royalty_table," is shown below in Figure 3.46.

R-factor		Royalty rate
>	<=	%
0.0	0.5	2.0%
0.5	0.8	5.0%
0.8	1.1	7.0%
1.1	1.5	10.0%
1.5	2.0	12.0%
2.0	2.5	14.0%
2.5	10 000.0	15.0%

Figure 3.46   Royalty rates based on R-factors, from the file "Ch3_roy_R_factor_1st_step.xls"

Next, we define the calculation of this example's R-factor:

R-factor in any given period = (R-factor revenue/R-factor costs)

where

R-factor revenue =
Project's PREVIOUS period's cumulative (sales revenue − royalty − income tax)

and

R-factor costs =
Project's PREVIOUS period's cumulative (opex + capex)

---

[9] We use quotation marks around "profitable" because we are using the example fiscal regime's regulatory definition of profitability. But outside this example's fiscal framework, definitions of profit are of course many and varied.

[10] Our example of how to calculate an R-factor-based royalty in this section will be useful in Chapter 8, as R-factors are also used for allocating profit oil under some production sharing contracts.

Note: Our present example assumes that the R-factor is calculated on an annual basis. Be aware, however, that some fiscal regimes calculate R-factors on semi-annual, quarterly or monthly bases.

Also, be aware that definitions of R-factor revenue and R-factor costs can vary, depending on the country. For example, in some cases, R-factor revenue might be on a pre-tax basis and / or might deduct opex (as opposed to including opex in the definition of R-factor costs, as in this example.) Whichever specific variant is used, the generic calculation approach discussed in this section is still relevant.

We stress that both the numerator and denominator are based on the *previous* period's (in this example, the previous year's) values, because if they were not – that is, if they were based instead on the *current* period's values – we would immediately have a problem: to know the royalty, we must know the R-factor; and to know the R-factor, we must know the R-factor revenue; and to know the R-factor revenue, we must know the royalty, which is our original question.

Avoiding circular references

This type of problem – which in simpler terms requires you to know A to calculate B, and B to calculate A – is known as a circularity, or, in Excel-speak, a **circular reference**. Let us look at a simpler example, in the file "Ch3_circularity.xls."

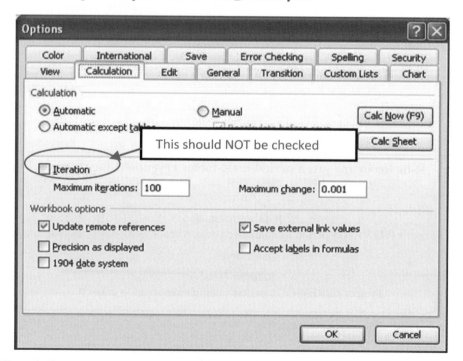

Figure 3.47   Ensuring the Iteration mode is disabled (Excel 2003)

First, be sure that Excel's calculation mode is *not* set to allow "Iteration," a method for attempting to solve circular references, which we will warn you more about soon. In fact, **the Calculation mode should *never* be checked to allow iteration, at least when you are using any of the modeling described in this book**. In Excel 2003, go to Tools/Options; the view under the Calculation tab should look like that in Figure 3.47.

(In Excel 2007, go to Office Button/Excel Options/Formulas/Calculation Options and ensure that "Enable Iterative calculation" is *not* checked. In Excel 2010, go to the File tab/Options/Formulas/Calculation Options and ensure that "Enable Iterative calculation" is *not* checked.)

Next, you should see the display in the workbook as in Figure 3.48.

	A	B	C
1			
2	This year's tax = this year's tax-last year's tax		
3			
4	Last year's tax	100	
5	This year's tax		

Figure 3.48   From "Ch3_circularity.xls"

Try to work out this year's tax. In cell B5, enter $=B5-B4$. You should immediately see the error message shown in Figure 3.49.

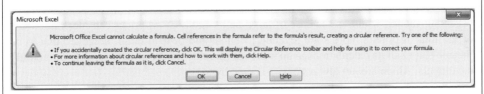

Microsoft Excel

Microsoft Office Excel cannot calculate a formula. Cell references in the formula refer to the formula's result, creating a circular reference. Try one of the following:
• If you accidentally created the circular reference, click OK. This will display the Circular Reference toolbar and help for using it to correct your formula.
• For more information about circular references and how to work with them, click Help.
• To continue leaving the formula as it is, click Cancel.

OK   Cancel   Help

Figure 3.49   Circular reference alert

Note that clicking "OK" would bring up a special toolbar to help you see where the circularity lies. This can be helpful when the circularity is subtle, but in this example, it is obvious – we are asking Excel to calculate in cell B5 something which depends on B5. Since we do not need the toolbar's help, click "Cancel." When you do so, you will see "Circular: B5" in the bottom left corner of your screen. This alerts you to the fact that the circular reference remains. Select cell B5 and press Delete on your keyboard. The "Circular: B5" message disappears.

Excel's iteration method is an attempt to solve circular references, such as the simple example above, as well as more complex ones like our royalty calculation. We urge you, however, **never to use this method**, for two reasons:

1. Iteration solutions can be volatile – that is, iteration can give you different answers at different times.

2. Once you allow one circular reference in an Excel file to be solved by iteration, Excel will not warn you if you accidentally insert any subsequent circular references, which can happen surprisingly easily. This can create potentially huge, even "fatal" problems, because a subtle circular reference, undetected in a complex spreadsheet, means the modeler can fail to understand what the model is doing, and produce bugs which – assuming they are even detected – take a long time to fix.

Another way to try to deal with circular references is to use Excel's Solver optimization add-in. We are also cautious regarding this approach, because, again, sometimes it can produce volatile solutions. In addition, some models may be too complex for Solver to be able to converge on a solution, which makes it difficult to rely on.

Our Preferred Alternative Method: Use Values from the Prior Period

Perhaps in recognition of the calculation challenges posed by circular references, some fiscal terms explicitly state that things such as our mutually dependent R-factor and royalty rates are to be based on the *prior* period's cumulative values. This makes the R-factor calculable without using iteration.

In other cases, however, fiscal rules do not address this, or actually insist that the circularity be calculated. In such cases we suggest the following approach: for a given period, base the calculations on the prior period values, but if you think that doing so might cause a significant error, consider building the model on a quarterly or, if need be, even a monthly basis. This will reduce the span of the error (and thus its magnitude) to at most one quarter or month, respectively. (Governments in fact tend to like basing R-factors on periods shorter than a year, as doing so can result in higher R-factors – and thus higher royalty rates – occurring sooner, which in the case of large fields and high oil prices can mean hundreds of millions of dollars more state revenue.) You should bear in mind, however, that to be meaningful in all its calculations, a quarterly or monthly model needs quarterly or monthly data inputs, which are not always easy to come by.

Calculating the R-factor in Two Stages

We'll use this preferred method in the example calculation by basing base the numerator and denominator for the R-factor on the cumulative *prior* year values.

Our assumptions in the file "Ch3_roy_R_factor_1st_step.xls" – in addition to the named range "Royalty_table" shown in Figure 3.46 – include:

- a 40% income tax rate in cell E26, which is named "Tax_rate";

- a production profile (row 31);

- capex and opex profiles, each with a multiplier switch (cells E34 and E38); and

- assumptions in rows 42–44 resulting in the oil price forecast in row 45.

Refer to Figure 3.50 in the file "Ch3_Supplement_to_roy_examples.pdf," which draws on the Excel file "Ch3_roy_R_factor_1st_step.xls."

First, we have to calculate the components of the R-factor numerator, i.e., the R-factor revenue, which is gross revenue − royalty − income tax. Gross revenue (row 53) is calculated in the usual way. But then immediately we have run into the circularity problem: how do we calculate the royalty rate (row 54), when the royalty rate depends on subsequent calculations?

The solution is to approach the model in two stages:

1. In this first stage, just type in any "dummy" values for the royalty rate as we've done in row 54; this gives the model something to "chew on" while we do the rest of the calculations. (You do not have to do this, but if you leave row 54 blank, it will be hard, as you do the rest of the calculations, to get a feel for whether the model is behaving sensibly.)

2. For the second stage, when we finally determine the actual royalty rates further down, we will simply "plug in" these actual rates into row 54. We will do this in our second file, "Ch3_roy_R_factor_2nd_step.xls."

Having entered the "dummy" values in row 54 for now – we have chosen 10% for each year, but you could use any percentage value between 0% and 100% – we can provisionally calculate royalty payments, and thus revenue, net of royalty (rows 57–58), as shown in Figure 3.50.

Next, we calculate the income tax liability (rows 60–69), using the given inputs for the tax rate and for opex and capex. (To keep this example simple, we assume all capex is expensed for tax purposes in the year it is incurred, i.e., not depreciated.) We also assume that royalty is tax deductible (which is why our revenue line in the tax calculation is revenue, net of royalty (row 61)), and that tax losses – as discussed in Chapter 1 – can be carried forward indefinitely.

Now we can calculate the **numerator for the R-factor**, which is the prior cumulative (gross revenue − royalty − income tax) in rows 73–76. For 2017, for example, the numerator is MOD $2331 mm (cell J76) when the model is set to the Base Scenario, using the button in row 43.

The **denominator for the R-factor** – the prior cumulative of (capex + opex) – is calculated in rows 79–82. For 2017, it is MOD $2408 (cell J82).

We now have all we need to calculate the R-factor and thus the royalty rate for each year:

- The formula for the R-factor for 2017 (cell J84), for example, is $=IF(I82 = 0, 0, I76/I82)$, where cell $I82$ is the *prior* year's R-factor denominator, and cell $I76$ is the *prior* year's R-factor numerator. (Note the error trap in the first part of the IF statement, which prevents Excel from displaying an error message if the denominator is zero.)

- The formula for the royalty rate for 2017 (cell J86), for example, is $=VLOOKUP(J84,$ Royalty_table, 3), where cell $J84$ is the R-factor for 2017, referencing column 3 of the named range, "Royalty_table" (cells C14:E20, not shown in Figure 3.50). For 2017, the resultant royalty rate is 5% (cell J86).

The final step – taken in the separate workbook "Ch3_roy_R_factor_2nd_step.xls" to make it easier to see what we have done – is simply to send the royalty rates calculated in row 86 up to row 54, to overwrite the temporary "dummy" values. This step is the only difference between the two files.

Thus, for example, the old dummy value of 10% for the royalty rate in 2017 (cell J54) should now be replaced with the formula $=J86$, which under the Base Scenario settings (again, triggered by the button in row 43) equals 5%.

Note that once you do this, you will see that many of the results starting from row 54 in this new file now differ from their counterparts in "Ch3_roy_R_factor_1st_step.xls." This is appropriate, as the new rates we have plugged into row 54 in the new file influence the calculations in subsequent rows.

A note on "down-and-up" calculation sequences

As a general rule, we strongly prefer calculation sequences which start at the top and always flow downwards. For example, a formula in row 2 references something in row 1; a formula in row 3 references something in row 2; etc. This is a "down-and-down" approach. Whereas the "down-and-up" approach, where something in row 1 depends on something in row 2, is to be avoided when possible, as it can be disorienting for a third party trying to understand the model. The R-factor calculation just described, however – just like tax calculations involving carryforwards, as discussed in Chapter 1 – is a case where the down-and-up method is unavoidable.

Interactive Analysis of the Royalty Based on the R-factor

This section appears in the file "Ch3_roy_R factor_exercises.pdf."

Further Practice

Try to calculate the royalty payments due under an R-factor regime by filling in the blank cells in the file "Ch3_roy_R_factor_exercise_setup.xls," in which we provide the assumptions (use that file's pre-set Base Scenario) and charts for displaying your results. Then compare your answers to those in the "Ch3_roy_R_factor_exercise_solution.xls" file.

3.10 ROYALTY BASED ON A MEASURE OF CUMULATIVE PROFITABILITY AND COMMODITY PRICES – CANADIAN OIL SANDS

Still other royalty regimes take into account both cumulative profitability *and* the oil price. Here is an example, based on rules which have been applicable to Canada's vast Alberta oil sands projects, which on a technical basis rival Saudi Arabia's oil resources in size.

This section appears in the file "Ch3_roy_Canadian_oil_sands.pdf," which concludes this chapter.

Chapter 4
Bonuses

4

Bonuses

4.1 INTRODUCTION

A **bonus** is an amount payable by a producer when a certain event occurs. The amount payable – whether in the form of cash or petroleum – is determined either by **fiat** (being stated in host country regulations, field licenses, or non-negotiable agreements between the producer and the state) or by **agent interaction** (negotiated between the producer and the state, or bid upon by potential producers).

The kind of bonus which often receives the most attention is the **signature bonus**, which, as mentioned in Chapter 1, is payable by a producer when it is awarded a license, permit or contract. These can be huge – in some West African countries (e.g., Angola and Nigeria) signature bonuses of several hundred million dollars have been paid for highly prospective exploration areas in recent times. Thus signature bonuses can strongly influence a producer's decision whether to proceed with a project, or even to bid for the right to do so. They can also act as barriers to entry, keeping the smaller entities out and limiting competition for the larger companies.

Other kinds of bonuses, however, sometimes represent only a small component of overall producer cashflows, and therefore are not always very consequential to the producer, but can be of greater significance to the government departments that receive them. Such bonuses are therefore important, and should not be disregarded or roughly approximated in models, for a number of reasons:

- First, they often represent the earliest payments made to a government (under the terms of all types of petroleum fiscal regimes – tax and royalty systems, as well production sharing agreements). Often these are paid long before production starts (e.g., signature bonuses, and commerciality bonuses, covered in this chapter). As such, they have huge symbolic significance to governments.

- Second, bonuses which are paid before or at the start of production represent early outflows in a cashflow profile and, although usually relatively small, can have larger impacts on project discounted cashflow (i.e., NPV) than their undiscounted size suggests. Such early bonuses are highly regressive because the sums involved tend to be fixed and paid regardless of whether commodity prices are high or low, or whether a small or giant field, or a low-cost or high-cost field, is involved in generating the cashflow.

- Third, some bonuses are paid to specific government departments which might not receive any of the other fiscal revenues raised from taxes or royalties. These bonuses are very important to the receiving entity, and need to be calculated accurately and paid promptly by producers in order to maintain good relations.

There are many different types of bonuses triggered by specified events, during or before field production, with different objectives in mind. Some countries have used several different types of bonuses triggered by different events over the life of a petroleum agreement (e.g., Egypt). Other countries do not use them at all.

Bonuses of all types are almost always denominated as monetary sums in inflated or "money-of-the-day" ("MOD") terms, as specified by law or relevant agreements. For this reason, all monetary values in this chapter's example fields should be assumed to be in MOD dollars. They are usually not tax deductible (and often not cost recoverable under production sharing contracts, which we introduce in Chapter 6).

Simplifications Used in this Chapter

We cover a number of bonus structures in this chapter. Note that here, as we are concentrating on showing the basic bonus calculation methods, we model them on a simplified, "standalone" basis, i.e., we do not consider commerciality issues like the economic limit test (ELT). But bear in mind that in properly integrated valuation models such as those we'll see in later chapters, the use of the ELT *will* matter – it will determine whether some kinds of bonuses (e.g., those linked to levels cumulative production) even get paid at all.

4.2   COMMERCIALITY BONUSES

A **commerciality bonus** is a bonus paid when the producer decides, with the state's approval, to develop a project on the grounds that doing so will be economically profitable, or "commercial." In a project which starts with exploration, this occurs after:

- the successful exploration well(s) – and perhaps subsequent appraisal well(s) – have been drilled and tested;

- the volumes discovered have been estimated; and

- it has been determined that there is enough petroleum available for production, under pre-vailing product price assumptions, to provide the producer with sufficient economic profit (usually defined from the producer's standpoint as positive NPV), to make development worthwhile. This determination, depending on the regulations, might be the result of pre-liminary economic modeling, a field development feasibility study, or even a full-blown field development plan, incorporating reserves, production and cost profile projections.

The point at which the producer considers the field to be commercial, and has persuaded the state that this is the case, is often called the "declaration of commerciality," or **commerciality** for short. It is after commerciality that the producer then starts spending development capex (capital expenditure). Therefore in our example models here, **we assume commerciality occurs in the period when development capex is forecast to be incurred for the first time**. Commerciality in our examples therefore precedes development, but comes after all exploration and most, if not all, appraisal expenditure is incurred.

We show how to model the timing of a commerciality bonus in the file "Ch4_bonus_commerciality_example.xls." When you open this (like all files discussed in this book) be sure to choose to enable macros if asked whether to do so.

In the Assumptions section, you will find:

- the commerciality bonus amount (MOD $25 mm in cell E5, named "Bonus");

- various exploration and development capex items, before any timing adjustment (rows 8–13);

- a capex timing delay factor (cell D16, in a cell named "Delay"), which postpones the start date of all of the unadjusted capex by up to two years (we have set this to 0 years for now); and

- a "Show Base Scenario" button (row 15) to restore the default inputs if need be.

In the Calculations section:

- All capex items are time-shifted in rows 21–26 according to the delay factor, using the OFFSET function the same way we have done in Chapter 1 and in Chapter 3 (this is the reason for the blank columns G–I). This step is not necessary, but it helps us check that the model is doing what it should.

- The exploration/appraisal and development portions of time-adjusted capex are summed for each year (rows 28–29).

- The commerciality bonus is then calculated in two different ways – refer to Figure 4.1.

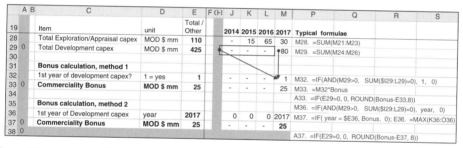

Figure 4.1   Commerciality bonus calculation, from the file, "Ch4_bonus_commerciality_example.xls"
Notes: (1) Some rows and columns are not shown. (2) Results shown reflect the Base Scenario.

Bonus Calculation Method 1

This is as follows:

- The annual formulas in row 32 determine whether the current year is the first year of development capex (which, again, we use as a proxy for the year of commerciality). In essence, the formulas check each year for whether there *is* development capex in the current year *and* whether there has *not* been any development capex in previous years. If both conditions are met, the answer is 1, meaning yes, it is the first year of development capex; otherwise, the answer is 0. Thus the formula for 2017 (cell M32), for example, is

$$=IF(AND(M29 > 0, SUM(\$I29{:}L29) = 0), 1, 0)$$

where $\boxed{\text{M29}}$ is 2017 development capex and $\boxed{\text{SUM(\$I29:L29)}}$ is the sum of all previous years' development capex. Row 32 will have at most only one year with a 1. The rest of the years will have a 0. In this case, 2017 is the first year of development capex (cell M32).

- The annual formulas in row 33 multiply the results in row 32 by the amount of the bonus. The MOD $25 mm commerciality bonus is thus paid in 2017 (cell M33).

- The checksum in cell A33 ensures that any commerciality bonus paid equals the amount it is stated to be in the Assumptions section.

Bonus Calculation Method 2

This is almost identical to Method 1:

- The annual formulas in row 36 give the *year* of commerciality, by checking each year whether there *is* development capex in the current year *and* whether there has been *no* prior development capex. If both conditions are met, the answer is the year; otherwise it is a 0. We see that the year is 2017 (cell M36).

- The formulas in row 37 say that if the current year is the commerciality year, as determined in row 36, then the answer is the amount of the commerciality bonus; otherwise it is 0. Again, we see that the MOD $25 mm bonus is paid in 2017 (cell M37).

- The checksum in cell A37 works the same way as the one in cell A33.

The checksum in cell A38 checks that the answer for both methods is the same.

Visual check

A simple visual check is provided in the chart which starts in row 40 (reproduced in Figure 4.2). Split the screen horizontally, so that you can see it in the bottom half and the delay factor (cell D16) in the top half. No matter which delay factor is chosen, the chart will show a commerciality bonus (a white column) occurring during the first year of development spending (as long as the commerciality bonus is not set to $0 (cell E5)).

Figure 4.2   Results under Base Scenario from the file "Ch4_bonus_commerciality_example.xls"

Exercises

- If you want practice calculating both the commerciality bonus and using the OFFSET function to simulate delays, go to the file "Ch4_bonus_com_offset_exercise_setup.xls" and fill in the blank cells.

- If you would prefer only to practice calculating the commerciality bonus, fill in the blanks in "Ch4_bonus_com_exercise_setup.xls." Note that until the exercise in this file is completed, the message in cell B1:C1 will indicate that there is an error; have a look at the formulas in the green-shaded checksum cells to see why.

Play with the delay factor while watching the chart provided in either file to see if the model seems to be behaving correctly, and then compare your results against those in "Ch4_bonus_com_exercise_solution.xls."

4.3 BONUSES PAYABLE AT FIRST COMMERCIAL PRODUCTION

Another, very common type of bonus is payable upon first **commercial production** (as distinct from early production from well tests).

Such bonuses, although often quite small in monetary terms, can be of great significance to governments. When a host government's head of state inaugurates a production facility at a high-profile ceremony, it is important that the government is seen to receive some immediate financial benefit associated with that event. A bonus paid at first commercial production can provide that largely symbolic immediate financial benefit.[1] Thus a bonus which the producer pays upon first commercial production helps offset the early perception that the producer is getting "too sweet" a deal.

Calculation/Exercise

This kind of bonus is calculated exactly the same way as the commerciality bonus, except that the "trigger" for the bonus payment is the period of first commercial production, rather than the first period of development spending. Try to calculate it in the file "Ch4_bonus_prod_exercise_setup.xls."

Again, until the exercise in this file is completed, the message in cell B1:C1 will indicate that there is an error. Check your answers against those in "Ch4_bonus_prod_exercise_solution.xls."

4.4 CUMULATIVE PRODUCTION BONUSES

As the name suggests, the trigger for these bonuses is when cumulative production reaches a specified level, also called a "milestone" or **threshold**.

---

[1] This can be especially important to governments using production sharing agreements, where – as we shall see later in Chapter 8 – the combined effect of cost recovery and profit sharing terms can mean that it is the producer, not the state, which receives most of the early cashflow.

Bonus #	Cumulative petroleum production threshold, mm boe	Bonus payment, MOD $ mm
1	20	10
2	30	15
3	40	40
4	50	60

Figure 4.3   Cumulative production bonus schedule, from "Ch4_bonus_prod_cuml_example.xls"

In Figure 4.3, from our example file "Ch4_bonus_prod_cuml_example.xls," is a typical cumulative bonus schedule for a combined oil and gas project, with production expressed in **barrels of oil equivalent ("boe,"** as explained in Section 1.2 of Chapter 1).

In the Assumptions section of the file, you will find:

- A factor for converting **cubic feet (cf)** of gas into boe (cell C11), which has been named "cf_gas_per_boe." This is set at a value of 6000, which is a commonly used approximation in the industry.[2]

- The bonus schedule (starting row 14), and shown in Figure 4.3 in which each threshold cell in column C has been named ("Threshold1," "Threshold2," etc.), as has each bonus payment cell in column D ("Bonus1," "Bonus2," etc.).

- In rows 22–23, unadjusted annual production assumptions for oil (in mm bbl, or mmb) and for gas (in **billions of cubic feet, or bcf**):

  o Note that columns F–K are for *forecast* production, from 2015 to 2020, while column E is for cumulative *historic* (i.e., as at December 31, 2014) production. The latter is important. Although when calculating NPV, we do not consider any *past* bonus payments which might have been based on historic production, we do consider any *future* bonus payments based on historic production (because historic production determines – and in some cases is the major share of – future cumulative production, which in turn is the trigger for future bonus payments).

  o Throughout the model, column D totals only the forecast years (except for cell D36, which is the maximum cumulative value of production, including historic production).

- A multiplier (cell C25) for adjusting the unadjusted production assumptions. Note that we adjust only forecast production, not historic production (which in a real model would be actual production historically recorded).

---

[2] In reality, each stream of natural gas is converted to boe based on its own unique energy content, which is determined by its chemical composition, and which is measured in terms of British thermal units (btu) per cubic foot (cf). More precise conversion factors in the range 5600–5800 cf/boe, linked to the exact composition of actual gas reservoirs, are also commonly used.

Calculation

In the first part of the Calculations section:

- future oil and gas production values are adjusted by the multiplier (rows 30–31);
- gas production is converted from bcf into mm boe (rows 32–33), which is then added to oil production (in mm bbl) to give, in row 34, total petroleum production (in mm boe);
- cumulative petroleum production (considering all years, history as well as forecast) is calculated in row 36. We have named the range E36:K36 – which includes historic as well as future production – "Cuml_prod." The result of 51.0 mm bbl in cell D36 is the maximum of cells E36:K36.

Next, we calculate the bonus payments. Refer to Figure 4.4.

The calculation method for all four bonus payments is identical. To save space, in Figure 4.4 we show only the calculations for Bonus Payments 1 and 2, and explain only Bonus 2 calculations in detail below.

The steps for all years, as well as for the History column, are as follows:

1. Determine whether the relevant threshold has been reached. For 2016 (cell G39), for example, the formula, $=IF(Cuml\_prod >= Threshold2, 1, 0)$ says that if cumulative petroleum production at the end of 2016 – referencing cell G36, by way of the named range, $Cuml\_prod$ – reaches or exceeds the threshold for Bonus 2 (which is $Threshold2$, in cell C16), then the answer is 1, meaning the threshold has been reached or exceeded; otherwise the answer is 0. In 2016, the result is 1.

	A	B	C	D	E	F G H	L M N O P
				Forecast Total / other	History (cuml.)	Forecast (annual) >>>	Typical formulae
	27	Calculations					
	28	Item	Unit			2015 2016 2017	
	34 0	Petroleum production	mm boe	30.4	20.6	9.2 7.5 6.2	G34. =G30+G33
	35						
	36 0	Cuml. petroleum production (incl. Historic)	mm boe	51.0	20.6	29.8 37.4 43.6	G36. =F36+G34
	37						
	38	Bonus 1 threshold reached?	1 = yes		1	1 1 1	G38. =IF(Cuml_prod>=Threshold1, 1, 0)
	39	Bonus 2 threshold reached?	1 = yes		-	- 1 1	G39. =IF(Cuml_prod>=Threshold2, 1, 0)
	42						
	43 0	Bonus 1 threshold reached for 1st time?	1 = yes	-	1	- - -	G43. =IF(AND(G38=1, SUM($E38:F38)=0),1, 0)
	44 0	Bonus 2 threshold reached for 1st time?	1 = yes	1	-	- 1 -	G44. =IF(AND(G39=1, SUM($E39:F39)=0),1, 0)
	47						
	48 0	Bonus 1 payment	MOD $ mm	-	10	- - -	G48. =G43*Bonus1
	49 0	Bonus 2 payment	MOD $ mm	15	-	- 15 -	G49. =G44*Bonus2
	50 0	Bonus 3 payment	MOD $ mm	40	-	- - 40	G50. =G45*Bonus3
	51 0	Bonus 4 payment	MOD $ mm	60	-	- - -	G51. =G46*Bonus4
	52	Total Bonus payments	MOD $ mm	115	10	- 15 40	G52. =SUM(G48:G51)

Figure 4.4 Calculation of cumulative production Bonuses 1 and 2, from "Ch4_bonus_prod_cuml_example.xls"
Notes: (1) Some rows and columns are not displayed. (2) Results shown here reflect a production multiplier (cell C25) setting of 100%.

2. Determine whether the relevant threshold has been reached *for the first time.* This step is to ensure that a given bonus is paid only once – i.e. the *first* year when its relevant threshold has been reached or exceeded – rather than *every* year it has been reached or exceeded. We could have included this step in step 1), but the result would have been a longer formula than we prefer. Here, the formulas are similar to those used in the Commerciality bonus calculation, in row 32 of Figure 4.1. Here, for 2016, for example (cell G44), the formula,

$$\boxed{\text{=IF(AND(G39 = 1, SUM(\$E39:F39) = 0), 1, 0)}}$$

says that if the Bonus 2 threshold has been reached in 2016 (meaning that cell $\boxed{\text{G39 = 1}}$) AND if row 39 has only zeroes for prior periods (including the History column), then the answer is 1, meaning, yes, 2016 is the first year the threshold has been reached or exceeded; otherwise the answer is 0. For 2016, the answer is 1. (Note: in the file you will see that the formula in E44 is unique in its row, as it doesn't reference prior years.)

3. Multiply the result in step 2) by the amount of the relevant Bonus payment. For 2016, the formula in cell G49 is $\boxed{\text{=G44*Bonus2}}$, where Bonus2 is the name of cell D16. The result is that the Bonus 2 payment of MOD $15 mm is paid in 2016.

Visual Check and Analysis

To see how the bonus payments behave under different production assumptions:

- scroll in the model so that the bonus schedule starting in row 14 is the first thing visible at the top of the screen;

- place the cursor in cell A27 and split the screen horizontally; and

- finally, scroll so that the chart starting in row 54 is visible in the bottom half of the screen. Be sure all columns are shown.

Note that the Y-axis scale is in MOD $ mm with reference to the bonus payments, and in mm boe with reference to cumulative production and bonus thresholds.

- Using the spinner control in cell C25, set the production multiplier to 0%. You will see that cumulative production is flat at 20.6 mm boe, reflecting only the historic production (which, again, is not affected by the multiplier). Because 20.6 mm boe is greater than the first bonus threshold of 20 mm boe, you will see that Bonus 1 is paid, but none of the others are.

- In steps of 10%, increase the multiplier from 0%. Note that in any year when one of the white diamonds reaches or crosses a threshold, the relevant bonus appears as payable in that year. For example, Bonus 2 finally appears in 2018, when the multiplier reaches 40%, which causes cumulative production in that year to reach 31.3 mm boe, crossing the Bonus 2 threshold of 30 mm boe for the first time.

- All four bonuses appear when the multiplier reaches 100%, as seen in Figure 4.5.

As you continue to increase the production multiplier, you will see that the bonuses occur sooner, sometimes even "doubling up" as more than one threshold is crossed for the first time

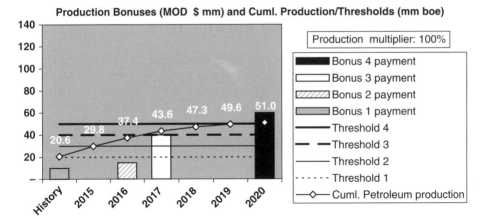

Figure 4.5 Cumulative production bonuses when production multiplier is set to 100%, from the file "Ch4_bonus_prod_cuml_example.xls"

in the same year – for example, when the multiplier is 180%, as shown in Figure 4.6. When the multiplier is set to 320%, the last three bonuses even "triple up" to all become payable in 2015.

It is key to this calculation to take historic production into account, to correctly determine cumulative production and thus to determine whether any past bonuses, based on the historic production, have already been paid.

Exercise

For practice, calculate the bonuses using the new assumed bonus schedule and production profile found in the file "Ch4_bonus_prod_cuml_exercise_setup.xls" and compare your answers to those in the file "Ch4_bonus_prod_cuml_exercise_solution.xls."

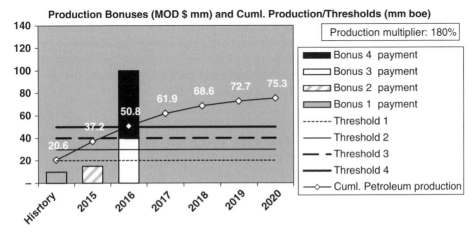

Figure 4.6 Cumulative production bonuses when production multiplier is set to 180%, from the file "Ch4_bonus_prod_cuml_example.xls"

4.5   BONUSES BASED ON THE CUMULATIVE VALUE OF PRODUCTION

Another kind of bonus, which we have seen used, for example, in Africa, is similar to the cumulative production bonus described above, in that bonus payments are triggered when cumulative production meets or exceeds specified thresholds. In this case, however, the *size* of the payment is not expressed as an absolute monetary amount, but rather as a percentage of the cumulative *value* of cumulative *production* at the time. Cumulative value for the example bonus regime used in this section is defined as cumulative gross revenue. An example is shown in Figure 4.7.

Production Bonus #	Cumulative production threshold, mm bbl	Bonus payable, % value of cuml. production
1	30	3.00%
2	60	2.00%
3	90	1.00%

Figure 4.7   Bonus schedule based on cumulative production value

Exercise/Analysis

An illustrative calculation based on this schedule is in the file "Ch4_bonus_cuml_value_prod_example.xls." The methodology is almost identical to that used in calculating cumulative production bonuses. Try filling in the blanks on the "Problem_setup" worksheet. Be sure to read the cell comments, and to apply the built-in multipliers (cells C16 and C17) to the forecast (though not historic) production and prices in rows 19 and 22, respectively. At the bottom of the sheet is a chart ready to display your results. Check your work against the "Solution" worksheet.

By playing with the spinners controlling production and prices while viewing the results, you can see that this type of bonus structure is progressive – to an extent, at least, in that it is based on gross revenue. The bonuses increase as the gross revenue from a given volume of production increases, while taking commodity prices into account – the producer pays a higher bonus on a given volume when prices are high, and a lower one when prices are low. It would be even more progressive if it were linked to some measure of "net revenue" (i.e., after deducting, say, any royalties and/or production costs from gross revenue), but we are only aware of countries using this method based on gross revenue.

4.6   BONUSES BASED ON THE PRODUCTION RATE FOR A SPECIFIED PERIOD

These are perhaps the most common type of production bonus. Calculating them is similar to calculating the two types of bonus we have just seen, in that you need to make bonuses payable when relevant thresholds have been reached or exceeded for the first time. In this case, however, the threshold is an *average* production rate, often expressed in barrels per day, over a certain period.

Again, to an extent, such bonus structures are progressive, in that they are only paid in a given period if the production thresholds are exceeded. But because these bonuses ignore prices and costs, it is possible sometimes for production volumes to exceed the threshold, requiring a bonus payment, even if low prices or high costs mean the production which triggers the payment has low or no profitability. Hence it is not a truly progressive mechanism.

Periodicity: Beware of "Averaging Out" Bonus Triggers

There is a potential calculation trap if there is a **periodicity mismatch** – that is, if the model is denominated in time periods which differ from the time periods on which the bonus thresholds are based.

An example is when you calculate, in an annual model, a bonus based on annual average production, even though the rules base bonuses on quarterly production.

It is often assumed as a matter of convenience – especially when the availability/quality of quarterly forecast data is not optimal – that the approximations inherent in annually modeling events which occur on more frequent basis are "close enough."

But some bonuses (as well as other fiscal elements) are required to be calculated on a monthly or quarterly basis for good reason: they can capture short-lived production or price spikes that would disappear when averaged over a full year.

Calculating everything on an annual basis, therefore, is only sound *sometimes*. Consider, for example, a simple case based on a Middle Eastern bonus regime, shown in Figure 4.8, in which a bonus is payable when production averages 25 m bbl/d or more for one quarter (cell C2). (Recall that the prefix "m" = 1000.)

	A	B	C	D	E
1					
2		Bonus is payable when production averages X m bbl / d for 1 quarter	25.0		
3		Days per year	365.0		
4		Quarters per year	4.0		
5		Days per quarter	91.3	C5. =C3/C4	
6					
7			Production		
8			m bbl / d	m bbl	
9		Quarter 1	3.0	274	
10		Quarter 2	17.0	1,551	
11		Quarter 3	29.0	2,646	
12		Quarter 4	27.0	2,464	
13		Annual	19.0	6,935	
14					
15			C13. =D13/C3	D13. =SUM(D9:D12)	

Figure 4.8 Potential error when mixing calculation and bonus threshold periods, from the "Simple_ QuarterlyVsAnnual" sheet of the file "Ch4_bonus_prod_monthly_avg_daily_rate_example.xls"

In the field's first production year, production starts low in Quarter 1, at an average rate of 3 m bbl/d (i.e., 3000 barrels per day), but quickly ramps up to average 29 m bbl/d by Quarter 3 (cells C9 and C11). In a quarterly model, this would be no problem – because 29 m bbl/d exceeds 25 m bbl/d, the bonus would be calculated as payable in Quarter 3. But an annual model would miss this payment, because production for the full year would average only 19 m bbl/d (cell C13).

"Well, true" – an analyst working for the producer, using an annual model, might argue – "but assuming that the next year's production rate levels out at around the rate of 27 m bbl/d seen in Quarter 4 of this year, the model will calculate the bonus as being payable the next year, so no great harm is done."

• This argument would certainly not impress a government that would have effectively not been paid a bonus when it was due.

• We would also counter that this distortion could in fact be material to a producer's NPV, because a bonus payment made this year would be discounted (by a discount factor) less heavily than a bonus payment made next year. So the annual model would understate the discounted value of the bonus, thus overstating NPV. Moreover, as we have seen in Chapter 1, the difference between two consecutive years' discount rates is more pronounced when those two years are early in the valuation period (as in our present example, concerning the first two production years) than when they occur later in the valuation period. So in this case, the annual model's result would be especially distorted.

Advice on dealing with periodicity mismatches

• Model annually (the gains in keeping the model at a manageable size are worthwhile) as long as there is no potential for material distortions like the one described here.

• If there is such potential, but it is because only relatively few special items in the model require calculations on a basis which is more frequent than annual, do not make the whole model annual. Rather, model only these special items on the time basis they require. Push your sources to supply data, or make credible estimates, for the relevant parameters in the time format needed, especially in the early valuation years.

• If you do calculate certain fiscal elements on a shorter timeframe, try to do it on a separate worksheet, which is fed inputs from, and which then feeds results back to, the main worksheet. Mixing timeframes on the same worksheet can lead to serious errors.

Exercise: Comparing Exact and "Close Enough" Bonus Calculation Methods, Using Data Supplied in a "Real-World" Format

The example above, based on one year of data and one bonus threshold, is short and simple. We provide a larger, more realistic data set on the "Assumptions sheet" of the file "Ch4_bonus_prod_monthly_avg_daily_rate_example.xls."

In addition to reiterating the point about the potential for distortions when mixing periodicity, this exercise also introduces two useful Excel functions: SUMIF and TRANSPOSE.

It also gives a useful taste of dealing with data received in a real-world format, as opposed to the relatively "clean" assumptions we have been spoiling you with so far.

On the "Assumptions" sheet of the file, you will find the bonus schedule shown in Figure 4.9. The first time the average *daily* production rate reaches or exceeds a threshold in the first column for *one month*, the corresponding bonus in the second column is payable.

Average monthly production, m bbl/d	Bonus, MOD $mm
10.00	1.0
15.00	5.0
20.00	10.0

Figure 4.9   Bonus schedule based on the average daily production rate for one month, from the "Assumptions" sheet of the file "Ch4_bonus_prod_monthly_avg_daily_rate_example.xls"

On the same sheet is a five-year production forecast, expressed in m bbl/month.[3] The raw data are in a vertical format and are depicted in Figure 4.10.

On the "Calculations" worksheet, our ultimate goal is to compare:

• the results when bonus payments are calculated based on monthly averages (i.e., following the rules strictly) against

• results based on the approximation of annual averages (i.e., the "should be good enough" approach).

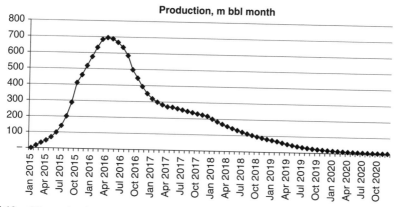

Figure 4.10   Oil production forecast, m bbl/month, from the "Assumptions" sheet of the file "Ch4_bonus_prod_monthly_avg_daily_rate_example.xls"

---

[3] This is not unrealistic – we have seen some engineers provide forecasts in rather unusual units, including barrels per 2.4 hours. In fact production data in many production accounting systems are reported routinely for each field or reservoir on a barrels/month basis, so reservoir engineers frequently fit production decline curves to this basis.

Links to sections

Adjustment of monthly data
Conversion to annual (using simple SUM formulae)
Conversion to annual (using SUMIF)
Conversion to bbl/day
Transposition to "landscape" format and bonus calculation
Comparison of monthly and annual methods

Figure 4.11   Steps involved in this exercise

Doing this takes a number of steps. There are hyperlinks to each step in cells B4:B9, shown in Figure 4.11.

As many of the steps are straightforward, with typical formulas displayed throughout the sheet, we will be selective about which ones we examine in detail here.

Adjustment of Monthly Data

This section merely uses a multiplier (cell C16 on the "Calculations" sheet) to adjust the raw monthly production data from the "Assumptions" sheet. The vertical format is retained.

Conversion to Annual (Using the Simple SUM Function)

This is just a matter of summing the adjusted monthly production volumes for each of the five years, using the SUM function. Use the audit function to trace the precedents for each of the five formulas in cells H19:H24 to see that they are correct. Because this is only a five-year production forecast, manually selecting the cells to sum is not hard, but if it were a more typical, 10–20(+)-year forecast, it would become tedious, and easy to make a mistake.

Conversion to Annual (Using SUMIF)

It is easier to convert the monthly data to annual data using the SUMIF function. As the name implies, this function sums values if they meet certain criteria. It works somewhat like a VLOOKUP or HLOOKUP function (discussed in Section 3.2 of Chapter 3), although rather than returning a single value within a specified range, it sums values within a specified range which meet specified criteria.

Although some find the SUMIF syntax to be slightly awkward, we find it a useful function for some modeling purposes. The syntax is:

=SUMIF ([a range of cells which may contain any number of different values, but includes a specified criteria value],

[the specified criteria value, i.e., an "instruction" of what to look for],

[a range of cells, corresponding to the range mentioned in the first expression, which contains the values to be summed])

	A	B	C	D	E	F	G	H	I	J K L
1	0	No errors found								
2		**Data**				**Calculations**				**Formulae used**
3		(Criteria)	(Criteria)	Value			Criteria	Summed Value		
4		Year	Quarter	$		Sum values by year – using SUM		$		
5		2017	1	33		Total for year...	2015	350		H5. =SUM(D10,D12,D13,D14,D16,D17,D20,D21)
6		2016	3	27		Total for year...	2016	187		H6. =SUM(D6,D9,D11,D19)
7		2017	4	9		Total for year...	2017	172		H7. =SUM(D5,D7,D8,D15,D18)
8		2017	1	52		Sum values by year – using SUMIF		$		
9	0	2016	4	45		Total for year...	2015	350		H9. =SUMIF(Years, G9, Values)
10	0	2015	2	97		Total for year...	2016	187		H10. =SUMIF(Years, G10, Values)
11	0	2016	4	71		Total for year...	2017	172		H11. =SUMIF(Years, G11, Values)
12		2015	2	79		Sum values by quarter – using SUM		$		
13		2015	3	49		Total for quarter...	1	163		H13. =SUM(D5,D8,D15,D17,D20)
14		2015	2	63		Total for quarter...	2	278		H14. =SUM(D10,D12,D14,D16,D21)
15		2017	1	55		Total for quarter...	3	120		H15. =SUM(D6,D13,D19)
16		2015	2	3		Total for quarter...	4	148		H16. =SUM(D7,D9,D11,D18)
17		2015	1	7		Sum values by quarter – using SUMIF		$		
18	0	2017	4	23		Total for quarter...	1	163		H18. =SUMIF(Quarters, G18, Values)
19	0	2016	3	44		Total for quarter...	2	278		H19. =SUMIF(Quarters, G19, Values)
20	0	2015	1	16		Total for quarter...	3	120		H20. =SUMIF(Quarters, G20, Values)
21	0	2015	2	36		Total for quarter...	4	148		H21. =SUMIF(Quarters, G21, Values)
22		↑								
23										
24		**Named ranges above:**				A9. =ROUND(H9-H5,8)		A18. =ROUND(H18-H13,8)		
25		**Name**	**Cells**			A10. =ROUND(H10-H6,8)		A19. =ROUND(H19-H14,8)		
26		Quarters	C5:C21			A11. =ROUND(H11-H7,8)		A20. =ROUND(H20-H15,8)		
27		Values	D5:D21					A21. =ROUND(H21-H16,8)		
28		Years	B5:B21							

Figure 4.12   From "Ch4_SUMIF_example.xls"

If that sounds a bit abstract, refer to the following example from the file, "Ch4_SUMIF_example.xls," shown in Figure 4.12.

In the Data columns, we have some dollar values (column D). They are meaningless; they are just for this example. The corresponding years and quarters are in a scrambled order. Some year + quarter combinations occur more than once, although with different dollar values. We want to sum the values two different ways: by year and by quarter (regardless of the year, i.e., we want to total all values which occur in, say, any third quarter).

Column H shows the calculations, using both the simple SUM function and the SUMIF function.

Using SUM is simple but tedious – each formula in cells H5:H7 and H13:H16 is unique and has to be "manually" constructed.[4]

Using SUMIF, on the other hand, is – once you get used to it – simple and fast. To make the example SUMIF formulas in Figure 4.12 easier to read and write, first we have prepared our raw data in columns B:D, by creating some named ranges. The names and the ranges they apply to are listed in cells B25:C28.

---

[4] One way to check that, for a given set of period calculations (e.g., for the yearly totals in cells H5:H7), you have used each data value in column D once, and only once, is to use Excel's Trace Precedents command (in Excel 2003: Tools/Formula Auditing/Trace Precedents; in Excel 2007 and Excel 2010: Formulas tab/Formula Auditing/Trace Precedents). Go to cell H5 and trace the precedents; then, without erasing the blue audit lines which will appear, do the same in cells H6 and H7. You will see that every value in column D has been referenced once. The lines can be simply erased when auditing is complete (in Excel 2003: by going to Tools/Formula Auditing/Remove All Arrows; in Excel 2007 and Excel 2010: Formulas tab/Formula Auditing/Remove Arrows).

As discussed in Chapter 1, we find these audit commands so useful generally that we have provided Excel macros which let you run the Trace Precedents command by pressing Ctrl+q; Trace Dependents with Ctrl+a; and erase lines with Ctrl+w.

Let us look at the SUMIF-calculated total for 2015 (cell H9) as an example. This uses the formula $\boxed{\text{=SUMIF(Years, G9, Values)}}$. It looks in the $\boxed{\text{Years}}$ range for the year specified in cell $\boxed{\text{G9}}$, which is 2015. Whenever it finds a 2015, it takes note of the value from the $\boxed{\text{Values}}$ range in the corresponding row and, in the end, sums these values. You can see that the result of this SUMIF formula, $350 (cell H9), matches that of the simple SUM function in cell H5.

Summing by quarter uses the same principle. To sum all values corresponding to all years' Quarter 1 (cell H18), for example, we use the formula $\boxed{\text{=SUMIF (Quarters, G18, Values)}}$.

Let us now put SUMIF to use in our royalty example file "Ch4_bonus_prod_monthly_avg_daily_rate_example.xls." Refer to Figure 4.13.

In cell U19, for example, we calculate 2015 total production with the formula $\boxed{\text{=SUMIF(Q\$19:Q\$90, T19, R\$19:R\$90)}}$, which looks in the range $\boxed{\text{Q19:Q90}}$ for the value of 2015 (cell $\boxed{\text{T19}}$) and sums the corresponding production values in the range $\boxed{\text{R19:R90}}$. In cell U27, you will find a checksum formula (not displayed in Figure 4.13) which shows that the result in cell U25 equals the result in cell H25 obtained by using the simple SUM formula in the previous step.

Exercise

To be sure you are comfortable with using SUMIF, try to fill in the blank dollar value cells on the "Setup" sheet of "Ch4_SUMIF_exercise.xls" where we have prepared 20 years of monthly values to sum, using both SUM and SUMIF. Compare your answers to those on the "Solution" sheet. We hope it will convert you seeing the SUMIF function's benefits.

Conversion to bbl/day

This step is needed to put both the monthly and annual production data into the same units as the bonus schedule. It is very simple. We assume that there are 365.25 days per year (cell AE15), and 365.25/12 = 30.44 days per month (cell AE16). We divide the monthly data (in m bbl) in cells AE19:AE90 by 30.44 and the annual data (in m bbl) in cells AH19:AH24 by 365.25, to get average production rates in m bbl/d.

Transposition to "Landscape" Format and Bonus Calculation

Recall that we have received our raw data in vertical format. We need to get the data into the horizontal format used in our model, i.e., we need to **transpose** the data. The following two simple examples – unrelated to our bonus calculation, and used for illustration only – show both the slow, tedious, manual way, and the fast, easy way using the TRANSPOSE function.

In Figure 4.14, taken from the "Transposition example" sheet of our file, we have raw data in cells A4:B8.

We have transposed the data manually in cells D3:H4. This requires entering a unique formula in each cell, as there is no easy, reliable way to write one formula for the job in cell D3,

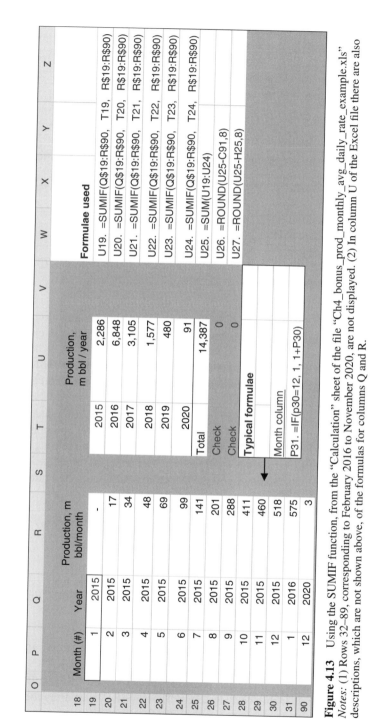

	Month (#)	Year	Production, m bbl/month		Production, m bbl / year		Formulae used
18							
19	1	2015	-	2015	2,286		U19. =SUMIF(Q$19:R$90, T19, R$19:R$90)
20	2	2015	17	2016	6,848		U20. =SUMIF(Q$19:R$90, T20, R$19:R$90)
21	3	2015	34	2017	3,105		U21. =SUMIF(Q$19:R$90, T21, R$19:R$90)
22	4	2015	48	2018	1,577		U22. =SUMIF(Q$19:R$90, T22, R$19:R$90)
23	5	2015	69	2019	480		U23. =SUMIF(Q$19:R$90, T23, R$19:R$90)
24	6	2015	99	2020	91		U24. =SUMIF(Q$19:R$90, T24, R$19:R$90)
25	7	2015	141	Total	14,387		U25. =SUM(U19:U24)
26	8	2015	201	Check	0		U26. =ROUND(U25-C91,8)
27	9	2015	288	Check	0		U27. =ROUND(U25-H25,8)
28	10	2015	411	Typical formulae			
29	11	2015	460				
30	12	2015	518	Month column			
31	1	2016	575	P31. =IF(p30=12, 1, 1+P30)			
90	12	2020	3				

Figure 4.13 Using the SUMIF function, from the "Calculation" sheet of the file "Ch4_bonus_prod_monthly_avg_daily_rate_example.xls" *Notes:* (1) Rows 32–89, corresponding to February 2016 to November 2020, are not displayed. (2) In column U of the Excel file there are also descriptions, which are not shown above, of the formulas for columns Q and R.

	A	B	C	D	E	F	G	H
1	Original data			Data transposed – manually				
2								
3	Year	Data		1900	1901	1902	1903	1904
4	1900	0		0	1	2	3	4
5	1901	1		Formulae used:				
6	1902	2		D3. =A4	E3. =A5	F3. =A6	G3. =A7	H3. =A8
7	1903	3		D4. =B4	E4. =B5	F4. =B6	G4. =B7	H4. =B8
8	1904	4						
9				Data transposed – using TRANSPOSE function				
10								
11				1900	1901	1902	1903	1904
12				0	1	2	3	4
13				Formula used in array:				
14				{=TRANSPOSE(A4:B8)}				

Figure 4.14   How to transpose, from the "Transposition example" sheet of the file "Ch4_bonus_prod_ monthly_avg_daily_rate_example.xls"

for example, which then could be copied to the rest of the cells. Imagine doing this for two columns of data spanning 20 years – that would be 40 individual formulas to enter and check.

Next, we have used the TRANSPOSE function in the range (or array) D11:H12. We have used a single formula – a special kind, known as an **array formula**, which we entered as follows:

- The original data, in cells A4:B8, are two columns wide by five rows deep, so place the cursor in cell D11 and select a range which is the opposite – five columns wide by two rows deep (here, the range D11:H12). (*Tip*: In Excel 2003, when you select a range which is larger than 10 columns by 10 rows, a small message box appears (sometimes at the extreme left side of the screen) which shows you the dimensions of the selected range. This is not the case, however, in Excel 2007.)

- With this whole range selected, type an "=" sign. This will appear at the start of the array (cell D11).

- After the "=" sign, type TRANSPOSE(A4:B8) .

- *Do not* press Enter; instead, press **Ctrl + Shift + Enter**. The data from cells A4:B8 will appear in transposed form in cells D11:H12. Note that the "Ctrl + Shift + Enter" command is used by Excel to enter formulas as **array formulas**.

Special characteristics of array formulas. After you have entered this array formula:

- Select, say, cell D11. In the formula bar, you will see {=TRANSPOSE(A4:B8)} . Note that the formula now appears within curly brackets. These mean it is an array formula.

- You will see the same thing in the formula bar, no matter which cell within D11:H12 you select.

- The cells within the array D11:H12 are now "locked together" – you cannot add rows or columns anywhere on the sheet which would cause the array to split up. For example, select cell E12 and, in Excel 2003, go to Insert/Rows, or Insert/Columns (in Excel 2007, go to Home/Cells/Insert/Insert Sheet Rows or Insert Sheet Columns), or select any cell inside or outside the array, but within columns E:G (such as H16), and try to insert a column. In any of these cases, you will get an error message saying, "You cannot change part of an array." **Thus the tradeoff against the benefits of using array formulas is that they limit your subsequent worksheet layout flexibility**. So think carefully where and when you use them. (For large amounts of data to transpose it can be worthwhile using a separate worksheet to perform the transposition, using the Transpose array function, and then Copy/Paste Special the data as input, unencumbered by the array formula constraints, into the main worksheet to be used for further analysis.)

* * *

With our bonus example in the "Calculation" worksheet, we have used the TRANSPOSE function in cells AR25:DK26 and AR55:AW56 to transpose, respectively, the monthly and annual production data (in m bbl/d) from vertical to horizontal formats.

Next, we have calculated the bonuses on a monthly and annual basis in the sections starting in cells AR28 and AR58, respectively. For each set of calculations, we use the same method as that used in Section 4.4 on cumulative production bonuses – we cause the bonus payments to be made in the periods when production reaches or exceeds, for the first time, the relevant thresholds from the bonus schedule. The only difference is that in Section 4.4 the bonus triggers were cumulative, absolute volumes, whereas here, they are average daily rates.

Total bonus payments are found starting in cells AO45 and AO69.

Comparison of Monthly and Annual Methods' Results

Finally, we can compare the bonuses calculated on each basis, in the section starting in cell AO79. The results confirm what we have already seen in our simplified example at the start of this exercise – that the annual basis, "close enough" shortcut method can be materially wrong.

Set the production multiplier (using a duplicate, in cell AP80, of the spinner control in cell C16) to 100%. The charts will look like those in Figure 4.15. The monthly average production curve crosses Threshold 3, but the annual average production does not reach it, as the highest values have been averaged down. As a result, bonuses total \$16 mm using the monthly method (cell AP83), but only \$6 mm using the annual method (cell AP84). You will also see discrepancies between the monthly and annual methods when the multiplier is set to 90%, 80%, 70% and 50%.

Exercise

Try calculating, at the very least, the production bonuses based on monthly average production rates, using the assumptions in the file "Ch4_bonus_prod_monthly_avg_daily_rate_exercise_setup.xls," which has a structure mimicking that of our example file. We have

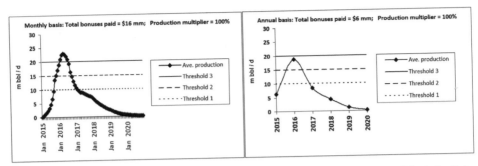

Figure 4.15   Comparison of monthly and annual total bonus calculations, from the "Calculation" sheet of the file "Ch4_bonus_prod_monthly_avg_daily_rate_example.xls"

provided the production data, the bonus schedule, the spinner controls and the charts – you only need to fill in the blanks. If you are in a sporting mood, also calculate the bonuses based on the (with respect) lazy and sloppy "close enough" method, based on annual averages. We promise some real drama for those who compare the results of the two methods when the multiplier is set at 100%. Check your results against those in "Ch4_bonus_prod_monthly_avg_daily_rate_exercise_solution.xls."

Chapter 5

Abandonment

5

Abandonment

5.1 INTRODUCTION

Basic Concepts and Terms

As discussed in Chapter 1, abandonment costs are the costs of abandoning wells and facilities and cleaning up and restoring the production site after production ends. They are also referred to as "decommissioning" or "site restoration" costs.

Although rules for funding abandonment take many forms, there are two basic kinds of abandonment regimes. One requires a single "lumpsum" payment at the end of the production. We term this payment an **abandonment payment**. For any given project, we will always express this in the singular. The abandonment payment can occur in the last year of economic production (or "commercial production" – we use the terms interchangeably) – or sometimes later, if there is a delay between this last year and the actual decommissioning activity.

The other kind of abandonment regime also requires a single abandonment payment to be made at the end of production, but requires – or permits – the payment to be funded in advance, by periodic contributions which the producer makes over the production period, before the actual abandonment payment is due. We term these periodic contributions **abandonment contributions**.

Avoid Double-Counting Cash Outflows

When modeling a regime in which there are no abandonment contributions, but rather only one lumpsum abandonment payment, the payment is counted as a cash outflow from the producer's perspective, and is discounted accordingly when determining project NPV.

In contrast, when modeling a regime in which abandonment contributions fund a later abandonment payment, it is important to bear in mind that – while we calculate both the contributions and the payment – we only count the periodic contributions as cash outflows. To count both the contributions and the payment would be double-counting:

- Once a producer has made an abandonment contribution to an account – either a normal bank account (or a purpose-specific escrow account, trust fund, bond, etc.) – the producer may no longer use it; it is no longer part of the producer's discretionary cash. Thus the dates when *contributions* are made are when the cash outflows, from the producer's perspective, occur; these contributions are what are discounted when calculating the producer's NPV.

- Whereas when the abandonment *payment* – which is made up of money to which the producer has already said goodbye – is made later, the payment does flow out of the account to pay the decommissioning contractor, but this is not an outflow from the producer's perspective, and is not discounted when calculating project NPV.

The only exceptions to these principles occur if, for whatever reason, the cumulative abandonment contributions either are too small to meet the actual abandonment costs, or exceed those costs. In these cases, adjustments that *do* constitute cashflows to the producer are necessary:

- If the abandonment contributions are too small, then the difference, to be made up at abandonment time, will be a cash outflow for the producer.

- If the abandonment contributions exceed requirements, then the difference will constitute a cash inflow for the producer in the form of cash returned, unless regulations state that those contributions are already assigned to the government to conduct the abandonment operations. Then, surplus funds may not return to the producer.

As the examples in this chapter show how abandonment contributions can be calibrated to ensure they match the amount needed for the abandonment payment, we do not treat these exceptional cases. But you should be aware of them. After all, our examples here are based on forecasts, which are inherently fallible.

How We Will Handle the Economic Limit in This Chapter

An abandonment payment occurs after economic production ends, which in turn depends on the economic limit, i.e., the last year in which production is economic. As we have seen in Chapter 1, determining the economic limit requires its own calculation (i.e., the calculation of the economic limit test, or "ELT"). Because in this chapter we want to concentrate on the mechanics of calculating abandonment funding, however, here **we will simply state the economic limit as an input assumption**. This is of course not sound practice for full economic models, but for these abandonment-focused illustrative models, it allows us to avoid unnecessary, distracting detail.

Thus in this chapter's models, you will see message boxes, with arrows pointing to input cells for the last economic production year, which say "normally this would be calculated," or words to this effect.

This will get our present lessons across, as the calculations we explain here depend on the economic limit date, not on whether that date is merely stated or properly calculated. (Just remember that when doing full modeling, the date does need to be properly calculated!)

5.2 LUMPSUM ABANDONMENT PAYMENTS

An example calculation of a lumpsum abandonment payment at the end of production, with no prior abandonment contributions, is shown in the file "Ch5_aband_lumpsum_w inflation.xls."

The basic strategy is as follows:

1. To use the economic life flag (ELF) to *time the abandonment payment*. Recall from Chapter 1 that the ELF is an expression of the economic limit, in the form of a row of annual 1s and 0s ("a binary flag"), where a 1 means the field is still economic and thus "alive," and a 0 means it is no longer economic and thus "dead."

2. To *adjust the size of the payment* according to an assumed inflation rate.

> Refer to the file "Ch5_aband_lumpsum_w inflation.xls," the Base Scenario of which is reproduced in **Figure 5.1**, found on page 1 of the file "Ch5_aband_supplement.pdf."

Our assumptions include:

- a production forecast (before considering the economic limit) in row 4;

- the economic limit in cell D5;

- whether the abandonment payment is paid in the same year as the last economic production year, or one year later (cell D7);

- the abandonment payment in Real 2015 $ mm (cell D8) – recall from Chapter 1 that this is the format in which analysts are most likely to receive abandonment cost estimates; and

- an inflation rate (cell D9), used to convert Real 2015 dollars into MOD ("money-of-the-day," or inflated) dollars.

In the Calculations section:

- The formulas in row 11 make the ELF a 1 in the years up to and including the last economic production year (cell D5, or 2021 in our Base Scenario example), and a 0 in the years thereafter. We have named the range F11:N11, "ELF".

- Post-ELF production in each year (row 13) equals pre-ELF production (row 4) times the ELF; this has the effect of truncating post-ELF production, in our example, to end in 2021.

- The timing of the abandonment payment is calculated in cell D14 as the sum of the last economic production year (cell D5) and any delay in making the abandonment payment (cell D7; or one year, in our example, meaning the payment will occur in 2022).

- The formulas in row 15 place the abandonment payment, in Real 2015 dollars (Real 2015 $50 mm in our example), in time according to the result in cell D14.

- The MOD dollar abandonment payment in row 17 (MOD $60.2 mm, in our example) is the inflated version of the results in row 15, calculated using a mid-year inflation index, as described in Section 1.2 of Chapter 1.

Split the screen so that the spinners which control the last production year, the abandonment payment delay factor and the inflation rate are visible at the top of the screen, and the interactive chart starting in row 27 (reproduced in Figure 5.2) is visible at the bottom. This will show you that the model is working as it should.

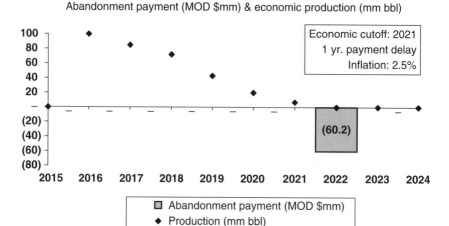

Figure 5.2   Basic lumpsum abandonment calculation, from the file "Ch5_aband_lumpsum_w infla-tion.xls"
Note: Reflects the Base Scenario settings.

(Note that the scale on the Y-axis (from -80 to 100) is in MOD $ mm when referring to the gray column, and is in mm bbl when referring to the black diamonds.)

Does production respond properly to changes in the economic limit? Does the payment timing? Does it make sense that the earlier the payment occurs, the lower its value is?

5.3   EQUAL ABANDONMENT CONTRIBUTIONS MADE OVER THE PRODUCTION PERIOD

As mentioned, producers are often required to fund the abandonment payment through periodic abandonment contributions, made prior to the actual decommissioning. According to one basic variant of this approach, the contributions must be the same size, and must be made each year of the economic production period.

It is important, in both this and the following sections, to clarify the term "production period." In an annual model, we define the **economic production period** as all years starting from the first year in which there is economic production, through the last year in which there is economic production, inclusive.

This might sound obvious, but we spell this out to emphasize that the economic production *period* is *not* defined simply as any period during which economic production occurs, because this definition would then exclude any intervening production "gap period(s)" during which there is no production, due to maintenance or some other interruption. (Granted, in an annual model, any year-long production gap(s) would be very unusual; nonetheless, it is good practice to make the model robust enough to handle them.)

This is important to get right because the number of abandonment contributions equals the number of years in the economic production *period*, not the number of years of economic production. For example, if the economic production period is 10 years, and includes one year of no production, there will be 10 equal abandonment contributions, not nine.

Calculation

> Refer to the file "Ch5_aband_eq pmnts over prod life.xls," the Base Scenario of which is reproduced in **Figure 5.3**, found on page 3 of the file "Ch5_aband_supplement.pdf."

As shown in Figure 5.3, the Assumptions section is the same as in the previous model. In the Calculations section, the basic strategy is:

- To use (as in the last example) the ELF (again, the economic life flag) to time the Real $ abandonment payment, thereby inflating it to MOD $.

- To define the economic production period, which allows us to:

   ○ divide the MOD $ value of the abandonment *payment* into the number of years in this period;

   ○ then use this to determine the number, timing and MOD $ value of equal annual abandonment *contributions*.

The steps shown in Figure 5.3 are as follows:

- The ELF and the post-ELF production profile (ending in 2021) are calculated straightforwardly in rows 10 and 12.

- Each of the annual cells in row 13 use the same formula to determine the <u>first year of the economic production period</u>.

   ○ For example, the formula for 2016 (cell G13) is

   =IF(AND(G12>0, SUM($E12:F12)=0), year, 0) .

   ○ This means that if production in 2016 (cell G12) is greater than 0, AND if the sum of production in all previous years – that is, the sum of cells $E12:F12 – equals 0, then the year corresponding to G12 is the first year of "non-zero" production; i.e. it is the year production starts.

      - When both conditions are met, the result of the formula is the corresponding year within the named range, year (cells F2:N2). Because both conditions are met in our example formula in cell G13, the answer in cell G13 is **2016**.

      - In each of the other annual cells in row 13, both conditions are never met simultaneously met, so the answer in each of these cells is 0.

○ Therefore, there will only one non-zero value in the annual cells of row 13, and this value will be the year of first production. This example's answer of **2016** is then "captured" in cell D13, with the formula =SUM(F13:N13).

○ Note that the annual formulae in row 13 all refer to the blank cell E12. This is intentional. This cell should be kept blank.

- Cell D14 equates the last year of the economic production period to the last economic production year as defined in cell D5 (so, 2021), unless there is no economic production at all, in which case the last economic production year is defined as 0. The latter provision is there in case the model user carelessly changes the production assumptions in row 4 to end before the last economic assumption year in cell D5.

- The annual cells in row 15 create binary flags to show whether a given year falls within the economic production *period* (as distinct from showing each year of economic *production*; as mentioned above, we would not want the model to be "fooled" by any gaps in economic production). If the year is between the economic production period start and end years, inclusive, the flag is a 1, meaning the year is within the economic production period; otherwise it is a 0. We will call this formula the Period-flag formula. The period flags are then summed in cell D15 to give the number of years in the period (six years in this example).

- The timing of the abandonment payment and its conversion from Real 2015 $ to MOD $ are determined in rows 16–19, in the same way as in the example from Section 5.2.

- The MOD $ value of each equivalent annual abandonment contribution is calculated in cell D20. It is equal to the MOD $ value of the abandonment payment (cell D19), divided by the number of years in the economic production period. In our example, this is MOD $60.17 mm/ 6 = MOD $10.03 mm. (Note in cell D20, for example, the use of the Error-trap expression =IF(D15=0, 0, ... to suppress error messages in case total economic production is 0.)

○ Note further that the abandonment *payment* delay factor of one year (cell D6) will not affect the *timing* of the annual abandonment *contributions* – these occur over each year of the economic production period, regardless of when the actual abandonment payment is made.

○ The delay factor, however, *will* affect the equal *value* of each annual abandonment *contribution*, because this value is based on the MOD $ value of the abandonment *payment*, which, due to inflation, will be lower in early years and higher in later years.

- The formulas in the annual cells in row 21 calculate the abandonment contributions as the value reached in cell D20, times the relevant year's economic production period flag (in row 15). The result in our example is that payments of MOD $10.03 mm are made between 2016 and 2021, inclusive.

- *Crucially*, note that the checksum formula in cell A21 ensures that the sum of the MOD $ abandonment contributions (cell D21) equals the MOD value of the abandonment payment (cell D17). Reaching that result is the point of the whole exercise!

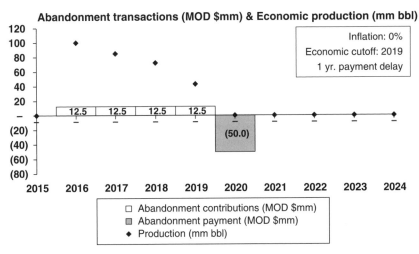

Figure 5.4 Implementing Step 5 (with economic cutoff set to 2019) in "Ch5_aband_eq pmnts over prod life.xls"

Visual Check

Arrange the screen so that rows 5–8 are visible, along with the chart starting in row 32, shown in Figure 5.4. (Note that only the white columns represent actual cash outflows from the producer's perspective, as discussed in the subsection "Avoid Double-Counting Cash Outflows," above.) Does the chart behave sensibly when you make the following cumulative changes?

1. Use the button in row 6 to show the Base Scenario. Scroll the economic limit (cell D5) from 2021 to 2016. (Are the absolute values of the two columns equivalent?)
2. Change the abandonment payment delay (cell D6) from 1 year to 0.
3. Set the economic cutoff to 2022.
4. Set the abandonment payment delay to 1.
5. Set inflation (cell D8) to 0%. These are now Real 2015 dollars. You can easily work out mentally that the abandonment contributions sum to the abandonment payment, when the economic cutoff year is set to 2020, 2019, 2017 or 2016.

Handling Cases with Prior Production, or When Forecasts Change

Be sure to account for any production years/abandonment contributions occurring prior to the period modeled. Just as such prior production was relevant to our calculation of fiscal mechanisms covered in Chapters 2 and 3, such as royalties and bonuses based on cumulative production, respectively, it matters here as well. This is because prior production determines the number of total years in the economic production period, thus influencing the size of each future annual contribution. Contributions already paid also influence the size of each future annual contribution. We will treat this soon in a new example.

Interpret the term "equal contributions" loosely. The size of each contribution equals the total abandonment payment (in MOD), divided by the number of years in the economic production period. This period, as the name suggests, is based on the economic (post-ELT) production forecast. Thus, in models where there is no prior production to account for (such as our last example), the producer must base the size of each annual contribution on its *forecast* of when the economic limit will kick in, triggering abandonment. In practice, this forecast will often change over the course of the field life, as more becomes known about actual costs and production capacity, as well as in response to the commodity price outlook. If the forecast of the abandonment date changes once production has started, then the annual contributions actually made will not be equivalent after all.

To illustrate, suppose that three years after a producer made the model shown in the last example, the producer decided that the economic limit would actually be in 2020, not 2021 as originally forecast. No other assumptions changed. On page 4 of the file, "Ch5_aband_supplement.pdf", Figure 5.5, from the file "mod_aband_02_eq pmnts over prod life_v07b_forecast changes.xls," shows how this new model, dated January 1, 2018, would look.

> Refer to the file "Ch5_aband_eq pmnts over prod life_forecast_changes.xls." Click the "Show Revised Base Scenario" button in row 8 to obtain the view reproduced in **Figure 5.5**, found on page 4 of the file "Ch5_aband_supplement.pdf."

As seen in the model, or in Figure 5.5:

- The years have been divided into two groups: History (columns F–H) and New forecast (columns I–N).

- Historic abandonment contributions have been value-pasted into cells F4:H4. Note that these match the forecasts made in cells F21:H21 of the previous model, as seen in Figure 5.3 (they were good forecasts).

- The inflation year numbers for the remaining forecast years (2018–2023) have been adjusted to reflect the new model date of January 1, 2018 in cells I5:N5.

- The economic limit, as mentioned, has been lowered from 2021 to 2020 (cell D7; provided you have clicked the "Show Revised Base Scenario" button in row 8).

- The remaining number of years (three) of the *forecast* production period are summed in cell D17.

- The rest of the model works exactly as before, except that the historic abandonment contributions in cells F4:H4 have been carried down to cells F23:H23. The forecast contributions (cells I23:N23) are still calculated as the value of the Real 2015 $ abandonment payment (inflated to 2021, when it will be made), divided by the number of remaining contributions to be made (i.e., the number of years remaining in the revised economic production life forecast). But now, they each equal MOD $11.49 mm, versus MOD $10.03 mm before.

- The important checksum in cell A23 shows that the sum of MOD abandonment contributions still matches the value of the MOD abandonment payment.

From row 23, you can see that the revised forecast contributions are equal to each other, but not to the historic contributions. Also, the total value of the MOD contributions (cell D23) falls to $54.4 mm from $60.2 in the old model, as the Real $ value of the abandonment payment is exposed to less inflation (due to the shorter time until the abandonment payment is made).[1]

Usually governments "forgive" such inequality of payments if the producer's reasons for revision appear reasonable, as governments are mainly concerned that the producer is making a good-faith, systematic effort to set aside enough money to fund the abandonment payment when that payment is actually required.

If the forecast of the abandonment date changes, then the only model in which the contributions are forecast to be equivalent would be the first model, before any revisions.

5.4 UNEQUAL ABANDONMENT CONTRIBUTIONS, BASED ON ANNUAL PRODUCTION AS A PERCENTAGE OF ULTIMATE PRODUCTION

Unlike the annual contributions we have just seen, annual contributions arising under this kind of abandonment funding regime, which we have seen used in Africa, are not equal. The contributions' value in a given year is based on that year's production, as a percentage of total economic production expected (i.e., forecast remaining reserves) over the life of the field, or **ultimate production**. This approach is sometimes referred to as the "**unit of production method**".

If, for example, a field's ultimate production is forecast to be 100 mm bbl (or mmb), the value of the abandonment payment is MOD $100 mm, and production in Year 1 is 10 mm bbl, the Year 1 abandonment contribution payment will be $\boxed{(8 \text{ mm bbl/100 mm bbl})*\text{MOD } \$100 \text{ mm} =}$ $\boxed{8\%*\text{MOD } \$100 \text{ mm} = \text{MOD } \$8 \text{ mm}}$. Thus the more the production in a given year, the higher the annual contribution. If (as is typical) production starts high and then declines, annual contributions will do the same, leading to a "frontloading" of abandonment contributions in the early years. In terms of discounted cashflow, this is not favorable for the producer.

Calculation

The basic calculation strategy is:

- to determine the timing and thus the MOD $ value of the abandonment cost, as we have done before; and then

- to calculate the annual abandonment contribution for each year of economic production, as just described above.

---

[1] Do *not*, incidentally, conclude from this that earlier abandonment payments are necessarily better from the producer's perspective than later ones, as we will discuss later.

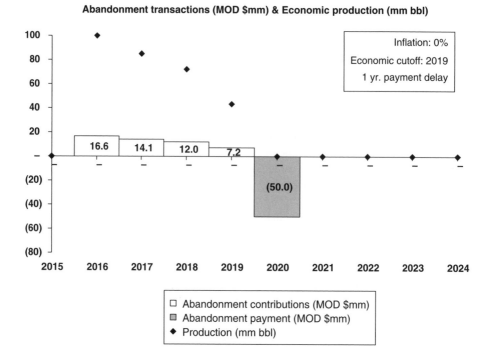

Figure 5.6   Frontloaded abandonment contributions, from the file "Ch5_aband_depletion_coeffs.xls," with model set as described below

Exercise

Try this one yourself. On the "Solution setup" sheet of the file "Ch5_aband_depletion_ coeffs.xls" are input assumptions. Set the economic cutoff to 2022, the abandonment payment delay to 0 years and inflation to 2.5%. Then fill in the Calculation section, which will cause results to show up in the chart we have prepared for you starting in row 22. Compare your solution for annual abandonment contributions against that provided on the "Solution" sheet.

Now set the economic cutoff to 2019, the payment delay to 1 year and the inflation rate to 0%. The chart should look like Figure 5.6, above. Compare it to Figure 5.5, which is based on the same assumptions. Note the marked "frontloading" of abandonment contributions in Figure 5.6.

5.5   EQUAL ABANDONMENT CONTRIBUTIONS, STARTING WHEN DEPLETION REACHES A SPECIFIED THRESHOLD

This method is based on **depletion**, which in a given year equals year-end cumulative production as a percentage of ultimate economic production. Equal annual contributions start once depletion passes a threshold, or "trigger" specified by legislation or contract.

Calculation

Refer to the file "Ch5_aband_cuml_prod_trigger.xls," which is reproduced in **Figure 5.7** on page 5 of the file "Ch5_aband_supplement.pdf."

In our example file, the percentage depletion threshold, or "trigger" for abandonment payments to start, is assumed to be 45% (cell D8, which is named "Cuml_prod_trigger").

Because the calculations shown in Figure 5.7 have many steps in common with the model "Ch5_aband_eq pmnts over prod life.xls" from Section 5.3, we will only treat the new steps here in detail:

- The economic production period is calculated in rows 14–16 using the first-period and period-flag formulas.

- Cumulative economic production in millions of barrels (row 17) is calculated in a way *designed to fall to and stay at 0 for each year after the end of the economic production period* (for reasons we will explain in a minute). For 2019 (cell J17), for example, the first part (in parentheses) of the formula $=(I17 + J13)*J16$ is the **Standard-accumulation formula**, i.e., the cumulative value of the prior year + the annual value of the present year, where, in this case, I17 and J13 are the cumulative and annual values for 2018 and 2019, respectively. The second part of the formula multiplies the result of the first part by the binary period flag in row 16, so that when the flag returns to 0 after production ends, cumulative production also returns a 0. We will call this modified formula the **Truncated-accumulation formula.**[2]

- Annual cumulative economic production as a percentage of the ultimate total is calculated in a straightforward way in row 18.

- The abandonment payment is timed and inflated in rows 19–22.

- Another binary flag – this one to show when abandonment contributions are due – is in row 23. For example, for 2019 (cell J23), this is calculated as $=IF(J18>=Cuml\_prod\_trigger, 1, 0)$, which means that if cumulative percentage production in 2019 (cell J18) equals or exceeds our specified 45% trigger, the answer is 1, meaning a contribution is due; otherwise, it is 0. In this case, cumulative percentage production is 92%, so the answer is 1.

- The size of each equal contribution is calculated in cell D24, as the MOD $mm abandonment payment, divided by the number of payments due. In this example, each payment is MOD $10.77 mm.

- Lastly, the annual abandonment contributions are calculated in row 25, as the size of any equal payment (cell D24) times the binary flag for the appropriate year in row 23. Thus, in this example, there are five payments of MOD $10.77 mm each, spanning 2017–2021, inclusive.

---

[2] Truncated-accumulation formulas do not have to use a flag, but in this case we already had the flag in row 16 handy, so it is easy enough to use it. Instead of a flag, you could multiply the standard accumulation part of the formula by anything that has the same effect. For example, you could rewrite cell the J17 formula, $=(I17 + J13)*J16$, as $=(I17 + J13)*IF(J13>0, 1, 0)$.

Now for the reason why, in the second step, we used the truncated-accumulation formula. We did so to prevent paying out too many contributions. If we had *not* done so, and instead had used the standard-accumulation formula, then cumulative production for 2022–2023 would have been recorded in cells M17:N17 as 327 million barrels. This would have caused 2022–2023 cumulative production, as a percentage of ultimate production, to equal 100% in the row below. This in turn would have resulted in abandonment contributions being flagged as due in 2022–2023 (cells M23:N23) and therefore to be paid out as two "extra" contributions of MOD $10.7 mm each (cells M25:N25). So in this case, the truncated-accumulation formula prevented this error (saving the producer MOD $21.2 mm in the process).

Visual Check

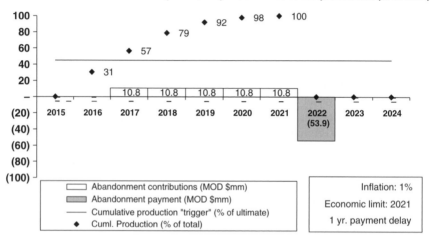

Figure 5.8   Results from depletion threshold-based abandonment regime, from the file "Ch5_aband_cuml_prod_trigger.xls"
Note: Results reflect the input assumptions shown in Figure 5.7.

The interactive chart starting on row 37 provides a visual check. It is reproduced in Figure 5.8.

Note that the labels on the Y-axis should be read:

- as MOD $ mm, with reference to the white abandonment contribution columns and the gray abandonment payment column;

- as percentages (with a range of 0–100%), with reference to:
  - the diamonds signifying cumulative production as a percentage of total ultimate production (again, bear in mind that once production stops, we make this return to 0%); and to
  - the black horizontal line showing the "trigger," expressed as a percentage of ultimate production, for abandonment payments to start. You will only see a white column below a diamond when the diamond is directly on, or higher than, the trigger line. Play with the trigger control (cell D8) while watching the chart to see this work.

5.6   EQUAL ABANDONMENT CONTRIBUTIONS STARTING FROM A SPECIFIED NUMBER OF PERIODS BEFORE ECONOMIC PRODUCTION ENDS

In Section 5.3 we saw an abandonment funding regime in which equal annual contributions are due each year of the entire economic production period. A common variant of this is to make equal annual contributions due only in a certain portion of those years. The portion is specified as the number of years before the end of economic production.

Calculation

The calculation is basically the same as in the Section 5.3 example model, with these additional steps:

- making sure the contributions start on time,

- while handling those cases when the economic production life is shorter than that implied by the specified contribution start year – for example, when the payments are to start in the seventh year of economic production, but economic production only lasts five years. In this context, we call this a **start-year conflict**.

> Refer to the file "Ch5_aband_eq pmnts_ over X yrs.xls" which is reproduced in **Figure 5.9**, found on page 6 of the file "Ch5_aband_supplement.pdf."

The formulas in this model, from the start through row 16, and in rows 21–25, work the same as in the Section 5.3 model. Here is what is new this time:

- The number of years of economic production life remaining at the start of each year is calculated in the annual columns of row 18. In essence, this is just counting down the number of years of economic life. In each year, the economic production period flags (in the prior row) for the current and all following years are summed. You can see this, for example, in the first part of the formula for 2019 (cell J18), =SUM(J17:$N17)*J17 . The second part of the formula, i.e., multiplying by the production period flag in cell J17 , makes the whole formula work like a truncated-accumulation formula (except that the accumulation works in reverse, starting with the highest value instead of ending with it), in order to prevent over-counting. For example, if in the formula for 2015 (cell F18) – a year before production begins – the sum was *not* multiplied by the flag of 0 in cell F17, the result would incorrectly read seven years.

- In cell D18, taking the maximum of the annual results in cells F18:N18 just serves as a check; the result needs to equal the number of years of the economic production period, as calculated in cell D17. The checksum in cell A18 tests if this is so.

- As mentioned, we need to account for any start-year conflicts. For example, the equal abandonment contributions are supposed to start when the economic production period has seven years left (cell D8), but the actual economic production life is only six years (cell D17). We have to choose the shorter of the two periods. So we calculate the number of annual contributions due in cell D19 as $\boxed{\text{=MIN(D17, D8)}}$. We have named cell D19 "Number_of_contributions."

Analysis

> Find this section in the file "Ch5_aband_sect5.6_analysis.pdf."

5.7 EQUAL ABANDONMENT CONTRIBUTIONS STARTING WHEN THE PRODUCER CHOOSES

Some countries require producers to make equal annual abandonment contributions over the economic production period, but allow the producer some discretion over when to start – for example, any year within the last seven years of economic production. Suppose a producer wants to know which year would be the best to start paying annual contributions. Here, we would define the "best" start year – all other things being equal – as the one which results in the lowest discounted value of the accumulated contributions.[3]

In light of material we have already covered, this is not hard to determine. Here is the basic solution strategy:

- Start with a model exactly like the one used in Section 5.6. Recall that this model lets the user set the abandonment contribution start year, in terms of the number of years before economic production ends. (Like that model, the one used here needs to be able to handle any start-year conflicts.)

- Once you have calculated the annual MOD contributions, discount them using the mid-year discounting method. This is done in rows 31–35 of our example model for this section, "Ch5_aband_eq pmnts_ over chosen X yrs.xls."

Exercise

Open the example model. Click the "Base Scenario" button in row 7. Note the assumptions for the economic cutoff year, the abandonment payment delay, the inflation rate and the discount rate (input in rows 6, 7, 11 and 12, respectively). Play with the spinner, which lets you determine when to start making annual abandonment contributions (cell D9) while watching the "Discounted value of abandonment contributions" result in cell D34, and the left chart which starts in cell B37.

As long as the discount rate is greater than 0%, the start year which results in the "best news" (i.e., the lowest present value of total contributions) will be the latest start year possible (i.e., the lowest value in cell D9). Thus in this example, the best course would be to make only one contribution, which would occur in 2021.

---

[3] Be aware, however, that in a full discounted cashflow model – as opposed to the shortened, simplistic one used for illustrative purposes here – you would also have to consider any NPV impacts from the tax deductibility of abandonment payments or – in a production sharing regime, as introduced in Chapter 6 – the cost recoverability of such payments.

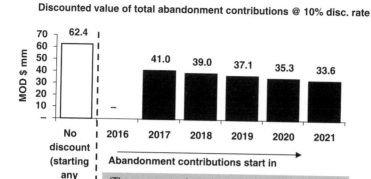

Figure 5.13   Base Scenario from the file "Ch5_aband_eq pmnts_ over chosen X yrs.xls"

This is because the fewer the number of years before the abandonment payment is due that you start making abandonment contributions, the later those contributions occur; and the later they occur, all other things being equal, the lower their discounted value will be.

Rather than scroll through the values in cell D9 while watching cell D34, you can use Excel's Data Table function (introduced in Chapter 1) to make a chart showing, all at once, the discounted value of total abandonment payments under different start-year scenarios. We have created this for you, starting in cell F37. It is shown in Figure 5.13, reflecting the results in the model when you select the "Base Scenario" button in row 7. Notice how, for example, the MOD $41.0 mm shown for 2017 matches the model's Base Scenario values in cells D29 and D34. The values in these two cells will match those shown for 2018 in the chart, if, for example, you change the value in cell D9 to 4.

(For the Data Table function to work, be sure Excel's calculation mode is set to automatic.)

Adjust the spinners in rows 6–12 to see whether the charts update sensibly. Note that there will be no black column or corresponding value label for years when there is not enough economic production life to permit abandonment contributions to start in that year.

Also, be aware that the gray caption at the bottom of the right chart can explain any start-year conflicts (here, the difference between the value in cell D9 and the number of black columns in Chart Y).

Can you guess/explain what happens when you vary:

- the economic cutoff (cell D6)?
- the abandonment payment delay (cell D7)?
- the number of abandonment contributions (cell D9)?
- the inflation and discount rates (cells D11:D12)?

The lesson from this short analysis is, as mentioned earlier, **that the time value of money means that producers often have a strong incentive to fund abandonment later rather than sooner, as this can minimize the discounted cost**.

5.8 MULTIPLE METHODS, USING WHICHEVER ONE MAKES ABANDONMENT CONTRIBUTIONS START EARLIER

Some regulators require more than one set of abandonment funding rules to be assessed. For example, we have seen one country with major offshore production which requires producers to model abandonment contributions two ways. The first way starts equal abandonment contributions a specified number of years before the abandonment payment, as shown in Section 5.6. We will call this **Method 1** in this section. The second method, **Method 2**, is based on a "depletion" regime of the kind covered in Section 5.5. The government requires the producer to apply whichever method results in earlier payments.

The modeling solution strategy is:

1. to model both methods, ignoring which will ultimately be applied; and then

2. to build in logic which chooses between the two.

This section continues in the file "Ch5_aband_sect5.8_analysis.pdf."

5.9 ABANDONMENT CONTRIBUTIONS WHICH EARN INTEREST (SINGLE RATE)

Our examples so far have ignored the fact that many countries allow abandonment contributions to earn and accrue interest from the time they are made until the abandonment payment occurs. This helps producers because, all else being equal, the accumulated interest provides a financial boost which lets them make smaller contributions to fund the same ultimate liability.

Here we provide an example that uses the basic abandonment funding regime from Section 5.3, in which equal contributions are made over the economic production period. Our example file for this section, "Ch5_aband_interest_single_rate.xls," is adapted from the Section 5.3 model, "Ch5_aband_eq pmnts over prod life.xls." Here is what is new in the present version, which you should set to the Base Scenario (cell K9).

- The abandonment payment delay (cell D7) can now extend up to three years. The cell has been named "Payment_delay."

- An assumed rate of interest, payable on abandonment contributions, is in cell D10, which has been named "Interest_rate". This single rate is assumed to be constant in all years. (It feeds what is essentially a duplicate of this cell (cell D24.))

- Determining the size of each annual contribution is now done with a more complex formula (cell D25) to be discussed soon.

- Other cells – which use formulas you have seen before – which have been named (to make the complex formula easier to understand) are "Number_of_contributions" (cell D19) and "Accumulated_funds_needed" (cell D22).

Calculation

The solution strategy consists of:

- using methods covered in Section 5.3 to calculate the timing and MOD value of the abandonment payment, and the number and timing of the MOD abandonment contributions;

- calculating the size of each equal annual abandonment contribution, so that, when taking into account interest earned on these contributions, total cumulative funds (contributions + interest) exactly match the value of the abandonment payment when it becomes due (this is where the complex formula comes in); and

- placing these contributions in time, and calculating the interest they earn.

> Refer to the file "Ch5_aband_interest_single_rate.xls," which is reproduced in **Figure 5.20**, found on page 7 of the file "Ch5_aband_supplement.pdf."

Using the PV Function to Find the Size of the Abandonment Contribution

The first formula used in this section's example model which we have not covered before is the most important and complicated one. It is in cell D25. It calculates the size of each equal abandonment contribution, taking into account that the contributions earn interest, and that the sum of the contributions plus accumulated interest must equal the abandonment payment. Here we call each such contribution a **levelized abandonment contribution**.

It is calculated in cell D25 as

> = IF(Number_of_contributions = 0, 0,
> (Accumulated_funds_needed/(1 + Interest_rate)^(Number_of_contributions
> +Payment_delay)/PV(Interest_rate, Number_of_contributions, −1, , 0))

Note the deliberate use of two commas near the end of the last expression, just before the zero. We shall explain this shortly.

Let us break this down into a few digestible steps. But before we do, be aware that while this long formula might be *challenging to understand*, the good news is that it is *easy to see that it works*. Skipping for a moment to the end result, we can see that, under our Base Scenario, the checksum formula in cell A30 shows a 0, which means that **the total funds (contributions + interest) accumulated at the abandonment payment date** (cell D30) equal MOD $66.2 mm – **exactly match the amount needed at that date** (cell D22). This is the whole point. You will see that this match is achieved, no matter what variables you choose in cells D6:D10.

There are four distinct parts to this levelized abandonment contribution formula:

1. $\boxed{\text{=IF(Number\_of\_contributions=0, 0, ..}}$. This simply returns a zero value if the model calculates that no contributions are required.

2. $\boxed{\text{(Accumulated\_funds\_needed/(1 + Interest\_rate)}^\wedge\text{(Number\_of\_contributions + Payment\_}}$ $\boxed{\text{delay) ...}}$. This is a discount formula which removes the interest payment contribution from the accumulated abandonment funds required. It does this by discounting the accumulated abandonment value, using the interest rate as the discount rate for the number of interest earning periods involved (in this case, nine: the six payment periods (or number of contributions), plus the three-year abandonment payment delay). This discounts the accumulated abandonment value back to its value at the start of the first contribution year, which is 2016, under the Base Scenario.

3. $\boxed{\text{PV(Interest\_rate, Number\_of\_contributions, -1, , 0)}}$ discounts the number of contributions using Excel's PV ("Present Value") function – the syntax of which is described below – using the interest rate as the discount rate. (You will soon see in this description that the two commas separating the −1 from the 0 are *not* typos, but rather are required by this Excel function's syntax. Note also that minus 1 in the third argument of the PV function ensures a positive number is returned by the calculation.)

4. Component 2 is divided by Component 3. Both numerator and denominator in this quotient need to be discounted by the same discount rate (i.e., the interest rate) to provide a levelized cost.

Notes

A. A **levelized cost** is the present value of a future cost or payment converted to equal periodic payments. Costs are usually levelized in real dollars (i.e., adjusted to remove the impact of inflation), which is what this formula achieves.

B. The Excel PV function uses this syntax:

PV(Rate, Nper, Pmt, Fv, Type), where
Rate is the interest rate per period.
Nper is the total number of payment periods required.
Pmt is the payment made each period (note that if Pmt is omitted, you must include the Fv argument).
Fv is the future value. (Note that if Fv is omitted, as it is in the formula used here, you *must* include the Pmt argument.)
Type is the number 0 or 1, which indicates when payments are due (0 means end of period; 1 means beginning of period). Do not get confused by the fact that we are assuming all payments occur at mid-year – in this case, the use of Type 0 means the *beginning* of the 12-month periods which start in the *middle* of the year when the abandonment payment is made.

Figure 5.21 is a screenshot which shows how these arguments work in our model under the Base Scenario. Note that "Invalid" next to the "Fv" box actually means that it has been omitted, as described above, and does not mean there is an error.

You can see this screenshot in the model by first selecting cell D25 and then, in the formula bar, placing the cursor after the "V" in "PV." Then (a) in Excel 2003, press the Function button f_x or, using the menu, go to Insert/Function; (b) in Excel 2007 and Excel 2010 go the Formulas tab/Insert Function f_x.

C. On the sheet, cells O44 to O46 show the calculation of Steps 2, 3 and 4 separately. Play with the spinners, particularly the interest rate and the economic limit, to satisfy yourself that you understand what the different components of this levelized cost formula are doing.

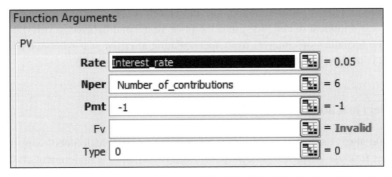

Figure 5.21   PV function arguments as used in cell D25, under the Base Scenario, of the file "Ch5_aband_interest_single_rate.xls"

Calculating the Contribution and Interest Payments

The last steps, thankfully, are pretty straightforward:

- Annual contributions (row 27) are assigned to the relevant years in the same way we have seen before – they equal the MOD $8.4 mm annual contribution in cell D25, times the corresponding annual binary economic production period flag (i.e., 1 or 0) in row 17 (which doubles here as a contribution payment flag for the relevant year). In our Base Scenario, example, this results in contributions of MOD $8.4 mm being made each year between 2016 and 2021, inclusive, and no contributions in the other years.

- Interest payments are calculated as follows, **taking as an example 2020 (cell K28)**, which uses the formula =IF(year>$D18, 0, Interest_rate*J29) :

  - Interest payments continue up to and including the year of the abandonment payment, which can be some years after the last abandonment contribution is made, depending on the delay factor (cell D7). Therefore the first part of the formula says that if the year of 2020 is after the abandonment payment year of 2024 (cell D18), the answer is 0. This is not the case, so the answer is not 0.

  - In any given year, interest payments are calculated as a percentage of the prior year's end balance of accumulated funds. Thus, in our example, the second part of the formula says that if the year of 2020 is before, or is the same year as, the abandonment payment year of 2024 specified in cell $\boxed{\text{D18}}$ – which is the case here – then the answer for 2020 is the $\boxed{\text{Interest\_rate}}$ (named cell D24) of 5%, times the balance ending in the previous year of 2019 (cell $\boxed{\text{J29}}$). This balance is MOD \$36.2 mm. So in this example, the answer for 2020 in cell K28 is 5% × MOD \$36.2 mm = **MOD \$1.8 mm.**

- A given year's end balance, in turn, is cumulative, calculated as the present year's contribution and interest, plus the prior year's end balance. Thus, for example, the cumulative 2019 balance which acts as the base for the next year's interest payment is calculated, in cell J29, as $\boxed{\text{=IF(year > \$D18, 0, J27+J28+I29)}}$. The second part of the formula sums – when the year is before, or is the same as, the abandonment payment year of 2024 found in cell $\boxed{\text{D18}}$ – the items just mentioned, i.e., the present year's contribution in cell $\boxed{\text{J27}}$, the present year's interest in cell $\boxed{\text{J28}}$, and the prior year's end balance in cell $\boxed{\text{I29}}$. The first part of the formula stops interest from accumulating after the year when the abandonment payment is made – in this case, in 2024 (again, found in cell $\boxed{\text{D18}}$).

Reminder: ask about tax implications

You should always ascertain whether (a) interest earned on abandonment contributions is counted as revenue for income tax purposes, and (b) whether abandonment contributions are income tax deductible (they usually are).

Visual Check

Figure 5.22 shows the chart found starting row 44 of the file. There will be both stacked columns and a dashed line each year, up to and including the year of the abandonment payment. Note that the total height of the stacked column (i.e., cumulative abandonment contributions + cumulative interest = total cumulative funds available) equals the dashed line in the last

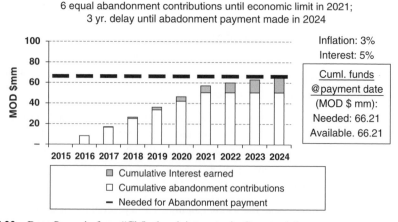

Figure 5.22   Base Scenario from "Ch5_aband_interest_single_rate.xls"

year. This is an important check that the model works. So are the matching "Needed" and "Available" values in the boxed caption on the right side of the chart.

Split the screen and, starting with the Base Scenario (use the button in row 8), play with the inputs while watching the chart and the levelized cost components (cells O42 to O44). Raise the interest rate (cell D10) to 10%. The total height of the stacked columns does not change, but, appropriately, the interest portion grows while the abandonment contributions shrink. This is because higher interest earned means lower contributions are needed to reach the target (i.e., the level of total funds needed when the abandonment payment is due).

Be sure you understand the effect on the chart of other changes, such as a change in the economic cutoff, the payment delay and the inflation rate.

Exercise

Because calculating the equally sized abandonment contributions is somewhat tricky, in that it involves a complex levelized cost formula, we have given you a practice example in the file "Ch5_aband_cuml_prod_trigger_exercise.xls," which is based on the model from Section 5.5. Assumptions and a chart are already in place on the "Setup" sheet. Have a try at filling in the blanks, and compare your answers to those on the "Solutions" sheet.

5.10 ABANDONMENT CONTRIBUTIONS WHICH EARN INTEREST (VARIABLE RATES)

Models like the last one assume, for convenience and simplicity, that the interest earned on abandonment contributions is the same every year. But if the analyst has a view of how interest rates will change over time, a more flexible model is needed. The one presented in this section accounts for variable interest rates, i.e., a different rate for each year.

This section continues in the file "Ch5_aband_sect5.10_analysis.pdf," which concludes the chapter.

Chapter 6

Introduction to Production Sharing Contract-Based Fiscal Regimes

6

Introduction to Production Sharing
Contract-Based Fiscal Regimes

6.1 OVERVIEW: PSCs AS A SPECIALIZED REVENUE SHARING FRAMEWORK

Fiscal systems based on **production sharing contracts** ("PSCs"; also called production sharing agreements, or "PSAs") are, in addition to the tax and royalty regimes we covered in Chapters 1 and 2, extremely common in the upstream petroleum industry, particularly in developing countries and some OPEC countries.

In one sense, to frame a distinction as "PSCs *versus* tax and royalty regimes" is misleading, because, as we shall see, many PSCs also make provisions for royalties and/or income taxes. Both types of regime can also include other common fiscal elements, such as bonuses, miscellaneous levies, special abandonment funding requirements, etc.

But in another sense, the systems are fundamentally different, with respect to how they distribute **gross project revenue**, which we define as the volume of production multiplied by the received price per unit of production. (We also refer to gross project revenue as **gross field revenue** or simply **field revenue**.)

Let us use some simplified examples to compare and contrast the essence of how typical tax and royalty and PSC regimes divide the gross revenue "pie." Note that for the purposes of this discussion:

- The example tax and royalty regime actually imposes both income taxes and royalties. (This might sound obvious, but, confusingly, the term "tax and royalty" is also used to describe regimes which *do not* impose royalties, such as the UK.)

- The example PSC regime also imposes a royalty (as do all other example PSC models in this book) though, in the real world, not all do.

- The company has a 100% equity interest in the field, meaning that however revenue is divided, the company pays for all field costs.

Under this example tax and royalty regime:

- First, a government and/or a third party or parties takes a certain percentage of gross revenue as royalty (any royalty going to a third party being called an "overriding royalty").

- We term the remainder, after deducting any royalty, **net revenue**, or sometimes **revenue, net of royalty**.[1]

- All of this net revenue flows to the investing oil company (or companies; for the sake of simplicity we will stick to the singular). Absent any external financing arrangements, this is what the oil company uses to pay for field costs (opex, capex, abandonment costs, etc.), miscellaneous levies and income tax.

- What remains of net revenue after these deductions is for the company to keep as its net cashflow, or **NCF**.

- The NCF for the government – since it has no equity interest, and therefore bears no share of field costs – equals the government's share of revenue, which consists of royalty, receipts from income tax, and income from any miscellaneous levies.

Whereas under a PSC, gross revenue is shared between the government and the investing oil company – which, as a signatory to a PSC, is usually called the **contractor** – in a fundamentally different way.

As with the example tax and royalty regime, the government takes a portion of gross field revenue as royalty, leaving net revenue as the remainder. Net revenue is then distributed as follows:

- The PSC specifies that a portion of net revenue will be the **maximum amount available to the contractor, to reimburse it for** designated eligible field costs it has incurred. These eligible field costs are called **recoverable costs**. The portion of net revenue which the contractor receives as reimbursement is called **cost oil** when the costs are related to the exploration, development and/or production of oil. If the costs relate to gas, this portion is called **cost gas**; and if the costs relate to both oil and gas, this portion is called **cost petroleum**. (As all of our examples assume that only oil is involved, we will use the term "cost oil.") The process of distributing cost oil is called **cost recovery**.

- Any portion of net revenue which is left after the contractor receives its cost oil is called **total profit oil**[2] (also sometimes called "gross profit oil" or "distributable profit oil".)

- Total profit oil, in turn, is distributed in some way, specified by the PSC, to each of the two parties, so that:

  ○ the contractor receives a portion of it as **contractor profit oil**;

  ○ the government receives the remaining portion of it as **government profit oil**.

---

[1] We stress that these definitions of "gross revenue" and "net revenue" used here are specific to this discussion. In practice, confusion can arise over the meaning of "gross" and "net." Sometimes they are used as defined above, to describe something before and after royalty payments, respectively. But other times, they refer to something quite different, namely, equity or working entitlement. At such times, for example, if field revenue is $100, and a shareholder has the right to 20% of it, then the field's "gross revenue" is $100, and the shareholder's "net revenue" is $20. Again, this is *not* what we mean by gross and net in this and the following chapters.

[2] Again, there can also be "profit gas" or "profit petroleum," etc.

Assuming – as we do in all of our PSC examples in this chapter – that there is a royalty, but there are no income taxes or miscellaneous levies, then:

- the **contractor's total share of PSC revenue** equals (cost oil received + contractor profit oil);

- the **government's total share of PSC revenue** equals (royalty + government profit oil); and

- the sum of contractor PSC revenue and government PSC revenue must equal gross revenue. It has to, because this is the "pie" we have been dividing to begin with.

  ○ This sounds quite basic, but we have seen "professional" models which do long, complex calculations of each component of each party's PSC revenue, which then failed to add up to gross revenue.

  ○ Your models should always check that they do.

Again, assuming the government bears no share of field costs:

- **contractor NCF equals** (contractor PSC revenue − *all* of the field costs);

- **government net cashflow (NCF)** equals government PSC revenue.

Keeping in mind the basic framework described in this section will help you navigate the next three chapters.

6.2 LOOKING AHEAD: ROAD MAP FOR THIS AND THE NEXT CHAPTERS

This, in a *very* simplified "nutshell," is how a basic PSC works. The general concepts are not difficult; neither are many of the calculations involved, though some involve some nuances to be aware of.

What is hard sometimes, however, is understanding how PSCs "behave", i.e., why the results of a PSC model change as they do, from the perspectives of the contractor, government or both, when input assumptions change.

- One reason is that some of the terminology used to describe certain results, such as the parties' shares of revenue and NCF, is sometimes vague.

- Another is that other results, such as the parties' revenue, NCF, NPV, and volumetric shares of production to which a PSC entitles them, are determined by a greater number of variables (some independent, some interdependent), or "moving parts," which can sometimes produce counterintuitive results.

Over the next three chapters, we aim to ease you into the modeling and analysis of PSCs with a very simple introductory model, which will, over different versions, evolve into a generic "core" PSC model, on which we will then base a number of other models which illustrate common variations among PSC regimes. We will focus on showing you how to calculate things, while pausing to present analysis exercises as we go.

In this chapter we will introduce PSC revenue distribution with a very simplified, single-year model focusing mainly on revenue distribution.

We will then present a (still-simplified) multi-year PSC model, in which we continue to illustrate key calculations, while also focusing on outcomes like each party's shares, or "**takes**" (used here as a noun, i.e., what each party takes) of revenue, NCF and volumetric entitlements.

In Chapter 7, we will examine the role of the economic limit test ("ELT") and depreciation, culminating with a detailed, reasonably realistic "plain vanilla" PSC example model. This is what we will call our **"core" PSC example model**. If you can replicate the parts of it in the chapter exercise, you will have a very good foundation for basic PSC modeling.

Finally, in Chapter 8, we will examine a number of more complex variations found in many common PSCs, different ways in which total profit oil is distributed, and forms of income tax levied under some PSCs.

6.3   SIMPLE EXAMPLE OF PSC REVENUE DISTRIBUTION

In this discussion, we assume:

- that royalties are applied;
- that a company has a 100% equity stake, or "working interest," meaning that:
  - the investing oil company pays 100% of non-fiscal costs, e.g., capex, opex, abandonment, etc.[3]; but
  - the company is *not* entitled to 100% of field revenue under either type of regime.

As discussed, under a simple tax and royalty regime, where the only fiscal payments required are royalty and income tax, the distribution of gross revenue is quite simple:

- The company's share of field revenue equals (gross revenue – royalty – income tax).
- The government's share of revenue equals (royalty + income tax).

Gross revenue distribution under a PSC, however, is more complex. We show an example of a PSC's multi-step revenue sharing mechanism in Figure 6.1, which comes from the simplified (one-year) model found in the file "Ch6_PSC_Revs_Single_Year.xls."

---

[3] Note that there have been examples of PSCs, such as Libya's "EPSA III" and "EPSA IV" PSCs, where the government pays a large share of opex, but these are the exception rather than the norm.

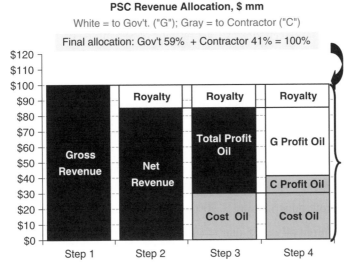

Figure 6.1 Simplified gross revenue distribution under an oil-producing PSC, from the file "Ch6_PSC_Revs_Single_Year.xls"
Note: Reflects the model's Base Scenario.

In Figure 6.1, we split the calculations – which we will detail later – for distributing gross revenue into four steps. We start with gross revenue, before any of it has been distributed, in Step 1 and end with the final revenue distribution in Step 4. Black columns or segments show revenue which, at a given step, has not yet been allocated; white segments show revenue allocated to the government; and gray segments show revenue allocated to the contractor.

Step 1 shows gross revenue, i.e., total field revenue, which is calculated in the usual way, as production volume × price. Here it is assumed to equal $100 mm.

In **Step 2**, we deduct royalty payable to the government. Here we have assumed a simple, flat-rate royalty equal to 15% of gross revenue (although, as we have seen in Chapter 3, royalties can be much more complex). Therefore $15 mm goes to the government in the form of royalty, leaving $85 mm in net revenue.

In **Step 3**, net revenue of $85 mm is, in turn, split into two parts:

• The contractor's **cost oil**. Despite the name, it is not a cost, but rather a revenue source for the contractor. Specifically, it is a portion of net revenue used to reimburse the contractor for certain costs (usually opex, capex and/or abandonment costs) which the contractor has incurred, and which the PSC and any other applicable accounting rules deem to be **recoverable costs** (i.e., costs eligible for reimbursement).[4] We will explain how cost oil is calculated shortly. For now, just note that cost oil equals $30 mm in the Base Scenario.

---

[4] The contractor's receipt of cost oil is called **cost recovery**. Because cost oil is received only by the contractor, we have not called it "contractor cost oil," but rather just "cost oil" for short.

- **Total profit oil** (also sometimes called "gross profit oil" or "distributable profit oil"). Any portion of net revenue which is not paid out to the contractor as cost oil becomes total profit oil. Thus in this Base Scenario case, net revenue of $85 mm − cost oil of $30 mm = total profit oil of $55 mm.

In **Step 4**, total profit oil is shared between the government and the contractor according to a mechanism defined in the PSC. In this example model, the mechanism is very simple: the contractor's share of total profit oil, called **contractor profit oil**, is defined as a constant percentage of total profit oil, with the rest of total profit oil becoming **government profit oil**:[5]

- In our Base Scenario, the contractor and government shares of total profit oil are assumed to be 20% and 80%, respectively. Therefore:

  ○ contractor profit oil is $55 mm × 20% = $11 mm; and

  ○ government profit oil is $55 mm × 80% = $44 mm (which could also be calculated as $55 mm − $11 mm).

Thus, under this simple PSC:

- contractor PSC revenue = cost oil of $30 mm + contractor profit oil of $11 mm = $41 mm;

- government PSC revenue = royalty of $15 mm royalty + government profit oil of $44 mm = $59 mm;

which together sum to $41 mm + $59 mm = $100 mm. Note that this matches the $100 mm in gross revenue we started with in Step 1. This is vital, as the primary objective of these calculations is to divide up gross revenue. **If the sum of government PSC revenue and contractor PSC revenue, as defined here, does not equal gross field revenue, this likely means there is a mistake in your calculations.** This is why we always check this in our PSC models, as you will see soon.

Note that one thing we have done to simplify this introductory model is to exclude income tax. As we will cover later, however, some PSCs include some form of income tax, which typically amounts to another revenue component for the government.

6.4   SIMPLISTIC (SINGLE-YEAR) MODEL REVENUE DISTRIBUTION CALCULATIONS, INCLUDING COST OIL DETERMINATION

In Figure 6.2, we show the underlying assumptions and calculations behind the results just discussed. (If you do not see the same values, click one of the "Reset to Base Scenario" buttons in row 2 of our example file.)

---

[5] We will see later how, in practice, profit sharing mechanisms are commonly more complex, as they are designed to accommodate changing different economic conditions.

Simple PSC example (single year model)

	A	B	C	D	E

Assumptions   Reset to Base Scenario

Inflation is ignored; ELT is not applied; Blue font = hard-coded values			**Comments**
Contractor working interest = 100%, therefore the Contractor bears all costs			
Field production	mmb	1.00	Don't change
Oil price received	$ / b	100.00	Max = 100
Royalty rate	%	15.00%	Max = 60%
Field revenue, net of royalty is referred to as "net revenue"			
Contractor recoverable costs	$ mm	30.00	Max = 90
Contractor non-recoverable costs	$ mm	0.00	
Maximum net revenue available as cost oil	%	65.00%	Max = 100%
Contractor profit share	%	20.00%	Max = 80%
Government profit share	%	80.00%	

Calculations

Gross field revenue	$ mm	100.00	
Royalty	$ mm	15.00	
Net revenue	**$ mm**	**85.00**	
Maximum net revenue available as cost oil	**$ mm**	**55.25**	
Contractor recoverable costs	$ mm	30.00	
Costs recovered by Contractor, i.e. cost oil	**$ mm**	**30.00**	
Memo: recoverable costs NOT recovered	*$ mm*	-	
Total profit oil	**$ mm**	**55.00**	
Contractor share of profit oil	$ mm	11.00	
Government share of profit oil	$ mm	44.00	
			PSC revenue "take"
Total Contractor PSC revenue	$ mm	41.00	**41.00%**
Total Government PSC revenue	$ mm	59.00	**59.00%**
Total PSC revenue	**$ mm**	**100.00**	**100.00%**
Check	0 = OK	0	0

Figure 6.2 Assumptions and calculations from the file "Ch6_PSC_Revs_Single_Year.xls"
Note: Reflects the model's Base Scenario.

Formulas used (note that the "•" symbol marks the end of a formula):D13. =1-D12•
D16. =D5*D6 • D17. =D16*D7 • D18. =D16-D17 • D20. =D11*D18 • D22. =D9•
D24. =MIN(D20, D22) • D25. =D22-D24 • D27. =D18-D24 • D28. =D12*D$27•
D29. =D13*D$27 • D31. =D28 + D24 • E31. =D31/D33 • D32. =D17 + D29•
E32. =D32/D33 • D33. =D31 + D32 • D34. =ROUND(D33-D16, 8)

Most of the calculations shown in Figure 6.2 are straightforward in light of the previous discussion. What we have not yet explained, however, is the calculation of cost oil.

We saw before, and see again in cell D24 in Figure 6.2, that in the Base Scenario, the contractor receives cost oil of $30 mm. Where does this result come from? In this simplified example, in which there is only one accounting period (the single year), there are two steps:

1. A certain maximum portion of net revenue is specified by the PSC to be available to be disbursed to the contractor as cost oil. Under our Base Scenario, it is 65% (cell D11). In dollar terms, then, the maximum portion of net revenue available as cost oil is 65% × net revenue of $85 mm (cell D18) = $55.25 mm (cell D20). When the contractor submits receipts for recoverable costs, this $55.25 mm is the *most* it can receive.

2. In any given accounting period, cost oil is the lower of:

   • the maximum portion of net revenue available as cost oil; and

   • the contractor's recoverable costs.

Let us consider two examples.

Simplistic Cost Oil Calculation – Example 1

In Figure 6.3, below:

• item b) is the maximum portion of net revenue available as cost oil, which, as we established above, equals $55.25 mm;

• the contractor's recoverable costs – item c) – total $30.00 mm;

• there are more funds available than are needed for the contractor to recover these costs;

• the contractor takes the lower amount – $30.00 mm – as cost oil, shown as item d);

• in the model, as seen in Figure 6.2, this is calculated in cell D24 with the formula =MIN(D20,D22), where D20 is item b), i.e., maximum net revenue available as cost oil ($55.25 mm), and D22 is item c), i.e., the contractor's recoverable costs ($30.00 mm).

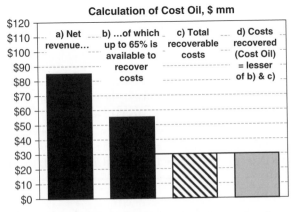

Figure 6.3 Calculation of cost oil under the Base Scenario, from the file "Ch6_PSC_Revs_Single_Year.xls"
Note: Reflects the model's Base Scenario.

This raises two issues:

- The contractor in this case recovers all its recoverable costs. As we will see later, this does not always happen.

- Because the contractor takes only $30.00 mm of the $55.25 mm available as cost oil, the $55.25 mm − $30.00 mm = $25.25 mm portion which the contractor does *not* take, contributes to total profit oil, which gets shared between the contractor and government in Step 4 of Figure 6.1.

Cost oil's effect on total profit oil

To be clear, there are two sources of funds contributing to total profit oil:

1. The portion of net revenue which is never made available as cost oil.

2. The portion which is potentially made available as cost oil, but ultimately is not distributed as cost oil, because the contractor's actual costs incurred were too low to justify its distribution. To be clear, this portion = $70 in the following example: if maximum net revenue available as cost oil is $100, and the contractor's recoverable costs are $30, the contractor receives $30 as cost oil, leaving $70 unused.

The **more complicated way to calculate total profit oil**, using our Base Scenario as an example, is as follows:

- Net revenue = $85.00 mm.

- The maximum portion of net revenue available as cost oil is 65% or, in dollar terms, 65% × $85.00 mm = $55.25 mm.

- The portion of net revenue which is never available as cost oil is therefore $85.00 mm − $55.25 mm = $29.75 mm; this will be the first of the two components of total profit oil.

- As we have seen, actual cost oil is $30.00 mm. After this cost oil is received by the contractor, what remains of the maximum portion of the $55.25 mm portion of net revenue available as cost oil is $55.25 mm − $30.00 mm = $25.25 mm; this will be the second of the two components of total profit oil.

- **Total profit oil** is therefore $29.75 mm + $25.25 mm = **$55.00 mm.**

Our preferred, **simpler way** to calculate total cost oil is used in our example model's cell D27, which contains the formula =D18-D24 . Thus:

- net revenue of $85.00 mm (cell D18), minus

- cost oil of $30.00 mm (cell D24), equals

- **total profit oil of, again, $55.00 mm**.

Thus, in the more complicated method, calculating the maximum portion of net revenue which is available as cost oil is just an interim step, which is no longer relevant after calculating cost oil.

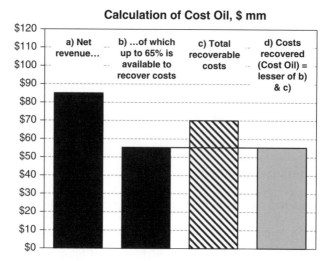

Figure 6.4 Calculation of cost oil under *adjusted* Base Scenario, from the file "Ch6_PSC_Revs_Single_ Year.xls"

Simplistic Cost Oil Calculation – Example 2

Figure 6.4 shows the determination of cost oil in our example model, after we have changed the amount of the contractor's recoverable costs, from the Base Scenario assumption of $30.00 mm, to $70.00 mm. (Change this yourself in the model, using either the spinner in cell D9 or the duplicate spinner in cell N4.)

- Now, the contractor's recoverable costs, item c), total $70.00 mm.

- Funds available, item b), which remains at $55.25 mm, are lower than the contractor needs to recover these costs.

The contractor cannot take more than is available in item b). Therefore it takes the lower amount, $55.25 mm, as cost oil.

- Again, this is calculated in the model's cell D24, as ⌐=MIN(D20,D22)⌐.

This has two implications:

- The contractor does not recover all its recoverable costs. (In this simplistic, single-year model, that is the end of the story; but as we will discuss below, in a multi-year model, costs which are not recovered in one period usually may be carried forward for potential recovery in later periods.) The portion of recoverable costs which are not recovered is represented by the part of the third column in Figure 6.4 which is above the horizontal line.

- Again, the amount of cost oil received impacts total profit oil. Having changed contractor recoverable costs from $30.00 mm to $70.00 mm, note in the model's cell D27 that total profit has fallen, from $55.00 mm in the Base Scenario to $29.75 mm. Satisfy yourself that you understand why.

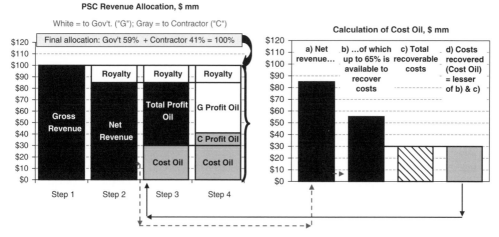

Figure 6.5   Simplified gross revenue distribution under an oil-producing PSC, from the file "Ch6_PSC_Revs_Single_Year.xls"
Note: Reflects Base Scenario.

In Figure 6.5, we present a screenshot from our example model, showing how both charts together explain all the determinants of PSC revenue sharing in our simplistic, single-year example, using the Base Scenario. Note the common Y-axis scales and the "flow" of the presentation. The dashed arrows, which start near the base of the net revenue column in the left chart, lead to the corresponding net revenue column in the right chart. This is our way of "breaking out" the cost oil calculation to the right chart. The right chart ends with the solid gray cost oil column. The solid arrow underneath it leads back to display the cost oil segment of the left chart's third column. Play with the spinner controls above the charts, in rows 3–5 of the model (which are not shown in Figure 6.5), to get a better feel for the dynamics.

Simplistic (Single-Year) Model: Cost Oil Determination Exercises

On the "Model" sheet of our example file "Ch6_PSC_Revs_Single_Year.xls," click either of the "Reset to Base Scenario" buttons in cell B2 or I1, and then arrange the view so that both charts are visible, along with the input assumptions and spinner controls in rows 3–5.

- Use the spinner in cell N4 to lower the "contractor recoverable costs, $ mm" (which we will simply call "recoverable costs") value in steps of $5 mm, from $30 mm down to $0. Note, in the right chart, how, over this range of costs, cost oil always equals recoverable costs. This is because recoverable costs are always lower than the maximum funds available for cost recovery.

- Next, increase recoverable costs until they reach $55. Now the right chart's last three columns are all the same height. This is because, if cost oil equals the "lower" of a) maximum funds available for cost recovery and b) recoverable costs, and a) = b), then cost oil equals both of them; there is no "lower" amount.

- Continue raising recoverable costs, so that they always exceed the maximum funds available for cost recovery. Cost oil will now always equal maximum funds available for cost recovery, because maximum funds available for cost recovery are now always lower than recoverable costs. In this case, the area of the right chart's third column, between the top of this column and the horizontal line, represents the amount of the contractor's unrecovered costs. This is calculated in cell D25 of the model itself.

Simplistic (Single-Year) Modeling Exercise

In the next section we will present some exercises to help you understand how changes in certain input assumptions flow through the PSC revenue distribution mechanism. First, however, to reinforce your understanding of the basic, underlying calculations, we suggest you try the following simple modeling exercise.

Open the file "Ch6_PSC_Revs_Single_Year_b_exercise.xls," which is simply a copy of most of our example file "Ch6_PSC_Revs_Single_Year.xls," only with the formulas in the Calculations section deleted. Click the button at the top of the model to be sure the Base Scenario input assumptions are used, and fill in the blank cells with formulas so that you reach the same answers as those in "Ch6_PSC_Revs_Single_Year.xls" under the Base Scenario.

Simplistic (Single-Year) Model PSC Revenue Distribution Exercises – Watching the "Moving Parts"

As you changed inputs in the cost oil determination exercises above, you will have noticed that the revenue distribution chart on the left updated whenever cost oil changed. We shall now examine how all the parts of our example model in "Ch6_PSC_Revs_Single_Year.xls" interact under more scenarios, focusing on the impact of changed assumptions on the contractor's and the government's PSC **revenue takes**. These "takes" are the values shown in the yellow-shaded caption at the top of the left chart and in cells E31:E32 of the model.

Clarifying terms – different kinds of "takes"

In upstream petroleum fiscal jargon, the term "take" is used as a noun, to mean which portion of something goes to one PSC party or another, i.e., what the party "takes away." There are different kinds of takes. Unfortunately, terms used to identify them are used differently by different people, or are unclear in other ways. Here is how we use the terms in this book.

PSC revenue take. A party's percentage share of total PSC revenue. (Because, as noted above, total PSC revenue equals total gross field revenue, the PSC revenue take is also each party's percentage share of total gross field revenue.) In our example model, "Ch6_PSC_Revs_Single_Year.xls," we calculate each party's PSC revenue take in cells E31 and E32. Under the Base Scenario, the contractor's PSC revenue take is 41%, and the government's is 59%. Note that the checksum in cell E34 checks that the two sum to 100%.

PSC cashflow take. We use this to mean each party's percentage share of the PSC's total net cashflow, or NCF (the calculation of which we will address later). Under the Base Scenario, the contractor's cashflow take is 15.7% (cell D44), and the government's is 84.3% (cell D45). Note that the cashflow take is not meaningful when the monetary value of one or both party's NCF is negative.

Confusingly, some people use the term "profit take" to mean PSC cashflow take, while others use "profit take" to mean a party's share of total profit oil (i.e., the values in cells D12 and D13) – which are quite different things.

We do not claim that our choice of terms in this book is the best, but we do define the terms clearly for our purposes. We do so because we want you to know what we mean, and – importantly – to **seek clarification** when someone uses these terms, especially unqualified versions of them, i.e., simply "contractor take" or "government take." (Without qualification, these takes are more likely to refer to revenue takes than profit takes, but it is hard to be sure if the terms are not defined.)

Split the Excel screen horizontally, and scroll/zoom out as needed so that you can see rows 2–42 in the top part of the screen, and the table which starts in row 84 in the bottom part. This table is reproduced in Figure 6.6. You will see a list of scenarios, one for each exercise.

For each, start by clicking the (duplicate) button in cell H84 to reset the model to the Base Scenario. Try to guess the impact on the contractor's and government's revenue "takes," compared to the Base Scenario – even if in only general terms, i.e., the direction of change – of setting the model to the gray-shaded parameters.

Reset to Base Scenario / Exercise #	Change the gray-shaded parameters as shown						Results	
	Oil price, $/b	Contractor recoverable costs $mm	Royalty rate	Max. Net Revenue avail. as Cost Oil	Contractor profit oil share	Gov't profit oil share	Contractor "Revenue take"	Gov't "Revenue take"
Scenario)	100	30	15%	65%	20%	80%	41.0%	59.0%
1	100	15	15%	65%	20%	80%		
2	100	60	15%	65%	20%	80%		
3	100	85	15%	65%	20%	80%		
4	100	30	5%	65%	20%	80%		
5	100	30	25%	65%	20%	80%		
6	100	30	60%	65%	20%	80%		
7	100	30	15%	85%	20%	80%		
8	100	30	15%	40%	20%	80%		
9	100	30	15%	25%	20%	80%		
10	100	30	15%	65%	10%	90%		
11	100	30	15%	65%	50%	50%		
12	50	30	15%	65%	20%	80%		

Figure 6.6   Gross revenue distribution exercises, from the file "Ch6_PSC_Revs_Single_Year.xls"

Then, using the spinner controls in rows 3–5 at the top of the charts, make these changes: that is, input the gray-shaded values while watching the charts change, and then record the answers in the table's Results columns on the left. Be sure you understand the impacts (again, at least the direction of the changes) for each scenario evaluated.

This should help you develop some intuition about the interaction of the various "moving parts" and their revenue impacts. It might not be easy at first, as the behavior of even this very simple PSC can be complex.

Hard-coded answers (in blue font) are shown in the next table in file "Ch6_PSC_Revs_Single_Year.xls," which starts in row 102, and are discussed in two versions of the same file, "Ch6_PSC_Rev_Sharing_Exercises.pdf" and the "flipbook" file called "Ch6_PSC_Rev_Sharing_Exercises.exe." You should proceed to one of these two files when you have finished.

Understand Revenue Determinants, but Keep the Cashflow Impact in Mind

The focus of the exercises which you should have just done has been percentage revenue takes. While it is important that you become comfortable with calculating and analyzing these, bear in mind that:

- revenue measured in percentage terms is not the same as revenue measured in absolute terms – a high percentage might sound impressive, but will be less so if it is a percentage of a low total; and

- revenue is only a stepping stone to the most important metric, which is cashflow. In the table starting in row 119 of "Ch6_PSC_Revs_Single_Year.xls," we have repeated the revenue take results of the exercise above, and added a column showing the contractor's cashflow in each case (column Q).

We show a scatter chart, or cross-plot, of the revenue and cashflow results in Figure 6.7.

Notice in this chart that in some cases there is a strong positive correlation between contractor PSC revenue take and contractor PSC cashflow, while in others there is none at all. The lack of correlation is due to the different ways that *costs* are considered in the calculation of contractor PSC revenue, versus in the calculation of contractor cashflow:

- contractor PSC revenue considers contractor costs only to the extent to which these costs determine cost oil, which in turn is only *the portion* of costs for which the contractor gets reimbursed; whereas

- contractor PSC cashflow considers *all costs* which the contractor incurs, whether the contractor gets reimbursed for them or not.

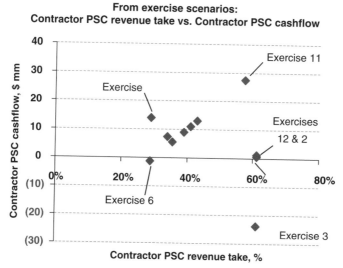

Figure 6.7   From the file "Ch6_PSC_Revs_Single_Year.xls"

We shall explore the dynamics of PSC cashflows (NCFs) and NPVs later, when we present a suite of multi-year, discounted cashflow models.

Cashflow reconciliation: another important check

Be sure to inspect the short "Reconciliation of Gross field revenue & PSC costs & cash-flow" section which starts in row 52. This is another important check which we suggest you use in PSC models. If necessary, see the explanation in the file's "Reconciliation_Check_Explained" worksheet.

6.5 INTRODUCING "ENTITLEMENT VOLUMES"

Under a PSC regime, the volume of petroleum to which a contractor is entitled is called, appropriately, its **entitlement volumes** or **net entitlement volumes**.

It is useful to explain how these are calculated, by comparison to how the analogous measure is calculated under a tax and royalty regime.

As covered in Chapter 1, under a tax and royalty regime, the volumes of production to which the investor may claim rights are its **working interest volumes**. Even though our simple example model in "Ch6_PSC_Revs_Single_Year.xls" is *not* a tax and royalty regime, for the purpose of comparison, we have calculated the working interest volumes in cell D50.

A	B	C	D
			Reset to Base Scenario
2	**Assumptions**		
5	Field production	mmb	1.00
6	Oil price received	$ / b	100.00
7	Royalty rate	%	15.00%
15	**Calculations**		
16	Gross field revenue	$ mm	100.00
17	Royalty	$ mm	15.00
18	**Net revenue**	**$ mm**	**85.00**
30			
31	Total Contractor PSC revenue	$ mm	41.00
47			
49	Contractor PSC entitlement volumes, net of royalty	mmb	0.41
50	Memo: Contractor working interest volumes, net of royalty	mmb	0.85

Figure 6.8 Working interest volume calculation, from the file "Ch6_PSC_Revs_Single_Year.xls"
Notes: Reflects Base Scenario; some rows are hidden.

To be economically meaningful, these working interest volumes should be reported on a net of royalty basis, i.e., after the deduction of royalty, as we have done in cell D50. As shown in Figure 6.8, under the Base Scenario, in which:

- the contractor has a 100% working interest in the **PSC permit**, also sometimes called the **PSC license**;

- gross field production is 1.00 mmb (or mm bbl); and

- the royalty rate is 15%;

then the working interest volumes equal 100% of

$$(1.00 \text{ mmb}) \times (1–15\%) = (1.00 \text{ mmb}) \times (85\%) = \textbf{0.85 mmb}$$

Thus in Figure 6.8, the working interest volumes, net of royalty,[6] of 0.85 mmb are calculated in cell D50 with the formula =D5*(100%-D7).

---

[6] As mentioned in Chapter 1, sometimes working interest volumes are reported on a gross of royalty basis, i.e., ignoring any royalty deductions. On this basis, the working interest volumes in this example would simply be 100% × 1.00 mmb = 1.00 mmb. This is not economically meaningful, however, as it ignores the very real deduction of royalty; the 15% of volumes deducted as royalty are never the company's to begin with. Still, some companies like reporting on a gross of royalty basis – misleadingly – because it makes their volumes look larger. Some stock exchange rules insist that volumes are reported net of royalty to avoid misleading the public.

"Barrels Worth of Revenue"

Note that we could have calculated these working interest volumes, net of royalty, another way, by framing the question as "Translated into barrels, how much net revenue is the company entitled to?" We would answer as follows.

First, if we consider that, generically,

$$\text{(volume)} \times \text{(price)} = \text{(revenue)}$$

then it is easy to see that

$$\text{(volume)} = \text{(revenue)}/\text{(price)}$$

In this case we are concerned specifically with volumes which are net of royalty. So – again, given that the company's working interest is 100% – we could also calculate it as 100% of

$$\text{(working interest volume, net of royalty)} = \text{(revenue, net of royalty)}/\text{(price)}$$

Plugging in the values from cells D18 and D6, respectively, would give us 100% of

$$\text{(working interest volume, net of royalty)} = (\$85 \text{ mm})/(\$100)$$

$$\text{working interest volume, net of royalty} = \textbf{0.85 mmb}$$

which matches our earlier answer.

This might seem obvious, yet the failure to understand this idea of "barrels worth of revenue" (or, when gas and other non-oil commodities are involved, revenue expressed as barrels of oil equivalent) is what sometimes causes people who are new to PSCs to struggle with the concept of PSC entitlement volumes, to which we now turn.

The formula used to calculate the contractor's PSC entitlement volumes, net of royalty, in cell D49 in Figure 6.9, is $=\text{IF(D6=0, 0, D31/D6)}$:

- The first expression IF(D6=0, 0 ...) is just a standard "error trap"; in a case where the oil price in cell $\boxed{\text{D6}}$ is $0, it has Excel display a zero, rather than a "#DIV/0!" error message.
- Otherwise, the answer is $\boxed{\text{D31/D6}}$, or the contractor's PSC revenue divided by the oil price, or **0.41 mmb**.

	A	B	C	D
				Reset to Base Scenario
2	**Assumptions**			
5	Field production		mmb	1.00
6	Oil price received		$ / b	100.00
7	Royalty rate		%	15.00%
15	**Calculations**			
16	Gross field revenue		$ mm	100.00
17	Royalty		$ mm	15.00
18	**Net revenue**		**$ mm**	**85.00**
30				
31	Total Contractor PSC revenue		$ mm	41.00
47				
49	Contractor PSC entitlement volumes, net of royalty		mmb	0.41
50	Memo: Contractor working interest volumes, net of royalty		mmb	0.85

Figure 6.9 Contractor PSC entitlement volume calculation, from the file "Ch6_PSC_Revs_Single_Year.xls;" some rows are hidden

This is exactly the same revenue, net of royalty/price formula we used in our second calculation of working interest volumes above. The only difference is how we have calculated the revenue, net of royalty :

- in the working interest volume calculation, revenue, net of royalty was gross field revenue, i.e., (field production) × (the oil price) – (a 15% royalty);
- whereas in the PSC entitlement volume calculation, the contractor's total PSC revenue, i.e.,

$$(\text{cost oil}) + (\text{contractor's share of profit oil})$$

is *already* net of royalty.

The reason why the contractor's PSC revenue, net of royalty is already net of royalty is that – as seen in the second column of Figure 6.10, which just repeats Figure 6.1 – net revenue (i.e., revenue, net of royalty) is the starting point for any PSC revenue which the contractor can receive. In other words, revenue has already been "netted out" (deducted) in Step 2, before the contractor can hope to see any share of remaining revenue.

Thus the contractor's PSC entitlement volumes are **0.41 mmb** (cell D49). This is a lot less than the working interest volumes of **0.85 mmb**.

- The 0.41 mmb in entitlement volumes accurately express the revenue, expressed as barrels, which the contractor receives under the PSC.
- The 0.85 mmb working interest volumes, on the other hand, are purely "notional" or, put more bluntly, economically meaningless, as they show what revenue, expressed as barrels, the PSC contractor would receive *if the fiscal regime were not in fact a PSC*.

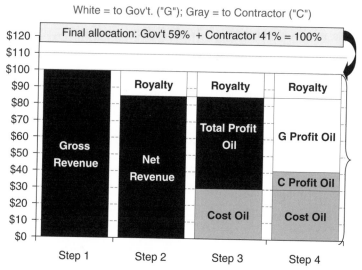

Figure 6.10   (Repeats Figure 6.1) Simplified gross revenue distribution under an oil-producing PSC, from the file "Ch6_PSC_Revs_Single_Year.xls"
Note: Reflects Base Scenario.

Still, some PSC contractors report their working interest volumes alongside their PSC entitlement volumes. A cynical view would suggest that this is in hope of misleading people who are unfamiliar with PSCs into thinking that the contractor's economic volumes are higher than they really are. It is important to keep this important difference in mind when considering volume entitlements.

Looking Ahead: Advanced Entitlement Topics

Contractor entitlement volumes are a key metric reported by companies which are party to PSCs. So far we have only introduced entitlement in a simplistic example. There are other noteworthy aspects which we have not addressed yet:

- In some countries, the entitlement calculation is subject to various regulations governing whether *any* entitlement volumes may be reported if the contractor's NPV is negative.

- Contractor entitlement can be easier to calculate than to analyze, because it varies with the oil price, sometimes in ways which are not always immediately intuitive or obvious.

- In some cases, a contractor's entitlement can rise while its NPV falls. This is why it is unwise to focus solely on entitlement volumes as a measure of "value."

We will address these topics later in the chapter.

6.6   SIMPLISTIC, MULTI-PERIOD PSC MODEL: THE CALCULATION OF COST OIL

So far, our single-year example model, "Ch6_PSC_Revs_Single_Year.xls," has helped us to explain the basics of PSC revenue distribution, revenue and cashflow takes, and entitlement volumes.

By modeling only one period, however, we have missed important nuances in the calculation of one item – cost oil – which we will cover here.

The basic principle we have seen, i.e., that cost oil is the lesser of:

- maximum funds available for cost recovery; and

- the contractor's recoverable costs,

still holds true.

Now, however, we need to **define the contractor's recoverable costs more fully**.

In any given accounting period designated by the PSC for the calculation of cost oil,

Contractor recoverable costs
=
(A) Contractor costs which become recoverable for the first time in the current period
+
(B) Any past contractor costs which were recoverable, but not recovered, in prior periods, and therefore are eligible to be carried forward to the current period

---

We elaborate as follows.

(A) Contractor costs which become recoverable for the first time in the current period

We will also refer to these as "newly recoverable costs" for short.

When these costs become recoverable depends on the cost recovery mechanism which the PSC specifies:

> *Variant 1.* In our single-year introductory model – and in a new, still simplistic but multi-year model which we shall introduce shortly – recoverable costs become recoverable for the first time in the period when they are incurred. This applies to all recoverable costs, whether they are opex, intangible capex, tangible capex,[7] abandonment payments, etc. This approach is simpler to calculate, although in practice is not very commonly used by PSCs for tangible capex, which often makes up a material part of recoverable costs. We will focus on this approach for now, however, because it will help us make our points more easily.

---

[7] See Section 1.6.5 of Chapter 1 for an explanation of the difference between tangible and intangible capex.

Variant 2. More often, however, PSCs make the tangible capex portion of recoverable costs recoverable, *not* when this tangible portion is incurred, but rather when depreciation charges relating to the tangible capex arise. In such cases, then, there are actually two mechanisms for determining when recoverable costs first become recoverable, depending on the type of cost:

- for tangible capex, it is when the related depreciation charges first arise;
- and for other recoverable costs, it is when they are first incurred, just like in Variant 1, above. In accounting jargon, such costs are said to be "expensed" in the accounting period in which they are incurred (i.e., rather than depreciated over time).

We will present an example model with Variant 2 in a later section.

(B) Any past contractor costs which were recoverable, but not recovered, in prior periods, and therefore are eligible to be carried forward to the current period

Recall how in some examples and exercises covered earlier, the maximum portion of net revenue available as cost oil was less than recoverable costs. In such cases, the contractor received the lesser of the two, i.e., it received the maximum portion of net revenue available as cost oil, but this was not enough to cover all of the recoverable costs. One such case is that shown in Figure 6.11, which simply repeats Figure 6.4 from the "Simplistic Cost Oil Calculation – Example 2" mentioned above.

Here, the contractor had to "swallow" the unrecovered portion of recoverable costs (represented by the portion of the third column which is above the horizontal line). What happened next? Because, in this example, there was only one year of activity, the answer is – nothing. The contractor never got a chance to recover this portion of costs, which hurt its cashflow:

- In the real world of multi-year projects, however, virtually all PSCs would permit the contractor to carry forward this unrecovered portion of costs to the next accounting period.

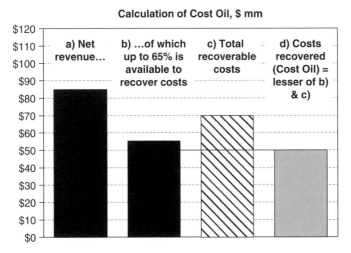

Figure 6.11   (Repeats Figure 6.4) Calculation of cost oil under *adjusted* Base Scenario, from the file "Ch6_PSC_Revs_Single_Year.xls"

- This means that the unrecovered portion would be added to the next period's newly recovered costs, to result in a new total of recoverable costs in this next period. In other words, it is like a credit: suppose last year you were owed $100 but only got $70, due to lack of available funds; this would entitle you to $30 this year. As always, if there are sufficient funds available in this next period, then the contractor will recover this new total, but if there are not, it will not, and the unrecovered portion of this new total will be carried forward to a *next* period.

- Most PSCs, in fact, permit unrecovered costs from one period to be carried forward for potential recovery (i.e., available funds permitting) to future periods indefinitely until they are fully recovered, or until the project life ends, whichever comes first. All our example PSC models assume this to be the case.

- Be aware that some PSCs, however, do limit how long costs incurred in a particular period can be carried forward, although these are less common.[8]

Multi-year Cost Oil: Interactive Example

Let us look at an example, taken from a new, multi-year example model, "Ch6_PSC_rev share_diagram.xls." It is essentially the same as our previous model, except that it has a five-year timeframe, and so calculates cost recovery on a multi-year basis. We will detail the underlying calculations shortly; for now, just focus on Figure 6.12. It is a screenshot of the chart which starts in cell M71, showing the results which appear after you click the "Scenario 2" button in cell B2.

In Figure 6.12:

- The captions at the top of the chart (which update to reflect input assumptions, which are changeable in rows 3–5) help explain where some of the values shown in the columns come from.

- The first two captions show assumptions which ultimately explain that, in each year, the maximum portion of each year's net revenue which is available as cost oil is $9 mm. This corresponds to the first (black) column for each year shown in the body of the chart.

- The third caption shows the assumption that newly incurred recoverable costs are assumed to be $15 mm per year. This corresponds to the second (white) column for each year. (Note that we are using Variant 1, as described above, i.e., we assume that all such costs become eligible for recovery in the year incurred.)

- Focusing for now just on the three columns for 2015, you should recognize that the format is similar to that in Figures 6.3 and 6.4, above, in that:

  - cost oil (the gray column) is always equal to the lesser of (a) maximum net revenue available as cost oil and (b) recoverable costs; and

---

[8] Modeling time-limited cost recovery can be rather tricky. While we do not detail it here, be aware that the methodology would be the same as that used to model a time-limited tax loss carryforward, which we treat in "Appendix III_Time_limited_tax_loss_carryforwards.pdf".

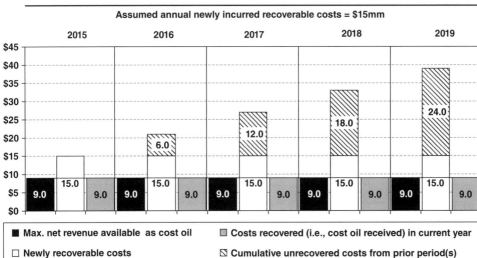

Assumed annual gross revenue of $20mm, less assumed 10% royalty = annual net revenue of $18mm; Thus assumed max. 50% of annual net revenue available as cost oil = $9mm

Figure 6.12   Multi-year cost oil determination, from Scenario 2 of the file "Ch6_PSC_rev share_diagram.xls"
Note: Results reflect Scenario 2.

○ the portion of the recoverable costs column which is above the horizontal line represents that year's unrecovered costs. In Figure 6.12, the data labels on the columns tell us that, at the end of 2015, **unrecovered costs** equal $15 mm in recoverable costs, minus $9 mm in costs recovered, or **$6 mm**.

The next difference between Figure 6.12 and Figures 6.3 and 6.4 is that Figure 6.12 shows what happens next to the unrecovered costs – they get carried forward to future periods for *potential* cost recovery.

- By "potential" we mean they are *eligible* to be recovered in the future periods.

- This is not the same, however, as *actual* cost recovery, which depends on whether there are sufficient funds from the revenue stream available. As we will now see, funds from the revenue stream are actually not sufficient in this example.

- Starting in 2016, the 2015 unrecovered costs of $6 mm get added to the middle column, in the form of the top segment with the diagonal line pattern.

- We can see that, in fact, every year, $15 mm − $9 mm = $6 mm of newly incurred recoverable costs (i.e., the portion of the white column which is above the horizontal line) are *not* recovered, which is why, starting in 2016, the *cumulative* unrecovered costs from the prior period(s) accumulate in multiples of $6 mm.

Let us look at a different scenario. In our multi-year example model, "Ch6_PSC_rev share_diagram.xls," split the Excel screen horizontally, so that you see the chart shown in Figure 6.12 in the bottom part of the screen, and the spinner controls in rows 3–5 (columns

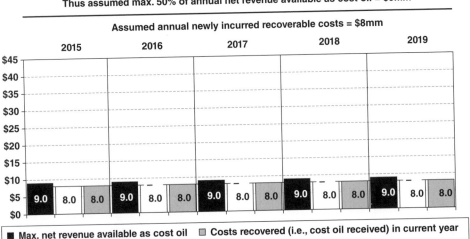

Figure 6.13 Multi-year cost oil determination, under new input assumptions, discussed below, from the file "Ch6_PSC_rev share_diagram.xls"

R and Z) in the top part. Starting with Scenario 2 still showing, use the spinner in cell R4 to lower the annual newly incurred recoverable costs, in steps of $1 mm, from $15 mm to $8 mm, watching the chart as you do so.

- With each $1 mm reduction in annual newly recoverable costs, the balance of unrecovered costs falls, because there are now less costs to recover to begin with.

- When annual newly recoverable costs reach $9 mm, they exactly match available funds, so that annual cost oil is $9 mm, and there are no unrecovered costs to carry forward.

- When annual newly recoverable costs reach $8 mm, the chart will look like Figure 6.13. Now, annual cost oil, being the lesser of funds available and recoverable costs, is also $8 mm, and there are no unrecovered costs.

Step back for a moment from our focus on just cost recovery, and test your knowledge of the wider workings of the PSC revenue distribution mechanism, by answering this: what happens to the $1 mm in net revenue which is not used as cost oil?

Exercise: Multi-year Cost Oil Determination

Use the spinners in rows 3–5 to scroll through the minimum and maximum permitted range of values for:

- annual gross revenue,
- annual newly incurred recoverable costs,

- the royalty rate, and

- the maximum percentage of net revenue available as cost oil

while watching the chart which starts in row 71. Be sure you understand why the chart changes as it does.

Also, consider the following. This simplistic model only looks at undiscounted monetary values. On this basis, the contractor's total (five-year) cashflow is unaffected by the timing of the contractor's cost recovery; all that matters is that it *does* recover its costs, at some point. Would this still be true if we consider total (five-year) discounted cashflow (i.e., NPV)?

Multi-year Cost Oil Calculation Details

As mentioned, most of the formulas used in our new, multi-year example model, "Ch6_PSC_rev share_diagram.xls," are the same as in our previous, single-year model, with the exception of those used to calculate cost oil, which we detail here. Select Scenario 2 and refer to the screenshot in Figure 6.14.

Note that, in this model, we have taken a shortcut by making annual gross revenue (cell C7) an explicit input assumption, rather than having separate assumptions for production and the oil price; this simplification will not impair our explanation.

	A	B	C	D	E	F	G	H	I
3	Scenario Shown:		2						
4	**Assumptions**			*All monetary values in $ mm*					
5		Inflation is ignored;	ELT is not applied;		Blue font = hard-coded values				
6		Contractor working interest = 100%, therefore the Contractor bears all costs							
7	Annual Gross Revenue		20						
8	Annual costs (all are recoverable)		15						
9	Royalty rate		10%	10					
10	Max. Net Revenue avail. as Cost Oil		50%	50					
11	Contractor profit share		20%	20					
12	Government profit share		80%						
13									
14	**Calculations**								
15			Total/other	2015	2016	2017	2018	2019	Key / typical formulae
16	Gross Revenue		100.00	20.00	20.00	20.00	20.00	20.00	F16. =C7
17	Royalty		10.00	2.00	2.00	2.00	2.00	2.00	F17. =F16*C9
18	Net Revenue		90.00	18.00	18.00	18.00	18.00	18.00	F18. =F16–F17
19	Max. Net Revenue avail. as Cost Oil		45.00	9.00	9.00	9.00	9.00	9.00	F19. =F18*C10
21	Newly recoverable costs		75.00	15.00	15.00	15.00	15.00	15.00	F21. =C8
22	Cuml. unrecovered costs from prior years			0.00	6.00	12.00	18.00	24.00	F22. =E27
23	Total costs recoverable in current year			15.00	21.00	27.00	33.00	39.00	F23. =F21+F22
25	Costs recovered i.e.. Cost Oil		45.00	9.00	9.00	9.00	9.00	9.00	F25. =MIN(F23,F19)
27	Unrecovered costs to be carried forward			6.00	12.00	18.00	24.00	30.00	F27. =F23–F25
29	Costs not recovered		30.00						C29. =C21–C25
30									A29. =ROUND(C29–H27,8)

Figure 6.14   Multi-year cost oil calculation, from Scenario 2 of the file "Ch6_PSC_rev share_ diagram.xls"

Note: Reflects Scenario 2.

Otherwise, the assumptions and calculations are much the same as in the single-year model, so that the determination of annual $9 mm maximum net revenue available as cost oil (in row 19) should be straightforward.

To calculate annual cost oil received by the contractor, we still need to know <u>total currently recoverable costs</u> (row 23). As discussed above, each year, these are the sum of two components:

- The first is annual newly incurred recoverable costs of $15 mm (row 21), which comes straight from the assumption in cell C8.

- The second component is <u>cumulative unrecovered costs from prior years</u>, calculated in row 22. We use two formulas in this row:

  ○ The first "formula" (in cell D22) is unique to the first timeline year of 2015. As indicated by the cell comment (visible within the Excel file), it is not actually a formula, but rather a hard-coded value of $0, reflecting the assumption that no recoverable costs were incurred before 2015.[9]

  ○ The second formula in row 22 is used for all years starting in 2016:

    – This part of the calculation requires a slight "twist," in that <u>we have to calculate down and then back up again</u>. Each annual result starting from 2016 equals the prior year's unrecovered costs (the calculation of which we shall explain soon). Thus in 2017, for example, total cumulative unrecovered costs from prior years of $12 mm (cell F22) simply equal the $12 mm value of costs which were not recovered in 2016 (cell E27), and which therefore get carried forward to the next year.

    – We have drawn arrows from the cells in row 27 to the following years in row 22 to emphasize this flow of the calculations.

Warning: slightly tricky calculation ahead

As we shall soon see, the fact that values in row 22 depend in part on values in row 27 makes the calculations potentially a bit tricky:

- as opposed to the usual practice of filling in a row with formulas to get the right answers for that row, before moving down to the next row,

- in this case, you have to fill in every annual cell in rows 22, 23, 25 and 27 before any of them show the right answers; once you fill in the last required annual cell in row 27, suddenly and all at once, all the annual cells in these rows will become correct.

---

[9] Note that in cases – which we will examine later – where recoverable costs *have* been incurred, but not recovered, *before* the start of the model's timeframe, one always must know the total cumulative amount of such costs, as at the start of the first timeline period.

This information should come from the contractor or perhaps the government. When there have been pre-timeline recoverable, but unrecovered costs, this is very important. Although past costs from before the model timeframe start costs are "sunk costs" which, seen in isolation, are not considered as future cash outflows to be discounted in a NPV calculation, such past costs *are* relevant, when, as is usually the case, they are recoverable in future years; in such cases they <u>impact cost oil received by the contractor</u> in the first timeframe period and/or in subsequent periods, and thus <u>*do*</u> impact future cashflows and NPV.

To conclude the calculation of total annual recoverable costs, in row 23, we sum the annual values in rows 21 and 22. Thus for 2017 (cell F23), total annual recoverable costs are the sum of current year costs of $15 mm and cumulative unrecovered costs from prior years of $12 mm, which equals $27 mm.

Next, in row 25, we calculate annual costs recovered by the contractor, i.e. cost oil. As we have seen before, in any given period, cost oil is the lesser of maximum funds available as cost oil, and total recoverable costs. Thus in 2017, for example, we calculate cost oil (cell F25) as the lower of these two items with Excel's MIN function, using the formula $\boxed{=\text{MIN(F23, F19)}}$. This gives the result of $9 mm for 2017 cost oil.

Recall that in the step before the last one, we carried forward unrecovered costs from row 27 to the following years in row 22. Now, in our next step, we calculate the underlying values in row 27 themselves. Both the principle and formula are simple:

In a given period,

Unrecovered costs to carry forward to the next period

=

Total costs recoverable in a current period

minus

Costs recovered (i.e., cost oil received) in this current period

---

In other words, what the contractor is owed, minus what it actually gets, equals what it is still owed. The answers in row 27 will be cumulative – it will show total amounts which the contractor is still owed from the time it first incurred recoverable costs. (These results correspond to the growing cumulative third column for each year starting in 2016 in the chart seen in Figure 6.12.)

For example, in cell F27, the $18 mm in unrecovered costs accumulated by the end of 2017, which are to be carried forward to 2018, is calculated as $27 mm (cell F23) minus $9 mm (cell F25).

As an intuitive check, note how the balance of unrecovered costs accumulates each year. In our simplified example, each year, maximum net revenue available as cost oil is $9 mm, or $6 mm less than annual current year costs of $15 mm. Therefore it accumulates by $6 mm per year – to total $6 mm at the end of 2015 (cell D27), and then $12 mm, $18 mm, $24 mm and $30 mm in each successive year.

Note the memo item in cell C29, showing that when the timeframe finishes at the end of 2019, the contractor has not recovered $30 mm of its total, newly incurred (from 2015) recoverable costs of $75 mm (cell C21). We calculate this $30 mm in cell C29 with the simple formula =C21−C25, i.e., as recoverable costs incurred from 2015 onwards, minus cost oil received from 2015 onwards. (You could adapt this formula to include pre-2015 unrecovered costs as well.)

Note also that the checksum result of zero in cell A29 verifies that the values in cells C29 and H27 (the final year of the timeframe) match.

This result in cell C29 has no dependents in the model, and so is for information only. However, the failure to recover all costs, as in this case, will, of course, be reflected in the contractor's net cashflow.

Exercise: Try These Calculations Yourself

In the file "Ch6_PSC_model_exercise.xls," go to the "Exercise" worksheet, set the model to Scenario 2, and then fill in the blank, orange-shaded cells with the appropriate formulas. Compare your answers to the Scenario 2 results on the "Solution" sheet.

6.7   TOPIC IN DEPTH: CONTRACTOR ENTITLEMENT

Having introduced PSC entitlement volumes earlier in this chapter, we now explore some related issues in detail.

Proceed to the file "Ch6_PSC entitlement.pdf," which is accompanied by the example model "Ch6_PSC entitlement_model.xls." This section concludes this chapter.

Chapter 7

More Realistic PSC Modeling

7

More Realistic PSC Modeling

7.1 INTRODUCING A MORE REALISTIC PSC MODEL

The simplified PSC models we have presented so far have helped us introduce a number of key concepts and methods, without the distractions of details which were not needed to make our points.

From now on, however, we will be using variations of a more realistic and sophisticated "core" model.

Looking Ahead: Moving Towards a "Core" Model

We will introduce this "core" model in two stages:

1. Most of the features in the models we will use henceforth are in the file "Ch7_PSC_basic_model_no_depreciation.xls," which we detail in this section.
2. The version of the model which we will present in the next section is essentially the same as the one just mentioned, except that it will use a cost recovery mechanism based on depreciation. This version will be what we will refer to as our final **core PSC model**, which, for the rest of our PSC-related material, will serve as the basis for other models which illustrate various facets of PSC regimes (e.g., different profit oil distribution mechanisms).

   - We choose this as our core model because depreciation-based cost recovery mechanisms are the norm in most PSC regimes.

   - The reason why we wait until a second "stage" to introduce this core model is that the depreciation calculations, done properly, are unfortunately rather detailed and take up a lot of space; we feel it would be too much at once to introduce this in this section, in addition to the new features used in the present section's model.

Tour of This Section's Model: Basic Controls and Assumptions

Open "Ch7_PSC_basic_model_no_depreciation.xls" and note the following.

Buttons for Custom Views

In row 12 are buttons which trigger macros that hide certain rows and split the screen, to make it easier to see and interact with various charts. In this model, two of the charts, which we will discuss later, will become standard in our core model. A third chart is specific to a short analysis we will present at the end of this section.

Note that these custom views will probably look best on a desktop monitor, as the charts were designed to be viewed, ideally, at a zoom resolution of 100%.

You can exit any of the custom views by clicking the "Show all rows" button in cell C12.

Time-related Assumptions

Starting with this PSC model, we will include the calculation of **discounted cashflows/NPVs, expressed in money-of-the-day ("MOD") terms**. Therefore, the section in rows 16–23 has cells for inputting inflation and discount rates, which in turn determine the values in the red-bordered, named ranges for the annual inflation and discount factors in rows 22–23 (which have been given the range names "Infl_index" and "Disc_factor" respectively). These use the mid-year convention, which we introduced in Section 1.2 of Chapter 1. The assumed last year of the PSC permit is in cell C19. We have locked this to 2024 (cell C19).

Fiscal and Field-related Assumptions

In row 28 are sensitivity multipliers, which we will use in later exercises to quickly see the impact of a change in a given input assumption. There are multipliers for the oil price, capex and opex (all of which are applied to the uninflated, i.e., Real $, versions of these parameters) as well as for production. The default setting – to which the model can be reset by clicking the "Reset assumptions to Base Scenario" button in cell B12 – for each of these multipliers is 100%. For example, changing the oil price multiplier (cell C28) from 100% to 105% will increase the assumed Real $ oil price (which can be input directly in monetary terms in cell C31) by 5%.

Basic fiscal assumptions are found in cells B33:C37. Note that this section will occupy more space in some of our later models; for example, when fiscal terms require tables which detail how profit oil is distributed according to sliding scales, rather than by the simple fixed percentages used here (cells C36:C37).

In cell C39 there is a switch to impose (or ignore) the positive NPV test to entitlement reserves, which was introduced in the last chapter's Section 6.5, and elaborated on in Section 6.7

Field cost assumptions are entered in cells L31:L36 in Real 2015 $ terms.

Note also that the field costs section includes an input cell (L33) for "sunk costs," i.e., recoverable costs incurred before the model's timeframe starts in 2015.

- In a narrow, *direct sense*, these are *irrelevant* to our ultimate NPV calculation, as NPV is the net present value of *future* cashflows, whereas "sunk" costs are by definition past costs incurred before the assumed valuation date (in this case, January 1, 2015).

- But in a broader, *indirect*, and yet very *relevant* sense, these sunk costs *will* affect NPV. This is because, in this example model, the sunk costs have not been recovered. They will be recovered, wholly or partially, resulting in cost oil for the contractor, sometime starting within the model's timeframe. This resultant cost oil will most definitely be a future cashflow, and thus will impact NPV.

All these costs are entered on a pre-sensitivity multiplier, Real 2015 basis, except for the pre-2015 sunk costs, which are entered on an inflated (i.e., MOD, or "money-of-the-day") basis. The adjacent cells in column M show the effects of the relevant multiplier settings.

Production volumes are entered on a pre-sensitivity multiplier, pre-economic limit test ("ELT") basis in row 42. Recall that the ELT (introduced in Chapter 1) determines when a specific field should be abandoned on commercial grounds, when the assumptions determining field revenue and the relevant deductions are taken into account. We have ignored it so far in our coverage of PSCs, for the sake of simplicity. This important addition to our current PSC model is applied in the model's Calculation section, as we will see soon.

Note the section "Memo: results of field assumptions in Real 2015 $/b, (pre-ELT basis)" in cells O27:R37. This shows basic field parameters (future revenue, costs and the resultant net field cashflow) and on an uninflated, undiscounted, per-barrel basis, ignoring both the ELT and all fiscal terms except for royalty.

- This is a useful quick-look reference, especially when changing input assumptions, to see whether the field generates positive cashflow on a "fundamental" level, before considering the "distorting" effects of the ELT, parts of the fiscal regime, and the time value of money.

- The view given by this section is only a starting point, but can still provide useful insights. For example, if you click the "Reset assumptions to Base Scenario" button in cell B12 and then set the real oil price assumption in cell C31 to $442/b, you will see that net field cashflow (cell R37) turns negative. This alone will tell you that Contractor NPV, for example, will almost certainly be negative at this price as well, without having to analyze the full fiscal model to see why. (Don't forget to reset back to the Base Scenario.).

Tour of This Section's Model: Results Summary

This part of the model, in rows 47–77, presents summaries of the following results, on a total life-of-field and, unless stated otherwise, post-ELT (i.e., considering the ELT) basis:

- the components of each party's PSC revenue;
- financial results – each party's total PSC revenue, total undiscounted net cashflow (NCF) and total discounted net cashflow (i.e., NPV) and their associated percentage takes;
- contractor IRR (i.e., internal rate of return, introduced in Section 1.2 of Chapter 1);
- the final production year, and the production life in years, on both a pre-ELT (i.e., ignoring the ELT) and post-ELT basis – comparing these shows the effect of the ELT on production life;
- volumetric outcomes, i.e., total pre-ELT and post-ELT gross field production, and the contractor's post-ELT working interest and entitlement barrels; and
- the reconciliation of gross field revenue, PSC costs and NCF, which serves as an important check.

Tour of This Section's Model: Pre-ELT Calculations and Determination of the ELT

This short section's purpose is to calculate the ELT, which is the economic cutoff year, i.e., the last when production is "economic" (commercially worthwhile). As explained in Section 1.8 of Chapter 1, this last economic year is calculated as the *earlier* of:

- the last year (cell C19) that the PSC permit, or license, is valid (which will always be 2024 in our examples in this and the next chapter, unless stated otherwise) and

- the year of peak cumulative **gross operating cashflow ("GOCF")**, which we define for ELT purposes, under the assumed fiscal regime, as gross field revenue less royalty and opex.

In essence, this test means that the field should be produced as long as permitted by the license term, but only if doing so increases total project GOCF.

For example, under our Base Scenario:

- Annual GOCF is calculated in inflated (MOD) dollars in rows 84–90. Total GOCF, when the field produces through to the end of **2024**, is **MOD $190.1 mm** (cell D90). Note that this total of MOD $1901.1 mm includes two negative annual results (i.e., GOCF losses) in 2023 and 2024.

- *Cumulative* GOCF is calculated in row 91. Note that the peak level of cumulative GOCF is **MOD $193.5 mm**, occurring in **2022** (cell M91). The cumulative peak occurs this year because, as just mentioned, GOCF is negative in the following two years. We "capture" (i.e., record) this cumulative peak value in cell D91, which uses the formula =MAX(F91:O91).

- Thus we see that by producing every year, through to the end of 2024, without regard for the ELT, the field under the Base Scenario generates MOD $190.1 mm, but when we pay attention to the ELT, we stop producing at the end of 2022, raising total GOCF to MOD $193.3 mm. Thus the ELT has done its job, which is to maximize GOCF.

We then combine the information that 2022 is the year of peak cumulative GOCF with information about the length of the license period, to determine the field's "ultimate" stopping year:

- First, we capture in row 94 the fact that 2022 is the year of peak cumulative GOCF:
  - In each annual cell of this row, we use a formula which answers with the year, if the year in question is the year when this peak value occurs; otherwise, the answer will be the text "n.a."
  - For example, the typical annual formula used in 2022 (cell M94) is =IF(M91 = $D91, year, n.a.), where M91 is cumulative GOCF in 2022, and D91 is the peak cumulative GOCF of all years. Since in this example 2022 is in fact the year when peak cumulative GOCF occurs, the answer in cell M94 is 2022, while the answer in the other years is "n.a."

○ We then capture the information that 2022 is the peak year in cell D94, which uses the formula $\boxed{\text{=MIN(F94:O94)}}$. This formula ignores the "n.a." text in the annual cells and so only records the answer of 2022.

• We express that 2022 is the last economic year – *ignoring the license length* – in row 95, in which each annual cell uses the formula $\boxed{\text{=IF(year < = \$D94, 1, 0)}}$, where $\boxed{\text{D94}}$ is the year of peak cumulative GOCF. In our Base Scenario, this results in values of 1 in each year up to and including 2022 (cell M95), and values of 0 thereafter. (Because the answer can only be a 1 or a 0, we call the range F95:O95 a **binary range** or "binary array".) You will see why we create this array in a moment.

• Similarly, we use a binary range in row 96 to create a license flag, i.e., a row where the annual cells show a 1 when the license term is ongoing, and a 0 otherwise. Each annual cell in row 96 uses the formula $\boxed{\text{=IF(year < = \$C19, 1, 0)}}$, where cell $\boxed{\text{C19}}$ is the assumed last year of the license. Because we assume the license is valid through to the last year in our timeline, i.e., 2024, every annual cell in row 96 shows a value of 1.

• Next, we express the economic lifespan, *considering* the license length – that is, the most sensible commercial lifespan which is permitted by the license length – with a third binary range, in row 97. This is our **economic life flag ("ELF")**.[1] A value of 1 means the field is "alive," and a value of 0 means it has been abandoned. Each annual cell of this row simply multiplies the ELF, ignoring the license flag (row 95), by the corresponding year of the license flag (row 96):

○ Thus, for example, in 2022 (cell M97) the typical formula $\boxed{\text{=M95*M96}}$ gives the answer of 1, meaning that, under this test, the field is "alive" because (a) it makes economic sense for it to be alive, and (b) the license length allows it to be alive.

○ In the next year of 2023, however, the answer is 0, meaning the field is no longer alive, because even though the license term permits it to be alive, it makes no economic sense to be so.

• We have named the red-bordered range F97:O97 "ELF." We will use the ELF in the next section of the model as a multiplier to truncate the field inputs (production, costs, etc.) to the economic lifespan, considering the license length. In other words, under the Base Scenario, the ELF will remove various post-2022 input assumption values from the model by multiplying them by 0, which will have the effect of modeling a field which shuts down in 2022.

Finally, we capture the last year of economic life, considering the license length, i.e., our "ultimate" stopping year, which from now on is what we will call the **last economic year** for short – in cell D98. We calculate this as follows:

• In each of the annual cells in row 98, we use a formula which, in essence, says, "If this year is the last year when the ELF equals 1, then the answer is this year (e.g., 2022); otherwise, the answer is 'n.a.'" To frame this as a formula:

---

[1] To clarify terminology, "ELT" is the economic limit test, which tells us the economic limit (i.e., the last year when it makes economic sense to produce); "ELF" is the economic life flag, i.e., the mechanism which communicates the ELT, combined with the license length, to the rest of the model.

- o we would expand this into, "If this year, the ELF equals 1, and in each of the following years, the ELF equals 0, then the answer is this year; otherwise, the answer is 'n.a.'";

- o which in turn expands into, "If this year, the ELF equals 1, and the sum of the ELF values in all following years equals 0, then the answer is this year; otherwise, the answer is 'n.a.'";

- o which we write as the following Excel formula (using the typical example of cell M98, for 2022): =IF(AND(M97 = 1, SUM(N97:$P97) = 0), year, "n.a.") .

- Under the Base Scenario, this results in a value of 2022 in cell M98, and the text "n.a." in the other annual cells in row 98.

- We capture this result of 2022 in cell D98 with the formula =MIN(F98:O98) , and name cell D98, "Last_economic_year".

Be sure you understand why the ELT and ELF are calculated this way. They are essential to any fully dynamic upstream petroleum valuation model.

Question to ponder

The version of the ELT used here and in other chapters is the one which is widely used in the upstream petroleum industry. It is based on total field revenues and opex – without any regard for the fact that field revenue and contractor PSC revenue can be quite different, as we have seen, and shall see again in later examples.

Given that it is usually the contractor which decides to abandon the permit when continuing to produce would be uneconomic from its perspective, does this version of the ELT seem entirely appropriate? Might it not be better for the contractor to use contractor PSC revenue in the formula, rather than total field revenue?

Because our aim in this book is to explain, rather than challenge, how the industry usually does things, we shall use the common version of the ELT. But do at least give this question some thought. We explore it more in "Appendix_IV_Knowing_when_to_quit_Alternative economic limit test.pdf" in the "Appendix_IV_Alternative_economic_limit_test" folder on the disk.

Tour of This Section's Model: Post-ELT Calculations

The remaining calculations, again on a MOD $ basis, are in the section under the heading "Post-economic limit basis" in row 99. These include:

- *The abandonment payment (row 101).* We had to calculate the last economic year in the ELT section in order to know when the field is abandoned. In our example models, we have chosen a simple variant of abandonment cost financing, whereby the entire MOD $ cost is spent as a lumpsum in the last economic year. (Other kinds of abandonment financing regimes are discussed in Chapter 5.) Thus a typical formula we use, for example, in 2022 (cell M101) is =IF(year = Last_economic_year, $M36*Infl_index, 0) , where cell M36 is the abandonment cost in Real 2015 $ mm, and Infl_index is the named range in row 22 which we use to convert Real 2015 $ values into inflated, MOD values. This inflates the Real 2015 $ value to the inflated, MOD value in the abandonment year.

- *Post-ELT memo items*: Field production (row 103) and the oil price (row 104) are calculated each year as the ELF times the respective pre-ELT versions of these items. These are used later in the model to calculate entitlement and working interest volumes.

- *Cost oil* (rows 106–128):

  ○ This section follows the cost oil calculation method as explained in the last chapter – that is, in the "Multi-year Cost Oil Calculation Details" subsection of Section 6.6 – except that, now, it uses post-ELT values. Thus gross field revenue (row 106), royalty (row 107), capex (row 113) and opex (114) are calculated as the ELF times the respective pre-ELT versions of these items.

  ○ Note that the abandonment payment (row 115) does not need to be multiplied by the ELF, because the way we calculated it already accounts for when the last economic year is.

  ○ Note further that in cells D127:D128, we calculate, as memo items, the dollar value and percentage of recoverable costs which are not recovered.

We have already explained all the remaining calculations listed below, in this chapter, the last chapter or Chapter 1. Still, it might be worthwhile inspecting the model's formulas (which are displayed in the descriptions starting in column S), as most will appear in the rest of the PSC models we cover. We also suggest that you read the cell comments, and understand what the checksums in red font do. The remaining calculations are:

- *Profit oil* for each party (rows 130–134).

- *Total PSC revenue and revenue takes* for each party (rows 136–145).

- *Discounted net cashflow ("NCF") and NCF takes* for each party (rows 146–169). Bear in mind that, because the contractor is assumed to bear all the costs:

  ○ total government NCF equals total government PSC revenue; and

  ○ total contractor NCF equals contractor PSC revenue minus total costs.

- *Discounted NCF/NPV and discounted NCF takes* (rows 178–182).

- *Contractor volumetric outcomes* (rows 185–189). These comprise contractor PSC entitlement volumes and contractor working interest volumes. The latter are presented for information only, because, as mentioned earlier, they are not economically meaningful under PSC regimes.

Calculation exercise: Try these yourself

This section's model covers/consolidates a lot of ground, relating not only to PSC-specific calculations, but also to nuances such as the ELT, Real vs. MOD dollars, and when to include sunk costs versus when to ignore them. We hope you have learned from our explanations, as well as from examining the model itself (which we always encourage; the transparency of a clearly written Excel model makes it a powerful learning tool).

Even if you have followed everything up to this point, a passive understanding of how a model works is not the same as the ability to build one yourself. Therefore, we issue a challenge. In the file "Ch7_PSC_basic_model_no_depreciation_exercise setup.xls," you will find a duplicate of this section's model, "Ch7_PSC_basic_model_no_depreciation.xls," only with the formulas in many key cells deleted, and shaded orange. With the model set to the Base Scenario, fill in these cells with the proper formulas, and check your answers against this section's model when it is also set to the Base Scenario.

As an extra check, change some input assumptions as follows: set the oil price sensitivity multiplier (cell C28) to 90%; the post-2015 opex multiplier (cell J28) to 120%; the oil production multiplier (cell M28) to 80%; the royalty rate (cell C33) to 20%; the maximum net revenue available as cost oil (cell C34) to 90%; and the contractor profit share (cell C36) to 55%. Then make the same changes in this section's model, and again compare answers.

Note that until you fill in all these cells correctly, cells A1, B1 and some of the checksums (i.e., the cells with red font) might show Excel error messages, or non-zero values (which will turn their shading green, also indicating some sort of error).

It would be exceptional if you got everything right the first time. Try, and learn from any mistakes you might make.

If you can match the results in this section's model, you will have a good foundation for calculating a basic, "plain vanilla" PSC model (although there is one more area – the impact of depreciation on cost recovery – which we will cover in the "core" PSC model later in this chapter).

Tour of This Section's Model, Continued: Standard Analysis Charts

Scroll to the top of the sheet and click the "Show PSC revenue/cashflow chart" button. Provided you have macros enabled, a horizontal splitter bar will appear. Above the bar are input assumption cells, and below it, starting in row 243, is the "Division of PSC Revenue and Cashflows, MOD $ mm" chart shown in Figure 7.1. Most of the rows in between will be hidden.

Depending on the size of your monitor, you might need to adjust the position of the bar, or scroll and/or zoom out a bit for the chart and the desired assumption cells to be visible (although the charts are designed to look best at a 100% resolution).

The PSC revenues and cashflow chart shown in Figure 7.1 depicts post-ELT, life-of-field outcomes on an undiscounted basis. We have seen similar charts before in the last chapter. In this version, we have added two columns (the last two, after the blue vertical dividing line) showing each party's NCF, and, above the last column, a caption indicating each party's NCF take. Notice that contractor cashflow (appearing in both the sixth and seventh columns) is the result of subtracting contractor costs (in the sixth column) from contractor PSC revenues (in the fifth column).

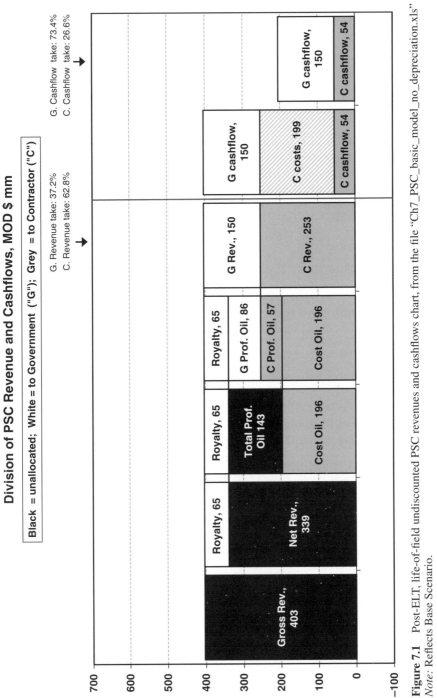

Figure 7.1 Post-ELT, life-of-field undiscounted PSC revenues and cashflows chart, from the file "Ch7_PSC_basic_model_no_depreciation.xls"

Note: Reflects Base Scenario.

All the captions and columns update when input assumptions above the splitter bar change. (Note that in this and some subsequent versions of the model which use Excel's Data Tables, the charts might update more slowly than usual.) This can be a useful way to play "what-if?" and quickly see what the model is doing, without the distortions introduced by discounting. We suggest you try changing some of the assumptions above the splitter bar and satisfying yourself that you understand what happens in the chart.

Exercise: be aware of the effects of the ELT

Reset the model to the Base Scenario. While still in the view resulting from clicking the "Show PSC revenue/cashflow chart" button in row 12, watch the chart – specifically, gross revenue in the first column – change as you increase the "Post-2015 opex" sensitivity multiplier in cell J28 from 100%. Note how gross revenue changes when the multiplier is set to the following values:

$$125\%, 155\%, 185\%, 220\%, 255\% \text{ and } 290\%$$

At first, this might look like an error in the model:

- We can appreciate that changing opex might affect *contractor's PSC revenue* (the gray segment in the fifth column), because contractor PSC revenue includes cost oil, which can be impacted by changing opex, which is assumed to be recoverable.

- But why would opex affect *gross field revenue*?

Let us see why:

- Exit the Custom View by clicking the "Show all rows" button in cell C12, manually split the screen horizontally below row 30, and scroll down in the bottom part of the screen so that you can see rows 87–97.

- Reset the model to the Base Scenario, and again change the opex multiplier as just described, this time watching the ELF in row 97. Note that the last year with a 1 in the ELF (row 97) is 2022. Now change the opex multiplier again as just described.

- Bearing in mind that a value of 1 in this row means the field is still economically "alive" in this year, notice how, at each of the increased opex settings mentioned, the field loses a year of economic life. This is because, as opex rises, the field's GOCF (row 90) becomes negative earlier and earlier; therefore cumulative GOCF (row 91) peaks sooner.

- Every time the field loses a year of economic life, i.e., is abandoned a year earlier, a year's worth of production is lost. This lost production in turn means lost gross field revenue,[2] which causes the first column in the chart to "bump down" a bit.

Reset the model to the Base Scenario and try the exercise again, but this time *lower* the opex multiplier in cell J28 from 100%. Notice in the chart how gross field revenue *increases*

---

[2] Do not forget, however, that stopping production due to the ELT while "losing" gross revenue results in a higher total project GOCF, and thus is the best choice from a GOCF maximization perspective. This is the whole point of the GOCF-based ELT.

when the multiplier is at 95% and 75%. Again, inspect the ELF in row 97. You can see that the increased revenue is a result of the longer field life, which results from the lower opex burden on GOCF.

When watching the chart while changing other parameters, the effect of the ELT might not be so obvious:

- For example, reset the model to the Base Scenario and watch the chart while lowering the oil price sensitivity multiplier in cell C28.

- At each lower setting of the oil price, gross revenue falls, which you would expect, given the direct link between the two. Notice, however, that gross revenue falls especially sharply when the oil price multiplier reaches these settings:

  80%, 65%, 50%, 45%, 35% and 30%

  especially the last one. This is because, at these multiplier settings, the field loses at least a year of economic life, which in turn reduces gross revenue. In fact, when the oil price multiplier is at 30%, the oil price is so low that producing in any year would mean a GOCF loss; therefore, to prevent such a loss, the ELT does not let the field produce at all, making the pre-production year of 2015 the last economic year.

- Similarly, note that gross revenue rises especially sharply when, starting from 100%, you increase the oil price multiplier to 105%, and then again to 130%. This is because the higher oil price extends the economic field life.

To help alert you to the potential impact of the ELT on the results, we have included, in the title "ribbon" (row 241) above the chart, a caption which records the last economic production year.

Try playing with other input assumptions while watching the chart. Try to make the last economic year change. To see why it does (or does not), inspect what is happening in rows 84–98.

The ELT is another important "moving part" of the more complex PSC models we will cover, so, again, be sure you are comfortable with how it works, and that you bear it mind when analyzing results.

To see another standard analysis chart we will be using in later PSC models, click the "Show Contractor cashflow/NPV charts" button in row 12, and scroll/zoom as needed, so that you see the version of the charts starting in row 304, shown in Figure 7.2, below, which displays the results of the model's Base Scenario.

These "waterfall charts" show the determination of post-ELT, life-of-field total contractor cashflows in MOD terms, on both an undiscounted basis (the left chart) and discounted basis (the right chart).

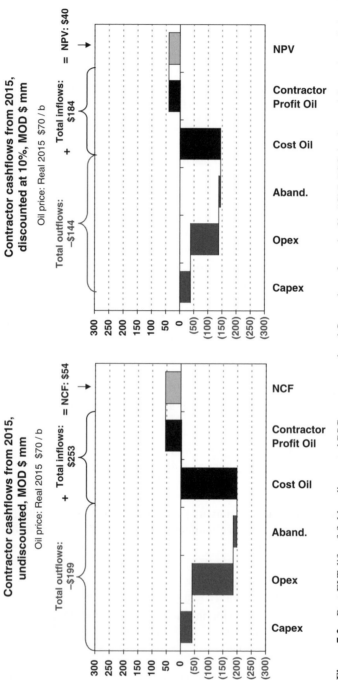

Figure 7.2 Post-ELT, life-of-field undiscounted PSC revenues and cashflows chart, from the file "Ch7_PSC_basic_model_no_depreciation.xls".
Note: Reflects Base Scenario.

Cash outflows appear in red, as negative values; cash inflows, in black, as positive values; and the resultant NCF (which in the case of the right chart is the NPV) in gray.

Note the cumulative picture given – the first item starts at 0 and, thereafter, each item starts where the previous one ends, so that the final item is the sum of all inflows minus the sum of all outflows.

Captions at the top of the charts update to show total inflows, outflows and the final results (e.g., in the left chart, under the Base Scenario, outflows of (−$199) + inflows of $253 = NCF of $54 mm), as well as the Real 2015 $ oil price assumed (in this case $70/b, or $70/bbl), for reference. As with the previous chart, the caption in the title "ribbon" (row 301) above the chart shows the last economic production year.

Notice that, because the "Division of PSC Revenue and Cashflows" chart (Figure 7.1) discussed above, and the left chart shown in Figure 7.2, both show results in undiscounted, inflated dollars, some of the values displayed in each match. For example, under the Base Scenario:

- "Total outflows" of MOD $199 mm in the caption of the left chart in Figure 7.2 equal the value shown for "C costs" (i.e., contractor costs) in Figure 7.1.

- The values represented by the left chart's black cost oil and contractor profit oil columns in Figure 7.2 match the values shown for these items in Figure 7.1.

- "Total inflows" of MOD $253 mm in the left chart's caption in Figure 7.2 equal the value shown for "C Rev" (i.e., contractor PSC revenue) in the Figure 7.1.

- "NCF" of MOD $54 mm in the left chart's caption in Figure 7.2 equals the value shown for "C Cashflow" (i.e., contractor PSC cashflow) in Figure 7.1.

The values shown in the right waterfall chart in Figure 7.2, however, will not correspond to those in Figure 7.1, as the former shows discounted values – unless you change the discount rate in cell C17 to 0% (in which case the left and right charts in Figure 7.2 will be identical).

As we shall see, these waterfall charts are another way to get a quick feel for – or identify questions about – how the various "moving parts" work together under the fiscal regime in question. The caveats regarding the sometimes subtle effects of the ELT apply here as well. We encourage you to play with some of the model's input assumptions while watching the charts update.

Exercise: Contractor Entitlement Versus NPV, Revisited with ELT

In the last chapter, we explored the impact of the oil price on contractor PSC entitlement volumes, in an example which was simplified in that – among other respects – we ignored the ELT. Here we briefly return to the topic, using the present section's model, "Ch7_PSC_basic_model_no_depreciation.xls," which includes the ELT.

Figure 7.3 is a screenshot of the chart in this model starting in row 196, which is visible, along with input assumptions, by clicking the "Show Contractor entitlement vs. NPV chart" button

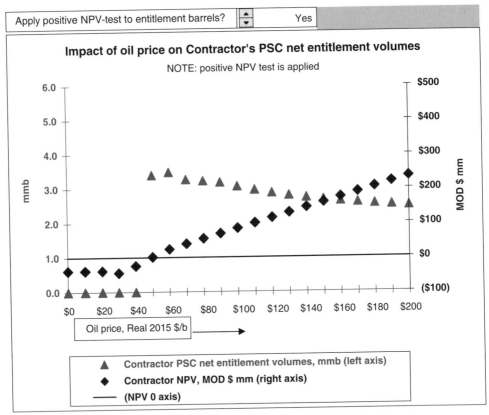

Figure 7.3 Contractor entitlement versus NPV, under the Base Scenario, from the file "Ch7_PSC_ basic_model_no_depreciation.xls"
Note: Reflects Base Scenario. Excel's calculation mode must be set to "Automatic."

in row 12. Be sure to reset to the Base Scenario – which includes using the positive-NPV test for entitlement – and to check that Excel's calculation mode is set (under "Options") to "Automatic," otherwise what you see in the file might not match Figure 7.3 until you recalculate the sheet manually by pressing F9.

The underlying data used for the chart come from the Excel Data Tables which start in row 214. These examine the results over the range of assumed oil prices, in $10 increments.

Figure 7.3 shows that, at oil prices (shown on the X-axis scale) of $50 or higher:

- contractor NPV (the black diamonds, referring to the right axis) always rises as the oil price rises, which makes intuitive sense (at least in this simple PSC – in others, as we shall see later, this is not always so);

- while contractor PSC entitlement volumes (the triangles, referring to the left axis) fall as the oil price rises. If you inspect the data underlying the entitlement volumes calculation, you will see that this is the same inverse relationship between entitlement and the oil price which we saw in the example in Section 6.7, in the cases when the oil price was over $70.

In summary, this happens because – although both the numerator and denominator in the entitlement equation (contractor PSC revenue and the oil price, respectively) rise as the price rises from $50/b, the denominator rises faster, resulting in falling entitlement volumes.

Notice, however, that at prices of less than $50, entitlement volumes are always 0 b. This is due to the positive-NPV test, whereby in order to classify entitlement volumes as reserves, they must be economic, i.e., they must generate positive contractor NPV. You can see in Figure 7.3 that:

- at prices from $0 to $40, NPV is negative (the black diamonds fall below the horizontal line); but

- when the oil price is $50, NPV turns just barely positive (this is hard to see in the chart, but cell H223 of the underlying Data Table shows that it is MOD $1.44 mm), causing entitlement volumes to "come alive" at this oil price.

Now turn off the positive-NPV test by adjusting the spinner so that cell C196 shows "No." You should see the chart reproduced in Figure 7.4.

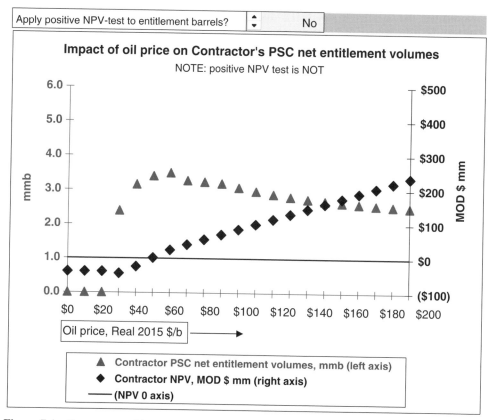

Figure 7.4 Contractor entitlement versus NPV, under Base Scenario but without positive-NPV test, from the file "Ch7_PSC_basic_model_no_depreciation.xls"
Note: Reflects Base Scenario, except that the positive-NPV test is not applied.

Note how, in Figure 7.4, there are entitlement volumes even when NPV is negative – at least sometimes, i.e., at oil prices between $30 and $40/b.

But since we've switched off the positive-NPV test, shouldn't we also see entitlement volumes at oil prices of $0–$20/b? The reason that we do not is not related to NPV at these prices. Rather, it is because at prices of $0–$20, field revenue, net of royalty, falls below opex, causing GOCF to be negative every year in our timeframe. When this happens, the ELT, which is designed to maximize total GOCF, never lets the field produce at all, "preferring" to let total GOCF equal $0, which is higher than the negative GOCF which would result from production at these prices.

One way you can see this in the underlying model is to leave the Custom View, by clicking the "Show all rows" button in cell C12, adjusting the oil price (cell C31), and inspecting the ELT calculations in the model as we did earlier.

- But an easier way is to stay within the Custom View (which, again, results from clicking the "Show Contractor entitlement vs. NPV chart" button in row 12), and adjust it, if necessary, so that the chart is visible beneath the horizontal screen splitter bar, and the "Oil price received, $/b – pre-multiplier" spinner in cell C31 is visible above it.

- Now lower the oil price in cell C31, which under the Base Scenario is Real $70/b, while watching, in the bottom part of the screen, not the chart itself (which, because it shows results from Data Tables which simulate different oil prices, will *not* change when you change the oil price), but rather the model's "live" result for "Last production year, post-ELT" which is shown to the right of the chart, in cell M201.

- As you lower the oil price, in steps of $2, watch this last production year get lower and lower until, at $20, it is 2015 – the start of the model's timeframe, and one year before any production is assumed to begin.

In other words, the ELT is telling us, at prices of $20 or less, not to produce at all, which of course means that entitlement volumes (or any other measure production) will be zero.

Main Points to Take Away

These are as follows:

- As we have seen before, there is often a tradeoff under certain PSCs between contractor entitlement volumes and contractor NPV; therefore it is unwise to think that an increase in entitlement volumes is necessarily good news for the contractor.

- The NPV positivity test and ELT can each influence the contractor's entitlement volumes.

- The form of the ELT commonly used in the industry, and used in this book, is not a safeguard against contractor NPV becoming negative:

  ○ This is because the definition of "economic" in this common "economic limit test" is based on maximizing total field basis, undiscounted gross operating cashflow, *not* on maximizing contractor NPV which, as the sum of discounted contractor net cashflows, is something quite different.

○ Note, for example, that when the oil price in cell C31 is $48:

    – the model's "live" result for contractor NPV, shown to the right of the chart in cell M200, is negative at MOD $(4.09) mm;

    – yet the last production year, as "recommended" by the ELT we use, is 2021 (cell M201).

○ In other words, this industry's common version of the ELT is effectively saying, "Go on and produce, from 2016 through to the end of 2021, as it will result in a cumulative total of undiscounted field basis GOCF of MOD $89.5 mm" (cell M202). This version of the ELT does not "know or care" that this would result in negative contractor NPV.

○ As mentioned earlier, it is not our aim in this book to challenge the commonly used industry ELT, but rather to prepare you to use it while understanding its shortcomings.

7.2   ARRIVING AT OUR "CORE" PSC MODEL

Having gradually added features to our example PSC models in this and the last chapter, we have progressed from a simple, single-year model to a multi-year one which is increasingly detailed and realistic.

The model which we present in this section adds one more feature, to make it a standard, or **"core" PSC model**, suitable for demonstrating variations among PSC regimes in this and the next chapter. This model is in the file "Ch7_PSC_basic_model_with_depreciation.xls."

The additional feature is the use of depreciation as a means of cost recovery for tangible capex. Specifically, we will use a common form of this, known as straight line depreciation, which we briefly introduce in Chapter 1, and discuss in detail in the file "Appendix_I_Depreciation.pdf" on the disk.

In our new, "core" model, we shall distinguish between:

• intangible recoverable capex, which – just like *all* recoverable capex in our *last* model – is "expensed," i.e., it becomes eligible for cost recovery in the year in which it is incurred; and

• tangible recoverable capex, which becomes eligible for cost recovery over time, via a depreciation mechanism.

In Figure 7.5, we show, in the *very* simplified example from the file "Ch7_Simple_example_depreciation_and_cost_recovery.xls," the difference between:

• how tangible capex has been treated for cost recovery purposes so far in this and the last chapter; and

• how tangible capex will been treated for cost recovery purposes in this section's new, "core" model, and in most of our remaining PSC example models.

	A	B	C	D	E	F	G	H	I	J
2										
3		$ mm	Total	2015	2016	2017	2018	2019	2020	2021
4		Tangible capex	80.0	–	80.0	–	–	–	–	–
5		Form and timing in which value of tangible capex ($ mm) becomes eligible for cost recovery								
6		Method A: used so far in text (uncommon)	80.0	–	80	–	–	–	–	–
7		Method B: Straight-line depreciation (rather common), assumed over 5 years	80.0	–	16.0	16.0	16.0	16.0	16.0	–

Figure 7.5 Simplistic comparison of ways in which tangible capex becomes recoverable, from the file "Ch7_Simple_example_depreciation_and_cost_recovery.xls"

Assume, as shown in Figure 7.5, that:

- in 2016, production (not shown) is ongoing;

- it continues through to the end of 2020; and

- in 2016, $80 mm in recoverable, tangible capex is incurred (cell E4).

Under Method A, all of the $80 mm in new recoverable tangible capex becomes eligible for recovery in the year incurred (2016; cell E6).

Under Method B – a simplified version of the method we will use in this section's model – one-fifth of the total value, i.e., the 2016 **depreciation charge** of $16 mm, becomes eligible for recovery in 2016, another fifth, in 2017, and so on, until the "fifth fifth" in 2020, after which this $80 mm item has been **fully depreciated**. (Let's leave this simplified model for now.)

In our full PSC models, the result of either method is used in the same way with respect to calculating *total* recoverable costs. That is, in any given year, the values calculated above are summed, along with any other recoverable costs incurred – for example, opex, intangible capex, abandonment payments, etc. – to calculate the values in the relevant model's "Total newly recoverable costs" row. An example from *this* section's main example model – "Ch7_PSC_basic_model_with_depreciation.xls" – is in rows 221–225, as shown in Figure 7.6.

In Figure 7.6, we jump ahead to the results of the depreciation calculation, to show you how these results feed the model's cost recovery section.

	A	B	C	D	E	F	G	H	I	J	K	L	M	N	O
133					Depreciation charge calculation										
218		e) Total depreciation charge, adjusted for terminal year write-off, POST-ELT basis (=a + d)	MOD $mm	28.4		-	3.0	3.5	3.5	3.5	3.5	3.5	7.6	-	-
219															
220		Contractor recoverable costs, and cost oil		Total/other		2015	2016	2017	2018	2019	2020	2021	2022	2023	2024
221		Tangible capex FROM ALL YEARS (via depreciation)	MOD $ mm	28.4		-	3.0	3.5	3.5	3.5	3.5	3.5	7.6	-	-
222		Intangible capex, incurred STARTING 2015	MOD $ mm	13.7		12.2	1.6	-	-	-	-	-	-	-	-
223		Opex, incurred STARTING 2015	MOD $ mm	145.2		-	28.7	24.8	21.8	19.5	17.9	16.7	15.9	-	-
224		Abandonment payment	MOD $ mm	12.5		-	-	-	-	-	-	-	12.5	-	-
225		Total newly recoverable costs	MOD $ mm	199.8		12.2	33.3	28.3	25.3	23.1	21.4	20.2	36.0	-	-

Figure 7.6 Depreciation charges in the context of other recoverable costs, from the file "Ch7_PSC_basic_model_with_depreciation.xls"
Note: Results reflect Base Scenario; some rows are hidden.

- The total depreciation annual charges are calculated in the rows preceding row 218 – which are hidden for the purposes of this screenshot – with the results shown in row 218. (Do not worry for the moment about how they are calculated; we'll discuss this soon; or why they are not all the same value, as in our simplistic example in Figure 7.5, above.)

- The same values in row 218 are used in row 221. These values in row 221 are then summed with those in rows 222–224 to give the annual "Total newly recoverable costs" in row 225.

To clarify an important point, tangible capex appears in two forms in our "core" PSC model, each of which serves a different purpose:

1. It appears in its depreciated form, as the depreciation charges shown in Figure 7.6, to be used in the calculation of each year's total recoverable costs, as just explained. Depreciation is a not a cash item; rather, it is a non-cash item which is used to help calculate a cash item. In this case, depreciation helps determine recoverable costs, which in turn help determine the cash item (the cash inflow) of cost oil received by the contractor.

2. It appears in its basic, "when incurred" form, as a cash item (a cash outflow) which is added to other cash outflows when calculating the contractor's net cashflow (NCF). In our "core" Excel model, annual tangible capex appears on a post-ELT, inflated basis in row 128, where it is added to other post-ELT, MOD basis contractor costs to give total contractor costs in row 131. This total is then used in row 260 in the contractor's NCF calculation.

How depreciation is calculated in the "core" PSC model

Although the concept of straight line depreciation is simple, the calculations involve a number of nuances, which – done correctly, and transparently enough without using "megaformulas" – unfortunately takes up a fair amount of model space.

We cover straight line depreciation in detail in the file "Appendix_I_Depreciation.pdf" on the disk. Even if you have some experience with this method, we strongly suggest that you turn to the portion of this appendix which covers straight line depreciation, or at least study the example Excel files it references, before proceeding with the rest of this chapter, as our approach is somewhat specific. We will use it in most of our remaining PSC examples, so you will need a good grasp of it.

Differences between the depreciation calculations in "Appendix I: Depreciation.pdf" and those in the "core" PSC model

One thing that the model which accompanies "Appendix_I_Depreciation.pdf," i.e., the model in the file "Depreciation_straight_line_example.xls," does *not* treat, but which we *do* treat in the "core" PSC model – i.e., "Ch7_PSC_basic_model_with_depreciation.xls" – is the depreciation of tangible capex incurred before the model's timeframe begins in 2015. Therefore you should be aware of the slight adjustments to the "core" PSC model made to accommodate this:

- Both the "FullExample" sheet in the "Depreciation_straight_line_example.xls" model and the "Model" sheet "Ch7_PSC_basic_model_with_depreciation.xls," i.e., the "core" PSC model, have sections entitled "Determination of when capex becomes depreciable," which deal with depreciable capex incurred before the first production year. In "Depreciation_straight_line_example.xls," this section starts in row 98. In the "core" PSC model, it starts in row 135. In the "core" PSC model, this section distinguishes, in rows 140–142, between depreciable capex incurred before and after the start of the model's timeframe.
- In each model, near the end of the depreciation calculations, there is a row captioned "b) Depreciable capex, when incurred." In "Depreciation_straight_line_example.xls," this is in row 182. In the "core" PSC model, it is in row 215. The only difference between the two is that, in the "core" PSC model, the total in cell D215 includes the pre-2015 depreciable capex, as stated in the cell note.

Having read and understood the relevant portions of **"Appendix I: Depreciation.pdf"** – and preferably having done the accompanying exercises as well – you should now recognize what is happening in the "Depreciation charge calculation" section of our "core" PSC model, in rows 133–218. Note that to keep the model easier to navigate, we have hidden these rows in our default view of the file. These rows can be revealed by clicking the [+] button on the right side of the screen in row 218.

As we saw in Figure 7.6, the depreciation charges calculated in row 218 of the "core" PSC model feed directly into tangible capex for cost recovery purposes in row 221. In Figure 7.7, we repeat the rows shown in Figure 7.6, and show a few more rows in the cost recovery section. These will make clear every one of the few differences between the "core" model's cost recovery section and that of the previous version of our PSC model, i.e., "Ch7_PSC_basic_model_no_depreciation.xls."

In addition to row 221, there are a few other differences between the cost recovery section of "Ch7_PSC_basic_model_no_depreciation.xls" and that of our "core" PSC model. These differences relate to pre-2015 recoverable costs.

	A	B	C	D	F	G	H	I	J	K	L	M	N	O
133		Depreciation charge calculation												
218	0	e) Total depreciation charge, adjusted for terminal year writE-off, POST-ELT basis (=a + d)	MOD $mm	28.4	–	3.0	3.5	3.5	3.5	3.5	3.5	7.6	–	–
219														
220		**Contractor recoverable costs, and cost oil**		Total/other	2015	2016	2017	2018	2019	2020	2021	2022	2023	2024
221		Tangible capex FROM ALL YEARS (via depreciation)	MOD $ mm	28.4	–	3.0	3.5	3.5	3.5	3.5	3.5	7.6	–	–
222		Intangible capex, incurred STARTING 2015	MOD $ mm	13.7	12.2	1.6	–	–	–	–	–	–	–	–
223		Opex, incurred STARTING 2015	MOD $ mm	145.2	–	28.7	24.8	21.8	19.5	17.9	16.7	15.9	–	–
224		Abandonment payment	MOD $ mm	12.5	–	–	–	–	–	–	–	12.5	–	–
225		Total newly recoverable costs	MOD $ mm	199.8	12.2	33.3	28.3	25.3	23.1	21.4	20.2	36.0	–	–
227		Intangible capex, incurred BEFORE 2015	MOD $ mm	10.2										
228		Opex, incurred BEFORE 2015	MOD $ mm	0.6										
230		Cuml. unrecovered costs from prior years	MOD $ mm		10.8	23.0	–	–	–	–	–	2.5	24.7	24.7
232		**Total costs recoverable in current year**	**MOD $ mm**		**23.0**	**56.3**	**28.3**	**25.3**	**23.1**	**21.4**	**20.2**	**38.5**	**24.7**	**24.7**
234		**Costs recovered i.e. cost oil**	MOD $ mm	**185.9**	–	**56.3**	**28.3**	**25.3**	**23.1**	**21.4**	**17.8**	**13.7**	–	–
236		Unrecovered costs to be carried forward	MOD $ mm		23.0	–	–	–	–	–	2.5	24.7	24.7	24.7
238		a) Memo: total recoverable costs	MOD $ mm	210.6										
239	0	b) Costs not recovered	MOD $ mm	24.7										
240		c) = a) / b)	%	11.7%										

Figure 7.7 Cost recovery section, from the file "Ch7_PSC_basic_model_with_depreciation.xls"
Notes: Results reflect Base Scenario; column E and some rows are hidden.

As shown in Figure 7.7, cells D227 and D228 show the split of pre-2015, "sunk" recoverable costs which are *not* tangible capex, i.e., intangible capex, and opex. These two are summed using the unique formula in cell F230. (Note that pre-2015 tangible capex is already accounted for in row 221.) In addition, the formula in cell D238, which is $\boxed{\text{=D225+D227+D228}}$, includes these "sunk" costs in the total of recoverable costs, which is then used to calculate the percentage of total recoverable costs which ultimately are not recovered.

Analysis: The Effects of Depreciation on Contractor PSC Revenues, Cashflows and NPV

We split the following analysis into two parts:

1. We will start with some very simplified examples – which are not found in our "core" PSC model, but rather in the file, "Ch7_simple_example_depreciation_and_cost_recovery.xls" which we saw earlier – to focus only on how using depreciation impacts cost recovery. We examine two effects separately, to prepare you for item 2, below:

   - the effects of discounting; and

   - the effects of the availability (or unavailability) of funds on cost recovery due to timing effects.

2. A comparison of total contractor PSC revenues, cashflows and NPV in our "core" model, i.e., "Ch7_PSC_basic_model_with_depreciation.xls," and its predecessor, i.e., "Ch7_PSC_basic_model_no_depreciation.xls." This part of the analysis is more complex, as there are more "moving parts" to consider.

This analysis is found in the file "Ch7_cost recovery_with_and_without_ depreciation.ppt," to which you should now proceed.

Looking ahead – variations on our "core" PSC model

In this and the next chapter, we will use the "core" PSC model presented in this section to show variations among PSC regimes.

Therefore, in the upcoming models, you should recognize the structure and formulas, except, perhaps, as these relate to the new variations being illustrated.

Also note that, in these models, input assumptions for items such as production, costs, oil price, etc., will not necessarily be the same as those used in the "core" PSC model, as we will sometimes vary these to make certain points. Therefore, in such cases, the results of these models and those of the core model will not be comparable.

7.3 "UPLIFTS" TO COST OIL

Some PSCs have mechanisms to give contractors incentives to spend sufficient capex, and to compensate them for spending it now, and recovering it (plus a return on that investment) some years later. This mechanism is known generically as an **uplift**, although other terms such as "investment credit" or "investment allowance" are also used. In many fiscal designs, uplifts, credits and/or allowances are applied to certain contractor investments, to give the contractor certain benefits:

- In cases where income taxes apply, an uplift can give the contractor extra income tax relief.
- In the example treated in this section, i.e., a PSC without any income tax, the uplift helps the contractor by effectively increasing the amount of recoverable costs to which the contractor is entitled – over and above the amount of recoverable costs which the contractor actually incurs. This gives the contractor the benefit of extra cost oil.

The uplift mechanism considered in this section is simple. It is expressed as a percentage addition to recoverable capex. This increases the potential amount of cost oil received by the contractor. For example:

- if a contractor incurs $100 mm in recoverable capex, and there is no uplift mechanism, the contractor will be entitled, funds permitting, to recover capex of $100 mm in the form of cost oil; but
- if a contractor incurs $100 mm in recoverable capex, and the PSC provides for a 20% uplift – which we will call a 20% **uplift factor** – the contractor will be entitled, funds permitting, to recover capex of $120 mm in the form of cost oil. In such a case, as we will see below, the extra $20 mm for the contractor will be at the government's direct expense.

Reminder: recoverable costs are not always recovered costs

Recall from our earlier discussion of PSC revenue sharing that, just because a contractor has a certain amount of recoverable costs, this does not mean the contractor will necessarily receive full reimbursement for this amount in the form of cost oil. The amount of cost oil actually received depends on the availability of funds to be disbursed as cost oil. This availability of funds, in turn, depends on:

(a) the amount of field revenue;
(b) the rate of any royalty payable; and
(c) the portion of (field revenue minus royalty) which is available as cost oil, and *when*.

Thus, timing matters. For example, if in the last year of production there is $10 mm available as cost oil, and recoverable costs – including an abandonment cost of $15 mm – are incurred, the contractor would only recover $10 mm, and would have to "swallow" the remaining $5 mm.[3]

---

[3] That is, unless the PSC has a special "carryback" arrangement to give the contractor some kind of fiscal benefit from the late-occurring abandonment costs, or unless it can offset such losses against revenue received from another permit area or field. We will not cover these here, but be aware that they are similar in principle, respectively, to the tax loss carrybacks discussed in the file "Appendix II_Tax_loss_carrybacks.pdf" and the fiscal consolidation of tax losses covered in Chapter 2.

Example Model and Calculation

The uplift in this section's example model – which is in the file "Ch7_PSCModel_with_ uplift.xls" – follows a commonly used form of uplift, whereby the uplift is a factor applied to tangible capex.

Because in this model – which is a variant of our basic "core" PSC model – the recovery of tangible capex is via the depreciation of tangible capex, the <u>uplift is applied to the depreciable value</u> of tangible capex, as follows:

- The uplift factor is expressed as a percentage, in the spinner-controlled cell G48, which we have named ⟦Uplift_factor⟧. In this example, the value in this cell is <u>the percentage addition to the depreciable value of tangible capex</u> incurred starting from 2015 (i.e., from the start of the model's timeframe).[4] Under the model's Base Scenario (to which the model can be reset by clicking the button in cell B12), the uplift factor is 0%.

- The uplift factor is applied in each of the annual cells in row 138, which is captioned "Depreciable value – including uplift – of tangible capex, incurred starting from 2015."

- The typical formula, for example, in 2016 (cell G138) is simply ⟦=G128*(1+Uplift_ factor)⟧, where ⟦G128⟧ is the value of tangible capex incurred in 2016.

- Under the Base Scenario, this is **MOD $47.0 mm**. If you change the ⟦Uplift_factor⟧ to 15%, the value in cell G138 changes to MOD $47.0 mm × 1.15 = **MOD $54.1 mm**.

Analysis – How Changing the Uplift Rate Impacts PSC Revenue Distribution and Cashflow

> Note: This section uses Excel Data Tables, which start in row 470. These can slow the model down. Therefore macros might run slowly, and charts might take a moment to update after you change input assumptions. Be sure Excel's calculation mode is set to Automatic.

Reset the model to the Base Scenario and click the "Show PSC revenues/cashflows chart" button in row 12. Adjust the horizontal splitter bar and/or scroll if necessary, so that you see row 48 in the top part of the screen, and the "Division of PSC Revenue and Cashflows, MOD $ mm" chart in the bottom part. (Using Excel's full screen viewing mode might let you see everything at our preferred 100% zoom resolution on a laptop.)

Use the spinner in cell G48 to change the uplift factor from 0% to 15%, while watching the chart. The changes you will see are summarized in Figure 7.8.

As you compare the results using 0% and 15% uplift factors, notice how the $10 mm increase in cost oil (row A of Figure 7.8) comes at the direct expense of total profit oil, which decreases by $10 mm (row I).

---

[4] Note that an uplift factor could also apply to recoverable "sunk" (pre-2015) tangible capex.

Index	Uplift factor	i) 0%	ii) 15%	ii) - i)
A	Contractor cost oil	191	201	*10*
B	Contractor profit oil	70	66	*(4)*
C	**Total Contractor PSC revenue**	**261**	**267**	**6**
D	Contractor costs	217	217	*0*
E	**Contractor cashflow**	**44**	**50**	**6**
F	Royalty	70	70	*0*
G	Government profit oil	105	99	*(6)*
H	**Total Government revenue (=Government cashflow)**	**174**	**168**	*(6)*
I	Memo: Total profit oil	175	165	*(10)*

Figure 7.8   Impact of change in uplift factor (monetary values in MOD $ mm), from the file "Ch7_PSCModel_with_uplift.xls"
Notes: This summary table does not appear in the Excel file. Results shown reflect the Base Scenario (except for the change of the uplift factor to 15% in the last column). Values are undiscounted.

Because, in this example model, the parties' shares of total profit are fixed percentages, the reduction in total profit oil, in turn, lowers the dollar value of both the contractor's and the government's shares of total profit oil, as seen in rows B and G.

For the contractor:

- the MOD $10 mm increase in cost oil (row A) exceeds the MOD $4 mm reduction in contractor profit oil (row B), resulting in a net increase in total contractor PSC revenue of MOD $6 mm (row C);

- although the "uplifted" value of the contractor's tangible capex (not shown in Figure 7.8) has increased, the actually incurred cash value of these costs (as well as that of other contractor costs) does not change (row D);

- thus the net effect of the MOD $6 mm increase in contractor PSC revenue, combined with static costs, is a **MOD $6 mm increase in contractor cashflow** (row E).

For the government:

- royalty income (row F) is unaffected by the change in the uplift factor;

- government profit oil, however, is reduced by $6 mm (row G);

- which means a net reduction in government revenue, and, because the government bears no costs, thus a net reduction in government cashflow of **MOD $6 mm** (row H).

Thus under the terms of this PSC, we have a "zero-sum" situation, i.e., one's party's loss is the other's gain. In this case, the government is ceding uplift to the contractor as a fiscal incentive, which in turn reduces the government's fiscal take.

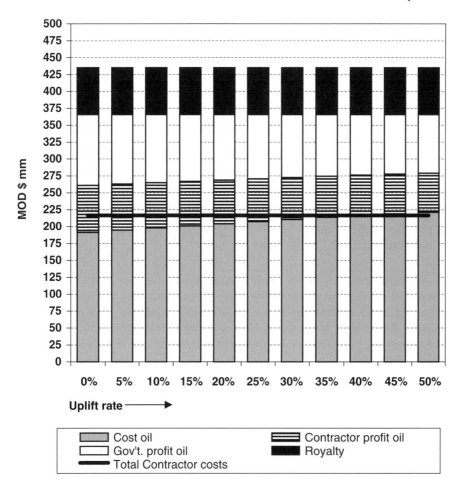

Figure 7.9   Impact of different uplift rates, undiscounted view, from the file "Ch7_PSCModel_with_ uplift.xls"
Notes: (a) Results shown reflect the Base Scenario (except for the changes of the uplift factor from 0% to 50%). (b) Because the underlying data shown in the charts come from Excel Data Tables, the chart will *not* change when the uplift factor is changed in the model.

Figure 7.9 makes it easier to see the impact of a range of uplift rates. It reproduces the chart located below cell B435, which was created using a number of Excel Data Tables.

The stacked columns in Figure 7.9 show the distribution of undiscounted PSC revenue, assuming different uplift rates. (In reality uplift rates rarely exceed 20%, but we have shown a range of 0–50% for illustrative purposes.)

The combined height of the column segments represents the sum of total PSC revenue, which is always the same, because the uplift rates do not determine the *total amount* of PSC revenue, but rather only its *distribution* between the parties.

The combined height of the bottom two segments represents the contractor's total PSC revenue, and the combined height of the top two segments represents the government's total PSC revenue.

As seen – perhaps most clearly by comparing the first (0% uplift) and last (50% uplift) columns – when the uplift rates increases:

- cost oil increases;

- contractor profit oil decreases;

- yet the increase in cost oil exceeds the decrease in contractor profit oil, so that the result is a net increase in total contractor PSC revenue; and

- as total contractor PSC revenue grows, the government's shrinks.

We have also plotted the contractor's actually incurred costs – which the uplift rate does not change – as a horizontal line. This shows us two things:

- When the line is above the top of the lowest segment, total contractor costs exceed the amount of cost oil taken by the contractor. Thus the space between this line and the top of the lowest segment represents the amount of any unrecovered contractor costs. Note that, by the point at which the uplift rate is 50%, not only does the contractor recover, in the form of cost oil, all of its recoverable costs, but also, its cost oil slightly *exceeds* its total recoverable costs.

- The difference between the combined height of the bottom two segments (which, again, represents total contractor PSC revenue) and the total costs line represents the contractor's cashflow. For example, in the 0% uplift stacked column on the far left, total contractor PSC revenue is around MOD $260 mm, and contractor costs are around $215 mm, so the contractor's cashflow is around MOD $45 mm.[5] Examining each column in this light shows us how – and why – an increasing uplift factor boosts the contractor's cashflow.

Now click the "Show sensitivity charts" button in row 12, and adjust the splitter bar and/or scroll as needed, so that you can see the post-2015 capex multiplier in cell G28 in the top part of the screen, and the chart on the left (which we saw in Figure 7.9) in the bottom part.

Focus on a stacked column in the chart – for example, the one corresponding to un uplift rate of 15% – and use the spinner control to increase the capex multiplier, from its Base Scenario setting of 100%, in increments of 5%. (Be sure that Excel's calculation mode is set to "Automatic," otherwise the chart will not fully update. Again, updating might take a moment, due to your computer's resources used by the underlying Data Tables.)

---

[5] The actual, more precise figures under the Base Scenario, in which the uplift factor is 0%, are visible in cells D259:D261 of the model. Contractor PSC revenue is MOD $261.0 mm; contractor costs are MOD $216.5 mm; and contractor cashflow is MOD $44.5 mm.

You will see that increasing the multiplier, thus increasing tangible capex available for cost recovery, has several effects:

- It magnifies the contractor PSC revenue benefit effect of the uplift. That is, the uplift is being applied to a higher level of capex, resulting in higher cost oil. As mentioned earlier, this higher cost oil reduces the contractor's share of profit oil, but the net result is higher total contractor PSC revenue.

- However, increasing the multiplier also *raises* contractor *costs*, at a rate which outweighs the increase in total contractor PSC revenue. This lowers contractor cashflow, as the surplus of total contractor PSC revenue over costs shrinks; and – when the multiplier is set high enough – ultimately vanishes.

  ○ Thus the uplift, while boosting contractor PSC revenue, does not *mean* that incurring higher contractor capex is an "easy ticket" to improving its net cashflow position – the laws of financial gravity still apply.

  ○ You can see this clearly by watching, for example, the 15% uplift column while increasing the capex multiplier. Watch the combined height of the bottom two segments rise, while the horizontal costs line rises faster. By the time the multiplier reaches 150%, this costs line overtakes the combined height of these two bottom segments, i.e., costs exceed contractor PSC revenue, which means contractor NCF turns negative.

- It lowers government PSC revenue (i.e., government cashflow), because more distributable revenue goes to the contractor as cost oil, at the direct expense of total profit oil, and thus at the expense of the government's share of profit oil.

The chart located below cell G435 shows the same trends on a discounted view. You can see the same dynamics just described, although they are muted by the effect of the time value of money.

Uplifts Are also Used to Give Contractors Income Tax Breaks

Although the PSC in this model does not levy income tax, recall, as mentioned at the start of this section, that uplifts are also used, in some fiscal regimes which *do* levy them, to reduce taxes payable. In such cases, the uplift works by increasing the depreciable value of capex, thus increasing depreciation charges, which are tax deductions, and/or by increasing the deductible value of capex (such as intangible capex) which is fully deductible in the year incurred.

Chapter 8

PSC Regime Variations

8

PSC Regime Variations

INTRODUCTION

In the last two chapters we have provided an introduction to the basic fiscal mechanisms governing production sharing contracts, or PSCs, and then showed how to build these into a basic though reasonably detailed "core" PSC model.

In this final chapter we show how to adapt this core model to illustrate a number of "variations on the theme" of production sharing which are in common use internationally. These variations involve the role of income tax, as well as different profit sharing mechanisms which react to changes in commodity prices, periodic production rates, cumulative production levels, and measures of project profitability.

An issue that arises with some production sharing mechanisms is that the contractor can be incentivized to actually spend more to enhance cashflow (a situation often referred to as "gold plating"). We provide an example of a PSC mechanism that could lead to "gold plating" behavior by the contractor, and discuss its implications and potential remedies.

8.1 PSCs WITH EXPLICIT INCOME TAX PROVISIONS

Introduction

Although we use the terms "tax and royalty" and "production sharing contracts" to describe two major different types of upstream petroleum fiscal regime, some PSCs include both income taxes and royalties. In fact we have already seen royalties in all the example PSC models discussed so far. In this section, we will present an example of a PSC which features income taxes as well.

Be aware that some PSCs state that the contractor is liable for paying income tax, but do not specify how the tax is levied; rather, they state that the contractor's income tax liability is considered to be fulfilled by the profit oil sharing provisions of the contract.

- In other words, the income tax which the contractor must pay is considered to be paid as part of the portion of total profit oil which the contractor does *not* receive.

- For example, if total profit oil is $100 mm, of which the contractor and government receive shares of $30 mm and $70 mm, respectively, some unspecified portion of the $70 mm of the government's share is considered to be income tax paid by the contractor.

We will call this a form of **implicit income taxation**.

In contrast, in most of this section, we will deal with a different situation – that is, one in which, in addition to the standard profit sharing (and cost recovery) mechanisms covered so far, the PSC also explicitly requires the contractor to pay income tax. Such **explicit income taxation** requires changes to how we calculate the contractor's and government's PSC revenue and revenue "takes." It can also change how the contractor's net entitlement volumes are reported.

Example Model

Our example file, "Ch8_PSC_with_income_tax.xls," is based on our "core" PSC example model. Apart from the additional rows for calculating income tax and for determining/ summarizing post-tax PSC revenue and contractor entitlement volumes, as discussed below, we have changed, for the Base Scenario, a few field input assumptions compared to those in the "core" model. Specifically, we have raised the received oil price (cell C31) and annual production volumes (row 54), and lowered opex, capex and the abandonment cost in cells L31:L32, L37, L40 and L43.

Income Tax Rate

The income tax rate is set in cell C43, which we have named "Tax_rate." In our Base Scenario, it is 35% in every year. Be aware, however, that some countries' PSCs use more complex formulas for tax rates, as discussed later in this section.

Prior Balance of Unused Tax Losses

Unused tax losses, arising from *before* the model's timeframe begins in 2015, are in cell C44, which we have named "Initial_prior_tax_loss." Although these occurred in the past from the standpoint of our model, which uses a valuation date of January 1, 2015, these will affect tax charges arising after this date, and so need to be accounted for.[1]

Notice that the value of these prior tax losses under the Base Scenario – MOD \$10.80 mm, shown in cell C44 – is *not* in blue font, meaning that it is not a hard-coded (typed-in) assumption, but rather is the result of a calculation. Here is where this value comes from:

- In this model, we assume that production only starts in 2016, so the assumed pre-2015, *directly* tax-deductible costs – specifically, opex and intangible capex,[2] found in cells L34 and L36 – were incurred before there was any field revenue.

- In the absence of pre-2015 revenue, these pre-2015 tax-deductible costs by definition create tax losses. Here, we have calculated these losses in cell C44 as =(L34*L33)+(L36*L33). This formula, which refers to cells in the costs assumptions section, translates as

---

[1] Tax losses, including the carrying forward of tax losses, are covered in Section 1.9.3 of Chapter 1.

[2] Note that, in addition to the pre-2015 opex and intangible capex, which are *directly* tax deductible, there is a third category of pre-2015 costs, namely, tangible capex, in cell L35. Following common industry practice, this will be treated as being *indirectly* tax deductible; that is, the related annual tax deductions will not be the tangible capex amounts when they are incurred, but rather will be the annual depreciation charges arising from this tangible capex, as we will discuss further below.

> (% of total pre-2015 cost which are opex × total pre-2015 costs)
>
> $+$
>
> (% of total pre-2015 cost which are intangible capex × total pre-2015 costs)

which under our Base Scenario equals the MOD $10.8 mm shown in cell C44.

Note that:

- As already discussed in Section 1.6.5 of Chapter 1 and "Appendix I: Depreciation.pdf," intangible capex is usually expensed for tax purposes, and not depreciated. This is the way we treat intangible capex here.

- We assume, as stated in row 45 of our example model, that unused tax losses can be carried forward indefinitely for use as deductions against future taxable income. (Such loss carryforwards are discussed in Section 1.9.3 of Chapter 1.)

- When modeling any regime which allows a carryforward of unused tax losses, it is necessary to know the balance of such unused losses as at the beginning of the model's timeframe.

Income Tax Base: Three Versions

We provide three different versions of the **income tax base**, which is the monetary amount, adjusted for any tax losses, which gets multiplied by the tax rate to result in the tax charge. You can choose the version of the tax base by using the spinner control in cell C47. Although the three choices are not an exhaustive list of variations, they do represent different kinds of tax bases commonly used under PSCs which impose income tax. The three options – whose impacts on valuation we will examine later in this section – are:

Version 1. Income tax is levied only on the contractor's share of profit oil, with no tax deductions permitted.

Version 2. Income tax is levied on the contractor's total PSC revenue (i.e., cost oil plus the contractor's share of profit oil), with no tax deductions permitted.

Version 3. Income tax is levied on the contractor's total PSC revenue, as in Version 2, but *with* tax deductions permitted. In this version, the tax deductions are assumed to be the standard deductions discussed in Chapter 1:

- opex;

- intangible (i.e., expensed) capex;

- abandonment costs;

- depreciation charges arising from tangible capex; and

- unused tax losses carried forward from prior tax periods.

Version 3 is the method we've seen mostly widely adopted in PSC regimes which levy income tax.

Note that the tax loss carryforward provisions discussed above are only relevant to Version 3. This is because, in Versions 1 and 2, there are no tax deductions permitted; therefore no tax losses can arise, and so there are no tax losses to carry forward.

Thinking ahead

Even before familiarizing yourself with this model's Base Scenario field assumptions, try to guess which of the three versions of income tax will likely result in the biggest total tax charge to the contractor, and why.

Depreciation Will Do Two Jobs in This Model

As mentioned, under Version 3, depreciation is a means of making tangible capex tax deductible.

Now, recall that our "core" PSC example model in Chapter 7 uses depreciation in another way – as a means of making tangible capex eligible for recovery by the contractor in the form of cost oil.

In this example, we have assumed that the same depreciation rules – as stated in rows 49–51 of our example model – apply to both (a) depreciation for income tax purposes and (b) depreciation for cost recovery purposes.

This means that the total depreciation charge in row 225 will feed both:

- the "Depreciation of tangible capex" row (row 291) in the Version 3 income tax section; and

- as always in this chapter's variations on our "core" PSC model, the "Tangible capex from all years (via depreciation)" row in the cost recovery section (row 228 in this section's model).

Be aware, however, that this is not always the case. Some fiscal regimes require one set of rules for depreciation income tax purposes and another for cost recovery purposes. By "rules," we mean:

- the type of depreciation (e.g., straight line, declining balance, double-declining balance, etc.);

- the useful lives when using the straight line method (e.g., 10 years for cost recovery purposes, versus 15 years for tax purposes); and/or

- the use of the terminal write-off provision for one purpose but not the other.[3]

In such cases, a different depreciation section must be modeled for each type of depreciation required. Fortunately, in our example model, the single depreciation section

---

[3] These items are all covered in "Appendix_I:_Depreciation.pdf."

(rows 140–225) – which follows the method already introduced in our "core" PSC example model – will serve both purposes.

Income Tax Calculation, Version 1: Levied on Contractor Share of Profit Oil, No Deductions Permitted (Used in Base Scenario)

The tax calculation in this section (rows 272–275) is simpler than the standard income tax calculation which we introduced in Chapter 1.

- Because no tax deductions are allowed, we do not consider any – which means, among other things, that we ignore carried forward tax losses, as these are a form of tax deduction.

- We also do not need any special formula logic to handle cases when taxable income becomes negative, because taxable income equals contractor profit oil, which can never be negative.

Therefore this section is very short. Taxable income (row 273; also called "taxable profit," as the two terms are often used interchangeably) equals post-ELT contractor profit oil (row 272). The contractor's income tax liability (row 275) simply equals taxable income times the income tax rate (row 274). Under our Base Scenario, the contractor's total tax charge under Version 1 is **MOD $43.0 mm** (cell D275).

Income Tax Calculation, Version 2: Levied on Contractor's Total PSC Revenue, No Deductions Permitted

This section (rows 279–282) is also short and simple, for the same reasons Version 1 is – there are no deductions (including loss carryforwards) to consider, and no logic is needed to handle negative taxable income, because taxable income – which in this Version 2 is contractor PSC revenue – can never be negative.

Taxable income (row 280) equals total, post-ELT contractor PSC revenue (row 279), which in turn is the sum of cost oil and contractor profit oil. The contractor's income tax charge (row 282) is, again, taxable income times the tax rate (row 281). Under our Base Scenario, the contractor's total tax charge under Version 2 is **MOD $111.0 mm** (cell D282).

Income Tax Calculation, Version 3: Levied on the Contractor's Total PSC Revenue, Deductions Permitted.

As mentioned, this version more closely resembles the standard income tax calculation introduced in Chapter 1. The main difference is that:

- whereas in Chapter 1, revenue was calculated as (the investor's post-ELT working interest share of production × the commodity price) – (royalty);

- here, revenue is calculated as the contractor's post-ELT PSC revenue (again, cost oil + the contractor's share of profit oil), found in row 286.

Most of the standard tax deductions, i.e., opex, intangible capex, abandonment costs and depreciation – all on a post-ELT basis – are collected in rows 288–291.

The last tax deduction – unused tax losses carried forward from prior periods – appears in row 292, and is calculated the same way, i.e., a "looping" method of calculations also involving rows 295 and 296, as explained in detail in Section 1.9.3 of Chapter 1.

Note the unique formula in 2015 (cell F292), which makes the loss carried forward to 2015 equal to the assumed value in the cell named "Initial_prior_tax_loss" (cell C44) which we mentioned earlier.

The various tax deductions for each year are summed in row 293. This sum is then subtracted from the contractor's PSC revenue, to result in taxable profit, in row 295.

- Note how the caption here is "Taxable profit/(untaxable loss)" as opposed to just "Taxable profit" in Versions 1 and 2. This is because here, unlike in Versions 1 and 2, negative values, i.e., tax losses, which are formatted in parentheses, are possible.

- A shorter term we sometimes use for "Taxable profit/(untaxable loss)" is simply "tax position."

The possibility of a loss in any given year requires the use of a logical IF statement when we calculate the contractor's tax liability, in the annual cells of row 298:

- Recall from Chapter 1 that current year tax losses are, as the term "untaxable loss" indicates, untaxable. Therefore, in years when tax losses arise, we need the income tax charge to equal 0.

- We accomplish this with a simple IF statement. For example, the formula for the typical tax year of 2019, in cell J298, is $=IF(J295<0, 0, \quad J295*J297)$. This means that if the tax position for the year, in cell $J295$, is less than 0, the answer is 0; otherwise, the answer equals the tax position (which will be 0 or positive) times the tax rate in cell $J297$.

- In 2019, the result is MOD \$5.4 mm, and total tax charges for all years (cell D298) equal **MOD \$41.9 mm**.

Income Tax Impact on PSC Revenue Distribution, NCF and NPV

Having just calculated three versions of the contractor's income tax liability, we can now choose which version is used in the model, using the spinner in cell C47, or its duplicate in cell F302. The chosen version's results will appear in the "Contractor's income tax liability" row (row 304), in which the annual cells use Excel's CHOOSE function.[4]

Note that for information purposes, in the next row (row 305), we express the volumetric equivalent of the tax charge in terms of millions of barrels of oil, by dividing the dollar value of the tax charge in row 304 by the received oil price in row 99. Under the Base Scenario,

[4] Excel's CHOOSE function syntax is as follows: CHOOSE([number of an item in a list], [listed item 1], [listed item 2], [listed item 3]...[etc.]). For example, =CHOOSE(2, A, B, C) would give the answer of B.

which uses income tax Version 1, the total tax charge is the equivalent of 0.484 mmb (or mm bbl) (cell D305).

We calculate the contractor's post-tax PSC revenue in row 311, as

$$(\text{cost oil} + \text{contractor profit oil} - \text{income tax})$$

Under the Base Scenario, the contractor's total post-tax PSC revenue equals MOD $247.2 mm (cell D311).

From the government's point of view, the income tax payment is additional revenue. Therefore "post-tax" government revenue takes account of the receipt of income tax paid by the contractor. The government's post-tax revenue is thus calculated in row 316 as

$$(\text{royalty} + \text{government profit oil} + \text{income tax})$$

Under the Base Scenario, the government's total post-tax PSC revenue equals MOD $322.7 mm (cell D316).

Interactive check

Let us check to see that the income tax charge works sensibly in the model. Summon the Base Scenario using the button in cell B12 and click the "Show PSC revenues/cashflows chart" button in row 12. Adjust the horizontal screen split bar and/or scroll as necessary so that you see the spinners for choosing the income tax rate (cell C43) and the income tax version (cell C47) in the top part of the screen, and the "Division of PSC Revenues and Cashflows" chart, which starts in row 376, in the bottom part.

Notice that this is an expanded version of this chart, compared to the one used in our "core" PSC example model.

- The differences here start in the fifth column, where we use the term "pre-tax" to describe the two parties' revenues. They are calculated the same way as government and contractor revenue are in the fifth column of the version of this chart in the "core" model; only the labels have changed. In this model, under the Base Scenario, government and contractor revenues are MOD $297.7 mm and MOD $317.2 mm, respectively.

- The sixth column is new. Comparing it to the fifth column, we can see how a tax charge of MOD $43.0 mm "takes a bite" out of the contractor's pre-tax revenue, reducing it to post-tax contractor revenue of MOD $274.2 mm.

- The MOD $43.0 mm tax charge from the fifth column is added to pre-tax government revenue of MOD $279.7 mm, resulting in total government post-tax revenue of MOD $322.7 mm in the seventh column.

Note how the chart updates when changing the tax rate. As you raise it, using the spinner (cell C43), in 5 percentage point steps, the tax "bite" widens until, at 100%, the contractor's undiscounted net cashflow goes negative. (Note that the use of Excel Data Tables in this model can make the charts a bit slow to update.) A 100% tax rate is of course unrealistic; this is just to check the model.

Classification of outflows

Although, to the contractor, a tax payment is as real a cash outflow as field costs, such as opex, capex and abandonment, we classify the tax outflow as a deduction from contractor PSC revenue, leading to post-tax contractor PSC revenue, from which we then deduct the field costs (in this version of the chart's second-to-last column, renamed "non-tax costs" for clarity). This classification of cash outflows as being tax or non-tax does not affect the "bottom line" of NCF or NPV, but it lets us distinguish between fiscal and non-fiscal costs, and so properly account for each party's PSC revenue.

Reset the tax rate to 35%, and then switch among the tax versions using the spinner in cell C47. You can see that Version 2 takes the biggest "bite" out of contractor PSC revenue, in both absolute and percentage terms. Version 2's tax charge is the largest because its tax base – total contractor PSC revenue, with no deductions – is also the largest of the three versions.

Exercise: Try This Yourself

Open the file "Ch8_PSC_with_income_tax_exercise_setup.xls." Fill in the blank, orange-shaded rows (rows 272–298) with the correct formulas. Set the model to the Base Scenario, and then compare your answers for the three versions of contractor tax liability to those in this section's example model, "Ch8_PSC_with_income_tax.xls."

Exercise: "Intuitive" Variance Analysis

To reinforce your understanding of how a simple change in a single input variable can influence not only the tax charge, but also the contractor's and government's net cashflows:

- In the file "Ch8_PSC_with_income_tax.xls" choose the Base Scenario, and then use the spinner in cell C47 to select the **Version 3** income tax method.
- Try to *guess intuitively* how increasing post-2015 opex by 5%, i.e., by changing the multiplier in J28 to 105%, might impact each party's NCF. For now, just guess whether either would increase or decrease. To guide your thinking, break out each party's NCF into its individual components and guess the direction of the change of each:
  - For the contractor, these components are non-tax costs, cost oil, contractor profit oil and the income tax payment.
  - For the government, they are royalty revenue, government profit oil and income tax revenue.

- Watch these components change on the "Division of PSC Revenues and Cashflows" chart as you switch the cost multiplier settings from 100% to 105% and back again. Can you explain all the changes? This is perhaps easiest if you work from left to right. That is, start by looking at the first column which is affected by the change in opex, i.e., the third column from the left; toggle the opex multiplier; understand what is happening with each segment in this third column; then move to the fourth column, repeating the process etc., through to the last column on the right.

Exercise: Precise Variance Analysis

Using small Excel Data Tables in rows 448–456 of the model in "Ch8_PSC_with_income_tax.xls," we've calculated each component of the contractor's and government's total (life-of-field) net cashflows (NCFs), and compared how changing the opex multiplier from 100% to 105% impacts each component, enabling us to explain changes in NCF. (Be sure Excel's calculation mode is set to Automatic.)

The results are shown Figures 8.1 and 8.2, which are screenshots of the analysis tables in rows 460–493. These collect the results of the Data Tables using the selected version of the income

Impact of opex change on Contractor NCF (uses Income Tax Version 3)			
Item	1	2	3
Cashflow item (MOD $ mm)	Opex sensitivity multiplier setting		105% opex setting: advantage / (disadvantage) to Contractor compared to 100% setting
	100%	105%	
a) Contractor Non-Tax Costs	195.7	203.3	(7.6)
b) Cost Oil	194.4	200.8	6.4
c) Contractor profit oil	122.8	120.3	(2.5)
d) Contractor tax payment	41.9	40.8	1.1
e) Contractor NCF = b + c - a - d	79.6	76.9	(2.7)
f) For Column 3 check: a + b + c + d + e			(2.7)
Column 3 check: f - e (0 means ok)			0

Note: Formula description for item e) does not apply to cell e3. Cell e3 = e1 + e2.

Comments by item
a) Higher opex increases Contractor non-tax costs.
b) Higher Contractor non-tax costs increase the amount recovered as cost oil (although not all of the increase is recovered.)
c) Higher cost oil lowers total profit oil. Because Contractor's share of profit oil is a fixed percentage of total profit oil, the dollar value of the Contractor's profit oil falls.
d) Higher opex means a larger income tax deduction, resulting in a lower income tax charge.

Figure 8.1   NCF variance analysis using Base Scenario and Version 3 income tax – contractor perspective, from the file "Ch8_PSC_with_income_tax.xls"

tax – we have used Version 3 income tax in this case – and add a variance analysis column, as shown above.

(Note that because the Data Tables simulate the opex multiplier settings of 100% and 105%, changing this multiplier manually will not *cause* the results in the Data Tables, or in the tables reproduced as Figures 8.1 and 8.2, to change.)

Figure 8.1 methodically explains the variance in contractor NCF when post-2015 opex increases by 5%:

- Note the columns which are labelled 1, 2 and 3. (These are our own labels, for the purposes of this figure; they are not Excel column labels, which would have been letters rather than numbers.)

- Column 1 shows the results of each component of contractor NCF when you set the model to the Base Scenario, with the opex multiplier to 100%.

- Column 2 shows the results of each component of contractor NCF when you set the model to the Base Scenario, and then set the opex multiplier to 105%.

- Column 3 shows how each Column 2 result differs from the Column 1 result.

  - Differences in Column 2 which benefit the contractor, compared to Column 1, e.g., higher cost oil, are shown as positive values.

  - Differences in Column 2 which disadvantage the contractor, e.g., higher non-tax costs, are shown as negative values.

For the reasons noted in the "Comments" section, the rise/fall in the various contractor PSC revenue components means some changes resulting from the higher opex work to the contractor's advantage, while others, to its disadvantage.

(Note that the comments do *not* update in the model; they are our "hard-coded" observations, based on choosing the Base Scenario, and then selecting income tax Version 3.)

In summary, as seen in the last column on the right:

- the higher opex means the contractor is disadvantaged by non-tax costs which are MOD $7.6 mm higher (item a)), and by contractor profit oil which is MOD $2.5 mm lower (item c));

- however, the higher opex also brings advantages: cost oil is MOD $6.4 mm higher than when the opex sensitivity multiplier is set to 100% (item b)), and the tax payment is MOD $1.1 mm lower (item d));

- so that overall, we can see that the net effect of raising opex by 5% (by having changed the opex sensitivity multiplier from 100% to 105%) is to **lower the contractor's NCF by MOD $2.7 mm** (item f)).

Impact of opex change on Government NCF (uses Income Tax Version 3)			
Item	1	2	3
	Opex sensitivity multiplier setting		105% opex setting: advantage / (disadvantage) to Government compared to 100% setting
Cashflow item (MOD $ mm)	**100%**	**105%**	
a) Royalty revenue	95.5	95.5	0.0
b) Government profit oil	184.2	180.4	(3.8)
c) Tax revenue	41.9	40.8	(1.1)
d) Government NCF = a + b + c	321.6	316.7	(4.9)
e) For Column 3 check: a + b + c + d			(4.9)
Check of Column 3: e - d (0 means ok)			0
Comments by item			
a) Higher opex does not effect royalty.			
b) Higher opex means higher Contractor non-tax costs. These increase Contractor's cost oil, lowering total profit oil. Because Government's share of profit oil is a fixed percentage of total profit oil, the dollar value of the Government's profit oil falls.			
c) Higher opex means a larger Contractor income tax deduction, resulting in a lower Contractor income tax payment to the Government.			

Figure 8.2   NCF variance analysis using Base Scenario and Version 3 income tax – government perspective, from the file "Ch8_PSC_with_income_tax.xls"

Figure 8.2 shows that the 5% increase in opex also lowers the government's NCF. Although royalty revenue is unchanged, government profit oil and tax revenue are MOD $3.8 mm and MOD $1.1 mm lower, respectively, for a total decrease in government NCF of **MOD $4.9 mm**.

Tax Rate Variations

In this example model, we have used a simple version of an income tax rate which is the same each year. In practice, however, as mentioned in Chapter 1, in some countries, income tax rates can vary, for example, according to:

- how many years a license has been producing;

- the production rate;

- whether the commodity produced is oil or gas (which under some systems can each require their own tax calculations);

- water depth, for offshore developments;

- a device known as the "R-factor," which is some measure of cumulative revenue divided by some measure of cumulative costs.[5]

Measuring Revenue Takes and Entitlement Volumes: Be Aware of Different Ways of Reporting

You will see that we have calculated the contractor's and government's PSC revenue and revenue takes on a *post-income tax* basis in rows 307–323.

---

[5] The generic concepts behind, and calculation of, R-factors are explained in detail in Section 3.9 of Chapter 3, which covers R-factors which determine royalties, and in Sections 8.5 and 8.6 of this chapter, which cover R-factors which determine the distribution of profit oil.

- We do so because revenue takes are intended to show how total PSC revenue is distributed, and the tax received by the state is clearly a distribution which needs to be accounted for.
- If we count income tax as an inflow to the government, of course we must then count it as an outflow from the contractor; if we did not, government and contractor revenue takes would not sum to 100%.

Entitlement volumes, however, can be calculated in different ways for reporting purposes, depending on the jurisdiction. They are commonly done on a *pre-income tax* basis for regulatory reporting purposes, as we have done in row 369, where the formulas divide each year's total pre-tax contractor PSC revenue (row 258) by the oil price received (row 126). Under the Base Scenario – which uses Income Tax Version 1 – total contractor pre-tax entitlement volumes are **3.52 mmb** (cell D369). Note that these volumes are net of royalty.

In contrast, other reporting regimes require that entitlement volumes be calculated on a *post-income* tax basis. We have done this in row 370. The annual formulas are the same as for the pre-tax basis entitlement volumes in row 369, except that for the post-tax volumes, the numerator is the value for post-tax contractor PSC revenue (row 311). Under the Base Scenario, total contractor pre-tax entitlement volumes are **3.04 mmb** (cell D370).

PSC Income Tax Liabilities and Reserves Entitlements in a Wider Context

In this chapter, we have focused on the contractor's NCF on a standalone basis, i.e. its NCF from a single PSC license, seen in isolation.

We have assumed that after:

- calculating the contractor's cash PSC revenue; and
- deducting its cash costs – including, in this section, income tax charges (which sometimes are specified within a PSC and, at other times, are set by separate tax regulations or laws); then

we reach a measure of NCF to the contractor, which is "the end of the story."

For contractors which are multinational companies, however, the "story" seldom ends there, as quite often the contractor is party to a PSC which is not in its home country. Sometimes, there are tax treaties between the contractor's home country and the PSC host country.

Such treaties are significant, as they can determine whether the contractor may deduct the payment (or deemed payment) of an income tax liability, under the terms of the PSC, against corporate income tax liabilities in the contractor's country of residence for tax purposes. Detailing these treaties is beyond the scope of this book. Be aware, however, that the tax impacts of this home country "angle" to the story can have a material impact on contractor NCF.

With expert tax advice, contractors usually try to negotiate the specific wording in the PSCs, so that any income tax paid, whether:

- directly, by the contractor from its share of revenue;
- from an allocated portion of project revenue; or
- by the government, from its revenue share on behalf of the contractor;

is accepted as a deductible charge for its corporate income tax in its home country.

Additionally, contractors try to include a reserves entitlement for any income tax deducted from the total project revenue stream.

From the reserves entitlement perspective, there are four common generic ways in which income tax paid under the terms of a PSC may be considered for reporting purposes in a contractor's home country:

1. The PSC explicitly states that the government – or the state-controlled national oil company ("NOC") which might be a party to the PSC – pays income tax (and any other taxes due) on the contractor's behalf, without specifying what those taxes are. The lack of definition of what the taxes are, or of what the rates and terms applied to those unspecified taxes might be, makes it hard for such taxes to be calculated as a deduction for home country corporate taxes, or to be allocated as a reserves entitlement. In such cases, it is likely that the contractor's total reported reserves entitlement would be based on a contractor's profit oil plus cost oil entitlement (i.e., essentially a post-tax basis, because the tax is rolled into the government's revenue take).

2. The PSC states that the government or NOC pays income tax on the contractor's behalf, with that income tax defined in the host country's tax law at known prevailing rates. (The PSC might also state, by way of offering fiscal stability, that if the tax rate were to change in the future, then the profit oil allocations would be adjusted to ensure that the contractor's take is not impacted by such changes.) In such a case, it *is* possible to calculate a value for that tax and a reserve entitlement, even though it is paid from the government's revenue stream. In these cases, it is likely that the contractor's total reserves entitlement would include an amount equivalent to the tax deemed to have been paid from the government's revenue stream, in addition to the reserves entitlement associated with the contractor's profit oil plus cost oil entitlements (i.e., the contractor's reserves entitlement would be essentially calculated on a pre-tax basis).

3. The PSC explicitly states that the contractor's income tax liability is discharged via a specified portion of the project revenue stream, calculated at a defined rate (defined in some PSCs as "tax oil"). The contractor never receives the tax oil revenue component, but if it is deemed to be an appropriately defined tax, it is likely to be considered as deductible for home country corporate tax purposes. In such cases, it is likely that the contractor's total reserves entitlement would include an amount equivalent to the "tax oil" in addition to the reserves entitlement associated with the contractor's profit oil plus cost oil entitlements (i.e., the contractor's reserves entitlement essentially would be calculated on a pre-tax basis in a way similar to case 2, above).

4. The PSC explicitly states that the contractor is liable to pay a defined income tax, at a specified rate, from its share of revenue. In this case, the contractor's total reserves entitlement would include an amount equivalent to the income tax paid in addition to the reserves entitlement associated with the contractor's profit oil plus cost oil entitlements (i.e., the contractor's reserves entitlement would be essentially calculated on a pre-tax basis).

Note that in cases 2, 3 and 4, reserves entitlements are calculated and reported on a pre-tax basis. In case 1 the reserves are calculated on a "post-tax" basis, although the taxes deemed paid have not been directly deducted from revenue components received by the contractor. **The variety of ways to measure entitlement volumes make it important to determine which one a contractor means when it reports them.**

Conclusions

Income tax payments under PSCs can be calculated in a number of ways, levied on a range of tax bases, and varied over time according to a number of different contract performance indicators.

As shown in this section, calculating income tax liabilities under a PSC is often quite straight-forward, if the rates and bases for the income tax are clearly defined, either in the PSC or in the associated tax legislation.

However, ambiguities do sometimes arise as to how PSC income taxes are to be treated for reserves entitlement purposes, and as to whether the taxes deemed to be paid are eligible for deduction against corporate taxes in the a contractor's host country. This latter issue is important to clarify, as the tax impacts can significantly affects the contractor's NCF, and thus NPV, from the producing assets.

8.2   PROFIT OIL SHARING BASED ON COMMODITY PRICES

In this section's example model, "Ch8_PSC_oil_price.xls," the contractor's and government's share of total (undistributed) profit oil varies as a function of the oil price. (The principles and calculations discussed here are the same as those which would be used for a gas-producing PSC, where the parties' profit gas shares vary as a function of the gas price.)

The profit oil sharing mechanism used is in the section of the model which starts in row 47, as shown in Figure 8.3. Note that the red-bordered range (visible in the Excel file) has been named "Profit_share_table."

Note the inverse relationship, from the contractor's perspective, whereby the higher the oil price is, the lower the contractor's share of profit oil will be, and vice versa. From the government's perspective, the relationship between prices and its share of profit oil is direct rather than inverse.

Distribution of total profit oil			
Oil Price at wellhead, $ (MOD) / bbl		% of gross profit oil (%)	
> =	<	Contractor	Government
0	20	90.0%	10.0%
20	40	75.0%	25.0%
40	60	60.0%	40.0%
60	80	45.0%	55.0%
80	100	30.0%	70.0%
100	150	20.0%	80.0%
150	no limit	15.0%	85.0%

Figure 8.3   Profit oil distribution scale, from the file "Ch8_PSC_oil_price.xls"

The idea behind such a profit oil sharing mechanism is to give the contractor incentives to develop and produce from the license area when prices are low, while giving the government an increasing share of PSC profits as prices rise.

Other Assumptions Unique to This Model

The assumptions used in this section's example model are identical to those in our standard "core" PSC model, except that the present model uses the profit oil distribution mechanism shown above, and that we use a different oil price assumptions section, which starts in row 66. This assumptions section offers a choice of five different oil price cases (as expressed in Real 2015 $/b, before the application of the oil price sensitivity multiplier). These cases are:

- *Price case 1: flat (row 67)* – the oil price is $70 every year. This case is used in the model's Base Scenario, which is summoned using the button in cell B12.

- *Price case 2: rising (row 68)* – the oil price starts at $40 in 2015 and rises annually until reaching $125 in 2021, where it stays thereafter.

- *Price case 3: falling (row 69)* – the oil price starts at $125 in 2015 and falls annually until reaching $40 in 2021, where it stays thereafter.

- *Price case 4: custom, calculated* – this lets the user set the oil price, by choosing inputs (cells C73:C75) for:

  - the initial (2015) oil price;

  - the direction of the change (rising or falling); and

  - starting in 2016, the annual percentage change on the previous year's price;

  resulting in the calculated custom price in row 76.

- *Price case 5: custom, typed-in (row 77)* – while the inputs just described for price case 4 are designed to make it easy to devise a price series which follows a specified trend for each year starting in 2016, they do not permit assumptions for irregular price trends. To give more flexibility, price case 5 lets you simply type in each annual price. This option is useful for modeling the impact of price spikes.

Choose the desired price case, which will appear in row 78, with the spinner control in cell C78.

Calculation of Profit Oil Shares

Calculating each party's annual share of profit oil is relatively straightforward. This is done in the section starting in row 269.

- Total (undistributed) profit oil is calculated in the usual way in row 270.

- The chosen oil price case, on a MOD, post-sensitivity multiplier basis, appears in row 272.

- The contractor's annual percentage shares of total profit oil are calculated using Excel's VLOOKUP function[6] in row 274. The formula used in the typical example year of 2019 (cell J274) is $\boxed{\text{=IF(J270=0, 0, VLOOKUP(J272, Profit\_share\_table, 3))}}$, which means that:

  ○ if total profit oil in cell $\boxed{\text{J270}}$ $= \boxed{0}$, then the answer is $\boxed{0}$%;

  ○ otherwise, the VLOOKUP function looks in column $\boxed{3}$ of the range, $\boxed{\text{Profit\_share\_table}}$ (i.e., the profit oil distribution table shown in Figure 8.3) for the contractor's percentage profit oil share corresponding to the oil price in cell $\boxed{\text{J272}}$. Under the model's Base Scenario (which uses price case 1), the 2019 oil price in cell $\boxed{\text{J272}}$ is MOD $76.52, resulting in a contractor share of 2019 total profit oil of **45%** (as found in cell D53 by the VLOOKUP function).

- The government's annual percentage shares of profit oil are calculated in row 275, as 100% minus a given year's contractor's percentage share (or as 0%, if that year's total profit oil is $0). Under the Base Scenario, the government's share in 2019 $= 100\% - 45\% = $ **55%** (cell J275).

- The annual MOD $ values of each party's share of profit oil are calculated in rows 277 and 278, as each party's percentage profit oil share times total profit oil (in row 270). Thus under the Base Scenario, in 2019, for example, the contractor's and government's shares of total profit oil of MOD $18.5 mm (cell J270) are, respectively, **MOD $8.3 mm** (cell J277) and **MOD $10.2** mm (cell J278).

- The annual values are summed in cells D277 and D278 to give each party's share of life-of-field total MOD profit oil. The **contractor's total is MOD $65.5 mm, and the government's is MOD $81.8 mm**.

- Each party's percentage shares of total profit oil over the life of the field are calculated by returning to rows 274 and 275, and, in the Total column, dividing each party's MOD total, life-of-field share of profit oil by the MOD total, life-of-field profit oil in cell D270. Thus under the Base Scenario, the **contractor's** total, life-of-field basis share of total profit oil is **44.4%** (cell D274), and the **government's** is **55.6%** (cell D275).

Checking the Model – And Your Understanding

Set the model to the Base Scenario using the button in cell B12, and then click the "Show profit oil and PSC revenues/cashflows charts" button in row 12. Drag the horizontal splitter bar down a few rows, and then scroll down so that in the top part of your screen you see the oil price assumptions in rows 66–80.

Let us create an intentionally extreme custom oil price forecast, to test the model. Use the spinner control in cell B78 to select price case 4 (custom, calculated). Use the spinners above row 78 to set the first year's oil price to Real 2015 $25.00/b (cell C73), rising thereafter (cell C74) by 21% per year (cell C75).

Below the horizontal splitter bar, the first chart on the left, starting in row 341, should appear as shown in Figure 8.4.

---

[6] The VLOOKUP function is explained in the self-contained file, "VLOOKUP_HLOOKUP_examples.xls" in the Chapter 1 folder.

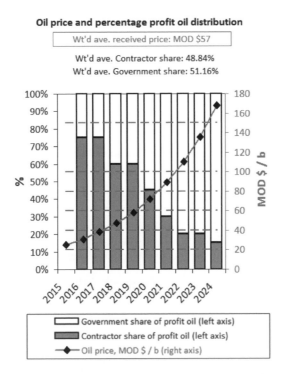

Figure 8.4   Oil price and percentage profit oil distribution under settings described above, from the file "Ch8_PSC_oil_price.xls"

In the chart reproduced in Figure 8.4, on a post-ELT basis:

- The line with the diamonds shows the MOD $ oil price, while the dashed horizontal lines show the different oil price thresholds from the profit oil distribution table. All these lines refer to the right axis. The weighted average received price over the life of the field appears in the boxed caption at the top of the chart. (Because it is the received price, it does not account for years when there is no production, such as in 2015 in this example.)

- The stacked columns show the contractor's (gray) and government's (white) percentage shares of annual total profit oil; these sum to 100% in each year, and refer to the left axis. Each party's weighted average shares of profit oil over the life of the field appear in the captions at the top of the chart, below the oil price caption.

Satisfy yourself that you understand what the chart shows – as the oil price "diamonds" exceed a new threshold, the shares of profit oil change; as the oil price rises, the contractor's percentage share of profit oil shrinks, while the government's grows.

The middle chart which starts in row 341 is similar to the left chart (just described), but instead of showing each party's percentage shares of total profit oil, it shows their dollar value shares of total profit oil, both annually in the columns and summed over the life of the field in the captions.

The chart on the right shows our standard depiction of life-of-field total PSC revenue distribution and cashflows for each party. Note that the values shown for contractor and government profit oil in the chart's fourth column match those in the captions of the middle chart.

To check your understanding of the model, try to answer the following questions:

- Choose oil price case 1. This is supposed to be a "flat" oil price time series. Why then is the oil price clearly not flat in the left and middle charts?

- Scroll through oil price cases 1, 2 and 3. Why does the number of columns in the left and middle charts change as you do so?

- Over the life of the field, does a higher contractor weighted average percentage share of total profit oil always result in a higher contractor dollar share of total profit oil? Why or why not? (Watch these metrics, in the left and middle charts' captions, while comparing, for example, oil price cases 2 and 3.) (Focusing on the captions in the right chart is useful, as this chart's scale updates automatically, which is sometimes distracting.)

- Over the life of the field, does a higher contractor weighted average percentage share of profit oil always result in higher contractor total PSC revenue? Why or why not? (Watch these metrics, in the left chart's caption, and the data label in the right chart's fifth column, while comparing, for example, oil price cases 1 and 2.)

- Over the life of the field, does a higher contractor weighted average percentage share of profit oil always result in higher contractor total undiscounted NCF? Why or why not? (Watch these metrics, in the left chart's caption, and the data label in the right chart's sixth column, while comparing, for example, oil price cases 1 and 2.)

(Requires some detailed analysis) Now scroll down so that, while keeping the oil price assumption rows in the top part of the screen, you see, in the bottom half of the screen, the charts, starting in row 415, which show the contractor's undiscounted and discounted net cashflows and their components. Switch again between price cases 1 and 2. Notice how:

- the last economic year, displayed in the caption in row 415, changes from 2022 under price case 1 to 2024 in price case 2;

- and yet, even though the price case 1 economic lifespan is two years shorter than that of price case 2, the contractor's MOD $38 mm NPV in price case 1 is higher than the MOD $35 mm NPV in price case 2. Why is this?

Special Technique: Using Crystal Ball Simulation/Optimization to Help Understand and Refine PSC Models

In many PSC fiscal systems, the revenue and cashflow splits to the contractor and government are driven by sliding-scale variables which involve much uncertainty over the project life cycle. This is particularly the case in this section's example, in which the variable is the oil price. If the oil price ends up varying a lot from year to year, the contractor's and government's percentage shares of total profit oil will vary widely too.

Stochastic Modeling: A Departure from Standard Scenario Analysis

In the version of this section's model discussed so far, we have tried to accommodate uncertainty about the oil price by creating several scenarios, including a fully customizable scenario which can be input in two ways.

This is useful, but only so useful, because, while it tells us the results of oil price scenario 1, 2, 3, etc., it does not account for our views – however fallible these might be – about *how likely* these scenarios, and thus the corresponding outcomes, are to occur.

As we show in this section, packages such as Crystal Ball – the Excel-compatible modeling software, of which a trial accompanies this book – are powerful ways to incorporate these views into our analysis. Crystal Ball quickly lets us analyze the impacts of price (as well as many other kinds of) uncertainty on how the fiscal regime in question "behaves," and how this effects key results.

In essence, Crystal Ball lets us easily model highly variable inputs, such as the oil price, *stochastically*. This means that, instead of expressing an oil price assumption as a single, fixed value – or as a time series in which each year is a single, fixed value, as we have done so far in this section in each of our oil price cases – we express the oil price assumption as a range of values, determined by a **probability distribution**.

Here is an example of such a probability distribution: suppose we expect that, at the extremes, the oil price can range between $30 and $250, but that these would happen only very rarely; most of the time, we expect it to be within a specified, narrower sub-range centered around $100, e.g., between $75 and $125, or, less symmetrically, between, say, $55 and $110.

A stochastic model in this case will run the model repeatedly, each time using a different oil price. The aim is to run the model enough times that the probability distribution is simulated reasonably closely (which is why stochastic models are also called "simulation models"). This can range from several hundred to several thousand times.

The use of repeated runs of the model, or "trials," means that the results will be a range of values.

Thus from our stochastic model, we will *not* get, for example, a single NPV; rather, we will get a *range* of NPVs, which we can then describe as having a minimum, a maximum and a most likely value, as well as quantifiable sub-ranges, e.g., there is a 90% chance that NPV will exceed $1 mm; there is an *X*% chance that NPV will be between $2 mm and $5 mm; there is a 10% chance that NPV will exceed $7 mm; etc.

Some people are uncomfortable with having a range of outcomes, as expressed in the title of a book on stochastic modeling, *Why Can't You Just Give Me The Number?*[7] Yet a range of outcomes not only is inevitable when incorporating risk into a model; it is actually much more

---

[7] *Why Can't You Just Give Me The Number? An Executive's Guide to Using Probabilistic Thinking to Manage Risk and to Make Better Decisions*, by Patrick Leach (Probabilistic Publishing, 2006).

useful to decision makers (who – like all of us – live in an inherently uncertain world) than simply creating, say, three fixed cases, designating them as "base," "low" and "high," and – as often happens – deciding, without any rigorous look at the underlying probabilities, that the base case is the "most likely" one.

Adapting Our Model to Incorporate Oil Price Uncertainty

We have adapted our example to work with Crystal Ball in a new version of this section's example model, "Ch8_PSC_oil_price_CrystalBall_part_1.xls."

> Unless you're already familiar with stochastic modeling and/or Crystal Ball ("CB" for short), we *strongly suggest* you review the self-contained tutorial files in the disk's "Appendix V_Introduction_to_probability_and_Crystal_Ball" folder on the disk before proceeding with this exercise. These explain all the basic concepts, terms and specific CB techniques discussed below. Otherwise, you might have trouble following the rest of this section.

If Excel is running, close it. Install CB if you have not done so already by following the instructions included with this book. Once CB has been installed and activated, launch it, which will in turn launch Excel. Click "Use Crystal Ball" on the CB welcome screen and, from within Excel, open the first version of our example file, "Ch8_PSC_oil_price_CrystalBall_part_1.xls."

Here we explain how we changed "Ch8_PSC_oil_price.xls" to arrive at "Ch8_PSC_oil_price_CrystalBall_part_1.xls." You can try to make these changes yourself, by making a copy of "Ch8_PSC_oil_price.xls" and following the same steps.

View the "Crystal_Ball_Settings" worksheet, which shows the general settings we have applied. In addition, we have made the following model-specific settings.

Input Assumption: Oil Price as a Lognormal Distribution

We assume the oil price will be lognormally distributed. We have done this by making the cell which determines the oil price multiplier – that is, cell C29 of the "Model" sheet, which under our Base Scenario settings equals 100 (meaning oil prices get multiplied by 100%) – a CB assumptions cell.

We selected this cell, clicked the "Define Assumption" button on the CB toolbar, chose the lognormal distribution from the Distribution Gallery, and set the parameters as follows: Location: 0; Mean: 100; Standard Deviation, 40. We then clicked Enter.

If you select cell C29 (which CB shaded green) and click the "Define Assumption" button, you will see – as shown in the screenshot in Figure 8.5 – that this input distribution will generate a wide range of oil prices, by setting the multiplier to values ranging from, effectively, 30% to over 250%, around a mean multiplier of 100%. The oil price – via this multiplier – is the only variable in the model which we have set to vary *stochastically*, i.e., by defining it to vary

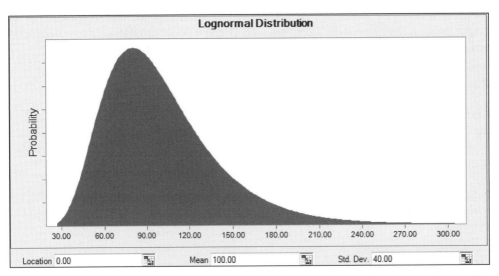

Figure 8.5 Assumed lognormal distribution for the oil price multiplier used in the file "Ch8_PSC_oil_price_CrystalBall_part_1.xls"

according to probability distribution (although other inputs could also be treated similarly to expand the analysis.)

In this example model, just **three outputs**, or results (which CB calls "Forecasts") calculated by the model are recorded by CB for each of 2000 trials to be performed in the simulation. (More trials could be added if deemed necessary.) These outputs are as follows.

Output 1: Government Discounted NCF (i.e., NPV)   This is in cell D320. We designated this as an output by selecting the cell, clicking the "Define Forecast" button on the CB toolbar, naming it "Gov Discounted CashFlow," specifying MOD $ mm as the unit, and clicking OK. CB then shaded this cell blue.

Output 2: Government Discounted NCF Take (%) in Trials Where Total Project Discounted NCF is Positive   This required a new cell to be set up (Cell D329) to record a modified version of the calculation in cell D326, i.e., to exclude outcomes when total discounted NCF is negative.

This modification is made in the formula in cell D329, which is $=IF(OR(D321<=0,$ $D320>D321), 1, D320/D321)$. This assigns all cases where either a) total project discounted cashflow is negative, or b) government discounted cashflow is greater than total project cashflow, to provide a value of 100%. (In other words, in case b), contractor cashflow is negative, so the government takes all of any positive cashflow that exists.)

We designated this as an output by selecting cell D329, clicking the "Define Forecast" button on the CB toolbar, and naming it "Gov Disc NCF Take." Again, CB shaded this cell blue.

Output 3: Contractor discounted NCF (i.e., NPV)   We designated this (cell D319) as an output the same way we did the other two, then named it "Contractor Discounted CashFlow" and specified MOD $ mm as the unit.

Running the Simulation

Reset the model to the Base Scenario using the button in cell B12 of the "Model" sheet, and on the CB toolbar click the "Reset Simulation" button (if it is not grayed out). Now the simulation is ready to run. Click the "Start Simulation" button on the CB toolbar. This will generate distribution charts for each of the three outputs in a matter of seconds.

Note that, after running the simulation, the state of the underlying model will reflect the last trial of the 2000 trials run. That is, the value of our stochastic variable – the oil price multiplier in cell C29.

Quick Analysis of Results

The three graphs shown at the top of the "TrialData" sheet to the right of column E illustrate the non-linearity of this fiscal regime:

- As the oil price in the trials rises towards each oil price threshold specified in the profit oil split table, it yields a higher contractor discounted cashflow and a lower government discounted cashflow and government take.

- As the oil price in the trials falls towards each oil price threshold specified in the profit oil split table, it yields a lower contractor discounted cashflow and a higher government discounted cashflow and government take.

- These trends are what is logically expected, but highlight that contractor and government takes are not easily predicted in detail in this fiscal regime. The full trial data from the simulation model highlight this characteristic of the fiscal regime. (We shall revisit these charts soon.)

Report 1 (Full Report). On the CB toolbar, we clicked "Create Report." In the "Reports" tab of the dialogue box which appeared, we chose "Full." Then in the Options tab, we specified that the report should go into the current workbook, typed "FullReport" for the sheet name, and then clicked "OK." This created a sheet with this name and pasted the report into it. (If such a sheet had already existed, CB would have added a suffix of 1, 2, 3, etc., for multiple sheets of that name.) The report includes a summary of the input and output assumptions, including charts showing key percentile boundaries.

Report 2 (Trial Data). We ran the simulation again, and then clicked the "Extract Data" button on the CB toolbar. In the Data tab of the dialogue box which appeared, we selected "Statistics" and "Trial Values," then selected "All" forecasts and assumptions. On the Options tab we named the destination sheet "TrialData" to go into the current workbook and clicked "OK."

Let us quickly review these results sheets.

The "FullReport" sheet generated for price case 1 (which the model used when we reset it to the Base Scenario) generates a summary of the simulation, which shows, among other statistics, the following. Values are expressed in MOD $ mm.

Government discounted cashflow (starting in row 142 of the "FullReport" sheet):

- Base case: 105.6 (i.e., the value of government discounted cashflow in the model before running the simulation, when the oil price multiplier is at 100%).
- **Mean (most likely): 123.6.**
- Median (or "P50"): 93.2.
- Minimum: 0.0.
- P90 (i.e., there is a 90% chance the value will be greater than or equal to this): 38.1.
- P10: 259.0.
- Maximum: 886.

Government discounted NCF take (i.e., in trials where total discounted project NCF is positive) (starting in row 86):

- Base case: 73.5%.
- **Mean: 84.2%.**
- Median: 81.6%.
- Mode: 100% (many low oil price cases generate no positive discounted profit for the contractor under the terms of this PSC; therefore, in such cases, 100% goes to the government).
- Minimum: 73.4%.
- P90: 74.5%.
- P10: 100%.
- Maximum: 100%.

Contractor discounted cashflow (values in MOD $ mm) (starting in row 30):

- Base case: 38.0.
- **Mean: 22.4.**
- Median: 30.1.
- Minimum: −(48.4).
- P90: −(17.4).
- P10: 43.0.
- Maximum: 124.6.

The "FullReport" sheet also shows charts of these three highly skewed distributions and the lognormal input distribution of the oil price multiplier.

The **conclusions** you could draw from this sheet are that, given the assumed lognormal distribution of the oil price:

- the government is likely to receive a share of discounted cashflow, under the field assumptions and range of oil prices, in excess of 80% and its share is unlikely to fall below about 75%; and

- the contractor's most likely NPV would be MOD $22.4 mm (the mean result), and it has a 90% chance of exceeding MOD $(17.4) mm (the P90) and a 10% chance of exceeding MOD $43.0 mm (the P10).

The "TrialData" sheet generated for price case 1 shows values of inputs and outputs for each simulation trial, and summary statistics for more detailed analysis. After CB generated these data, we reformatted and ranked them based on the oil price (low to high), and manually created the three charts which are shown below.

From Figure 8.6, we can see that, in general, contractor discounted cashflow (i.e., NPV) rises with the oil price. The trend, however, is punctuated by some "bumpiness," which occurs as

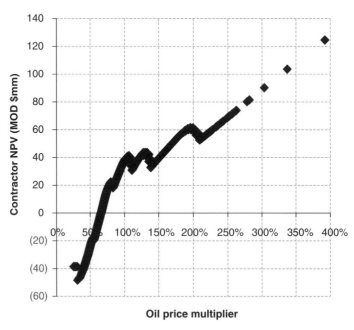

Figure 8.6 Oil price vs. contractor discounted cashflow, from the "TrialData" sheet of the file "Ch8_PSC_oil_price_CrystalBall_part_1.xls"
Note: Results reflect the model's Base Scenario, except for the oil price multiplier's variation from 100%.

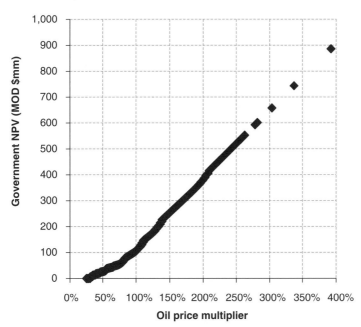

Figure 8.7 Oil price vs. government discounted cashflow, from the "TrialData" sheet of the file "Ch8_PSC_oil_price_CrystalBall_part_1.xls"
Note: Results reflect the model's Base Scenario, except for the oil price multiplier's variation from 100%.

the oil price passes through bands of the profit oil distribution mechanism, i.e., the one shown in Figure 8.3, above, causing the contractor's percentage share of profit oil:

- to fall, when the oil price first crosses a new threshold in the profit sharing table; but then
- to resume climbing once the benefits of the higher oil price are great enough to outweigh the lower percentage share of profit oil.

The trend in government discounted cashflow also shows some irregularity, but in general is much smoother, as shown in Figure 8.7. This is because the government's cashflow consists of not only its share of profit oil – which is also subject to some "bumpiness" as rising oil prices change its percentage share of profit oil – but also royalty revenue, which rises steadily in line with the oil price, filling in the "bumps."

Comparing the Y-axis scales of these last two charts makes it clear that the government's NPV is much higher than the contractor's.

When, as in Figure 8.8, the government's NPV is expressed as a percentage of total NPV, the irregularity in the government's take is easier to see. (You might need to change the chart's X-axis scale to 0%-400% to match the view shown in Figure 8.8.)

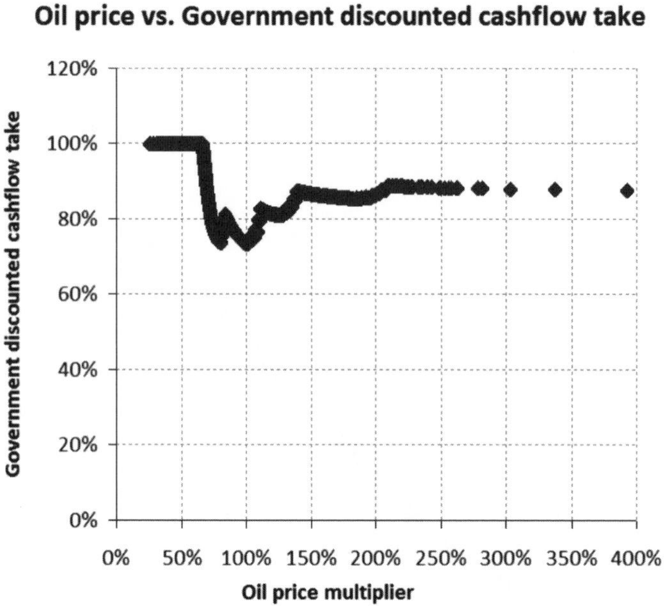

Oil price vs. Government discounted cashflow take

Figure 8.8 Oil price vs. government share of positive total project discounted cashflow, from the "TrialData" sheet of the file "Ch8_PSC_oil_price_CrystalBall_part_1.xls"
Note: Results reflect the model's Base Scenario, except for the oil price multiplier's variation from 100%.

This irregularity partially reflects the fact that it is a percentage of *total* discounted project cashflow, which in turn is irregular because it is the sum of the "smooth" and "bumpy" discounted cashflows shown in the previous two charts; the combination of the two still leaves some "bumpiness."

The PSC involves some steep ramps of increasing government take versus the oil price (e.g., at multiplier settings of between around 100% and 112%, and between around 128% and 140%). At oil price multiplier settings of below about 66%, the government takes all of the profits (if any).

There is much additional information in the simulation trial data we will not analyze here. Suffice it to say that the few minutes of effort needed to set up the simulation can provide considerable insight into the detailed behavior of a fiscal system.

Applying Crystal Ball's Optimizer to Fiscal Design

CB's **OptQuest** optimization tool – which we introduced in the third of the three self-contained tutorial files in the "Appendix V" folder on the disk – can be used to help find optimum solutions to an array of fiscal design objectives, such as getting parties to the PSC to agree on certain negotiated terms.

We will use the model in "Ch8_PSC_oil_price_CrystalBall_part_1.xls" to illustrate a simple example.

We saw in the "Quick Analysis of Results" section above that in the simulation analysis, just conducted, of a wide range of oil prices, the government can expect to achieve a mean (most likely) percentage discounted NCF take, when total project NCF is positive, of 84.2%. Let us suppose the government wants to increase this to 88%.

We can use CB's OptQuest tool to help find ways to achieve this, by changing parameters of the fiscal system. In this case, we will change the percentage shares of total profit oil, which, as we have seen, are defined in the table starting in row 47 of the "Model" sheet (and which we reproduced in Figure 8.3).

Preparing the Model for Use with OptQuest

For OptQuest to work, we first needed to define "Decision" variables, i.e., the values in the profit oil distribution table which we want to change, to reach the government's mean 88% goal, or objective.

In this example, our decision variables will be cells D53:D55 in the profit oil distribution table – which is repeated in Figure 8.9.

OptQuest will run a number of simulations of 2000 trials each. That is:

- It will try a new combination of percentages in these three cells (which are circled in Figure 8.9), run 2000 trials, and record the resultant mean of our objective, the government's discounted cashflow take (in cell D329).

- If the combination of new values does not result in a mean value of 88%, OptQuest tries a new combination of values in cells D53:D55 in a new simulation.

- If it *does* result in 88%, it also tries again, to see if there is a different way to reach the same answer. This can be very useful, in cases where we like a result, but not how it is reached. (We explain in a moment how to tell OptQuest when to stop.)

	B	C	D	E	F
47		Distribution of total profit oil			
48	Oil Price at wellhead, $ (MOD) / bbl		% of gross profit oil (%)		
49	> =	<	Contractor	Government	
50	0	20	90.0%	10.0%	
51	20	40	75.0%	25.0%	
52	40	60	60.0%	40.0%	
53	60	80	45.0%	55.0%	
54	80	100	30.0%	70.0%	
55	100	150	20.0%	80.0%	
56	150	no limit	15.0%	85.0%	

(Cells C51–C53 annotated: "Decision variables for OptQuest")

Figure 8.9   Profit oil distribution scale, from the "Model" sheet of the file "Ch8_PSC_oil_price.xls" (repeated from above)

We designated the cells circled in Figure 8.9 as decision cells, and specified how much they may change, by – one cell at a time – selecting each cell, clicking the "Define Decision" button on the CB toolbar, and entering, in the dialogue box which appeared, the following permitted ranges we want OptQuest to try:

- cell D53 (which refers to oil prices >= $60/barrel to < $80/barrel): 30% to 40%;

- cell D54 (which refers to oil prices >= $80/barrel to < $100/barrel): 20% to 30%;

- cell D55 (which refers to oil prices >= $100/barrel to < $150/barrel): 15% to 20%.

Each time, under "Type," we selected "Continuous." This means that the decision can be any decimal value between the stated range, e.g. 30.00%, 30.01%, 30.001%, etc.

After a cell was designated as a decision cell, OptQuest shaded it yellow. If you select any of these three yellow cells in the model, and then click the "Define Decision" button on the CB toolbar, you will see the settings just described.

Next, we defined cell D329 – which displays the government's discounted cashflow take – as our objective. On the CB toolbar, we clicked the "OptQuest" button, and, in the Objectives menu of the OptQuest dialogue box which appeared, clicked "Add Objective." Under the "Objectives" heading, we entered:

> "Set Target for Mean of Gov Disc NCF Take to 88%."

We then clicked the "Add Requirement" button, and under the "Requirements" heading, entered:

> "The Mean of Gov Disc NCF Take must be greater than or equal to 88%."

If you select cell D329 and click the "OptQuest" button on the CB toolbar, you will see these settings in the Objectives menu of the dialogue box which will appear.

For this simple optimization, no additional constraints were needed, but others could be entered in this menu for more constrained cases, as we shall see later.

Finally, before running the optimization, we need to specify a few additional OptQuest settings. Under the OptQuest dialogue's Options menu, set the following:

- Optimization control: Run for 30 simulations.

- Type of optimization: With simulation (stochastic).

- Decision variable cells: Leave set to original values.

Running OptQuest: First Pass

With everything prepared, scroll within the model so that you can see cells D53:D55. Click the "OptQuest" button on the CB toolbar, and then click Run at the bottom of the OptQuest menu which appears.

The OptQuest Results window appears. OptQuest tries 30 different sets of decision variables, one set for each of the 30 simulations. If necessary, move this window so that you can see the new values in the Excel model's cells D53:D55 which OptQuest is trying out.

On a medium-spec, 2011 laptop, the 30 simulations take less than a minute.

When they are done, choose Solution Analysis from the View menu of the OptQuest Results window. You will see the table shown in Figure 8.10.

This screenshot shows a list of 15 **feasible solutions**, namely, the Decision Variables (i.e., the suggested new values to use in the Excel model's cells D53:D55) which are within the ranges we specified, and which met our objective of achieving a government discounted NCF take of at least 88%.

Let us test OptQuest, by:

- manually inputting the Decision Variables from the top-ranked solution shown in Figure 8.10 into our Excel model (as shown in Figure 8.11, below); and

Rank	Solution #	Objective Set Target Mean = 88.0% Gov Disc NCF Take	+ Requirements Mean >= 88.0% Gov Disc NCF Take	− Decision Variables		
				D53	D54	D55
1	26	88.0%	88.0%	34.7%	21.8%	16.1%
2	25	88.0%	88.0%	34.6%	21.8%	16.1%
3	24	88.0%	88.0%	34.6%	21.8%	16.1%
4	23	88.1%	88.1%	34.5%	21.9%	16.1%
5	22	88.1%	88.1%	34.4%	21.9%	16.1%
6	29	88.1%	88.1%	35.2%	21.2%	15.3%
7	21	88.1%	88.1%	34.1%	22.0%	16.1%
8	20	88.2%	88.2%	33.6%	22.2%	16.2%
9	4	88.4%	88.4%	32.5%	22.5%	16.3%
10	13	88.4%	88.4%	31.3%	22.6%	18.4%
11	27	88.6%	88.6%	31.4%	22.7%	16.3%
12	28	88.7%	88.7%	30.6%	23.4%	16.3%
13	30	88.7%	88.7%	30.0%	23.6%	16.9%
14	5	88.9%	88.9%	31.3%	21.3%	15.6%
15	2	89.4%	89.4%	30.0%	20.0%	15.0%

Figure 8.10   Solutions view from the OptQuest Results window after running OptQuest with the file "Ch8_PSC_oil_price_CrystalBall_part_1.xls"

	B	C	D	E	F
47	Distribution of total profit oil				
48	Oil Price at wellhead, $ (MOD) / bbl		% of gross profit oil (%)		
49	> =	<	Contractor	Government	
50	0	20	90.0%	10.0%	
51	20	40	75.0%	25.0%	
52	40	60	60.0%	40.0%	
53	60	80	34.7%	65.3%	
54	80	100	21.8%	78.2%	
55	100	150	16.1%	83.9%	
56	150	no limit	15.0%	85.0%	

(Annotation in table spanning rows 51–53: "Manually typed-in Decisions from OptQuest's "best" solution" with arrow pointing to cell D53)

Figure 8.11   Revised profit oil distribution scale, using OptQuest's top-ranked solution, in the file "Ch8_PSC_oil_price_CrystalBall_part_2.xls"

- running a simulation, to see if the resultant mean government cashflow take is indeed the 88% which OptQuest says it should be.

We did this in a new copy of the model – the file, "Ch8_PSC_oil_price_CrystalBall_part_2.xls" – in which the only difference compared to the previous file consists of the shaded values shown in Figure 8.11. (You won't see these changes to cells D53:D55 in the version of this file on the disc; you will have to make them yourself.)

Note how the decisions in cells D53, D54 and D55 differ from their respective, prior Base Scenario values of 45%, 30% and 20%. It makes intuitive sense to suppose that, when we use these lower contractor shares of total profit oil, government cashflow take will rise from its Base Scenario, simulated mean of 84.2%, but let us run a simulation with these new values in place, to see if they actually result in the mean government cashflow of take of 88% which OptQuest claims.

Click the CB toolbar's "Reset Simulation" button if it is green, and then click the "Start Simulation" button. From the Forecast: Gov Disc NCF Take window which appears after the simulation has finished, you can see that the mean is in fact 88%, as shown in Figure 8.12.

OptQuest was right. You can test any of OptQuest's other proposed feasible solutions this way.

Taking the Contractor's View into Account – Running OptQuest a Second Time

The design of PSCs in their final, signed form rarely happens in isolation, with the government simply decreeing changes unilaterally; rather, PSC terms are subject to negotiations between both sides.

As we saw above in the "Quick Analysis of Results" section, before we ran OptQuest and used its top-ranked solution in the profit oil distribution table, the contractor's mean NPV was MOD $22.4 mm. After using this OptQuest solution, however, it fell to MOD $15.8 mm. You can see this yourself, by rerunning the simulation we just ran, and inspecting the "Forecast: Contractor Discounted Cashflow" chart which appears when the simulation finishes.

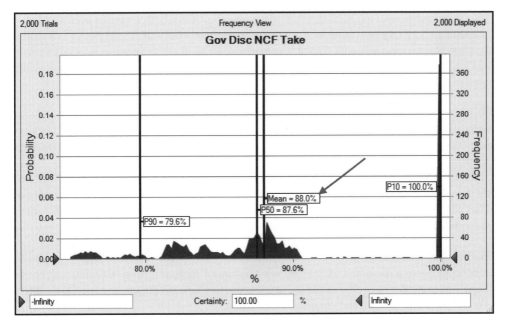

Figure 8.12 Simulation results for government NCF take using OptQuest top-ranked solution and the model in the file "Ch8_PSC_oil_price_CrystalBall_part_2.xls"

The contractor, understandably, was not happy to see its NPV fall. After some bargaining between the two sides, it was agreed to try to revise the profit oil distribution table, so that the government could still achieve a mean discounted cashflow take of 88%, while also giving the contractor a mean NPV of at least $18.0 mm.

We tried this in yet another copy of the model – "Ch8_PSC_oil_price_CrystalBall_part_3.xls." We added the following **new requirement**, entered, as before, by clicking the "OptQuest" button on the CB toolbar, and, under the Objectives menu, clicking the "Add Requirement" button, and under the "Requirements" heading, entering:

> "The Mean of Contractor Discounted Cashflow must be greater than or equal to 18.0 MOD $ mm."

We then:

- reset the Excel model to the Base Scenario by clicking the button in cell B12 – which replaced the OptQuest solution values for cells D53:D56 with the model's original values;

- clicked the "Reset Simulation" button on the CB toolbar, if the button was not grayed out;

- clicked the "OptQuest" button on the CB toolbar again; and

- clicked Run.

After 30 simulations, OptQuest did *not* find a way to achieve both a mean government discounted cashflow take of at least 88%, and a mean contractor NPV of at least MOD $18.0 mm. We know this because when OptQuest was finished, we went to the Solution Analysis view in the OptQuest Results window and saw that there were 30 "infeasible solutions" but 0 "feasible solutions."

We tried again, this time giving OptQuest more time. In the Options menu of the OptQuest dialogue box, under "Optimization control," we changed the settings, from having OptQuest run 30 simulations, to having it run for 10 minutes. We ran OptQuest for the full time – but still without success.

We then tried changing some parameters, to give OptQuest more flexibility to find a solution. After a bit of **trial and error** – which can sometimes be necessary with OptQuest, depending on model complexity and the desired objectives – we tried the following.

First, we changed the range of permitted values for each of the three decision variables in cells D53:D55 to a minimum of 0% and a maximum of 50%, selecting "Continuous" as the "Type" for each. We were able to edit these cells, one at a time, by clicking on the CB toolbar's "Define Decision" button, and entering these changes.

Next, we added a fourth decision variable – cell D56, which is the contractor's percentage share corresponding to oil prices of MOD $150 and higher. Again, we selected this cell, clicked the "Define Decision" button, and gave this cell the same setting as the other three decision cells, i.e., a minimum of 0%, a maximum of 50%, and a "Continuous" distribution type. When we finished, OptQuest shaded this cell yellow, like the three cells above it.

Thus the new decision variables and their settings are as summarized in Figure 8.13, which is a screenshot of the "Decision Variables" view from the main OptQuest dialogue box.

Note that the figures in the "Base Case" column are those which are in cells D53:D56 before running OptQuest. Again, these are the default figures from our Base Scenario.

We needed one more adjustment. Because we allowed each of the four decisions to "float" anywhere between 0% and 50%, this could disrupt the descending order designed in the original PSC – that is, it could result in cell D56 having a higher value than cell D55, cell D55 having a higher value than cell D54, etc. We wanted to preserve the descending order, and, in fact, to ensure that there was at least a 1 percentage point difference between the values.

Decision Variables	Lower Bound	Base Case	Upper Bound	Type
D53	0.0%	45.0%	50.0%	Continuous
D54	0.0%	30.0%	50.0%	Continuous
D55	0.0%	20.0%	50.0%	Continuous
D56	0.0%	15.0%	50.0%	Continuous

Figure 8.13   OptQuest decision variables used in the file "Ch8_PSC_oil_price_CrystalBall_part_3.xls"

To add these conditions, we used the Constraints menu of the OptQuest dialogue box. Rather than entering several constraints (e.g., D56 must be at least 1 percentage point lower than D55, D55 must be at least 1 percentage point lower than D54, etc.), we entered, in **cell H56** of the "Model" sheet, a formula which gives the answer of 1 when all these conditions are met, and otherwise gives an answer of 0. The formula is

$$=IF(AND(D56+1\% < D55, D55+1\% < D54, D54+1\% < D53), 1, 0)$$

Then, in the OptQuest dialogue's Constraints menu, we clicked Add Constraint, specified "H56 = 1," and clicked Close. This tells OptQuest that the value in H56 must equal 1 if a solution is to be valid, i.e., feasible.

We ran OptQuest again. Within about 20 seconds, it started finding feasible solutions. We stopped OptQuest after three minutes, by which time it had found 37 feasible (and over 300 infeasible) solutions. We captured these results in Excel format by clicking the Extract Data option, found under the Analyze menu item of the OptQuest Results window. (In the dialogue box which appeared, under the OptQuest Data tab, we checked both checkboxes, and under the Simulation Data tab, we unchecked all the items.)

The results, which we have reformatted, appear in the "OptQuestSolutions2" worksheet of the file "Ch8_PSC_oil_price_CrystalBall_part_3.xls," and are depicted in Figure 8.14.

The contractor's percentage shares of profit oil for the relevant oil price bands, from the Base Scenario and from our first OptQuest run, appear for reference in the two skinny rectangular

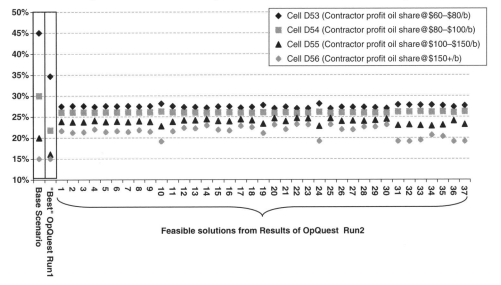

Figure 8.14 Summary of feasible OptQuest solutions, from the "OptQuestSolutions2" worksheet of the file "Ch8_PSC_oil_price_CrystalBall_part_3.xls"

boxes on the left side of Figure 8.14. The remaining data points show the 37 feasible solutions suggested by the second OptQuest run. Note how they compress the range of percentages to around 19–28%. From these 37 solutions, the highest resultant government cashflow take was **88.06%** (from solution #37 on the chart), and the highest resultant contractor NPV was **MOD $18.73 mm** (solution #14). (These results are not visible in the chart, but are on the underlying worksheet, in rows 46 and 23, respectively.) This meets each party's objectives.

We could designate more tranches of the profit oil table as decision variables, to give OptQuest even more alternative solutions.

In real life, it would be prudent to run this analysis for a wide range of potential field sizes and production, price and cost assumptions before finalizing the values.

Governments and contractors can use optimization techniques like those shown here to help negotiate mutually acceptable fiscal terms. Note that OptQuest works with both stochastic simulation models, i.e., those which have input assumptions which are not static values, but rather are represented as probability distributions, like the oil price in our present model, as well as with "normal" deterministic models, e.g., in which input assumptions *are* static values.

We encourage you to explore using OptQuest with other fiscal design optimization targets using this and other models.

8.3   PROFIT OIL SHARING BASED ON THE PRODUCTION RATE

Introduction

Some countries distribute profit oil to the contractor and government based on the license's production rate, usually measured in volume per day over a certain period.

In our example model for this section, found in the file "Ch8_PSC_production_rate.xls," we have assumed that the measurement period is one year. In cases where the period is more frequent, the model's timeframe should be denominated to match.

In our example model – which is based on the "core" PSC example model – we have assumed that profit oil distribution is based on average annual oil production rates, measured in thousands of barrels per day (mb/d, or m bbl/d) shown in the scale in Figure 8.15. This is taken from rows 52–61 of the model. The cells with values in the middle four columns have been given the range name "Profit_share_table."

(Note that the last column is not formally a part of the distribution table, but we have created it to help with our calculations, as discussed below.)

Note the **inverse relationship**, whereby the lower the production rate is, the higher the contractor's share of profit oil will be, and vice versa. For the government, the production rate/profit share relationship is direct rather than inverse.

Distribution of gross profit oil					
Tranche #	Annual ave. production rate, (100% WI basis), m b / d		% of gross profit oil		Vol. in tranche, m b / d
	> =	<	Contractor	Gov't	
1	0	25	80.0%	20.0%	25
2	25	50	70.0%	30.0%	25
3	50	75	60.0%	40.0%	25
4	75	100	50.0%	50.0%	25
5	100	125	40.0%	60.0%	25
6	125	150	30.0%	70.0%	25
7	150	1.E+07	20.0%	80.0%	999999850

Figure 8.15   Profit oil distribution scale, from the file "Ch8_PSC_production_rate.xls"
Note: The "1.E+09" value in Tranche 7 of the third column is space-saving, scientific notation for 1 billion. We have used this value to signify that there is effectively no upper limit to this tranche, i.e., that 20% and 80% contractor and government shares, respectively, correspond to any production rate which is greater than 150 mb/d.

Because often production profiles, after an initial ramp-up, tend to peak in the early years and then decline over time, in such cases (excluding the ramp-up periods) this profit oil distribution mechanism will give the contractor a lower *percentage share* of profit oil in early years than in later ones. Bear in mind, however, that these lower, early percentages will be applied to *total* profit oil which is higher in *absolute terms*, giving the contractor a high *dollar value* share of profit oil in these early years.

"Top-Rate" vs. "Tranches" Approaches

As we discussed in Chapter 3, where we encountered a similar, production rate-based scale for determining royalties, there are two variations of this type of mechanism. You need to be sure which one the PSC intends, as they produce different results.

This section's example model calculates the parties' shares of profit oil using both versions, as discussed below, and lets the user choose which will be used in the model, using the spinner control in cell M54.

- A *"top-rate"* version. In this version, only one row of the scale shown in Figure 8.15 is relevant for the period in which the shares of profit oil are being calculated, i.e., the row corresponding to the <u>average annual production rate</u> for the year in question.

  ○ For example, assume production in a period averages 35 mb/d. We can see that this falls between 25 and 50 mb/d in the second row of the table. Therefore the contractor's share of profit oil that year would be ⌐70%⌐ and the government's, 30%.

  ○ This can be calculated with a simple formula using Excel's VLOOKUP function, as we'll show later.

- *A "tranche" or "blended rate" version.* In this version, the contractor's percentage share of profit oil is calculated as a weighted average of the percentages which correspond to every step of the scale, or "tranche," through which the period's production passes. For example, assume again that annual average production is 35 mb/d:

  o In this case, 35 mb/d "passes through" or "straddles" Tranches 1 and 2.

  o The portion of the 35 mb/d production which falls within Tranche 1 is the portion from 0 to 25 mb/d. The portion of total production within Tranche 1 is thus $25/35 = \mathbf{71.4\%}$. Considered on its own, this would result in a contractor profit share of **80%**.

  o We have accounted for 25 mb/d of the total 35 mb/d. The remaining $35 - 25 = 10$ mb/d would fall within Tranche 2. Thus the portion of total production within Tranche 2 is $20/35 = \mathbf{28.6\%}$, which, considered on its own, corresponds to a contractor profit share of **70%**.

  o The "blended" or weighted average contractor share of total profit oil in this case would be calculated as $\mathbf{(71.4\% \times 80\%) + (28.6\% \times 70\%)} = (57.1\% + 20\%) = \boxed{\mathbf{77.1\%}}$.

  o Rather than do a separate weighted average calculation for the government's share, we can simply calculate it as 100% minus the contractor's 77.1% share, or 22.9%. (You can see we did these calculations off to one side, in cells M56:P60.)

Notice how, in this example, the contractor's 77.1% share of profit oil, calculated using the tranche method, is higher than the 70% resulting from the "top-rate" method. This will always be the case when:

(a) there is an inverse relationship between production rates and the contractor's share of profit oil; and

(b) the production rate for the period in question "straddles" more than one tranche.

This is because the tranche method will take into consideration the portion(s) of total production which are lower than the top rate, and thus the corresponding higher contractor percentage shares of profit oil. These higher rates in turn boost the weighted average.

Example Model: Other Assumptions

In addition to adding the profit sharing table to the basic "core" PSC model and letting you choose between tranche and top-rate methods, we have added to this section's model a second assumed production case, for comparison. Each case produces a total of 206.6 mmb, but, as shown in Figure 8.16, production timing differs:

- Production Case 1, which is used in our Base Scenario, starts production at a peak rate of 160.2 mb/d and then declines quickly.

- Production Case 2 starts the same year, but at a rate of 72.3 mb/d, which it maintains in a multi-year plateau, before a slow decline starts in 2021.

Each case's data are entered as hard-coded values, expressed in mmb per year, in rows 65 and 67, and then converted to mb/d in rows 66 and 68, using an assumed 365.25 production days per year (cell C45, which we have named "Prod_days_per_year").

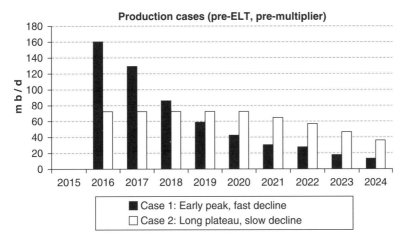

Figure 8.16   Production cases used in the model, from row 72 of the "Model" sheet in the file "Ch8_PSC_production_rate.xls"

You can choose which case feeds the model using the spinner in cell B90, and duplicates of it elsewhere.

Both cases are shown in Figure 8.16, before the application of (a) the production sensitivity multiplier (which under the Base Scenario is set to 100%) and (b) the economic limit test (ELT).

Note that under the Base Scenario's economic assumptions, the field does not shut down on commercial grounds in either case before the end of the pre-ELT lifespan; therefore, under these assumptions, the pre-ELT and post-ELT volumes are the same. (You can see this by splitting the screen and toggling between the cases while watching the economic life flag (ELF) in row 143.)

Note also that production in this example model is deliberately higher than in our standard "core" PSC model, so that when using the tranche method, production will pass through several tranches of the profit oil distribution table, to make the example more interesting.

We have made other changes to the "core" model here:

- In cells H33:M47, fixed opex, capex and abandonment costs have been scaled up to be realistic in light of the higher production volumes.

- We have also made the structure of opex more variable than fixed, as you can see in cells R33:R34. We have done this because it will give each production case the same post-ELT production lifespan. This means one less "moving part" when we compare the results of the two production cases later.

Profit Oil Distribution Calculations in the Model: Top-Rate Method

Shares of profit oil using this method are calculated in the section entitled "1) Calculation of profit oil shares: top rate method" in rows 284–293.

The contractor's annual <u>percentage shares</u> of total profit oil are calculated in row 289. For example, for 2019, the typical formula in <u>cell J289</u> is

---

=IF(J282=0, 0, VLOOKUP(J287, Profit_share_table, 3))

This means that if 2019 profit oil (cell $\boxed{\text{J282}}$) equals $\boxed{\$0}$, the answer is $\boxed{0\%}$; otherwise, the answer is found in the red-bordered range named $\boxed{\text{Profit\_share\_table}}$ (cells G55:J61). Specifically:

- in this range's row which corresponds to 2019 average annual production, in mb/d, which is found in cell $\boxed{\text{J287}}$; and

- in this range's column number $\boxed{3}$.

Under our Base Scenario, average annual production for 2019 in cell $\boxed{\text{J287}}$ is 58.9 mb/d.

The VLOOKUP function understands that this falls within the row of $\boxed{\text{Profit\_share\_table}}$ for 50–75 mb/d production rates (i.e., row 57), and returns the answer found in the range's third column, which is a 60% contractor share of profit oil (cell I57).

In row 290, the government's share of profit oil in 2019 is calculated as $100\% - 60\% = 40\%$ (cell J290). Here again we use an IF statement which answers 0% if total profit oil is $0.

In the rows 292–293, we calculate the <u>dollar value</u> of the contractor and government shares of total profit oil, multiplying the respective percentage shares by total profit oil. Thus in the Base Scenario in 2019, of total profit oil of MOD $1056.6 mm (cell J282), MOD $634.0 mm goes to the contractor (cell J292), and MOD $422.6 mm goes to the government (cell J293).

In cells D292:D293, we sum the annual dollar values of each party's share of profit oil over the economic life of the field, giving us totals, under the Base Scenario, of MOD $3984.1 mm for the contractor and MOD $5,117.6 mm for the government.

Having calculated each party's percentage of profit oil annually, we can now do so as an average over the economic life of the field. We do this in cells D289:D290, by dividing the dollar value of life-of-field, total profit oil (MOD $9101.7 mm under the Base Scenario (cell D282)) by each party's dollar value share. Under the Base Scenario, the top-rate method gives the contractor an economic life-of-field basis 43.8% share of profit oil (cell D289) and the government, 56.2% (cell D290).

Profit Oil Distribution Calculations in the Model: The Tranche Method

We calculate profit oil shares according to the tranche rate method in rows 295–375 of our example model. Note that this section could have been shorter if we had used "megaformulas," which would be challenging to write and read. Instead, we have split the calculation into smaller but more numerous steps.

Let us review the four basic steps we took in calculating the contractor's share of profit oil in the simple tranche rate example in the "'Top-Rate' vs. 'Tranches' Approaches" section of the text a few pages ago. These were to:

(a) identify the tranche(s) in which a given period's production falls;

(b) calculate the percentage of the period's production falling within each relevant tranche;

(c) calculate the contractor's "blended" percentage share of profit oil for the period, using a weighted average formula; and

(d) subtract the contractor's "blended" percentage share from 100% to get the government's share of profit oil for the period.

Basically, the calculations in rows 295–369 just perform these four steps, and then multiply the results – i.e., each party's percentage share of profit oil – by total profit oil, to get the dollar value of each party's profit oil.

Because the formulas are designed to accommodate changing assumptions, however, they are more nuanced than those in the simple example in the "'Top-Rate' vs. 'Tranches' Approaches" section of the text.

Cross Reference to Chapter 3

You might be able to understand the model's formulas in light of the foregoing explanation, just by looking at them or their descriptions in column Q.

If not, note that the calculation method is the same as the one we used in Section 3.6 of Chapter 3, where we used the tranche-based production rate method to calculate royalty rates. The only difference in this section's model is that there are more tranches in the PSC distribution schedule than in the royalty schedule. Thus here we will use the same generic formulas as in the royalty model, but in more rows.

Rather than repeat the full explanation of the detailed tranche method calculations here, instead we present, in Figure 8.17, a summary of the tranche method calculation steps taken in our example PSC model, their counterparts in the relevant royalty model, and the sections of the text in Chapter 3 which explain the royalty calculations.

If needed, review this Chapter 3 material. Once you are comfortable with it, you will immediately understand the corresponding sections of our present example model.

Quick Visual Check of Tranche Allocation

To provide a visual check, we have created a chart starting in row 321 of our PSC example model, which shows the allocation of annual production to tranches from the profit oil distribution table.

a) PSC model and relevant sections	b) Analogous royalty model and relevant sections	c) Section of Chapter 3 text which explains b)
Ch8_PSC_production_rate.xls	Ch3_roy_prod_rate_example.xls	n.a.
"2a) Allocation of annual production (m bbl/d) to tranches" (rows 297–316)	"1a) Allocation of annual production (m bbl/d) to tranches" (rows 65–73)	"Calculating the production rate-based royalty, assuming a tranche regime – version 1 (longest)" – "Step 1a"
"2b) Allocation of annual production (% of total) to tranches" (rows 357–366)	"2b) Allocation of annual production (% of total) to tranches" (rows 140–146)	"Calculating the production rate-based royalty, assuming a tranche regime – version 2 (shorter)" – "Step 2b)"
"2c) Calculation of 'blended rate' shares of profit oil" – "Contractor share of profit oil" (row 371)	"2c) Calculation of blended royalty rate (2 ways)" – "Blended royalty rate – using SUMPRODUCT function" (row 152)	"Calculating the production rate-based royalty, assuming a tranche regime – version 2 (shorter)" – "Step 2c)"

Figure 8.17 Steps of the tranche method profit oil share calculation taken in "Ch8_PSC_production_rate.xls," their counterparts in the tranche method royalty model of Chapter 3, "Ch3_roy_prod_rate_example.xls," and accompanying explanations in the text of Chapter 3

Use the duplicate of the production case selection spinner (in cell B333) to switch between Case 1 and Case 2. Notice from the chart the different number of tranches which production passes through in each case. (What might this mean for contractor percentage shares of profit oil in each case?)

You can also use the copy of the oil production sensitivity multiplier (in cell B329) to raise or lower each year's annual production. Watch the chart while scrolling from 50% to 150%. Do the changes in the chart make sense to you?

Reset to the Base Scenario using the button in cell B14 when you are done.

Model Results

The results of the tranche-based calculations are found in Section 2c) of our example model, in rows 371–375.

- Under the Base Scenario, using the tranche method, the contractor's life-of-field share of profit oil is 64.8% and the government's, 35.2% (cells D371:D372).
- This is a big difference, in the contractor's favor, to the results of the top-rate method, which gives the contractor a 43.8% share and the government, 56.2% (cells D289:D290). As mentioned, this happens because the tranche method considers the impact of production in various, lower production rate tranches, which correspond to higher shares of profit oil for the contractor.

Visual Check of Results

Reset to the Base Scenario, and then click the "Show profit sharing & PSC revenues/cashflows charts" button in row 14, adjusting the view as necessary so that you can see rows 448–476 in the bottom part of the screen.

(Note that these charts were designed to be viewed within Excel at a zoom setting of 100%. If you have trouble seeing everything on your monitor, we have reproduced screenshots from the following discussion in the file "Ch8_Supplement_to_Sec_8_3.pdf." When viewed in full screen mode, these pages might actually make it easier to see the things we will be comparing.)

The left chart shows, in the Base Scenario (which includes Production Case 1):

- annual average post-ELT production in mb/d, represented by the red line which refers to the right axis; and

- stacked columns representing the percentage shares of total profit oil of the government (white) and the contractor (gray), which sum to 100% and refer to the left axis.

There are life-of-field profit oil percentage captions at the top of the chart.

Use the spinners above the chart to select, for example, Production Case 1 (cell B450) and the tranche method (cell C450). The contractor and government profit oil captions will show 64.8% and 35.2%, respectively. The area in the chart covered by columns will be 64.8% gray and 35.2% white in this case.

The right chart repeats the red production line, which again refers to the right axis, while the stacked columns show the MOD $ value of the parties' profit shares, using the same colors and axis as in the previous chart.

The bottom chart repeats the visual check of how production is allocated to tranches when the tranche method is used.

Let us compare Production Case 1 results under both the tranche and top-rate methods, either by viewing the charts in the Excel file while switching between methods with the spinner in cell C450, or by viewing the comparative screenshots on page 2 of the file "Ch8_Supplement_to_Sec_8_3.pdf":

- In the top left chart, using either profit oil allocation method, the inverse relationship between the production rate and the contractor's percentage share of profit oil is easy to see. As the production rate falls, the contractor's share rises. The direct relationship between the production rate and the government's share is also evident – both fall together.

- Next, compare the *degrees* to which the party's shares change, depending on the profit oil allocation method chosen. As we mentioned, the tranche method gives the contractor a higher percentage share of profit oil than the top-rate method does, because the tranche method considers production rates which correspond to higher contractor shares. Thus under the tranche method, the charts' columns are more gray than white, while under the top-rate method, the opposite is true.

Next, choose <u>Production Case 2</u> (cell B450), and then again toggle between the tranche and top-rate methods (or view page 3 of the PDF supplement):

- The same relationships between production rate and each party's share of profit oil still hold true, though the trends are less "dramatic" here. This is because the production profile is more stable, and the production decline less marked, than in Production Case 1.

The reason that under Production Case 2 the differences between the two methods' results are smaller than they were under Production Case 1, is because – as seen in the bottom chart, starting in row 477 – in Production Case 2, the production profile passes through fewer tranches than in Case 1.

Exercise: Calculate These Yourself

The exercise file "Ch8_PSC_production_rate_exercise_setup.xls" is a copy of this section's example model, with empty, orange-shaded cells starting in row 289. Fill these in with the correct formulas, and then check your answers against those in the example model.

Note that at certain stages you might see that some checksums, including the master checksum in cell A1, show non-zero values and turn green to indicate there are errors. Any error messages should disappear when you have filled in all the cells correctly.

Exercise: Variance Analysis

Let us <u>compare the two production cases, focusing only on the tranche method results</u>, but expanding that focus to include differences not only in the contractor's share of profit oil, but also in the contractor's undiscounted and discounted cashflows.

In the file "Ch8_PSC_production_rate.xls," reset to the Base Scenario assumptions, which among other things selects Production Case 1 and the tranche method. The captions of the charts which start in row 448 show that, on an economic life-of-field basis:

- the contractor's share of total profit oil is 64.8%;
- total profit oil is MOD $9.10 bn (which, incidentally, can be verified against the "Division of PSC Revenue and Cashflows" chart starting in cell G452);
- resulting in <u>Production Case 1 life-of-field contractor profit oil</u> of 64.8% × MOD $9.10 bn =<u>MOD $5.89 bn</u>.

Next, select Production Case 2. Still using the tranche method, on an economic life-of-field basis:

- the contractor's share of total profit oil is 71.8%;
- total profit oil is MOD $9.44 bn;

- resulting in <u>Production Case 2 life-of-field contractor profit oil</u> of 71.8% × MOD $9.44 bn = <u>MOD $6.78 bn.</u>

Thus, using the tranche method, **the contractor's profit oil** is <u>MOD $6.78 bn − MOD $5.89 bn = **MOD $0.89 bn**</u> higher in Production Case 2 than in Production Case 1.

Now toggle between the cases, while watching either of the identical, gray "C cashflow" (contractor undiscounted NCF) columns in the "Division of PSC Revenue and Cashflows" chart. Note that the difference between <u>Production Case 2 NCF of MOD $7.26 bn</u> and <u>Production Case 1 NCF of MOD $6.37 bn</u> is also **MOD $0.89 bn.**

Now press the "Show Contractor revenue/NCF/NPV charts" button in row 14. In row 549, above the charts, you will find new duplicate versions of the switches for selecting the production case and the profit oil allocation method. Be sure that the tranche method is still chosen. Toggle between Production Case 1 and Case 2. Notice how one chart moves much more than other. Notice also the details (collected in Figure 8.18) in the captions above the last column of each chart.

	Production Case 1	Production Case 2
NCF, MOD $ bn	6.37	7.26
NPV, MOD $ bn	4.19	4.13

Figure 8.18 Contractor's undiscounted and discounted total (life-of-field) cashflows, tranche method, compiled from the file "Ch8_PSC_production_rate.xls"

Production Case 1 has a materially *lower NCF*, but a marginally *higher NPV*. **Why?**

<u>Hint</u>: To put the problem into perspective, we suggest that you do the following:

- Click the "Show profit sharing & PSC revenues/cashflows charts" button in row 14, and reset to the Base Scenario.

- Watch the "Division of PSC Revenue and Cashflows" chart while switching back and forth between the two production cases.

- You will see that all the values in the chart change. This is due to the <u>effects of inflation</u>. (Bear in mind that these are undiscounted values, so discounting effects are ignored.) Even though, in each production case, total production is the same, the difference in production *timing* means that the inflated values of annual gross field revenue, and annual variable opex, will differ between the two cases. The resultant differences will "ripple" throughout the model:

  ○ Differences between the inflated value of the two cases' gross revenue causes differences in their net revenue, and thus in total profit oil, and then in each party's share of profit oil.

  ○ Differences between the inflated value of the two cases' variable opex causes differences in their contractor costs, and thus in their cost oil (and, again, in total profit oil).

To aid your investigation, try removing these inflationary impacts by setting the annual inflation rate (cell C18) to 0%.

The underlying dynamic remains. If you again press the "Show Contractor revenue/NCF/NPV charts" button in row 14, and toggle between the two production cases, you will see that Production Case 1 still has the lower undiscounted contractor NCF, but the higher contractor NPV.

Setting inflation to 0% thus preserves the trend we are investigating, while helping reduce the number of "moving parts."

Keep inflation at 0%. You will also see this if you press the "Show profit sharing & PSC revenues/cashflows charts" button in row 14, and again toggle between the two production cases, this time watching the "Division of PSC Revenue and Cashflows" charts:

- Now, in each case, gross field revenue, net revenue, contractor costs, cost oil and total profit oil are exactly the same in each production case.

- The differences only start to appear in the fourth column, and this is due to the movement of the contractor profit oil ("C Prof. Oil") segment. All other changes follow on from this.

So, having removed the distortions of inflation, we see that:

- the only difference between the two cases, on an underscored basis, is due ultimately to the different distribution of profit oil;

- this different distribution is due to the different production rates; and

- this different distribution explains why, in Production Case 2, contractor undiscounted *NCF* is higher than in Production Case 1.

So **why**, in Production Case 2, is the contractor's *NPV* lower than in Production Case 1, even with inflation taken out of the picture?

8.4   PROFIT OIL SHARING BASED ON CUMULATIVE PRODUCTION

Note that portions of this section are extremely similar to the previous Section 8.3, to help reduce the number of cross-references in this section.

Introduction

In this section's model, we will examine an example of a PSC which allocates profit oil to the contractor and government based on the license's cumulative production, measured at the end of the accounting period. We use annual periods for this section's example model, "Ch8_PSC_cumulative_production.xls." The table showing the profit sharing mechanism starts in row 47, as reproduced in Figure 8.19.

	B	C	D	E	F	G
47	Tranche	Distribution of gross profit oil				
48		Cumulative field production (100% WI basis), mm b			% of gross profit oil (%)	
49	#	> =		<	Contractor	Government
50	1	0		35	90.0%	10.0%
51	2	35		70	75.0%	25.0%
52	3	70		105	60.0%	40.0%
53	4	105		140	45.0%	55.0%
54	5	140		175	30.0%	70.0%
55	6	175		210	20.0%	80.0%
56	7	210		999,999,999	10.0%	90.0%

Figure 8.19 Profit oil distribution scale based on year-end cumulative total license production, from the file "Ch8_PSC_cumulative_production.xls"
Note: Reflects Base Scenario assumptions. Columns F and G are merged.

To make later formulas easier to read, we have named the range C50:G56, "Profit_share_table," and the range B50:G56, "Enlarged_Profit_share_table."

Distribution schedules like this tend to work in the "opposite direction" to the profit sharing scales based on average production rates, which we covered in the last section:

- In the typical example in Section 8.3, the inverse relationship between the production rate and the contractor's percentage share of total profit oil meant that when production rates were high, the contractor's percentage share of profit oil was low, and vice versa. Because life-of-field production for newly developed oil fields usually starts high and then declines, the contractor in such cases would receive lower percentages of total profit oil in the early production years and higher percentages in the later years. For the government's percentage share of profit oil, the opposite would be true.

- In contrast, the mechanism based on cumulative production shown in Figure 8.19 gives the contractor a higher percentage share of total profit oil in the early years, which falls as cumulative production grows over time. For the government's percentage share of profit oil, the opposite is true.

Modeling period versus accounting period

As was the case with the production rate-based profit oil distribution mechanism, the frequency with which profit oil is allocated to the PSC parties can vary among PSCs. In this example, we assume that profit oil is allocated annually, although it can be more frequent (e.g., semesterly (i.e., half-yearly), quarterly or even monthly). For the most accurate results, the model's timeframe should match the frequency with which profit oil is calculated, although:

- our standard caveat about the scarcity, in some cases, of long-term input data on a more frequent than annual basis applies here as well;

> - when the "tranche" method (discussed below) is used, modeling profit oil distributions on a less frequent basis than specified in the PSC (e.g., modeling annually when it is supposed to be calculated quarterly) can provide a reasonable approximation – but only if production changes at a constant rate, and other factors ultimately influencing profit oil (e.g., oil prices, royalties and costs) are roughly even – over the period modeled.

"Top-Rate" Versus "Tranche" Methods (Again)

In Section 8.3, we described two possible interpretations of the profit oil distribution schedule. Both are applicable here as well.

The "top rate" method. This is the simpler of the two. For the period under consideration, it uses only one row from the schedule shown in Figure 8.19. For example, assume that at the end of the period cumulative production is 75 mmb. This falls within the 70–105 mmb range of the table (row 52), which corresponds to a $\boxed{60\%}$ share of profit oil for the contractor and a 40% share for the government. No more information or calculation is needed.

The "tranche" method. This can require more information and steps to calculate, as a "blend" of percentage shares can sometimes apply, if cumulative production has moved among or between more than one band, or "tranche," of the schedule over the period in question. Consider two examples, each assuming that <u>cumulative production at the end of the period is 80 mmb</u>:

- *Example 1.* If production at the <u>start of the period is 71 mmb</u>, then cumulative production over the period has ranged from 71 to 80 mmb. The start and end values both fall within the 70–105 mmb range of the distribution schedule; this would result in a $\boxed{60\%}$ share of profit oil for the contractor and thus a 40% share for the government. This is the same result obtained from the top-rate method.

- *Example 2.* If, however, production at the <u>start of the period is (i.e., at the end of the previous period) 65 mmb</u>, then cumulative production over the period has ranged from 65 to 80 mmb. We can see that this <u>total production in the period</u> of $80 - 65 = 15$ mmb falls within, or "straddles," two of the tranches, Tranches 2 and 3. We therefore need to split the period's total production into two parts:

  - The first portion of cumulative production – from 65 mmb to just under 70 mmb – falls within Tranche 2 (cells C51:D51). This portion of production within Tranche 2 is $70 - 65 = 5$ mmb. Of the period's total production of 15 mmb, this 5 mmb makes up $5/15 = \mathbf{33.33\%}$. This portion within Tranche 2 corresponds to a contractor profit oil share of **75.0%** (cell E51).

  - The second portion of cumulative production – from 70 to 80 mmb – falls within Tranche 3 (cells C52:D52). This portion of production within Tranche 3 is $80 - 70 = 10$ mmb. Of the total period's production of 15 mmb, this 10 mmb makes up $10/15 = \mathbf{66.67\%}$. This portion within Tranche 3 corresponds to a contractor profit oil share of **60%** (cell E52).

Under the tranche method, the contractor's share of profit oil for the period would thus be calculated as a weighted average, or "blended," percentage, i.e., as $\mathbf{(33.33\% \times 75\%)}$ +

$(\mathbf{66.67\% \times 60\%}) = 25\% + 40\% = \boxed{65\%}$. The government's share would be $100\% - 65\% = 35\%$.

Note that the contractor's share of profit oil using the tranche method (65%) exceeds its share using the top-rate method (60%). As was the case with the production rate-based profit oil sharing mechanism discussed in the last section, this will always be the case when:

(a) there is an inverse relationship between cumulative production and the contractor's share of profit oil; and

(b) cumulative production over the period in question passes through more than one tranche.

The tranche method result in such cases will be higher than the top-rate result, because the tranche method will take into consideration lower, historic cumulative production levels, which correspond to higher contractor percentages of total profit oil.

This section's example model calculates each party's share of profit oil on an annual basis using both the tranche and top-rate methods, and lets the user choose which method to use, using the spinner in cell I54 and its duplicates elsewhere in the model. Under the Base Scenario, the version used in the model is the tranche method by default.

Example Model: Other Assumptions

In the current section's model, "Ch8_PSC_cumulative_production.xls," we have made a few changes to the input assumptions compared to our "core" PSC example model (i.e., the model in the file, "Ch7_PSC_basic_model_with_depreciation.xls").

In the current section's model, "Ch8_PSC_cumulative_production.xls," to make levels of cumulative production pass through enough realistic profit oil sharing tranches to make the example instructive, we have increased the field's total, pre-ELT production to 222 mmb (row 62). We have also increased field costs (starting in cell M31) accordingly. Despite these changes, pre-ELT, field net cashflow (ignoring the fiscal regime) of Real 2015 $20.22/b (cell S37) is the same as in the "core" PSC example model.

Profit Oil Distribution Calculations in the Model: Top-Rate Method

Shares of profit oil using this method are calculated in our present example model, the section entitled "1) Calculation of profit oil shares: top rate method" in rows 258–267.

The contractor's annual percentage shares of total profit oil are calculated in row 262. For example, in 2019, the typical formula in cell K262 is

=IF(K256=0, 0, VLOOKUP(K260, Profit_share_table, 3))

This means that if 2019 profit oil (cell K256) equals $0, the answer is 0%; otherwise, the answer is found in the red-bordered range named Profit_share_table (cells C50:G56). Specifically:

- in this range's row, which corresponds to 2019 year-end cumulative annual production mmb in cell K260; and

- in this range's column number 3.

Under our Base Scenario, 2019 year-end cumulative production in cell K260 is 161.4 mmb. The VLOOKUP function looks within the corresponding row of Profit_share_table (row 54, which spans the range of 140–175 mmb), and returns the answer found in the range's third column, which is a **30% contractor share** of profit oil (cell E54).

In row 263, the government's share of profit oil in 2019 is calculated as $100\% - 30\% = 70\%$ (cell K263). (Note that the formula here contains an IF statement which gives the answer of 0% if total profit oil is $0.)

In rows 265–266, the dollar value of contractor and government shares of total profit oil is calculated, by multiplying their respective percentage shares by total profit oil. Thus under the Base Scenario in 2019, of total profit oil of MOD $777.2 mm (cell K256), MOD $233.2 mm goes to the contractor (cell K265), and MOD $544.0 mm goes to the government (cell K266).

We sum, in cells E265:E266, the annual dollar values of each party's share of profit oil over the economic life of the field, giving us, under the Base Scenario, MOD $2817.1 mm for the contractor and MOD $3297.6 mm for the government.

Now we can calculate the parties' total percentages of profit oil over the economic life of the field. We do this back up in cells E262:E263, by dividing these two figures by the dollar value of life-of-field, total profit oil of MOD $6114.7 mm (cell E256). Thus under the Base Scenario, the top-rate method gives the contractor a life-of-field-basis 46.1% share of profit oil (cell E262) and the government, 53.9% (cell E263).

Profit Oil Distribution Calculations in the Model: Tranche Method

We calculate profit oil shares using the tranche rate method in rows 268–326 of our example model. Let us review the four basic steps we took in calculating the contractor's share of profit oil in the simplified tranche rate Example 2, above. These steps were to:

(a) identify (in the process, counting) how many tranches the cumulative production during the period passes through;

(b) calculate the percentage of the period's production falling within each relevant tranche;

(c) calculate the contractor's "blended" percentage share of profit oil for the period, using a weighted average formula; and

(d) subtract the resultant contractor's "blended" percentage share from 100% to get the government's share of profit oil for the period.

The calculations down through rows 322 perform these four steps, and then multiply the results, i.e., each party's percentage share of profit oil, by total profit oil to get the dollar value of each party's profit oil in rows 324–325.

Although the objective of each step is easy to understand, some of the formulas used – of which typical examples appear as captions in column R of our example model – are necessarily complex in order to accommodate a variety of input combinations. The basic formula used in Section 2c) in particular is a bit tricky (and is among the longest formulas used in this book).

Cross Reference to Chapter 3

The calculations use the same methods which we used in Section 3.5 of Chapter 3, where we calculated royalty rates using a tranche-based cumulative production method. The only difference here is that there are fewer tranches in the PSC distribution schedule than in the royalty schedule (meaning we still use the same generic formulas as in the royalty model, but in fewer rows here).

Rather than repeat the full explanation of the detailed tranche method calculations here, instead we present, in Figure 8.20, a summary of the tranche method calculation steps taken in our example PSC model; their counterparts in the relevant royalty model; and the sections of the text in Chapter 3 which explain these calculations in the royalty model.

If necessary, review this Chapter 3 material. Once you are comfortable with it, you will immediately understand the corresponding sections of our present example model.

Results and Check of Tranche Method Calculations

The results of the current section's tranche-based calculations are found in Section 2e) of our example model, in rows 318–326 of our example file.

Under the Base Scenario, using the tranche method, the contractor's life-of-field share of profit oil is 53.8% (cell E321) and the government's, 46.2% (cell E322).

- Note that this is a material difference, in the contractor's favor, to the results of the top-rate method, which gives the contractor 46.1% share (cell E262) and the government, 53.9% (cell E263). (You can also see this in cells E333:E334 while toggling the spinner in cell C330.)

- This is due to the reason explained earlier: the tranche method considers the impact of production in various tranches which correspond to higher contractor profit oil sharing rates.

For a visual check, choose the Base Scenario (cell C12), and then click the "Show profit sharing/sensitivity charts" button in row 12. Below the screen split you should see a section with three charts, starting in row 397.

The chart on the left shows year-end cumulative post-ELT production in mmb, represented by the red line, which refers to the right axis. The stacked columns represent the percentage

a) PSC model and relevant sections	b) Analogous royalty model and relevant sections	c) Section of Chapter 3 which explains b)
"Ch8_PSC_cumulative_ production.xls"	"Ch3_roy_cuml_prod_ CROSSOVER_full_ example.xls"	"Section 3.5 Royalty based on cumulative production throughout the period" – "Tranche method – more complex example"*
2) Calculation of profit oil shares: tranche method (row 268)	2) Calculations – Tranche method (row 37)	n.a.
2a) Determination of relevant tranches (rows 270–284)	2a) Determination of relevant tranches (rows 38–60)	Calculations: model Section 2a): Determination of relevant tranches
2b) Numbering of relevant tranches (rows 286–295)	2b) Numbering of relevant tranches (rows 62–75)	Calculations: model Section 2b): Numbering of relevant tranches
2c) Allocation of volumes (barrels) to tranches (rows 296–306)	2c) Allocation of volumes (barrels) to tranches (rows 76–95)	Calculations: model Section 2c): Allocation of volumes (barrels) to tranches
2d) Allocation of volumes (percentages) to tranches (rows 307–317)	2d) Allocation of volumes (percentages) to tranches (rows 96–110)	Calculations: model Section 2d): Allocation of volumes (percentages) to tranches
2e) Calculation of "blended rate" shares of profit oil (rows 318–326)	2e) Calculation of blended royalty rates, and royalty payments – b) Blended rate (using SUMPRODUCT function) (row 115)	Calculations: model Section 2e): Calculation of blended royalty rates, and royalty payments

Figure 8.20 Steps for the tranche method profit oil share calculation taken in "Ch8_PSC_ cumulative_production.xls," their counterparts in the tranche method royalty model of Chapter 3, and accompanying explanations in the text of Chapter 3
*Optional reading in Chapter 3: "Introduction: Top-Rate and Tranche Methods" and "Calculation Strategy."

shares of total profit oil of the government (white) and the contractor (gray), which sum to 100%, and refer to the left axis. Note the profit oil percentage captions at the top of the chart.

The middle chart shows the same information, profit oil shares in absolute terms.

Use the (duplicate) spinner in cell E399 to toggle between the tranche and top-rate methods. The relationships between cumulative production and the contractor's share (inverse) and the government's (direct) are clear in both charts, using either profit oil allocation method. Also note how the contractor's share is higher under the tranche method in both percentage terms (as shown in the screenshots in Figures 8.21 and 8.22) and absolute terms.

Adjust the (duplicate) oil production multiplier spinner in cell J399 from 50% to 150%. Satisfy yourself that you understand the resultant changes in the charts. (Note that the chart on the right will not update, as we will explain shortly.)

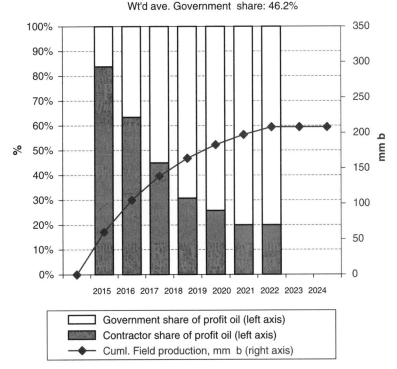

Figure 8.21   Profit oil distribution and cumulative production under Base Scenario (including tranche method), from the file "Ch8_PSC_cumulative_production.xls"

Impacts on Cashflows and NPV: Keeping the Bigger Picture in Mind

Focusing on the left chart alone might lead one to think that lower production is better for the contractor, as it leads to a higher *percentage share* of profit oil. But this narrow view is wrong – whether the tranche or top-rate method is chosen – as seen in the following:

- The "Life-of-field Contractor revenue vs. cumulative field production" chart on the far right (starting at column M, row 400), which shows the contractor's *total* PSC revenue in dollar terms (i.e., contractor profit oil plus cost oil) under various oil post-ELT, life-of-field production scenarios. This shows that, as production increases, the contractor's percentage PSC revenue take falls, but its total, absolute PSC revenue in dollar terms rises.[8]

---

[8] Note that this chart draws on values from Data Tables in cells U437:Z448. This means the chart will not update if you increase the oil production multiplier. It will, however, reflect other changes in the model, if Excel's calculation mode is set to Automatic. This mode can cause the model to take a moment to update after a change is made.

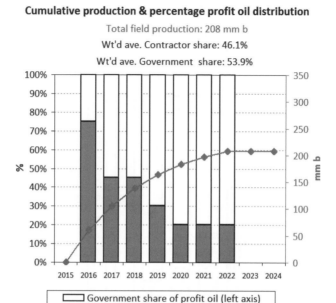

Figure 8.22 Profit oil distribution and cumulative production under Base Scenario (but then set to top-rate method), from the file "Ch8_PSC_cumulative_production.xls"

- The "Division of PSC Revenue and Cashflows" chart starting in row 453, which you can quickly see by pressing the "Show PSC revenues/cashflows chart" button in row 12. Using the (duplicate) spinners for choosing the profit oil distribution method and oil production multiplier at the top of the chart, you can see that under either method, when production rises, the contractor's percentage shares of profit oil and total PSC revenue fall, but their absolute values rise. The dollar value of contractor undiscounted net cashflow also rises as production rises.

- The "waterfall charts" starting in row 511, which you can see quickly by pressing the "Show Contractor cashflow/NPV charts" button in row 12. By adjusting the (duplicate) spinners above the charts starting in row 514, you can see that more production results in higher contractor undiscounted NCF, and NPV, regardless of which profit allocation method is used.

Exercise: Calculate These Yourself

The exercise file "Ch8_PSC_cumulative_production_exercise setup.xls" is a copy of this section's example model, with empty, orange-shaded cells between rows 260 and 325. Fill in these cells with the correct formulas, and then check your answers against those in the example model.

Note that at certain stages you might see that some checksums, including the master checksum in cell A1, show non-zero values and turn green to indicate there are errors. Any error messages should disappear when you have filled in all the cells correctly.

8.5   INTRODUCTION TO PROFIT SHARING BASED ON A MEASURE OF CUMULATIVE PROFITABILITY: THE "R-FACTOR"

In Section 3.9 of Chapter 3, we covered royalties based on a "R-factor," a measure of cumulative profitability. When this profitability has not been achieved, or is low, the fiscal regime is more lenient to the investor, but as profitability grows, the regime is less lenient.

- As concerns royalties, "lenient" meant a lower royalty rate payable by the investor;

- In this section, as concerns contractor profit oil, "lenient" means allocating a higher share of total profit oil to the contractor.

Let us review how this commonly works in a PSC, by summarizing a simplistic example from Chapter 3. Assume that an investor makes an initial investment of $10, and thereafter never has any more costs, and over the next three years has annual revenue of $5.

R-factor based on current year cumulative revenues and costs					
	Year	**1**	**2**	**3**	**4**
A	Annual revenue	0.0	5.0	5.0	5.0
B	**Cuml. annual revenue**	**0.0**	**5.0**	**10.0**	**15.0**
C	Annual costs	10.0	0.0	0.0	0.0
D	**Cuml. annual costs**	**10.0**	**10.0**	**10.0**	**10.0**
E = B/D	**R-factor**	**0.00**	**0.50**	**1.00**	**1.50**

Figure 8.23   Simplistic R-factor example

As seen in Figure 8.23, the R-factor – the ratio of cumulative revenue to cumulative costs – grows each year.

- In each year, we calculate the ratio of cumulative revenues to costs arising *since the beginning of the project*, and on an undiscounted basis, reflecting the most common practice in the industry.

- In Year 3, the R-factor of 1.0 means the investor has exactly broken even.

- In Year 4, the R-factor of greater than 1.0 means the investor is now profitable by this measure.

R-factor mechanisms in many PSCs use an <u>inverse relationship</u>, whereby the contractor gets a higher percentage share of total profit oil when the R-factor is low, and a lower share when the R-factor is high. For example – again, simplistically – the PSC might use a scale whereby the contractor gets:

- 75% of total profit oil when the R-factor is 0.5 or less (leaving 25% for the government);

- 50% of total profit oil when the R-factor is over 0.5, but less than or equal to 1.0; and

- 25% of total profit oil when the R-factor is greater than 1.0.

This is intended to let the contractor recoup its investment relatively early, while giving the government a greater share of total profit oil once the investment has become profitable.

As was the case with royalties based on R-factors, profit oil distributions based on R-factors have the potential for circularity problems in their calculation. Consider how the following shows the potential for circularity in R-factor calculations:

R-factor = (cumulative revenue)/(cumulative costs)

and

Cumulative revenue = (cumulative cost oil + cumulative contractor profit oil).

Therefore,

R-factor = (cumulative cost oil + cumulative contractor profit oil)/(cumulative costs).

* * *

Contractor profit oil is based on the R-factor

* * *

Therefore,

R-factor = (cumulative cost oil + something based on the R-factor)/(cumulative costs)

This last statement reveals the essence of the circularity: that is, to know the R-factor, you have to already know the R-factor.

In an acknowledgement of the potential for such a circularity, most PSCs avoid this problem by calculating the *present* period's R-factor as the cumulative revenue at the end of the *prior* period, divided by the cumulative costs at the end of the *prior* period. We adjust the example shown in Figure 8.23 for these timing considerations in Figure 8.24.

	R-factor based on prior year cumulative revenues and costs				
	Year	1	2	3	4
A	Annual revenue	0.0	5.0	5.0	5.0
B	**Cuml. annual revenue**	0.0	5.0	10.0	15.0
C	Annual costs	10.0	0.0	0.0	0.0
D	**Cuml. annual costs**	10.0	10.0	10.0	10.0
E = (prior B / prior D)	R factor	0.00	0.00	0.50	1.00

Figure 8.24 Simplistic R-factor example, adjusted to use prior period values
Note: Year 1 R-factor is exceptional as it is specified by the PSC to equal 0.

This, however, leaves the problem of how to calculate the R-factor for the first year, when by definition there is no prior year. Many PSCs deal with this by stating that, in the first year, the R-factor will equal a specified value (often one which corresponds to the highest contractor share of profit oil in the scale).

Introducing the R-factor Example Model

We have adapted our "core" PSC model to use R-factors to determine the profit oil distribution between the contractor and government, in the files "Ch8_PSC_R_factor_Step_1.xls" and "Ch8_PSC_R_factor_Step_2.xls." We have broken the calculation into two steps, just as we did when calculating the royalties based on the R-factor in Chapter 3.

Let's start with "Ch8_PSC_R_factor_Step_1.xls." The model assumes that the R-factor is calculated – and that profit oil is therefore distributed – on an annual basis, according to the table starting in row 48 of the model and shown in Figure 8.25.

The range B51:D58 is named "Profit_share_table."

The PSC in our example states that in the first production year, the R-factor is assumed to be within the first row of the scale, i.e., that it is a positive value less than or equal to 0.75. Therefore, for modeling purposes, we assume, in cell E60, that this value is equal to 0.1 (although for modeling purposes you could pick any other value within this range). Cell E60 is named "Rfactor_in_1st_prod_year."

Refer to Figure A on page 2 of "Ch8_Supplement_to_Sec_8_5.pdf," or to rows 250–284 of the file "Ch8_PSC_R_factor_Step_1.xls," for the following discussion of how we calculate the annual distribution of profit oil in this model.

	B	C	D	E	F
48	Profit sharing				
49	R-factor		Share of total profit oil		
50	>	<=	Contractor	Government	
51	0.00	0.75	60.0%	40.0%	
52	0.75	1.25	55.0%	45.0%	
53	1.25	1.50	50.0%	50.0%	
54	1.50	1.75	45.0%	55.0%	
55	1.75	2.00	40.0%	60.0%	
56	2.00	2.25	30.0%	70.0%	
57	2.25	2.50	20.0%	80.0%	
58	2.50	No limit	10.0%	90.0%	

Figure 8.25 Profit oil distribution based on annual R-factors, from the file "Ch8_PSC_R_factor_Step_1.xls"
Notes: Reflects Base Scenario. In rows 50–58, columns E and F are merged.

Calculating Contractor Profit Oil

The goal of this section of the model is to calculate the contractor's share of total profit oil. Once we have determined total profit oil (calculated in the usual way, in row 263), we immediately face the problem referred to above: in order to calculate the R-factor, one of the things we need to know is the contractor's percentage share of total profit oil, but this depends on the R-factor. Even though our example PSC states that the R-factor is based on prior period values, the calculation can be a bit tricky and/or disorienting.

To deal with this, at this stage of the calculation we just type in hard-coded "dummy" percentage values for the contractor's share of total profit oil in row 265. This is not strictly necessary – you could just leave the annual cells in this row blank – but we prefer, as we build the rest of the section, to have some values, even temporary ones, in place for the model to "chew on."

> **Bear in mind that, for now, all results in rows 265, 267, 270–271, 279 and 282–287 are temporary, and will change once we finish this section's very last step**, which we show in the next model, "Ch8_PSC_R_factor_Step_2.xls."

Next, in row 267, we multiply the annual total profit oil values in row 263 by these "dummy" percentage values in row 265 to get annual dollar values for contractor profit oil. In 2019, for example, it is MOD $3.9 mm (cell J267).

We then add the annual cells in row 267 to the annual cost oil values, which are calculated in the usual way in row 250, to get annual total and cumulative contractor PSC revenue in rows 270 and 271, respectively. The cumulative value will be the numerator for the R-factor calculation. For short, we term the numerator "X."

We then calculate the denominator for the R-factor formula – cumulative contractor costs – which we term "Y" in row 276. Note the unique formula in cell F276, which includes pre-2015 costs in the cumulative total of costs incurred as at the end of 2015.

Annual R-factors are calculated in row 279. For 2019 (cell J279), for example, we use the formula

> =IF(year=First_depreciation_year, Rfactor_in_1st_prod_year, IF(I276=0, 0,I271/I276))

- Because depreciation starts in the first production year, in the depreciation section of the model, we named the cell D152 – where we determine the first production year – First_depreciation_year. Thus the first IF statement in the formula above actually means that if it is the first *production* year, then the R-factor equals the assumed value of 0.10 which is in the cell named Rfactor_in_1st_prod_year (cell E60, as mentioned above.) Because 2019 is not the first production year, this condition does not apply in cell J279.

- The first part of the second IF statement is just a standard error trap, which prevents a "#DIV/0!" message from appearing if I276 – the previous year's denominator – is $\boxed{0}$. This is also not the case, so, again, this condition is inapplicable in cell J279.

- Therefore, the answer in cell J279 is that the R-factor for 2019 is the prior year's "X" (cell $\boxed{I271}$) divided by the prior year's "Y" (cell $\boxed{I276}$), or **1.03**.

Having calculated the annual R-factors in this way, we use them to determine the contractor's annual percentage shares of total profit oil in row 282.

In the example year of 2019, the formula in cell J282 is

$$=IF(J263=0, \ 0, \quad VLOOKUP(J279, \quad Profit\_share\_table, \quad 3))$$

The second expression is the most important. It uses the VLOOKUP function to find, in column $\boxed{3}$ of the range $\boxed{Profit\_share\_table}$, the contractor's percentage share of total profit oil which corresponds to the R-factor in cell $\boxed{J279}$. In this case, the R-factor of 1.03 lies within the 0.75–1.25 band (row 52) of $\boxed{Profit\_share\_table}$, resulting in a contractor percentage profit share of **55%**.

The dollar value of annual contractor profit oil is calculated in row 283 as the percentage in row 282 times total profit oil in row 263. In 2019, for example, it equals MOD $ 10.7 mm (cell J283).

As mentioned, most of the rows starting with row 265 contain temporary results at this stage, due to the "dummy values" in row 265. This causes the checksums in row 284 to show non-zero values and turn green, indicating errors. These checksums test whether the annual dollar values of contractor profit oil in row 283 and row 267 are the same. They aren't – yet.

We now fix this with our final step, which we have performed in an otherwise identical copy of the model. This new version is the file "Ch8_PSC_R_factor_Step_2.xls."

Refer to Figure B on page 3 of "Ch8_Supplement_to_Sec_8_3.pdf," or to the file "Ch8_PSC_R_factor_Step_2.xls," for the following discussion.

The change we make to the companion model is simple. We merely replace the annual "dummy" values in row 265 with the calculated annual results in row 282, by linking to these results with equals signs. For example, the "dummy" value in cell J265 is now replaced with the formula "=J282."

Because the "down-then-up" flow of calculations is unusual, we make it clear what we have done:

- in Figure B in the PDF, by displaying the audit lines which trace the precedent of each annual cell in row 265; and

- in the Excel file, by adding explanations to the captions in rows 259 and 265.

Having completed this last step, we can see that the values in rows 265, 267, 270–271, 279 and 283 – and in cell D282 – have changed as a result, and that the checksums in row 284 are now "happy," displaying the zeroes against a non-green background, indicating that the annual values in rows 283 and 267 are now the same.

When you build similar models, there is no need to do the last step in a new version of the model. We have done so only because it makes it easier to show you how the model should look before and after the last step.

The Calculations Look Circular, But Are Not

Watching the flow of calculations, you might initially think that they are circular, as the annual values in row 265 both determine and are determined by those in row 282.

But notice – even assuming that Excel, as we always recommend, is set to *not* permit iterations (as discussed in the "Avoiding Circular References" subsection of Chapter 3's Section 3.9) – that if you make in "Ch8_PSC_R_factor_Step_1.xls" the same change we just made in "Ch8_PSC_R_factor_Step_2.xls," you will *not* see a warning that a circular reference has occurred.

The reference is not circular because the R-factor for a given year, while it does determine the contractor's share of profit oil in that year, is based on the prior year's "X" and "Y" values; notice again that the R-factor for 2019, in cell J279, for example, is referencing prior year values in column I.

Calculating Government Profit Oil

Having determined the contractor's share of total profit oil, determining the government's share is a simple matter of subtracting the contractor's share from the total. In steps not shown in Figure A or Figure B of the file "Ch8_Supplement_to_Sec_8_3.pdf," we do this in percentage terms in row 285 and in dollar terms in row 286.[9]

Exercise: Try This Yourself

Open the practice model "Ch8_PSC_R_factor_exercise.xls."

Set this model to the Base Scenario, using the button in cell B13.

Fill in the orange-shaded, blank cells in rows 265–286 with the correct formulas. Then compare your answers against those in "Ch8_PSC_R_factor_Step_2.xls."

There are not that many items to fill in, as the point is only to practice the profit oil distribution calculations.

---

[9] Note that, in row 285, we have used logic which returns the answer 0% if total profit oil is $0; if we had not, the answer in row 285 would be 100%. While this would still be literally true – the government would have a 100% share of $0 profit oil – we prefer here that both government and contractor shares of a total of $0 be displayed as 0%.

Note that, until you finish, some checksums, including the master checksum in cell A1, might show a non-zero value and turn green, signifying an error has been detected. Doing the exercise correctly will make these error messages go away.

Exercise: Checking the Model, Analyzing Results

We have designed three scenarios for the finished model in "Ch8_PSC_R_factor_Step_2.xls" to help show that the model is working correctly. These scenarios can be summoned using the buttons in cell B13. The only differences between them are settings of the sensitivity multipliers[10] in row 29.

- In the Base Scenario, all four multipliers (for the oil price, capex, opex and production) are set to 100%.

- Scenario 2 has higher oil prices and lower costs than the Base Scenario. The oil price multiplier is set to 150%, the capex multiplier, to 90%, and the opex multiplier, to 35%.

- Scenario 3 has lower oil prices and higher costs than the Base Scenario. The oil price multiplier is set to 80%, the capex multiplier, to 105%, and the opex multiplier, to 110%.

Choose the Base Scenario, and click the "Show Annual R-factors/Comparative results" button in row 13, or otherwise split/arrange the screen so that you can see the multipliers (row 29) in the top part of the screen, and the charts starting in row 475 in the bottom part.

(You will also find screenshots of the views we are discussing starting on page 4 of the PDF supplement "Ch8_Supplement_to_Sec_8_5.pdf." We do not reproduce them here because of the colors they use.)

The "Determinants of R-Factor" chart on the left shows:

- cumulative annual contractor PSC revenue (the gray line with triangles) – which is the "X" numerator for the R-factor equation, in MOD $ mm – referring to the chart's left axis;

- cumulative annual contractor costs (the black line with circles) – which is the "Y" denominator for the R-factor equation, in MOD $ mm – again referring to the chart's left axis; and

- the annual R-factor (the red line with diamonds), referring to the right axis.

As discussed, each year's R-factor equals the *prior* year's X value divided by the prior year's Y value (except, as mentioned, in the first production year of 2016, where the R-factor is designated as 0.10).

---

[10] Recall that the multipliers do not effect historic (pre-2015) items.

We have added data labels showing the 2024 R-factor, and 2023 X and Y values on which it is based:

- As seen in the chart, MOD $270 mm/MOD $211 mm = a 2024 R-factor of 1.3.

- Note that there is nothing special about this choice of 2023/2024 annual values, other than to help you see one example calculation in the chart, which would have become messy if we had used data labels for all years.

Before we look at the next chart, let us also examine Scenarios 2 and 3 on the "Determinants of R-factor" chart. Do this either in the model, by pressing the appropriate scenario buttons in row 13, or by viewing pages 4–6 in the PDF supplement:

- In Scenario 2 (page 5), higher prices and lower costs mean that the relative gap between the X and Y lines widens over the producing life, resulting in higher annual R-factors than in the Base Scenario.

- In Scenario 3 (page 6), lower prices and higher costs mean that the relative gap between the X and Y lines is very narrow over the producing life, resulting in lower R-factors than in the Base Scenario. (The blue line is not shown in the Excel file.)

Now, look to the right, at the "Annual R-factors and distribution of total profit oil" chart on the right. Select the Base Scenario in the model (or return to page 4 of the PDF supplement). Note the following:

- the red R-factor line, which is repeated from the left chart, still referring to the right axis;

- the columns showing the contractor's (white) and government's (black) annual percentages of total profit oil, summing to 100%, and referring to the left axis; and

- the caption box at the top of the chart, showing these percentages on a life-of-field basis. (Note that the contractor's 54.72% share means that 54.72% of the combined area of the stacked columns is white.)

Now, recall the inverse relationship, in which a higher R-factor results in a lower contractor percentage share of total profit oil, and vice versa. We can see this, using the Base Scenario (page 4), in the right chart, in which the dashed red lines are the R-factor thresholds from the PSC's profit oil distribution table (cells C51:C58). Whenever the red dots move onto or cross these lines from one year to the next, the contractor (and thus government) percentage profit oil shares change. For example:

- In 2016, i.e., the first production year, the R-factor is, as discussed, assumed to be 0.10, placing it in the first band of the table (since it falls between 0.00 and 0.75), resulting in a contractor profit share of 60%, shown by the chart's first white column.

- In 2017, the R-factor is 0.95, and so has moved into the second band of the table (as it falls between 0.75 and 1.25), resulting in a contractor profit share of 55%, shown by the chart's second white column.

- Under the Base Scenario, the right chart is informative, but not very dramatic, as the annual R-factors have a generally narrow range, passing into only three bands of the profit oil sharing table.

- Scenario 2 (page 5) shows a bit more action. The R-factor passes into a few different bands over the production life. (The red data labels make it clearer, starting in 2019, which side of the top threshold the R-factor is on.)

- Scenario 3 (page 6) is the dullest, with the R-factor passing through only two bands.

Now let us view the charts under all three scenarios again, to reinforce our understanding of the profit sharing mechanism's general intent, i.e., to help the contractor when "times are hard," by providing a greater percentage share of total profit oil, while lowering this share when "times are good":

- Under the Base Scenario, the left chart shows that the contractor's cumulative PSC revenues are moderately ahead of cumulative costs over most of the producing life, resulting in a life-of-field profit share for the contractor of **54.72%** (as shown in the right chart's boxed caption).

- Under Scenario 2, the left chart shows that the contractor's cumulative PSC revenues are well ahead of cumulative costs over most of the producing life. By this measure, "times are good," resulting in a life-of-field profit share for the contractor of **35.73%**.

- Under Scenario 3, the left chart shows that the contractor's cumulative PSC revenues are just barely ahead of cumulative costs over most of the producing life. By this measure, "times are bad," resulting in a life-of-field profit share for the contractor of **57.48%**.

Keep the Big Picture in Mind

To reiterate the point we have made several times before – single outcomes, such as a contractor's percentage share of profit oil, are important to understand, but should not be viewed in isolation, as they are only one of many steps needed to calculate the most important outcome for investors, i.e., NPV. As shown in the results of all three scenarios, collected in Figure 8.26, it would be quite misleading to judge the attractiveness of a scenario simply by profit oil shares.

For example, Scenario 3 gives the contractor the highest percentage share of profit oil (57.5%). But – as we saw in its "Determinants of R-factor" chart – it also has the narrowest gap between contractor revenue and costs, leaving very little total profit oil, in absolute terms, for either party, no matter what percentage shares they get. Higher costs and lower prices trigger the economic limit early, giving Scenario 3 the shortest economic production life, at six years, and the lowest contractor NPV, at MOD $15.5 mm, of any of the scenarios.

Scenario 2 has by far the lowest contractor percentage share of total profit oil (35.7%).

- But Scenario 2 also has materially lower field costs, higher received field revenue, the longest economic production life (nine years), and easily the highest contractor NPV, at MOD $118.2 mm, of any scenario.

Results of Scenarios (compiled by macro)	Base Scenario	Scenario 2 (higher oil price, lower costs)	Scenario 3 (lower oil price, higher costs)
Inputs: Real 2015$ / b (pre-ELT basis)			
Oil price	70.00	105.00	56.00
Net field revenue	58.80	88.20	47.04
Total field costs	38.58	19.86	41.77
Total field NCF	20.22	68.34	5.27
Results (post-ELT basis)			
Government prof. oil share	45.3%	64.3%	42.5%
Contractor prof. oil share	**54.7%**	**35.7%**	**57.5%**
Government prof. oil, MOD $ mm	69.2	277.4	34.2
Contractor prof. oil, MOD $ mm	83.7	154.2	46.2
Government total PSC rev. share	33.2%	58.5%	27.2%
Contractor total PSC rev. share	66.8%	41.5%	72.8%
Government total PSC rev., MOD $ mm	133.7	381.8	82.8
Contractor total PSC rev., MOD $ mm	269.5	271.0	221.2
Government NPV share	65.6%	69.0%	79.7%
Contractor NPV share	34.4%	31.0%	20.3%
Government NPV, MOD $ mm	97.3	262.6	61.1
Contractor NPV, MOD $ mm	**51.1**	**118.2**	**15.5**

Figure 8.26 Results of all three scenarios, from row 477 of the file "Ch8_PSC_R_factor_Step_2.xls"

- Scenario 2 is the most attractive scenario for the contractor (as well as for the government), in terms of the dollar value of both undiscounted total PSC revenue and NPV.

Our point, again, is that you should understand how individual "moving parts" of the PSC cash distribution mechanism work, without losing sight of the big picture.

Variations among R-factor Mechanisms: Different Distribution Scales and Definitions of "R"

Distribution Scales

The profit oil distribution table which starts in row 48 uses <u>discrete bands</u> or tranches of R-factors. Others, however, use an <u>interpolation method</u>, whereby two specified R-factor ranges will result in "ceiling" and "floor" rates for the contractor's share.

For example, assume that when:

- any R-factor of less than 1.0 gives the contractor a 90% share of total profit oil; and
- any R-factor of 2.0 or greater gives a 10% share,

then at R-factors between 1.0 and 2.0, the contractor's share will move along a "sliding scale" between 90% and 10% in a linear fashion.

We give an example of this in the next model, which is covered in **Section 8.6**.

Definitions of R

There are different ways to calculate the R-factor. Here, and in the next example model, we use the common definition of

> (Contractor cumulative PSC revenue)/(Contractor cumulative costs)

Some fiscal regimes, however, use

> (Project cumulative revenue)/(Project cumulative costs)

Applying the latter to our example models, where we assume that the contractor bears all costs:

- the denominator would not change, as contractor costs equal "project costs";
- but the numerator *would* change, as contractor PSC revenue is less than "project revenue," which typically means some measure of 100% working interest basis, total *field* revenue.

Variations among R-factor Mechanisms: Frequency of Calculating "R"

In this example model, we have assumed that the R-factor and the resulting profit shares are determined annually, i.e., at the end of year, using "X" and "Y" values which represent cumulative totals from the start of the project.

In practice, however, some countries use more frequent periods, e.g., semesters (i.e., half-years), quarters or even months. This makes profit oil sharing sensitive to changing conditions (e.g., higher prices causing a sudden jump in cumulative revenues, or additional costs causing a sudden increase in cumulative costs).

Governments, in fact, often prefer basing R-factors on periods shorter than a year, as this can result in higher R-factors occurring sooner, giving the government a higher share of profit oil earlier than it would get in an annual calculation.[11]

Refer to Figure 8.27 for a new, simplistic comparison of a quarterly and R-factor calculation in two scenarios. One is a base case, and the other adds an extra cost in the third quarter. This

---

[11] Note, however, that in certain cases, the shorter accounting period can also work in the contractor's favor, depending on the timing of incremental investments or maintenance costs.

	G	H	I	J	K	L	M	N	O / P (Typical formulae)	R
553	Simplistic example: effects of timing of R-factor calculation and profit oil sharing									
		Assumptions (monetary values in $ mm)								
555	"X" in Q1	$100	"Y" in Q1			*Q1 R-factor*		*1.54*		
556						Maintenance capex		$30		
557	X & Y normal 1/4ly growth rate	5%								
558	**Scenario: no extra spending**								**Typical formulae**	
559				Q1	Q2	Q3	Q4	Annual		
560	X (Contractor's cuml. PSC rev.)			$100	$105	$110	$116	$116	L560. =K560*(1+$J$557)	N560. =M560
561	Y (Contractor's cuml. costs)			$65	$68	$72	$75	$75	L561. =K561*(1+$J$557)	N56. =M5611
562	**R-factor, prior period (X/Y)**			**1.54**	**1.54**	**1.54**	**1.54**	**1.54**	L562. =K560/K561	N562. =M560/M561
563		Contractor profit share								
564	Calculated annually							45%	N564. =VLOOKUP(N562,Profit_share_table,3)	
565	Calculated quarterly			45%	45%	45%	45%		L565. =VLOOKUP(L562,Profit_share_table,3)	
566		Goverment profit share								
567	Calculated annually							55%	N567. =1–N564	
568	Calculated quarterly			55%	55%	55%	55%		L568. =1–L565	
569	**Scenario: maintenance capex in Q3**									
570				Q1	Q2	Q3	Q4	Annual		
571	X (Contractor's cuml. PSC rev.)			$100	$105	$110	$116	$116	L571. =K571*(1+$J$557)	N571. =M571
572	Y (Contractor's cuml. costs)			$65	$68	$102	$107	$107	L572. =(K572*(1+$J$557))+N557	N572. =M572
573	**R-factor, prior period (X/Y)**			**1.54**	**1.54**	**1.54**	**1.08**	**1.08**	L573. =K571/K572	N573. =M571/M572
574		C profit share								
575	Calculated annually							55%	N575. =VLOOKUP(N573,Profit_share_table,3)	
576	Calculated quarterly			45%	45%	45%	55%		L576. =VLOOKUP(L573,Profit_share_table,3)	
577		G profit share								
578	Calculated annually							45%	N578. =1–N575	
579	Calculated quarterly			55%	55%	55%	45%		L579. =1–L576	

Figure 8.27 Simplistic example: effects of timing of R-factor calculation and profit oil sharing, from the file "Ch8_PSC_R_factor_with_timing_example.xls"

screenshot comes from the "Timing example" section which starts in row 550. Take a moment to study the formulas' captions.

The example shown in Figure 8.27 looks at one year during the production phase of a PSC license, on both a quarterly and an annual basis. It uses the same R-factor tranches discussed in the last section, but otherwise the inputs are notional:[12]

- We assume that in the first quarter ("Q1"), the contractor's "X" and "Y" – which, again, are the contractor's PSC revenue and costs, calculated cumulatively from the start of the project – are $100 mm and $65 mm, respectively (cells H556 and J556).

- We also assume that the contractor's Q1 R-factor (which is based on assumed, but not shown, X and Y values from Q4 of the previous year) is 1.54 (cell N556).

- (Note how these three assumed values start off the model in each of the two scenarios, in cells J560:J562 and J571:J573.)

- In the base scenario (i.e., no extra spending on maintenance capex), all of the contractor's "Y" costs are opex. In the maintenance capex scenario, the contractor's "Y" costs account for this $30 mm item (cell N557), assumed spent in Q3 (cell L572).

- In both scenarios, opex and the contractor's X are assumed to grow at 5% per quarter (cell J557).

Now, consider the base scenario:

- Because X and Y always change at the same 5% quarterly rate, the contractor's quarterly R-factors, calculated as the previous quarter's (X/Y), is always the same, at 1.54 (row 562).

- The Q4 X and Y values in cells M560:M561 are cumulative results since the start of the project through to the end of Q4. Because the *annual* values in cells N560:N561 are cumulative from the start of the project through to the end of the year, i.e., also through to the end of Q4, the values in cells M560:M561 equal those in cells N560:N561.

- Note further that the annual R-factor in cell N562 is calculated as (M560/M561), i.e., as the (Q4 X value)/(the Q4 Y value), again because these Q4 values are cumulative through to the end of the year.

Therefore:

- on an annual basis:

  ○ the R-factor is 1.54;

  ○ according to our example model's profit oil distribution scale (starting in row 51, not shown in Figure 8.27), a R-factor of 1.54 gives the contractor a 45% share of annual profit oil;

---

[12] The term "base scenario" used in this section – i.e., "Variations among R-factor Mechanisms: Frequency of Calculating 'R' " – is distinct from the "Base Scenario" (summoned with the button in cell B12) which is used in the rest of the model.

- o therefore the contractor gets a 45% share of the whole year's profit oil, and the government, 55% (cells N564 and N567);

- on a quarterly basis, the R-factor for Q1–Q4 is always 1.54, so, each quarter, the contractor is entitled to 45% of that quarter's profit oil, again leaving 55% for the government (rows 565 and 568).

Thus in this base scenario, the parties' shares of profit oil for the year are the same, whether calculated on an annual or quarterly basis. So far this example this is not very interesting, although it does make clear how the R-factor and resulting profit shares are calculated on a quarterly basis.

But now consider the second scenario, in which we assume that, in Q3, the contractor incurs maintenance capex of $30 mm. This is reflected in the gray-shaded Q3 Y value of $102 mm in cell L572, which is calculated as ((Q2 Y value × 105%) + $30 mm).

- Note that the annual R-factor (cell N573) is down to 1.08, compared to 1.54 in the first scenario (cell N562).

- According to our profit oil distribution scale, a R-factor of 1.08 corresponds to a contractor profit oil share of 55%, which is higher than the 45% in the base scenario.

Therefore, in the second scenario:

- On an annual basis:

- o The R-factor of 1.08 gives the contractor a 55% share of the whole year's profit oil, and the government, 45% (cells N575 and N578).

- o Is this "fair"?

- o Or, to rephrase the question, if the idea behind basing profit oil distribution on R-factors is to help the contractor – in the form of a higher share, when the contractor's "times are bad" – does the contractor really "deserve" 55% of the *entire year's* profit oil, when it was in fact having a "bad time" in *only one of the four quarters*?

- On a quarterly basis, help in the form of a higher share of contractor profit oil is limited to the only single quarter when the contractor is actually having a "bad time," due to the capex expenditure:

- the R-factor (row 573) for Q1, Q2 and Q3 is always 1.54, giving the contractor a 45% share of each of those three quarter's total profit oil, leaving 55% for the government;

- the R-factor for Q4, which takes into account the *prior* quarter's extra spending, is 1.08 (cell M573), giving the contractor a 55% share of Q4 profit oil, leaving 45% for the government (cell M579).

Although this is a further simplification, due to all the "moving parts" at play, suppose that annual total (undistributed) profit oil were equal in each quarter. In this case, in the second scenario:

- calculating R on an annual basis, the contractor would get **55%** of the year's total profit oil, and the government, the other 45%;

- but calculating R quarterly, the contractor would get

$$(45\% \times 25\%) + (45\% \times 25\%) + (45\% \times 25\%) + (55\% \times 25\%) =$$
$$(11.25\%) + (11.25\%) + (11.25\%) + (13.75\%) =$$

47.50% of the year's total profit oil, and the government, the other 52.50%.

In other words, the annual basis calculation method "overcompensates" the contractor because it takes into account only its end-year position, and lets this "stand for" the entire year, ignoring variations in this position throughout the year.

Periodicity as a Modeling Issue

In the case of real-world large fields and high oil prices, the combined effect of enough such periods of "overcompensation" can mean the loss of tens or even hundreds of millions of dollars in government revenue. This is particularly true when there are brief oil price spikes, which will be more promptly reflected in shorter-period R-factor calculations than annual calculations. Therefore, governments prefer R-factors to be based on more frequent "snapshots" of the contractor's position, such as quarterly (or, again, semesterly (half-yearly) or monthly) R-factors.

This is why you should note the potential importance of modeling on a time basis which matches the requirements of the fiscal regime.

Having said that, we have seen cases when there was no material difference between the results of (a) a quarterly R-factor-based regime, modeled quarterly, and (b) a quarterly R-factor-based regime, modeled annually.

A host of variables are at play, and often one does not know how different the outcomes will be until actually modeling both ways.

The safest route would seem to be to make the model's time denomination match the fiscal regime's, although, as noted in Chapter 3, to be meaningful in all its calculations, a semesterly, quarterly or monthly model needs semesterly, quarterly or monthly data inputs, which are not always easy to come by.

8.6   R-FACTORS AND THE "GOLD PLATING" EFFECT

Introduction: R-factors and Bizarre PSC Model Behavior

The example just discussed makes it easy to imagine how an unscrupulous contractor might take advantage of the PSC terms, e.g., by timing expenditure to maximize its share of profit oil.

This is not the only vulnerability of R-factor-based profit oil distribution mechanisms, some of which can cause PSC revenue distribution to "behave" in quite counterintuitive ways.

For example, profit oil R-factors which have been designed a certain way can in fact end up rewarding contractors for spending more than necessary. This is known as **gold plating**. (Imagine that if spending more benefits a contractor, an unscrupulous one would not buy ordinary pipelines, but rather gold-plated ones, if allowed to get away with it.)[13] Thus, for example, it can happen that <u>spending more capex will actually *increase* the contractor's NPV,</u> which is extremely unusual.

Governments are aware of such potential for abuse, and to prevent it usually use rigorous budgetary approval, auditing and cost reporting procedures.

Nevertheless, it still can be hard to counter the more subtle gold plating strategies of canny contractors, who technically speaking are not breaking any rules. This points to an inherent weakness in certain R-factor designs. It is hard to eliminate fully the potential for gold plating while allowing the R-factor to achieve its intended goal, which is to reward contractors with higher percentages of profit oil before they "break even" than after.

Contractors, governments and third-party analysts (including you) need to be able to understand this strange phenomenon. When a model says that higher costs = higher contractor NPV, the modeler has some questions to answer. An inability to do so damages the model's and modeler's credibility.

Example PSC R-factor Gold Plating Model

To explain gold plating in detail – and enable you to as well – we illustrate it in a new file, "Ch8_PSC_R_factor_gold_plating.xls." It is based on a real field and fiscal regime we have encountered, although we have changed the scale of the production profile and costs, as well as a few fiscal items, to protect proprietary information. The model still behaves as strangely, and in the same way, as the original field model.

Regarding <u>field assumptions</u>, this section's model differs from the "core" PSC example model, in that in the current model:

- it is assumed the contractor makes a commercial discovery after an initial, two year (2015–2016) exploration and appraisal period (the second year of which overlaps with the start of the development period);

- production starts in the sixth year of the valuation period (2020), versus the second valuation year in our "core" model – so be aware of the stronger discounting effects here; and

- there is a long, flat production plateau (row 29), in contrast to the short, fast-peaking, generally fast-declining production profiles assumed in our other PSC models. The plateau is the result of a phased multi-well development strategy, which – accounting for the variations in *individual well* output over time – spreads out well drilling from 2017 through the end of 2021, in a way designed to keep *total* production flat as long as possible.

---

[13] Note that, in addition to R-factors, other fiscal mechanisms in which rates are based on scales of some profitability measure have the potential for gold plating.

R Factor (calculated on annual basis)		Contractor Profit
>	<=	Share (%)
0.00	1.00	90%
1.00	2.00	90%–(90%–10%) * (R–1)/(2–1)
2.00	999,999	10%
During first production year, by contractual definition, R will be a positive number <1; so for modeling purposes, in that year R = 0.1		

Figure 8.28 R-factor-based profit oil distribution, using linear interpolation, from row 68 of the file "Ch8_PSC_R_factor_gold_plating.xls"

Some key Base Scenario fiscal terms (found in the section starting in row 54) are as follows:

- the royalty rate is 15%;

- 75% is the maximum portion of net revenue available as cost oil;

- all costs are recoverable;

- there are no "sunk costs" from before the model's timeframe begins in 2015; and

- the contractor pays no income tax.

Unlike the "core" PSC model, this model has no depreciation. The "core" model used depreciation to help calculate the cost recovery of tangible capex. In this model's fiscal system, however, all costs *including* tangible capex are eligible for cost recovery, funds permitting, in the year in which they are incurred.[14]

Also note that, whereas the last section's model, "Ch8_PSC_R_factor_Step_2.xls," used discrete bands of R-factor thresholds in the profit oil distribution table, here this example uses a linear interpolation method between a stated minimum and maximum. See Figures 8.28 and 8.29.

The formula in the third column of Figure 8.28 is the linear interpolation function. This means that when it applies – which is when the R-factor is greater than 1.0, but effectively less than or equal to 2.0 – the resultant contractor share of profit oil will be at a point somewhere between 90% and 10%. (Note that "999,999" is our modeling shorthand in this case for no upper limit.)

The exact point will depend on how far the R-factor in question lies between 1.0 and 2.0. If it is exactly mid-way between 1.0 and 2.0, i.e., if it is 1.5, then the resultant factor will be exactly halfway between 90% and 10% – that is, it will be 50%. Figure 8.29 shows the straight line (hence the term "linear interpolation") which is seen between R-factors from 1.0 to 2.0, when these are plotted against the corresponding contractor profit shares.

---

[14] This is the method used in Chapter 7's example model, "Ch7_PSC_basic_model_no_depreciation.xls."

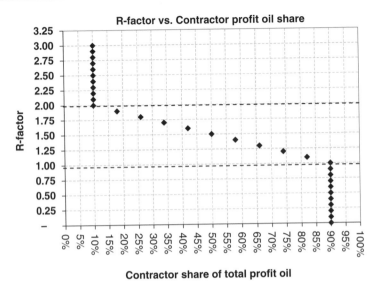

Figure 8.29   R-factor-based profit oil distribution using linear interpolation, from row 770 of the file "Ch8_PSC_R_factor_gold_plating.xls"

Section continues in PDF file

To permit the use of larger graphics, we continue the rest of this section in PDF.

Turn to "Ch8_Supplement_to_Sec_8_6.pdf," which draws on the example model, "Ch8_PSC_R_factor_gold_plating.xls." If viewed on-screen, the PDF will look best in full screen mode. This PDF section concludes this chapter.

Index

Index of certain topics in the materials on the disk

In most cases, the presence of topics covered in materials on the disc is "flagged" in the text of the physical book; therefore these topics can be found in the main index. This is not the case, however, with certain items. To make it easier to locate such topics, we present the following selective, supplementary index of electronic material.